THE ARMS RACE IN THE 1980s

THE ARMS RACE
IN THE 1980s

Edited by
David Carlton and Carlo Schaerf

St. Martin's Press   New York

ISBN 0-312-04946-3

Library of Congress Cataloging in Publication Data

Main entry under title:

The Arms race in the 1980s.

  Includes bibliographical references and index.
  1. Arms control—Addresses, essays, lectures.
2. Disarmament—Addresses, essays, lectures.
I. Carlton, David, 1938–   II. Schaerf, Carlo.
JX1974.A7696   1982   327.1'74   81–21303
ISBN 0-312-04946-3   AACR2

Contents

Preface   vii
List of Abbreviations   ix
Notes on the Contributors   xiii
List of Course Participants   xviii

1. Summary of Discussions   1
    William F. Gutteridge

PART I THE CENTRAL ARMS RACE

2. Disarmament, Security and Public Confidence   23
    William F. Gutteridge

3. Some Peculiarities of the Arms Race on the
    Threshold of the 1980s   31
    M. A. Milstein

4. Disarmament: Phoenix and Hydra   42
    Komarraju Ravi

5. Arms Control: The Bankruptcy of the Strategist's
    Approach   48
    Trevor Taylor

6. Military Parity, Political and Military Detente   62
    Max Schmidt

7. Disarmament-supporting Measures: Conceptual
    Innovation and Institutional Reform of the National
    Arms Control and Disarmament Machineries   82
    H. G. Brauch

8.   The Maintenance of Peace is the Most Important
     Problem of Today   105
     V. S. Emelyanov

9.   Is the SALT Era Over?   114
     Gloria Duffy

10. Technological Misinformation: Fission and Fusion
     Weapons   124
     Alexander De Volpi

PART II   THE PROBLEM OF PROLIFERATION

11. International Strategies for Managing the Nuclear
     Fuel Cycle   145
     Ian Smart

12. Non-proliferation of Nuclear Weapons as an
     Essential Step towards Nuclear Disarmament   168
     V. S. Emelyanov

13. The Dilemmas of Non-proliferation Policy:
     the Supplier Countries   175
     Pierre Lellouche

14. Non-proliferation and Developing Countries   205
     Olga Šuković

PART III   REGIONAL STUDIES

15. The Dilemma of European Theatre Nuclear Arms
     Control   235
     Lawrence Freedman

16. Nuclear-weapon-free Zones: the Latin American
     Experiment   252
     Félix Calderón

17. International Security Regimes: the Case of a
     Balkan Nuclear-free Zone   273
     Athanassios G. Platias and R. J. Rydell

18. Greece and Nuclear Weapons   299
     Kosta Tsipis

19. Nigeria's Nuclear Potential   314
     Robert D'A. Henderson

Index   332

Preface

The chapters in this volume were presented to the eighth course of
the International School on Disarmament and Research on Conflicts (ISODARCO), held in Venice, Italy, between 26 August and
5 September 1980.

The organisation of the course was made possible by the
generous collaboration and financial contributions of many
organisations and individuals. For their financial contributions we
wish to express our gratitude to:

The Ford Foundation, in particular Enid Schoettle;
The Italian National Research Council — National Committee
    for Juridical and Political Sciences;
The Italian Ministry of Cultural Affairs;
The University of Rome, in particular Professor Antonio
    Ruberti and Professor Giorgio Tecce;
The Pugwash Conferences on Science and World Affairs.

We wish to acknowledge the dedicated collaboration, before and
during the course, of Mimma Mauro, Gabriella Fascetti, Marzia
Mauro, Bruno Pellizzoni and Anna Petrelli. For administrative
work our thanks are due to Fernando Pacciani and Luciano Fiore.
For hospitality in Venice we are indebted to the Domus Ciliota.

The editors are grateful to the University of Wisconsin Press for
permission to publish a revised version of an article by Pierre
Lellouche first printed in *International Organization*, winter
1981.

All opinions expressed in the chapters and in the summary of
discussions are of a purely private nature and do not necessarily

represent the official view either of the organisers of the School or
of the organisations to which the writers may be affiliated.

D. C.
C. S.

List of Abbreviations

ABM	Anti-ballistic Missile
ACDA	Arms Control and Disarmament Agency (United States)
ADM	Atomic Demolition Munition
AECL	Atomic Energy of Canada Limited
ALCM	Air-launched Cruise Missile
BWR	Boiling Water Reactor
CCD	Conference of the Committee on Disarmament
CD	Committee on Disarmament (Geneva)
CEA	Commissariat Énergie Atomique
CIA	Central Intelligence Agency (United States)
CPSU	Communist Party of the Soviet Union
CSCE	Conference on Security and Co-operation in Europe
CTBT	Comprehensive Test Ban Treaty
ECOWAS	Economic Community of West African States
EDF	Electricité de France
EEC	European Economic Community
EURATOM	European Atomic Energy Community
FBR	Fast Breeder Reactor
FBS	Forward-based Systems
FMG	Federal Military Government (Nigeria)
GDR	German Democratic Republic
GLCM	Ground-launched Cruise Missile
HEU	Highly Enriched Uranium
HWR	Heavy Water Reactor

IAEA	International Atomic Energy Agency
ICBM	Intercontinental Ballistic Missile
IISS	International Institute for Strategic Studies
INFCE	International Nuclear Fuel Cycle Evaluation
IRBM	Intermediate-range Ballistic Missile
ISODARCO	International School on Disarmament and Research on Conflicts
KWU	Kraft Werke-union
LMFBR	Liquid Metal Fast Breeder Reactor
LRTNF	Long-range Theatre Nuclear Forces
LWR	Light Water Reactor
MBFR	Mutual Balanced Force Reduction
MIRV	Multiple Independently-targetable Re-entry Vehicle
MLR	Multilateral Force
MRBM	Medium-range Ballistic Missile
NATO	North Atlantic Treaty Organisation
NGO	Non-Governmental Organisation
NNPA	Nuclear Non-proliferation Act (United States)
NNWS	Non-nuclear-weapon State
NORAD	North American Air Defense
NPT	Non-proliferation Treaty
NSC	National Security Council (United States)
NUMCO	Nigerian Uranium Mining Company
NWFZ	Nuclear-weapon-free Zone
NWS	Nuclear-weapon State
OECD	Organisation for Economic Co-operation and Development
OPANAL	Agency for the Prohibition of Nuclear Weapons in Latin America
OPEC	Organisation of Petroleum Exporting Countries
PHWR	Pressurised Heavy Water Reactor
PWR	Pressurised Water Reactor
QRA	Quick Reaction Alert
SAS	Special Ammunition Storage Sites
SALT	Strategic Arms Limitation Talks
SIPRI	Stockholm International Peace Research Institute
SLBM	Submarine-launched Ballistic Missile
SSBN	Nuclear Ballistic Missile-Firing Submarines
TEL	Transporter–Erector–Launcher
TNF	Theatre Nuclear Force

TNT	Tri-nitro-toluene
UNESCO	United Nations Educational, Scientific and Cultural Organisation
USICA	United States International Communications Agency

Notes on the Contributors

Hans Günter Brauch (West German) is Research Associate at the Institute of Political Science at Heidelberg University and a Teaching Associate at Tübingen University. He was formerly a Teaching Associate at Darmstadt University. He has published extensively in German on problems of international security and of arms control.

Félix Calderón (Peruvian) is a Peruvian diplomat. After serving in the Peruvian Ministry of Foreign Affairs in Lima and as a Second Secretary in the Embassy of Peru in London, he is currently Peruvian Representative at the International Atomic Energy Agency in Vienna. He is also preparing an academic dissertation on the subject of Nuclear-weapon-free Zones.

David Carlton (British) (co-editor) is Senior Lecturer in Diplomatic History at the Polytechnic of North London. He holds a Ph.D. degree from the University of London. He is author of *MacDonald versus Henderson: The Foreign Policy of the Second Labour Government* (Macmillan: London, 1970); of *Anthony Eden: A Biography* (Allen Lane: London, 1981); and of numerous articles on modern international politics. He is co-editor of five previous volumes in this series.

Alexander De Volpi (US) is Manager of the Diagnostics Section in the Reactor Analysis and Safety Division of the Argonne National Laboratory, Illinois. He holds a Ph.D. degree in Physics from the Virginia Polytechnic Institute. Among his many publications is *Proliferation, Plutonium, and Policy: Impediments to Nuclear Weapons Propagation* (1979).

Gloria Duffy (US) is Program Fellow, Arms Control and Disarmament Program, Stanford University and a Consultant to the Rand Corporation. Her publications include *Power Politics: The U.S. Nuclear Industry and Nuclear Exports* (1978) and *Soviet Nuclear Policies: Nuclear Energy and Nuclear Exports* (1979).

V. S. Emelyanov (Soviet) is a Corresponding Member of the Academy of Sciences of the USSR and a Hero of Socialist Labour. He has held prominent positions on the Scientific Consultative Committee of the United Nations and in the International Atomic Energy Agency. He is also Chairman of the Commission on Scientific Problems of Disarmament of the Academy of Sciences of the USSR and is a regular participant in the Pugwash Conferences on Science and World Affairs.

Lawrence Freedman (British) is Head of Policy Studies at the Royal Institute of International Affairs in London. He was formerly a Research Fellow at Nuffield College, Oxford, and a Research Associate at the International Institute for Strategic Studies. He is author of three books: *US Intelligence and the Soviet Strategic Threat* (Macmillan: London, 1977); *Britain and Nuclear Weapons* (Macmillan: London, 1980); and *The Evolution of Nuclear Strategy* (Macmillan: London, 1981).

William F. Gutteridge (British) is Professor of International Studies and Head of Political and Economic Studies Group at the University of Aston in Birmingham. He was formerly Senior Lecturer in Commonwealth History and Government at the Royal Military Academy, Sandhurst. He is author of *Armed Forces in New States* (1962); *Military Institutions and Power in the New States* (1965); *The Military in African Politics* (1969); and *Military Regimes in Africa* (1975).

Robert D'A. Henderson (Canadian) is a member of the Department of Government at the National University of Lesotho. He was formerly Lecturer in International Relations at the University of Ife, Ife-Ife, Nigeria. He specialises in African security issues and has contributed articles on these themes to *Journal of Modern African Studies*, *The World Today*, *Government and Opposition*, and *Journal of Strategic Studies*.

Pierre Lellouche (French) is Head of European Security Studies at the Institut français des relations internationales in Paris. He is author of *Internationalization of the Nuclear Fuel Cycle and Non-Proliferation Strategy* (Praeger: New York, forthcoming). He has also contributed articles to *The Washington Quarterly*, *Foreign Affairs*, and *International Organization*.

M. A. Milstein (Soviet) is a Chief of Section at the Institute of Canadian and US Studies of the Soviet Academy of Sciences. He has published, *inter alia*, in Russian (and in translation) a study of *Contemporary Bourgeois Military Science*. He is a retired General of the Soviet Union.

Athanassios G. Platias (Greek) is a Fellow of the Peace Studies Program at Cornell University. He is registered as a Ph.D. candidate in the Department of Government at the same university. He was formerly a Fellow at the Center for Science and International Affairs, Harvard University. He is a graduate of the Law Faculty of the University of Athens.

Komarraju Ravi (Indian) is Lecturer in Strategic Studies at Andhra University, Waltair, India. He has published various articles on Indian politics, specialising in problems relating to Andhra Pradesh. He is co-author of a forthcoming book, *Government and Politics in Andhra Pradesh*. He is also interested in disarmament and arms control.

R. J. Rydell (US) is a political scientist at the Lawrence Livermore National Laboratory and is currently studying the causes and effects of the proliferation of nuclear weapons. He was previously a Research Fellow at the Center for Science and International Affairs at Harvard University. He was educated at the University of Virginia (B.A.), the London School of Economics (M.Sc.), and Princeton University (M.A. and Ph.D.). His doctoral dissertation, entitled 'Decision Making on the Breeder Reactor in Britain and the United States' will be published as a book by the University of California Press.

Carlo Schaerf (Italian) (co-editor) is Professor of Physics at the University of Rome. He was formerly a Research Associate at Stanford University and on the staff of the Italian Atomic Energy

Commission. With Professor Eduardo Amaldi he founded in 1966 the International School on Disarmament and Research on Conflicts (ISODARCO). He was appointed Director of ISODARCO in 1970. He is co-editor of five previous volumes in this series.

Max Schmidt (East German) is Director of the Institute of International Politics and Economics of the German Democratic Republic. Professor Dr Schmidt was formerly a Member of the Executive of the National Board for Political Sciences in his country. He is author of many books and articles on East–West relations with particular reference to economics, the arms race, and disarmament.

Ian Smart (British) is now a consultant, specialising in international energy affairs. He served as member of the British Diplomatic Service between 1958 and 1969. Subsequently he was Assistant Director of the International Institute for Strategic Studies and Director of Studies at the Royal Institute of International Affairs in London. His publications include *Future Conditional: The Prospects for Anglo-French Nuclear Co-operation* (1971); *The Future of the British Nuclear Deterrent: Technical, Economic and Strategic Issues* (1977); *and Multinational Arrangements for the Nuclear Fuel Cycle* (1980).

Olga Šuković (Yugoslav) is Director of the International Law Department at the Institute of International Politics and Economics in Belgrade. She was formerly an Assistant Lecturer at Skopje University and a Research Fellow at the Stockholm International Peace Research Institute (SIPRI). Under SIPRI auspices, she was author of *Force Reductions in Europe* (1974) and co-author of *Laws of War and Dubious Weapons* (1976). She has also published extensively in Serbo-Croatian.

Trevor Taylor (British) is Principal Lecturer in International Relations at North Staffordshire Polytechnic. Dr Taylor was editor of, and a contributor to, *Approaches and Theory in International Relations* (Longman: London, 1978). He has also written several articles on arms transfers and NATO standardisation. He is currently preparing a book, with the assistance of a NATO Fellowship, on co-operation in the North Atlantic area in arms procurement.

Kosta Tsipis (US) is Associate Director of the Program in Science and Technology for International Security at the Massachusetts Institute of Technology. He was previously associated with the Stockholm International Peace Research Institute. He is author of three books and 42 articles on international security themes.

List of Course Participants

Venice, 26 August–5 September 1980

Abdel-Moneim, Mohamed (Egyptian) Ministry of Foreign Affairs, Tahrir Sq., Cairo, Egypt.

Annequin, Jean Louis (French) Institut Français de Polémologie, Hotel des Invalides, 129, rue de Grenelle, 75700 Paris, France.

Behar, Nansen (Bulgarian) Institute for Contemporary Social Studies, Bulgarian Academy of Sciences, Pionersky put 21, 1635 Sofia, Bulgaria.

Berglund, Gregory (US) Mas Roussier Entremont, 13100 Aix-en-Provence, France.

Bjornerstedt, Rolf (Swedish) SIPRI, Sveavägen 166, S-113 46 Stockholm, Sweden.

Brauch, Hans Günter (West German) Alte-Bergsteige 47, D-6950 Mosbach, West Germany.

Burzynski, Andrzej (Polish) Institute of State and Law of the Polish Academy of Sciences, Nowy Swiat 72, Warsaw, Poland.

Caldéron, Félix (Peruvian) Peruvian Embassy, Wien, Austria.

Calogero, Francesco (Italian) Istituto di Fisica dell'Università di Roma, P. le Aldo Moro 2, 00185 Roma, Italy.

Carlton, David (British) Department of History, Philosophy and European Studies, Polytechnic of North London, Prince of Wales Road, London, Great Britain.

Celentano, Guido (Italian) C. so Vittorio Emanuele 168, 80121 Napoli, Italy.

De Andreis, Marco (Italian) Aviazione e Difesa, Via Tagliamento 29, Roma, Italy.

De La Riva, Careaga Ion (Spanish) Villa Berriz-Emen, c/Bermudez Cañete 1, Madrid 16, Spain.

De Volpi, Alexander (US) Bldg. 208, Argonne National Laboratory, Argonne, Illinois 60439, USA.

Dona' Dalle Rose, Luigi F. (Italian) Istituto di Fisica, Univ. di Padova, Via Marzolo 8, Padova, Italy.

Duffy, Gloria (US) Arms Control Program, Stanford University Bldg. 160, Stanford, California 94305, USA.

Elzen, Boelie (Dutch) Twente University of Technology, PB 217, Enschede, The Netherlands.

Emelyanov, V. S. (Soviet) Leninskiyi Prospect 17, Academy of Science, Moscow, USSR.

Fabiyi, Edwin (Nigerian) Institute of Peace Law and International Department, Université de Nice 9, Av. de Fabrón, 06200 Nice, France.

Feld, Bernard T. (US) Physics Department, MIT, Cambridge, Massachusetts 02139, USA.

Ferm, Ragnihild (Swedish) SIPRI, Sveavagen 166, S-113 46 Stockholm, Sweden.

Frankowska, Maria (Polish) Polish Academy of Science, Institute of State and Law, Noury Surat 72, Warsaw, Poland.

Freedman, Lawrence (British) RIIA, Chatham House, 10 St James's Sq., London, Great Britain.

Ghantus, Wolfgang (East German) Institute of International Politics and Economics, Breite Strasse 11, 102 Berlin, German Democratic Republic.

Gusmaroli, Franca (Italian) Defence Today, Via Tagliamento 29, 00100 Roma, Italy.

Gutteridge, William (British) Political and Economic Studies Group, University of Aston, Birmingham, Great Britain.

Henderson, Robert D'A. (Canadian) National University of Lesotho, Lesotho, Africa.

Kaplan, Richard Alan (US) 1912 Elliott Drive, Vallejo, California, 94590, USA.

Leifer, Jeffrey (US) Yale School of Organization and Management, 135 Prospect St, New Haven, Conn. 06520, USA.

Lellouche, Pierre (French) IFRI, 6 Rue Ferrus, 75014 Paris, France.

Löhmannsröben, Hans (West German) Robert Koch Str. 38(913), 34 Göttingen, West Germany.

Luciani, Giacomo (Italian) Istituto Affari Internazionali, Viale Mazzini 88, Roma, Italy.

Mack, Newell (US) U-Consultants, 100 Leonard St, Belmont,

Massachusetts 02178, USA.

Milstein, M. A. (Soviet) Academy of Sciences of the USSR, Klebny 2/3, Moscow, USSR.

Moro, Daniele (Italian) Direzione Nazionale del PSI, Intern. Dept., Via Tomacelli 146, 00100 Roma, Italy.

Nabil, A. Eissa (Egyptian) Physics Dept., Faculty of Science, Alazhar University, Nasr City, Cairo, Egypt.

Nakai, Yoko (Japanese) USICA, American Embassy Tokyo, 10-5, Akasaka 1-Chome, Minato-Ku, Tokyo, Japan 107.

Ooms, Jack (Dutch) Prins Maurits Laboratory TNO PO Box 45, 2280 AA Ryswyk, The Netherlands.

Pascolini, Alessandro (Italian) Istituto di Fisica, Univ. di Padova, Via Marzolo 8, Padova, Italy.

Pascu, Ioan Mircea (Romanian) Institute of Political Sciences, 1–3 Armata Poporucui, Sector 6, Bucharest, Romania.

Patania, Annino Aldo (Italian) Johns Hopkins University, 1740 Massachusetts Ave., NW, Washington DC 20036, USA.

Pfeifenberger, Werner (Austrian) Österreichisches Institut für Politische Bildung, A-7210 Mattersburg, Austria.

Platias, Athanassios (Greek) Peace Studies Program, Cornell University, 180 Uris Hall, Ithaca, NY 14853, US.

Ravi, Komarraju (Indian) Department of Politics and Public Administration, Andhra University, Waltair, Andhra Pradesh, India.

Réti, Gÿorgy (Hungarian) Hungarian Institute for Foreign Affairs, 1016 Budapest, Hungary.

Schaerf, Carlo (Italian) Istituto di Fisica dell'Università di Roma, P. le Aldo Moro 2, Roma, Italy.

Schmidt, Max (East German) Institute of International Politics & Economics, 102 Berlin, Breite Strasse 11, German Democratic Republic.

Schoettle, Enid (US) The Ford Foundation, 320 East 43rd Street, New York, NY 10017, USA.

Silvestri, Stefano (Italian) L'Europeo, Via della Mercede 37, Roma, Italy.

Skons, Elisabeth (Swedish) SIPRI, Sveavagen 166, S-11346 Stockholm, Sweden.

Smart, Ian (British) Grosvenor Avenue, Richmond, Surrey, Great Britain.

Smit, A. Wim (Dutch) Center for Studies on Problems of Science and Society, Twente University of Technology, PB 217,

Enschede, The Netherlands.

Šuković, Olga (Yugoslav) Institute of International Politics and Economics, Makedonska 25, 11000 Belgrade, Yugoslavia.

Taylor, Trevor (British) Department of International Relations and Politics, North Staffordshire Polytechnic, College Road, Stoke on Trent, Staffordshire, Great Britain.

Thompson, Susan (British) Centre for Disarmament Geneva Unit, UN Office at Geneva, Palais des Nations, 1211 Geneva, Switzerland.

Tromp, Hylke (Dutch) Polemological Institute, PO Box 121, Haren (Gr.), The Netherlands.

Tsipis, Kosta (US) Room 26 402, MIT, Cambridge, Massachusetts 02139, USA.

Vogt, Margaret (Nigerian) Nigerian Institute of International Affairs, GP Box 1727 Lagos, Nigeria.

Wiedmeyer, Hans (West German) Phil.-Theol. Hochschule, St. Georgen Offenbacher Landstr. 224, D-6000 Frankfurt 70, West Germany.

Wright, Steve (British) Richardson Institute, Politics Department, University of Lancaster, Bailrigg, Lancaster, Great Britain.

Ziai, Iradj (Iranian) POB 1512, Tehran, Iran.

Zoppo, Ciro Elliott (US) Political Science Dept., University of California, Los Angeles, California 90049, USA.

OBSERVERS

Castelli, Antonio (Italian) Collegio Navale Morosini, S. Elena 30122, Venezia, Italy.

Elkin, Natan (Argentinian) Pl. Université 1, 1348 Louvain-la-Neuve, Belgium.

Gurevich, Sergio (Argentinian) 27, rue de Luxemburg, 1150 Bruxelles, Belgium.

Jacchia, Enrico (Italian) Piazza dell'Orologio, 7, 00186 Roma, Italy.

Note One author of a paper was unable to attend the course, namely R. J. Rydell.

1 Summary of Discussions

William F. Gutteridge

Introduction

The eighth course of the International School on Disarmament and Research on Conflicts (ISODARCO) was held in Venice, Italy, between 26 August and 5 September 1980. A major part of the proceedings was devoted to the topic 'Disarmament and Arms Control — Present Situation and Future Prospects'.

The preconditions for more successful disarmament negotiations came under scrutiny from the outset. The unprecedented increase in military expenditure in this century, and particularly during the last 30 years, has created an apparently absurd situation, especially at a time when up to one-third of the world's population are lacking the essentials for a proper existence. It was generally agreed, however, that it is not military expenditure which worries people, but the prospect of war. It is clearly the case that much in international relations is being determined by military power. The unseating of Idi Amin in Uganda resulted from an exercise of military force. Israel survives as a state because of its use of military power. Military expenditure and effective military power are, however, not necessarily correlated. In these circumstances a more realistic approach to the problem of disarmament and arms control is clearly required. Such an approach would depend on an ability to reduce the sense of insecurity between states and it was argued that the Tanzanian example, of a country which had begun with basic military forces, in 1961, and subsequently expanded in order to deal with the perceived threat from its Ugandan neighbour, is a very good case in point. Similarly, states in Africa are alarmed by the possibility of South Africa developing

1

nuclear weapons, and this contributes to their sense of insecurity and to raising the level of armaments which they feel to be necessary. The fact that political influence and military force in the world tend to go together led some participants to contend that arms control is a more important concept than disarmament. Disarmament could only be, in any case, of a limited character and would perhaps follow upon deliberate attempts to diminish international tension and some of the more dangerous aspects of the arms race. The two main objectives are clearly the avoidance of nuclear war, on the one hand, and the management of local conflicts which might be consolidated by arms control measures on a regional basis, on the other.

The important point was made that the acquisition of weapons and the escalation of the arms race depends on different factors in different circumstances. The Israeli approach to an expanded and well-equipped military establishment is clearly the product of an unambiguous state of acute conflict. This is not the case in the relationship between the United States and the Soviet Union. The conflict, which they each perceive, certainly does not justify, in security terms, the level of nuclear weapons which they have acquired. In their particular case deep feelings of distrust justify the continual search for new weapon systems calculated to provide them with greater protection. Under the circumstances it was suggested that there is, as yet, no agreed set of rules which would make possible a relationship which might be defined as interdependence and in the intervening period, before this set of rules is established, the use of war and force would clearly be seen in some quarters to have validity.

International Security

A realistic assessment of the causes of the present arms race involves a recognition of the fact that acceptance of arms limitation depends on perceptions of security. A reappraisal of the whole concept of security may be necessary. It was asked, for example, whether the fact that different states in Europe belong to two opposing blocs enhances their sense of security or not. As a practical measure there was general agreement that a freeze would very quickly result in mutual reductions and certainly in delaying modernisation and the process of replacement.

If the concept of security is paramount, then general and complete disarmament is almost certainly an unattainable goal. Even arms limitation and substantial reductions in the level of weapons and expenditure are themselves probably long-term objectives. Campaigns by non-governmental organisations are in themselves unlikely to be capable of being sustained long enough to produce important effects. Previous disarmament campaigns probably failed because of the belief that solutions to conflict problems and security issues were at hand and feasible. Defusing potential crises is, however, probably more important than attempts to find a cure for the problems which give rise to them.

The opening discussion was followed by a more detailed examination of the concept of security. The view that, with continuing research and development, stability could be provided by a form of balance between weapon developments on either side was discounted on several grounds. First, the existing political situation may not continue indefinitely, since third or fourth parties, including terrorists, or, in some cases, small states intent on the proliferation of nuclear weapons, may engender destabilisation; reliance on this sort of technical stability would, in fact, put any degree of disarmament even further into the future. The best chance of minimising the risk is to do something about the basic international set-up; in other words, to do something radical. Otherwise, expansion in the number of nuclear weapons, in whatever hands they were, would create ever-increasing problems of control and enhance the risk of nuclear war arising from the kinds of quick decision which would be necessary at lower levels in the chain of command. The possibility of general and complete disarmament, though remote, could result in a less secure world than that which at present exists. To consider disarmament in such terms might well be counterproductive; what is needed is a serious approach to arms limitation and arms reductions. Arms reductions, nevertheless, will always be of advantage to some and disadvantageous to others. Consideration, therefore, needs to be given, as already suggested, to overt means of preserving national sovereignty and independence, the minimum requirement even for a small neutral country like Sweden. So the search for an equitable basis for security has to go on; the UN Charter alone does not provide an adequate guarantee of security.

The decoupling which is taking place between the superpower strategic relationship on the one hand, and the European system, on the other, was thought to be an indication of a changing perception in some quarters of the concept of security. In this context it is certainly not surprising that individuals and groups are becoming more active in attempting to change the position with regard, at least, to nuclear disarmament. The distinction which had been made by one participant, between arms controllers as concerned essentially with the maintenance of stability, and disarmament-seekers looking for security, was strongly contested. Both groups have to be concerned with security, and direct negotiation is only one part of the essential political processes. Negotiation, history has shown, can only take place on two bases: either that of fear and apprehension and the sense of desperation, or that of strength and a sense of security. Only the second of these would be likely to lead to constructive bargaining with lasting results. It was held that many actions by states were clearly a reaction to a sense of insecurity. For example, the Indian nuclear explosion – whether, in fact, the test was of a weapon or a peaceful nuclear device – was widely seen as an indication of the feeling of insecurity to which many of the less powerful states were no less subject.

There was little support for the view which had been expressed by some disarmament negotiators in the past that there was now such a great quantity of fissile material available in so many countries that it would not be possible to achieve nuclear disarmament, on the grounds that verification would be impracticable. It was pointed out in this connection that verification is not part of the biological weapons convention and that, in any case, it might be unduly pessimistic to suppose that such a possibility was scientifically unattainable. There was also some debate about the blurring of the distinction and the bridging of the gap between nuclear and conventional weapons which was taking place in two directions. One danger may be that, in some circumstances, nuclear battlefield weapons might seem more attractive on the grounds of cost-effectiveness. In general, however, it was felt to be vital that the distinction between nuclear and conventional weapons was maintained, and this was generally regarded as not beyond the ingenuity of those concerned.

Nuclear Proliferation

The question of nuclear proliferation was discussed at some length. The view was expressed that the Non-Proliferation Treaty

(NPT) had become a neglected subject, with the Second Review Conference proceeding in Geneva virtually unnoticed. The West German–Brazilian deal on nuclear reactors, which had at one time provoked a great deal of discussion, was now scarcely mentioned, and it had been reported that, for example, the United States was providing nuclear fuel to India. There is now a wide acceptance of the view that Israel and India have become, as it were, unofficial nuclear weapon states, whilst Pakistan, Iraq, Argentina and South Africa are probably on the brink. A number of problems of control remained unresolved while advancements in enrichment, technology and breeder technology have taken place.

An important factor in the situation is that economic forces are encouraging a form of protectionism, especially on the part of West Europeans. They are having to take action to protect their own nuclear industry, and to keep the industrial base of that industry alive. One way of doing this, particularly noticeable in the case of West Germany, is through exports. In a number of cases the suppliers of nuclear technology are in a vulnerable position with regard to energy supply. For example, in dealing with Iraq, a major oil supplier, the pressures upon Italy or France to supply nuclear reactors or technology were at one time considerable. A position such as that described could only be coped with in the long term by reinforcing the NPT, as far as possible, in order to avoid its collapse; by strengthening security, especially in the Third World where the temptation to acquire nuclear weapons might become strong; and by providing fire-breaks which would prevent a nuclear exchange in a particular part of the world spreading across the globe.

The question of internationalisation and international control through a variety of institutions was at first discounted, but in subsequent discussion, a more positive view eventually emerged. In the process certain important principles were established. First, it was recognised that fission will be used for an increasing amount, and an increasing proportion, of the world's electricity supply. This could amount, by the beginning of the next century, to 20 per cent of the primary energy equivalent. Non-proliferation policies must take this fact into account. Military proliferation could not be eliminated by abandoning nuclear power, nor would policies with regard to nuclear power ultimately be determined by the attitude towards military proliferation. To stop or freeze the development of nuclear power or the proliferation of nuclear weapons by direct methods would be seen as discriminatory even within the industrialised world itself. There was no prospect of success unless non-proliferation policies aimed at military security and energy security were addressed together, and seen to converge. On the military side, the inhibition of the spread of nuclear weapons must be seen to be effective. It was, as in other matters concerning security, a matter of confidence.

The discussion on the means of controlling and monitoring the process involved much detailed consideration of the practicability of restricting access to materials. The opportunity to prevent the dissemination of information on processing and enrichment had long since passed even if it had ever existed; even in the 1950s this was to all intents and purposes technically and politically impossible. It might be possible to delay access to new countries wishing to instal nuclear technology, but only at high cost in that if it were done in a restrictive way, seen as discriminatory, bitter international competition would be bound to ensue.

At this point it was argued that internationalisation and machinery for international control were not as novel or theoretical as they appeared to be. In fact, state interest in the management of energy and multinational institutions for the purpose had a long history; it might well be possible, within the framework of such a system, to discourage or reduce the dangers of diversion of nuclear technology from civil to military use simply because several countries were involved in the process. It was also noted that, in this as in other fields, direct undertakings to other governments might well be respected. The process of simplification of verification might proceed, and means might also be provided for governments practically to demonstrate their commitment to restraint. The fact had to be faced, also, that the larger the scale of the plant, the more likely a lower unit cost was to be achieved. There would, therefore, be attractions to states to become involved in such a multinational process for the sake of economy, and by this means the processes of technical education and dissemination of information might be more effectively controlled. The experience of recent years, in a number of countries, had inevitably engendered a sense of insecurity with regard to energy supply, and avoidance of disruption was therefore a fundamental precondition if confidence in a controversial policy were to be achieved. If fear of future proliferation is to be effectively restrained, it will need to be accompanied by a guarantee of energy supply within a relatively symmetrical situation. Any international institution which is set up should have the narrowest range of objectives possible consistent with the achievement of its goal, so that effort would not be too dispersed and opportunities for distrust generated.

Though there had been some ideological tensions involved in the process, current International Atomic Energy Agency (IAEA) investigations in two fields — namely, international plutonium storage and international spent-fuel management — were showing some promise. But the obvious fact was that the international rules always involved some overriding of national operations, and some countries, notably the United States and France, were particularly sensitive and reacted in a predictable way when threatened, as they perceived it, in terms of their national interest. In such circumstances the question as to who is to make decisions in certain conditions on the release of materials also inevitably arises. The choice before the world in this respect seems to be a direct one between a frank, bitter, competitive rivalry, and equal access with co-operation rather than conflict.

During further discussions the experience of the Law of the Sea Conference, with regard to seabed mining, and the steps which have been taken towards international satellite communication control were considered, and felt to be encouraging. It was argued that competing private companies might be an obstacle to such an arrangement but in reply it was pointed out that direct government involvement would be indispensable, at least in the decision to set up such international organisations. The creation of effective international machinery would be a very lengthy process, and any agreement between suppliers would have to be complemented by a broad consensus among users. The risks involved in internationalisation, including the great distances over which sensitive materials would have to be transported, and the problem of organising effective regional storage arrangements, were emphasised. Above all, an international regime would have to be honest and not discriminatory. This had been put very clearly in a powerful Egyptian statement on the problem. Cairo had pointed out that not only was there a danger in viewing the problem of nuclear proliferation from the standpoint of existing nuclear powers and existing suppliers of nuclear technology, but there was a tendency to regard some countries as sensitive and some as not.

The suggestion was made that in this field there were 'no sensitive technologies, only sensitive countries' and this was substantiated by reference to the lack of concern in the case of transfer of technology to some highly developed industrial countries within the framework of existing alliances, as contrasted with the alarm expressed about developments within the Third World countries. The problem of nuclear non-proliferation is central to the concept of security and is subject to the same conditions relating to the development of trust and confidence as are other attempts at arms control or arms limitation.

The Soviet point of view on the issue of non-proliferation resulted in an interesting debate. It was first pointed out that the Soviet Government took the view that a continuation of the present escalation of nuclear weapons would almost inevitably lead to major war, with an unprecedented number of casualties and devastation. It was, it was claimed, for this reason that the Soviet Union had earlier proposed force reductions of 1000 tanks and 20,000 men in Central Europe. This, however, had not achieved the response Moscow had hoped for. Nevertheless, the Soviets still set some store on the prospects for non-proliferation based on the original NPT which, however, had involved exceptionally complex negotiations.

The question of the negotiations for a Comprehensive Test Ban Treaty (CTBT) was raised, and in this connection it was thought vital to ensure that nuclear tests in space were eliminated. A review of the position, in relation to peaceful nuclear explosions, covered the variation in attitudes which had taken place over the years. There had, for example, been a phase during which the Soviet approach to peaceful nuclear explosions had been more positive than that of other powers.

When the question of a choice of nuclear cycles was raised — for example, whether a thorium cycle would be preferable to a plutonium cycle — it was pointed out that the prospect of fast-breeder reactors had changed the conditions, and would especially alter the conditions for further negotiations over the NPT in the 1980s. There was also at this point an indication of Soviet optimism about the prospect of fusion energy possibly being established as a viable means of power production by the end of the century. Others expressed considerable scepticism about this, but there was at least a tentative agreement that if this could be achieved, then it would be cheaper and safer than fission. For this reason a massive effort should be made, as in other directions, to find alternatives to what was clearly still, in some respects, a dangerous source of power.

With regard to the export of nuclear materials and technology, there was a discussion on the quality of the guidelines which had been devised for the London Suppliers Group — of which guidelines the Soviet Union had been a principal initiator and was a supporter. Whether full-scope safeguards on top of these guidelines would, in fact, add anything to safety and a sense of security in these matters, seemed doubtful. A number of participants suggested that there might not be any real purpose in these, given the existing safeguards. They would not be much help in the face of anyone who was deliberately intending to bypass the provision and develop nuclear weapons. This, of course, raised the question as to who it is, in the chain of command within the political structures in different countries, who is capable of using nuclear weapons — that is, in the sense of being able morally to justify and take the decision to use them. What were the conditions in which they might be encouraged or feel it necessary to take such an appalling decision? A full examination of this question, and a public debate upon it, might in itself serve to reveal the futility of any such action, and help in the building of confidence. In the end, security was the prime requirement, and it was noted that each of the papers given and also much of the discussion had effectively, but not always directly, led back to this point. There was no alternative, in other words, to adopting policies which people, and states, and the leadership of those states, would perceive to be in the direct interest of their survival and the preservation of their integrity. It seems, incidentally, that even the Soviet Union with its vast land mass is now concerned about the disposal of nuclear waste and the problems connected with its transportation over long distances to storage areas, as well as the long-term possibility of those storage areas being interfered with as a result of seismic upheavals.

Political and Military Detente

The discussion on political and military detente, and the concept of military parity, predictably led to a sharp division of opinion. In general, however detente was defined, there was agreement that it was a precondition for successful arms limitation or disarmament negotiations. In other words, security comes first. But the problem of parity was differently perceived. It was recognised that a concept of parity, in general, required that there should be a rough or approximate balance of all aspects; in other words that the weapon systems on either side should be, numerically and in terms of fire-power, roughly equivalent, and that the possibilities of a surprise strike should be taken into account. Equitable security, a term which recurred during the discussions, would involve not seeking to out-match the other side. It seemed, however, that that was precisely what each side perceived to be happening.

Interventions from supporters of the Warsaw Pact were, in essence, a mirror image of what was presented by those holding military perspectives deriving from the North Atlantic Treaty Organisation (NATO). It was claimed that American policy was to remain the strongest nation, and involved the building up of strong forces in such a way as to deny the concept of strategic parity. This was to be achieved by the relative invulnerability of strike systems, and by the development of what were categorised as 'invisible aircraft' which would be able to elude detection. It was suggested that part of this process was the reduction, through the impending introduction of the Pershing II, of the early warning margin from 30 minutes to 4 or 6 minutes. It was consistently claimed that the NATO decision to deploy this system, in 1983, along with a number of long-range cruise missiles, would amount to a fundamental change in the strategic situation in Europe. Medium-range weapons could be used, because of the different geographical position of the Soviet Union and the United States, to change the balance; this is not just modernisation of an existing system, it was claimed, but a new system, and the risk of general war was being increased by the dangerous and invalid concept of limited nuclear war. The states of the Warsaw Pact felt threatened as a result. There was no doubt about their capacity, to devise new types of weapon to combat this new threat, but they were not anxious to engage in an arms race which would be of a renewed and distinctively different character. In particular, Warsaw Pact states felt that, because of enhanced quality and quantity, the cost of weapon systems was proving a considerable strain on national economies and getting dangerously near a point of crisis.

In discussion, there was a clear division between those who

viewed the impending deployment of new American weapons systems in Europe as aimed at re-establishing military parity, and those who claimed that military parity already existed. It was argued that the perception from Eastern Europe did not seem to take account of the fact that the Soviet Union was already well into the process of deploying the weapon known as the SS-20 on a regular basis. At the same time there was a focus of criticism by Warsaw Pact supporters on the forward-based American nuclear systems. There clearly has to be a beginning of negotiation about the situation in Europe, arising primarily from the deployment of medium-range weapons, but it was argued that a freeze at present levels of development, procurement and deployment might well be a precondition for real success. Only in this way could the different perceptions about the present 'balance' be prevented from prejudicing the negotiations.

Some held the view that the concept of parity was a sterile one. On the one hand it could be claimed that approximate strategic parity, rather than detailed parity, had been achieved and that there was no real need for it in any case. It was further suggested that the usefulness of the concept was greatly limited by the fact that it was often used as an excuse for improving capability, before proceeding to negotiations. There was the repeated suggestion, on both sides, that the balance had shifted to their disadvantage. In the end it was clear that the whole issue was a question of good faith and trust and hence new ideas were required. They were certainly required in relation to aspects of confidence-building measures in the light of manoeuvres which were currently taking place in the German Democratic Republic without the presence of Western observers. These issues would need to be explored at the forthcoming Madrid review conference. Freezing of the nuclear forces and weapon systems at existing levels, which had already been mentioned, was endorsed from both points of view as a new idea which should be explored.

Aspects of this discussion were continued in response to a paper which suggested that the Soviet threat had been built up and magnified by the media and by political elites in Western countries, and had not much to do with national security. This view was questioned. Indeed, it was even asked whether it would be in such circumstances rational of the Soviet Union to wish to negotiate with the United States, which seemed to be perceived as set upon a fixed and predetermined course. It was pointed out that in practice, during the 1970s, the US budget had declined for military purposes by 35 per cent in real terms, and the number of strategic weapons had actually been reduced, while at the same time the Soviet Union had been developing and eventually deploying the SS-20 and the Backfire bomber.

Potential Destabilisation Resulting From Radically New Weapon Systems

It was decided to consider the potential for destabilisation by concentrating on a particular example, namely the possible use of lasers as weapons. The criteria which could lead to their development and employment were accordingly systematically discussed. Laser weapons essentially involve the transmission of destructive energy directly to the target at the speed of light, with an accuracy of about 1 metre. In ideal conditions it has been demonstrated that a laser could destroy a militarily significant target. In battlefield conditions there is considerable doubt about effective feasibility. But the real questions are whether a new capability could be developed? Whether there is a need for it? What the long-term implications would be? Whether laser weapons would be essentially offensive or defensive and affect the strategic nuclear balance, the stability of that balance, and arms limitation efforts as between the United States and the Soviet Union? Basically, there are three possible military uses for lasers at present: anti-satellite, anti-aircraft, and anti-missile. Extensive tests have shown that in laboratory conditions it is possible to shoot down an aircraft or a missile. This can be done in a variety of ways which are set out in some detail in the relevant paper.

The lessons of the experiment so far suggest, however, that laser weapons could in present circumstances be defeated very cheaply; they would be very vulnerable, especially as far as their sensors are concerned. Moreover, no completely new mission for them has been envisaged, nor one in which they could achieve a particular objective more effectively than existing weapons. There would also be a problem of cost-effectiveness. There is no doubt at all, however, that many potential developments will be re-examined, in the light especially of the current shift towards war-fighting as opposed to deterrent concepts. In discussion it was concluded that, in spite of the difficulties, there is certainly some battlefield potential in the development of lasers, which has probably gone already quite far, and that in other defence connections the anti-satellite rôle from aircraft is within reach and achievable. One of the incentives to develop such weapons might arise from the fact that researchers in this field may be finding it easier to get money for military research purposes than for civilian applications, whatever their real objectives.

Technological Information and Misinformation

The question of technological information and misinformation with regard to the development of fission and fusion weapons was also considered, especially in relation to its effect on the stability, or otherwise, of the existing position and on proliferation of nuclear weapons. As on previous occasions, the possibility of technological developments aimed at curtailing proliferation was raised. It was stressed that both proliferation itself, especially the cost of acquiring nuclear weapons and maintaining them, and counter-proliferation techniques are very expensive. On the other hand, some of the methods of limiting the dangerous usage of radioactive materials are only superficially attractive. The amount of material, for example, needed for isotopic de-naturing or 'spiking' would be enormous in relation to the effectiveness achieved.

There was also discussion about the benefits of test bans and test ban verification, and it was conclusively argued that it was highly improbable that all horizontal proliferation could be prevented. On the other hand many nations, though obviously not all, might be prevented from acquiring nuclear weapons and it should be possible, with rigorous safeguards, to obstruct the diversion of weapons and the more sophisticated technology to terrorists.

In discussion the need to avoid alienating, through non-proliferation campaigns, the protagonists of peaceful nuclear energy was stressed. The reality of the now inevitable development of peaceful nuclear energy had to be faced. It is, therefore, important that those who are primarily concerned with non-proliferation of nuclear weapons, and those whose prime concern is for the peaceful use of nuclear energy, should find common ground. In this connection, references to British investigations had shown that, for example, the thorium cycle is not necessarily any less dangerous than the plutonium cycle. It was suggested that denaturing was only one of a number of technical palliatives and is in itself not ultimately irreversible: the problem of producing sufficient denaturing material was again referred to. There is no single answer to the technical problems related to proliferation, and technology in itself will certainly not prevent the proliferation of nuclear weapons. Hence it is vital to approach all these problems by a variety of methods, both technical and political. In this connection the current pessimism about arms control and its achievements should not be allowed to go too far. Like other instruments, it is one of a range of options which must be applied simultaneously in order to attempt to introduce some rationality into the present absurd situation.

SALT and Arms Control Prospects

The discussion on SALT and other arms control negotiations began with an attempt to assess the current position especially in so far as Europe was concerned. The remark 'the more one eats the more one's appetite grows' was quoted with the suggestion that negotiators' appetite for arms control had steadily increased, in that they had become more and more ambitious and, therefore, more frequently than was necessary encountered a failure. What was needed was limited and modest activity aimed at clear and specific tasks; otherwise arms control negotiations were almost inevitably doomed to be counterproductive. The essential thing was to know beforehand what the general objective of any negotiations might be. In Europe the essential reality was that SALT and theatre nuclear forces had become entangled. Theatre and strategic systems realistically had probably to be merged for negotiating purposes. The threats from imbalances 'were mainly a matter of perception'. In tackling the European situation, however, it was probably unworkable to include weapons which were from their locations unable to reach the United States. New European negotiations about medium-range systems in Europe and any resumed SALT talks might be more usefully kept distinct.

It was further suggested that the strategists' view was essentially bankrupt. Though the deterrence of major attacks and major war between the superpowers might now have become relatively easy in political terms, technological development of weapon systems had continued unabated for 10—15 years, with potentially disastrous consequences even in the economic field. It is time for negotiation, but negotiation on arms control measures involves a realistic appreciation of their limitations. Arms controllers should realise that they have a range of tasks, all of which might seem to be inter-active. Their first duty is to minimise the chance of war; their second to reduce the horrors of war, if it occurs; and their third to reduce the peacetime costs of war-preparation. Their function needs to be identified more clearly as reflecting the general interest in avoiding war, already referred to. It was suggested that it was unlikely that the proposal for a nuclear free zone in Europe would attract much support, because the threat of the horror of war in Europe is a deterrent in strategic terms. On the other hand, it was certainly necessary to develop, probably at the Madrid Con-ference, new confidence-building measures focusing on such questions as early warning times and demilitarised zones. Though major force reductions seem difficult to achieve, arms control should aim initially at restrictions in military strength in such a way that those restrictions could be seen to match political objectives and aspirations.

In discussion, it was forcibly argued that what was needed was a clearer public perception of the real objectives of the major parties, however antagonistic those objectives might initially appear to be. This involved, as had already been indicated in the context of international security, the emergence of definite rules of detente following clear and frank discussions which must aim at revealing the nature and extent of competition and rivalry. Large-scale arms control requires more than declarations on non-use of force. There has to be some way of inspiring confidence that there will not be radical attempts to promote unacceptable changes in existing social systems. The notion of confidence-building measures aimed at establishing the ground rules of detente was emphasised. Reference to such issues recurred in different con-texts.

The achievements of the SALT era and its historic rôle were examined. The loss of momentum which had followed earlier achievements in the field of arms control was probably inevitable. It might even be possible to take a thoroughly pessimistic view, and to argue that the world situation would have been better rather than worse without SALT. This was not an argument which found any favour. There had been distinctive, if limited, gains even if SALT II were never to be ratified. One of these was a break-through in relation to Soviet secrecy which had resulted in the possibility of a continuing dialogue on military issues. Even so SALT II ratification had probably been doomed in the United States before the Afghanistan crisis of December 1979. For a variety of reasons attitudes in the United States had moved towards giving primacy to the security of that country and maybe to its military superiority before giving priority to arms control. In this connection it was again emphasised that both in America and the Soviet Union the real concern was with each others' stance and attitudes. It was, therefore, important to discover, for example, whether the Soviets would be prepared without the ratification of SALT II to go forward to other negotiations. The response to this was simply that 'we don't believe each other' and that the most important way of establishing confidence would be for SALT II to be ratified. It was argued from the Soviet standpoint that new negotiations could not have effect unless or until SALT II was ratified. At this point the fear experienced by the different parties about their security and about the prospect of nuclear war in relation to it was raised again in different forms. If fear has increased, will it necessarily this time be capable of being reversed, or will, in the event, polarisation of attitudes be confirmed, and the renewal of negotiations on a reasonable basis made even more difficult than their initiation in the first instance? It was generally accepted, however, that the arms control culture, as it was described, was a product of the American system, and that its institutionalisation within that system was an important factor in a movement towards stability in world affairs. It was important that steps should be taken especially to prevent total disillusionment in that quarter. It was agreed that there was probably a corresponding problem in the Soviet Union as a result of the non-ratification of SALT II.

Finally, on this subject, the question of what arms control is capable of doing was looked at again. The development of such concepts as 'mutually assured destruction' had deceived many people into believing that the control of the technological race was a very difficult political manoeuvre. It was too readily assumed that experts really know and that technology really works. Technological development was in fact sanctified by the development of strategies and doctrines. This sanctification of technological development led to escalation because there are always counter-technologies even if their only use is to generate confusion.

Another assumption had implicitly been made, and that was that success in negotiations could only be at the expense of the other side. In fact, in arms control negotiations success could only be judged in terms of both sides. Arms control negotiations and their product would be bypassed unless there was respect for the golden rule that each must feel secure. For this reason, the concept of verification, though marginally useful in some cases, was an essentially futile approach, because verification was unlikely to be effective unless trust existed and the political will to respect the agreements prevailed. Verification is also too heavily vulnerable to technological innovation.

To some extent the conventional arms race, especially in Europe, was tending to drive the nuclear arms race. The situation in Europe could be seen in two ways: either it was on the verge of a further dangerous period of expansion and deployment on both sides, or it could proceed to negotiations aimed at some form of nuclear disarmament in Europe, leaving for the time being the strategic weapon systems. The important thing was to renew the dialogue, and with the present situation over SALT II it was perhaps most likely that Europe and European-orientated talks would provide the better prospect.

Confidence-Building Measures – a Specific Proposal

A discussion on confidence-building measures concentrated on a particular proposal. It was suggested that arms control negotiations have codified the arms race, and that, except for the Biological Warfare Convention, no real disarmament has taken place. The argument, however, that the upgrading of what might be termed the 'arms control bureaucracies' could seriously affect the issue did not meet with much enthusiasm. Though there was a general acceptance of the importance of small groups of specialists, specifically concerned with the technicalities and processes of arms control, it was thought to be extremely important to permeate the whole of the governmental systems relevant to defence and military matters with attitudes which would encourage them to review all measures in the light of the prospect for peace, and possible eventual arms limitation and reduction. Indeed, the separateness of arms control agencies and organisations was criticised. This would tend, some participants felt, to reduce the emphasis on the avoidance of war as the priority. The institutionalisation of procedures might well lead people to suppose that these matters were already in safe hands and would be promoted, and that they themselves could, therefore, shrug off the responsibility. While the purposes of arms control and its objectives needed to be redefined and asserted if a radical change was to take place, only a freeze on military budgets with possible subsequent reduction, or some such radical measure to draw attention in political and popular terms to the issues, might be effective. Political leaders, and especially heads of state, needed a direct stake in arms control negotiations. They should not be spectators; only in this way would they be able to deal with opposition and attempts to bypass the agreements which were made. In a sense, the various arms control bureaucracies which had been established in a few countries had served a very useful purpose, but they had not necessarily contributed to the establishment of a proper constituency for thinking on arms control. This was because of the tendency to separate their professional concerns from the realities of national and international security interests, and as in the case of energy interests and movements towards non-proliferation this division could well prove stultifying.

The Position of the Third World

The discussion on international security and arms control ended with an examination of the problems of the Third World. This began with references to the NPT as a discriminatory agreement favouring the established nuclear countries — an argument which many felt to be unconstructive. Piling up criticism against the NPT was not thought to be helpful; what was necessary, was an alternative political approach to the problem to parallel that treaty and attempts to enforce it. The example of the acceptance by the United States and Great Britain of the IAEA regime for the peaceful uses of nuclear technology was quoted as a potential breakthrough which might be generally applied. It was nevertheless agreed that on a number of these issues there was no reason to feel that international discussion could not be initiated by less significant states. Ireland's initiative on non-proliferation, taken as long ago as 1958, had already been referred to. On the other hand, it was vital to tackle problems of regional security. Southern Africa has been mentioned as an area in which potential nuclear proliferation was probably affecting the military attitudes of a number of countries in the region, but this applied to several parts of the world. Also relevant was that a number of Third World countries had a considerable problem in meeting their needs in terms of economic survival. The costs of crude oil, for example, might be directly related to a drive to acquire nuclear technology with a consequent heading towards nuclear weapon proliferation. There were, however, countries like Niger with considerable supplies of uranium who needed to be helped to play a full and responsible rôle within the framework of the international community, with the guarantee that they could use the raw materials in their soil for their own purposes or to their own direct advantage.

The discussion on non-proliferation merged with a discussion on wider security issues. It was argued that non-alignment was really the surest way to security for Third World countries because dependence on foreign military aid, in particular, limited foreign policy·options. There was some doubt, however, whether the indigenisation of arms production, which had been possible in some countries — especially those few which had an imperial legacy of such production — was, in fact, a factor assisting security in all respects.

The example of Latin America and the Treaty of Tlatelolco in relation to the establishment of a nuclear free zone was quoted, and the potential of nuclear free zones as an aspect of regional disarmament was discussed. On the whole, whilst nuclear free zones obviously had their uses, as in the wider fields of arms control, the prime requirement was for arrangements which would guarantee security.

On several occasions the special problems of Africa were raised. Nigeria, for example, had an interest in developing its nuclear potential in the peaceful field, and at the same time creating a situation in which the countries of West Africa around it were encouraged to establish freedom of action. Nigeria, it was argued, was reluctant to respond to threats in the sub-region from forces outside; France was sometimes seen in such an interventionist rôle and was felt by some countries in that area to have been providing a stimulus to what would in economic terms be 'a debilitating process of arms acquisition'.

Conclusion

The whole range of discussions on disarmament proposals and prospects was notable for its concern for the basic political aspects of security, and its emphasis on the importance of establishing the right priorities. It was unlikely that disarmament, even very limited disarmament, would be a first step. What was required was a new phase in international relations in which major powers would establish, firmly, the rules by which they intended to conduct themselves internationally, and in which on a regional basis other countries, especially Third World countries, would, in fact, be encouraged to devise regional security agreements based initially and particularly on the promise of non-intervention from outside.

PART I

THE CENTRAL ARMS RACE

2 Disarmament, Security and Public Confidence

William F. Gutteridge

International crises, especially during presidential election campaigns in the United States, tend to harden the attitudes of the key actors on the world's stage. They encourage positive and uncritical political responses to the 'worst case' analyses which it is the undoubted professional responsibility of the military to supply. The polarisation which ensues generally not only leads to increased military expenditures, which may not be of paramount importance in itself, but enhances the risk of war, by sensitising international relationships. In these circumstances the exploitation of inherent human insecurity becomes easier and the justification of tougher defence policies is facilitated. Popular anxieties faithfully reciprocate the stances of political leaderships who not only play upon the natural concern for national survival but effectively manage the dissemination of information relevant to it.

Crises over Afghanistan, the oil-producing states of the Persian Gulf, Angola or Vietnam come and may go, and are largely accommodated psychologically because of a tacit assumption that in due course 'normality' will return, in the shape of tension at a conventionally acceptable level. In some ways such an assumption is essential if the international community is not to live permanently in the grip of fears which might precipitate global war at any time. It does, however, presuppose the reversibility of any acute deterioration in international relations and it also fails to take account of the innovations in weapons and doctrines for their use which are part of the response and are not usually withdrawn once initiated. If, for example, the gap between the announcement of the intended acquisition of new weapon systems such as cruise missiles or Trident missile submarines and their deployment was to prove, as it might, of real significance in terms of debate and negotiation then a breakthrough in halting spiralling arms rivalry might have been achieved.

That such a breakthrough is desirable is probably self-evident. That disarmament can only be achieved by a mutual enhancement of security may not be self-evident. The present potentially disastrous and yet manifestly absurd situation has been on the cards for at least 25 years during which time the resources devoted to military purposes have trebled in the world as a whole. It was President Dwight Eisenhower who first commented percipiently on the so-called military–industrial complex and referred in 1953 to the nuclear arms race as 'the disastrous rise in misplaced power'. Today the proliferation of independent states, as well as the rivalry between the United States and the Soviet Union, has contributed to an unprecedented level of arms and military expenditure at a time of alleged peace, when much of the globe's still rapidly increasing population lack the necessities of life. Perhaps this indicates an inherent human inability to develop the necessary institutions for the control of technology and to tackle problems on this scale. There is no doubt about the essential facts even though the precise figures from time to time may be the subject of futile argument. There has been a vast increase in military expenditure in this century. Today we devote, in real terms, twenty times the resources that were devoted to military expenditure in the run-up to the First World War. Military expenditure has quadrupled at least since the end of the Second World War and risen particularly steeply since 1970. Quite apart from the risk to peace which is involved in maintaining the equivalent of about a million and a quarter Hiroshima bombs, it is reasonable to argue that there must have been a massive diversion of resources away from humane social purposes.

Today in the world about 25 million men are under arms and well over 50 million men and women are employed directly or indirectly for military purposes. One in four of all research scientists and technologists actually employed in research and development are employed in military research and development. In the case of physicists, and some types of engineer, working in research and development, the proportion may be as high as one in two. With involvement on that scale the moral responsibility cannot lie solely with the politicians.

The social implications of this great growth in military expenditure are often obscured by an aggregation of the figures by totting up the global statistics and then taking a percentage. Only 6 per cent of the world's output, the world's income, the total of the world's gross national products is devoted to this purpose. On the face of it this is, perhaps, not an outrageous proportion but in the case of individual countries the figure ranges from 0.9 per cent to 30 per cent. But that 6 per cent of the world total is, in fact, the rough equivalent of the total income of the 1500 million poorest of the world's population, living in South-East Asia, the Far East and Africa. At 1979 prices one Trident submarine would have cost the total national income of a country like Jordan.

Clearly such a military burden has disabling effects, especially in less developed countries. Technically trained manpower is diverted from other rôles. Though thousands of jobs may be available in armaments industries in developed countries, there is no doubt that they are relatively poor employers because they are erratic and capital-intensive, and often too dependent on one consumer. The effect of the revolution in Iran on factories producing tanks in places like Gateshead, Great Britain, is sufficient evidence of this. We are also told that military expenditure is inflationary. So why do we not disarm? Why has disarmament, at least until now, not become a popular cause with consistent mass support?

There are many reasons. In the first place, arms and armies are associated with national pride and loyalty. They are there to provide at least notional protection against perceived threats, whether real or imaginary. The problem as a whole is seen as too large and intimidating to be solved and is, therefore, ignored or fended off. Piecemeal arms control measures tend to treat the symptoms of the problem rather than to dig out the roots. Politically the ratification by the American Senate of SALT II, the agreement on strategic arms limitation, was desirable. The agreement remains a possible basis for future negotiations by the Ronald Reagan Administration. Even so, the SALT II negotiations were so prolonged that an agreement, which actually allowed for increases in certain categories of strategic weapons, was only achieved at the expense of concurrent increases in both American and Soviet military expenditure. In the end, technical arguments, such as those which have hindered the Mutual Force Reduction talks in Vienna for 13 years confirm the bystander's impression that, in relation to the capacity to wipe out mankind, debates about the allowable levels of nuclear and other categories of weapon are irrelevant.

All these factors tend to discredit arms control and to make disarmament a negative issue − a reduction in jobs and security, rather than an addition to the well-being of mankind. How can it be made positive? Clearly new political priorities are needed, especially the reallocation of resources to development and other social needs, and for this international incentives are required. One suggestion is to impose, through the United Nations and a general agreement, a ceiling on military expenditures. An agreement to freeze at present levels would apparently be in everybody's interest. If connected with a limitation on the introduction of new weapon systems, and especially if inflation continued, reductions would soon follow. Another device which has already been examined is a tax on military expenditure; a fund, with the proceeds devoted to development and other social purposes. A 10 per cent tax generally applied would enable international agencies to tackle problems like the universal supply of clean drinking water and the irrigation of semi-arid areas. This would give some credibility to the process of disarmament and arms reduction as a positive act in the interests of mankind as a whole. Less directly it would ensure that there was more publicity, and increase the pressure to publicise what actually happens in the military field, particularly the processes of selling arms and providing training for other people's armies. Publicity as a form of restraint has been underplayed. Even retrospective information would exercise some influence on the development and elaboration of defence policies. But even so, little progress will be made until more account is taken of the fundamental issues.

Why arm? Why do so few countries, even those who cannot possibily defend themselves, actually resist the temptation to develop armies beyond those which are absolutely strictly necessary in size and sophistication for normal security? Costa Rica might be mentioned, or The Gambia, and they are scarcely significant examples. The case of Tanzania could be quoted where 6 months before independence in the former Tangyanika Julius Nyerere was on the point of dispensing with armed forces. But then he decided to have them. At first they only amounted to two battalions inherited from the colonial power, which were eventually expanded to meet the threat from Idi Amin's Uganda. But why arm in the first place? − presumably because armed forces are symbols of nationhood and power. It was Joseph Stalin who once enquired: 'but how many divisions has the Pope?' and put it all into the perspective of 'realpolitik'.

Behind the arms race and the futile acquisition of more and more dangerous weapons lies the perception of threat, real or imaginary, and with it the possibility of conflict and a sense of insecurity. In the end, though pressures for arms control and disarmament need to be sustained, any radical improvement will depend on a political approach to security.

A survey and article in *New Society* dealt with the question of popular reactions in Britain to current defence policy and the rôle of nuclear weapons.[1] Nuclear weapons seemed in the public mind to be overshadowed by economic issues and the cost of living, but there was clear evidence of a growing concern about nuclear war. Civil defence was not rated highly, with 70 per cent of the population convinced that they would not survive a nuclear war. They are probably right and there are others who would not want to survive in those conditions. Roughly the same proportion, according to this report, however, feel that Britain should retain her nuclear weapons and are convinced that a policy of deterrence is the only answer. Most significantly, 85 per cent — the highest positive response to any question — are convinced that the Soviet Union poses a serious military threat to Great Britain and Europe. This is the key fact that the political leadership fosters, or at least is dependent upon for the justification of defence expenditure, especially when imposing increases in such budgets in times of recession.

The protagonists of disarmament, whether general, nuclear, multilateral, unilateral or European, cannot ignore this feeling of insecurity by whatever means it is generated and the part that it plays in sustaining a deterrence policy, for that policy derives its strength from the belief that it will both thwart the enemy on the one hand, and avoid the nuclear holocaust on the other. So, there is continuing attention paid to the Soviet threat and to means of defence against it.

In the process there are a number of questions which remain largely undiscussed. On what practical or moral basis could, in the last resort, a nuclear holocaust be regarded as preferable to Soviet expansion? What, indeed, is the likelihood of Soviet expansion into, and of an occupation of, Western Europe in any circumstance? If nuclear war is wrong and suicidal, is it not also wrong and immoral to threaten it in response? Even in military terms, have nuclear weapons utility? Lord Mountbatten, in one of the final speeches of his career, actually raised this question. The whole question must be seen from the standpoint of a potential enemy: the view expressed in many quarters in the Soviet bloc is in effect a mirror image of that emanating from the Pentagon at its most hawkish. They see themselves surrounded by a hostile world, threatened by subversion, with serious domestic weaknesses; the proceedings of the Madrid Conference have demonstrated that the Soviet Union and her allies feel threatened by the kinds of pressure on human rights and other issues which have resulted from sub- scribing to the Helsinki Final Act, and which are highlighted by events in Poland. A gun is a defensive weapon seen from behind; it does not look that way when it is pointed at you! The SS-20, for example, can easily be presented in the Soviet Union as no more than a response to an earlier generation of Western nuclear weapons. The cruise missile and Pershing II are the West's response to it. The process is endless.

Disarmament will not begin without a shift away from mutual distrust towards mutual confidence. However serious the Soviet threat, however extensive their arms build-up, the opportunity has to be left for a change in attitude to have effect and for the genuineness of an initiative, verbal or otherwise, to be tested.

Security is not a 'zero-sum' game. In other words, security can- not be achieved at the expense of that of a potential enemy. The security of one is the security of the other. In spite of the claim that the deployment of cruise missiles and Pershing II missiles is necessary to redress the balance upset by the deployment of the Soviet SS-20, in a more general sense rough parity at present exists, a sufficient parity, as it were, between East and West. The con- tinued deployment of the Soviet system is, however, inevitably undermining this. The moment has been reached and will soon pass for a freeze at present levels of deployment and development while negotiations proceed. The reduction of nuclear weapons systems deployed in Europe could then be the aim of the next stage. Without a freeze the negotiations themselves will probably come to nothing, because in the meantime all parties will be trying to get themselves into a position of additional strength from which to negotiate.

In the meantime, in order to promote further developments, serious confidence-building measures of a deliberate kind relating to military and political aspirations must be devised and implemented. A system by which the subscribing countries to an agreement make open declarations of their intentions should be instituted. Notification, before or soon after the event, should operate not only for troop manoeuvres but for deployment and for major arms transfers. Surface naval movements, which in any case are observable by satellite, might be included. Discussion of the technicalities relating to the equivalence of different weapon systems should be subordinate to the devising of procedures which safeguard against the possibility of war. The reduction of fear and distrust and the avoidance of a war that nobody wants, demands a level of discipline in international relations which has not yet been achieved. A determination not to overreact to the actions and rhetoric of the other side is one essential prerequisite.

The resurgence in Great Britain and elsewhere, in spite of governmental resolve to the contrary, of a diversity of peace movements is itself an encouragement to a more rational approach. In some senses these peace movements divide against themselves. The World Disarmament Movement may not subscribe to the immediate objective of the Campaign for European Nuclear Disarmament. It may, in turn, not want to get too closely involved with the Campaign for Nuclear Disarmament. But the mere diversity of these movements has already created an important debate; a debate started within the peace movement which has already brought in people who have not so far been involved. People whose influence derives from their independence may see in this diversity the opportunity for focusing publicly on the real issue of the avoidance of nuclear war. Starting with Mountbatten, there have already been some members of the scientific and military establishment willing to give credibility to the debate which is taking place. In the media in Great Britain there were, by mid-1980, signs of a real debate in which participants of a wide range of opinion were being caused to state their common ground. A groundswell of mass popular protest in the West covering a wide spectrum of views is unlikely to be matched by a similar spontaneous movement in the Soviet Union; the Communist system would preclude it. But in due course the Soviet leadership may have to live up to its own peace rhetoric, in response to clear evidence of good faith and intentions in the West. The unquestioning acceptance of defence policies, which is now being challenged, is based on the maintenance of political stereotypes and on the continuance of historic fears and international suspicions.

There is unlikely to be complete agreement about the methods by which a nuclear war is to be avoided. Some people in the West will be pacifists, some people will be very far from being pacifists, some people will think that the Soviet Union is a benign power, others will think it is a determinedly aggressive power; that is not the point. The point is that to focus on the avoidance of war by the best means available requires a greater realism and a recognition of the needs and aspirations of others. Protest against military preparations and nuclear proliferation may be categorised as self-indulgent unless it is based on a recognition of the implications of disarmament. It might be accompanied by a new concept of defence and resistance making use of the precision and reliability of the new generation of conventional weapons. It is necessary to get away from the conviction that the choice lies between subjugation and wholesale destruction. Protest on its own is liable to breed pessimism. C. P. Snow once wrote 'when men believe that events are too big for them, there is no hope'. Constructive and acceptable alternative policies which are realistically concerned with international security are the necessary concomitant of opposition to nuclear escalation. Is military power the only recognised basis for power and influence? Is its utility not demonstrably declining? It is not inconceivable that the Western European nations, if they could effectively combine in matters of foreign policy, could demonstrate the potential of civilian power derived from economic and cultural strength?

Note

1. *New Society*, 25 Sept. 1980.

3 Some Peculiarities of the Arms Race on the Threshold of the 1980s

M. A. Milstein

Appraising the past decade from the point of view of achievements in stopping the arms race, one should acknowledge that the 1970s were marked by definite results in the limitation of the arms race and in disarmament. Thus international agreements prohibiting the deployment of mass destruction weapons on the seabed and ocean-floor, banning bacteriological weapons and limiting natural environment modification techniques were signed; and draft agreements on limiting strategic armaments and preventing nuclear wars were reached. A number of measures, aiming at strengthening mutual confidence in Europe, began to materialise in the same years. A system of negotiations on problems of disarmament, both on a bilateral and multilateral basis, was created. This produced a number of resolutions still awaiting implementation. The Soviet Union has been one of the major sponsors of, and an active participant in, all these actions, aiming at the limitation of the arms race.

On the whole one can say that the past decade was not wasted for the limitation of the arms race. At the same time one should not think that the aforementioned developments mitigated unworthy rivalry in this field and still less that they stopped the arms race. On the contrary, at the turn of the decade, as the result of the actions taken by the United States and some other NATO countries aimed at undermining detente, and at causing an escalation of the arms race and of military preparations, a sharp spiralling of the arms race took place which enhanced the danger of an outbreak of nuclear war.

The myth about the 'Soviet military menace' widely circulated in the West by all available means has served as a pretext and cover for all these steps. Thus the increase of the military budgets of NATO countries is mainly justified by the allegation that the Soviet Union is regularly increasing its military spending and allocates for military purposes much more than is required for its defence. But in fact it is common knowledge that the Soviet Union is steadily reducing its spending, confining itself to its national security needs. The United States explained the decision speedily to develop and deploy the MX mobile missile, in particular, by the Soviet Union's alleged acquisition of a first-strike capability through modernisation of its long-range missiles which makes American land-based missiles vulnerable. But it is known, and the Soviet leaders have stated this more than once, that the Soviet Union is against the first-strike concept and is not seeking this capability.

Using the pretext of 'the Soviet military menace', and acting under American pressure, NATO took a decision on the production and deployment in Western Europe of medium-range missiles. Hence, the myth about 'the Soviet military menace' is widely and continuously used at all levels as a justification for all the measures and actions recently envisaged in American military doctrine and policy.

What are the main features of the present-day arms race? First to be noted is the geographical scope of this sinister phenomenon which has acquired global proportions and which has a complex nature. The number of states entering the vicious arms race is growing. The major powers are followed down the road of creating considerable military arsenals by a large number of medium-sized and small countries.

Nuclear weapons, of monstrous destructive capacity, present the greatest danger. According to American estimates, nuclear weapons on our planet are equivalent to more than 1,350,000 atomic bombs of the type dropped by the United States on Hiroshima in 1945. According to some American data they exceed 50 billion tons of TNT. The available stocks of nuclear weapons are sufficient for the manifold annihilation of every living thing on the Earth. Meanwhile, weapons of mass destruction are continuously modernised and their numbers are growing. The production of nuclear armaments proceeds alongside the output of conventional arms thus leading to the unrestrained, ever-growing accumulation of the instruments of death and destruction.

So-called conventional weapons are no less dangerous. Many modern types of conventional weapons, developed on the basis of the latest achievements of science and technology, possess colossal destructive power. According to some estimates, the armies of the world are now armed with 124,000 tanks, 35,000 combat aircraft, 12,400 warships and other types of military equipment.

Results of the scientific—technical revolution are widely applied for military purposes. Nearly one-fourth of the world scientific personnel is engaged in military research and development. Nearly 40 per cent of research funds are invested in this.

On the whole, it is possible to note that on the threshold of the 1980s the arms race and the rate of arms stockpiling reached a point at which critical alternatives are faced: either the arms race is stopped and reversed or we enter upon a new era of perilous brinkmanship with all the ensuing consequences for mankind. It is no coincidence that many Western experts regard the 1980s as a period of supreme importance and, to a certain extent, a critical one for the prevention of new, dangerous spirals in the arms race. Simultaneously, it is stressed that if we fail to take resolute and effective measures, aiming at a real curbing of the arms race in this decade, if we miss the chances, however small they may be, to achieve this, the world might start to slip irreversibly into the abyss of a nuclear catastrophe.

Bernard Feld, a noted American physicist and former Secretary-General of the Pugwash Movement, has written that the chances of nuclear weapons being used in case of a conflict before 1984 are, roughly, one to three and of a nuclear war in the remaining 16 years of our century are more than fifty—fifty. As the statement from the 30th Pugwash Conference, held in August 1980, emphasised 'never before has mankind been in such grave peril'.

Considering the concrete features of the modern state of the arms race, it is necessary to note that its main peculiarity is a shift of central emphasis from the quantitative to the qualitative aspect. This is especially true for development in strategic arms. In this connection the qualitative arms race, initiated as before by the United States, might be viewed as the motive force of the modern state of the arms race. Though formally it is whipped up with the pretext of the 'Soviet military threat', its real cause is the striving of definite circles in Washington to depart from the state of parity and to achieve military—technical, in other words, qualitative, superiority over the Soviet Union in the decisive dimensions of strategic arms. According to Carter's Secretary of Defense, Harold Brown, the short- and long-term programmes in science and technology are so balanced as to secure American technical superiority over its possible adversaries.

The qualitative improvement of nuclear missiles is especially dangerous, because such innovations at a time of scientific— technical revolution, especially in nuclear weapon systems, may have far-reaching strategic and political consequences. Any attempt to reach superiority in strategic forces may destabilise the situation and increase the danger of nuclear war. In other words, there is no further rationale either in the quantitative or the qualitative arms race.

Improvements in the accuracy of the means of delivery is the most dangerous trend of the qualitative arms race. (Accuracy is usually measured by the so-called circular error probable, that is equal to the radius of the circle centred at the target that contains 50 per cent of the warheads aimed at it.) Specifically, the case in point is further improvement of the Minuteman-3 missile-guidance system through introduction of the MK-12A warhead and a new guidance system NS-20. Accelerated development of the new generation of warheads for intercontinental missiles capable of manoeuvrability and control in the final portion of the flight trajectory, is under way (the so-called MARV system). With the introduction in 1979 of the MK-12A the accuracy of the Minuteman-3 missile doubled in comparison with the earlier Minuteman-3 missile; the Poseidon naval missile (1971) doubled compared with Polaris; and the Trident-1 missile, which will be introduced at the beginning of the 1980s, will be nearly four times more accurate in comparison with the Polaris missile.

Work continues on the MARV system for the Trident and MX missiles. This system can change direction in the final stages of the flight trajectory and ensure the accuracy of missiles. With the considerable improvement in accuracy, the destructive power of the warhead increases. The introduction of long-range cruise missiles, which can be equipped with nuclear or conventional warheads and super-accurate guidance systems, will be fraught with equally serious consequences.

Emergence of considerable quantities of missiles of high accuracy are leading the United States to revise in the most dangerous way a number of basic military–strategic concepts and especially those which relate to the consequences of a nuclear war and the employment of nuclear missiles in such a war. We are in fact here confronting the fundamental issues of nuclear strategy. Can nuclear weapons be effectively used for the settlement of foreign problems? Could victory be gained in a nuclear war? Is limited nuclear war possible and what would its price be? In other words, there is a straightforward question: should there be a nuclear war or not? It is common knowledge that for a long time there was a widespread opinion in the United States that nuclear war is 'unthinkable', that there can be no winners in such a war, that a nuclear war will mean the end of civilisation, and that to start such a war means to commit suicide. Nuclear forces were regarded, at least in official declarations, as a means to deter and avert a nuclear war and not to be used in combat operations.

Official US documents and verbal statements of Administration officials repeatedly stressed that the huge American nuclear stockpile served as a sort of stern warning to the other side, reminding it that the United States was at all times in a position to deliver a powerful retaliatory blow causing unacceptable manpower and economic losses to the other side. This is the essence of the 'assured destruction' concept, which was advanced by Robert McNamara, Secretary of Defense way back in the 1960s. Time passed. Presidents came and went, and so did the names of American doctrines – 'massive retaliation', 'flexible response', 'realistic deterrence' – and still the 'assured destruction' concept remained a starting point, a fundamental concept of the American military doctrine.

But since there has existed a recognised parity of strategic forces it has been assumed that the other side had similar 'assured destruction' capabilities and that there is an objective possibility of 'mutual assured destruction', although it was not officially recognised. At the same time American experts admit that this meant mutual deterrence and the recognition of the impermissibility of nuclear war, since the use of nuclear weapons would pose a potentially grave threat to the United States itself.

So at the beginning of the 1980s the United States has adopted a new strategy. What is new now is not only that the priority in targeting is shifted from the cities and industrial centres of the Soviet Union to its military and political targets, but what is more important and dangerous is the recognition of the possibility of waging nuclear war, a possibility that has been accepted at the very highest levels of the American Government — the acceptability of nuclear war and the possibility of victory in such a war. The new strategy by no means could be called a strategy of deterrence. It is a strategy of waging and fighting nuclear war with victory in such a war in view.

Colin Gray, the leading Research Fellow of the Hudson Institute in the United States, in an article published in the Summer 1980 issue of *Foreign Policy* expressed the view that, as he pointed out, now exists in the so-called defence community of the United States: 'The United States should plan to defeat the Soviet Union and to do so at a cost that would not prohibit the United States's recovery.' It is unnecessary to stress the dangerous impact of such statements.

The new strategy gives a new definition to 'limited nuclear war', emphasising the selectiveness of targets and the 'limited' collateral damage that would ensue in comparison with a strike against cities and industrial centres. The new concept, which provides for the use of strategic offensive forces mainly against military targets, may in effect be regarded potentially as a concept of the first strike, that is a disarming strike, since the constant process of improving accuracy and the introduction of invulnerable mobile systems provide material backing for this concept.

Soviet military doctrine is that nuclear weapons will never be used unless an aggressor uses them first. The Soviet Union believes that nuclear war will bring no advantage to anyone and may even lead to the end of civilisation; and the end of civilisation can hardly be called 'victory'. Soviet doctrine regards nuclear weapons as ones that must never be used. They are not an instrument for waging war in any rational sense. They are not weapons with which one can achieve foreign policy goals. But, of course, if the Soviet Union is forced to use them in reply to their first use by an aggressor, they will be used, with all their consequences, as a punishment of the aggressor. The Soviet Union does not believe there can be such a thing as 'limited' nuclear war and considers that any nuclear conflict is bound to be catastrophic in its consequences.

What is behind the extremist development in American military policy? As a pretext to justify steps and actions envisaged in recent American military doctrine much has been made of the myth about the 'Soviet military threat'. First, the concept of 'Soviet military threat' is widely held among various groups of people throughout the West, and particularly in the United States. It is not a temporary phenomenon but a very stable opinion. Actually this concept appeared not today, not yesterday, but long ago almost at the same time as the emergence of the Soviet state. Of course since then this concept has undergone some evolutional changes but it has preserved its main features. This concept served in the past and is serving now as a pretext for justifying what the US Government or any other NATO country wants to do in the military field.

This concept is widely believed not because there is a real military threat but because such opinion is artificially built up by politicians, military establishments and the mass media for reasons which usually have nothing to do with real threats or national security. As Henry Steele Commager wrote on 26 August 1980 in his article in the *International Herald Tribune*:

> We [the United States] are threatened by a paranoia that sees the Soviet Union as a mortal enemy, bent on the destruction of the United States and free nations everywhere, and by the military policies that this paranoia dictates. There never has been and there is not now any basis for this fantasy.

Nevertheless this concept has its fluctuations. It is particularly widely disseminated and advertised at a time when there is a debate going on about a military budget, or about a new weapons programme, or about a new doctrine. Actually all military programmes — increases in military expenditure, military build-ups in general, everything in the military field — are usually presented as a reply to 'the Soviet military threat'. Particularly interested in propagating this myth are those who are protecting the interests of the military—industrial complex of the United States. So we should not expect that this myth will disappear, no matter what the Soviet Union will do.

Actually the real causes of the new and more dangerous trends in American military doctrine and military policy are entirely different. They are, above all, shaped by a serious shift in the American foreign policy course as a whole towards the policy of *Diktat* and expansionism. American foreign policy is sharply moving towards militarisation, whereby any foreign-policy task is intended to be solved only with the help of military force, either through the threat of force or its actual use.

Those circles in Washington which mainly advocate the interests of militarism and the industrial—military complex have gained the upper hand in the military field. Those circles have long favoured a sharp build-up of American military might; they have always sought ways to emerge from the state of parity with a bid to establish military superiority over the Soviet Union through ever-new initiatives in the arms race and through the slowing-down of arms control talks. Some of them believe that the United States is already overwhelmingly superior in technological development.

The interests of the election campaign play a definite rôle here. To please rightist circles Carter whipped up military hysteria in the country so as to avoid accusations from the Right of 'neglecting' national interests and the security of the United States. There is no doubt that the myth about the 'Soviet military threat' has been deliberately used by American aggressive circles to bring pressure on Congress in order to push new military programmes through. Such is the principal explanation for the adoption of the new military strategy. The United States is thus obviously adopting as its basic concept one of using strategic forces in a 'counterforce' rôle. In the 1980s this will undoubtedly be further developed. The adoption of this approach signifies that the possibility and accept-ability of a nuclear war is officially admitted. It is not accidental that in his annual report to the Congress, the US Secretary of Defense, Brown, said that 'the strategy of the USA and NATO takes into account the possibility of being the first to employ nuclear weapons, if it becomes necessary'. Simultaneously, it is stressed that it is indispensable to maintain combat preparedness not only for security needs but for 'execution of offensive opera-tions as well'.

Concerning technological aspects of disarmament, one should not overlook that alongside the development of new destabilising models and types of nuclear weapons and of other types of mass destruction weapons, the creation of the scientific–technical and industrial nuclear potential is taking place in an increasing number of countries. The NPT, which is a sound basis for inter-national co-operation in the peaceful use of atomic energy, still lacks the participation of more than 30 states. Among them are the Republic of South Africa, Brazil, Argentina and some other countries which are capable of manufacturing nuclear explosive devices or are on the threshold of this capability. Nor are two nuclear powers, the People's Republic of China and France, signatories of the Treaty.

As was mentioned earlier, serious changes are taking place in conventional arms development: a series of new types of weapon with explosive, fragmentation and incendiary effects have been developed and have been used in aerial bombing by the United States in the war against Vietnam with total destructive effects which approach the destructive and annihilating consequences of nuclear weapons. Employment of these and of other new types of conventional weapons, coupled with unproved means of accurate guidance, may mean that the differences between nuclear and non-nuclear weapons will be eliminated and this may lead to a higher risk that a conventional conflict will turn into a nuclear war.

It should be stressed again, however, that the nuclear arms race presents the greatest danger. The development of a new generation of nuclear weapons at a time of arms limitation talks, with an emphasis on nuclear arms, undermines these talks, increases mutual distrust and aggravates military confrontation. As previously stressed, the particular danger of the new technological race is that it gradually spreads the opinion in the West that nuclear weapons and the means of their delivery are no longer weapons of deterrent, 'inconceivable' weapons, but have become 'possible' weapons, 'conceivable' weapons.

One should also mention that never before has the technological arms race in Europe been so fraught with such dangers for the people of Europe as it is nowadays. One should never forget that there is no other area in the world with such a large concentration of armed forces and armaments. Here are two combat-ready and opposed military–political groupings with all types of modern weapons, including huge stocks of missile-nuclear weapons. That is why the introduction of new types of nuclear weapons, in Europe, represented by medium-range missiles and the neutron weapon, would render detente more difficult and lead to a new and dangerous spiral in the arms race; it would greatly increase the danger of a nuclear catastrophe in Europe and all over the world. In any case, there are no sound political or military–strategic reasons to justify, in modern conditions, the arming of NATO with new, additional systems of nuclear weapons, especially such systems which can greatly destabilise the situation and invalidate the efforts of many years, aimed at normalisation of relations and at the development of detente in Europe. The emergence of new nuclear weapons and the changes in American military—strategic concepts are thus effecting dangerous changes in the military—strategic concepts of NATO.

What developments in strategic offensive weapons are particularly alarming? First, in the 1980s, the accuracy of warheads and guidance systems will be further improved. This will open up the possibility of hitting small targets and, consequently, the possibility of 'limited' employment of nuclear weapons against military targets and the possibility of adopting the concept of 'counterforce' as a basic one.

Secondly, this period will see armies equipped with destabilising strategic weapons which are represented by mobile ground-based and under-water systems armed with intercontinental missiles. The accuracy of these systems can be reduced to a few dozen metres.

Thirdly, all this provides the potential for a disarming first strike, that is the possibility of putting out of action the retaliatory forces of the other side. Hence the temptation to make a first nuclear strike grows.

Fourthly, air-, sea- and ground-based cruise missiles can become widespread thus leading to the acquisition of a strategic potential by some European countries and to the danger of a further proliferation of nuclear weapons.

Fifthly, the possibility of 'limited' employment of nuclear weapons in a theatre of war will increase due to the improvement of accuracy of so-called tactical nuclear weapons and their further miniaturisation.

Sixthly, in the 1980s the danger of proliferation of nuclear weapons will in general grow and in particular the nuclear potentials of Great Britain, France and especially China will be consolidated. For example, providing the submarine forces of Great Britain with 'Trident' missiles will greatly increase its nuclear potential. Again, China's nuclear potential will be considerably consolidated when it gets intercontinental missiles.

Hence the character and consequences of the strategic arms race in the 1980s will basically differ from the past. It will be, mainly, a qualitative arms race marked by the possibility of increasing ineffectiveness of means of control and verification. Within the same period the definition of strategic parity and equal security might need reappraisal because the old dimensions of these concepts may change.

In these circumstances, the first priority is probably to seek a complete halt to the qualitative and quantitative growth of armaments. A new agreement banning the development and production of new types and systems of weapons of mass destruction would be particularly important.

The Soviet Union stands for the total banning of nuclear weapons. The proposal to halve production of all types of nuclear weapons and to reduce gradually stocks up to their complete elimination was made with that aim in view. The Warsaw Treaty states have proposed early negotiations of the five nuclear powers − the Soviet Union, the United States, Great Britain, France and China − with the aim of withdrawing from the arsenals of states all forms of nuclear weapons and using nuclear power exclusively for peaceful purposes. Early ratification of SALT II and transition to SALT III would be a positive contribution to halting the arms race, including its qualitative aspects and to lessening the danger of nuclear war. Real agreement in the Vienna talks would also play a positive rôle in this process.

Finally, supplementing political detente with the military aspect presupposes the adoption not only of concrete measures aimed at curbing the arms race but also of limitations regarding military−strategic concepts which hinder detente and even whip up the arms race. Realities of our life urgently demand that circles in the West which are drawing up military policy and strategy should stop thinking in terms of war, in general, and in terms of a nuclear war in particular. Any attempt to increase the range of 'applications' of nuclear weapons greatly increases the danger of a nuclear catastrophe.

4 Disarmament: Phoenix and Hydra

Komarraju Ravi

The post-1945 era brought in its wake independence to many Third World nations and also renewed hopes for disarmament and arms control. In the nascent dawn of newly found freedom the Third World nations wanted peace, having understood from the recent past what devastation wars can really bring. Not only this, they were dominated by the 'Western-security' syndrome; that their security needs would be fulfilled by their erstwhile colonisers to an extent at least. Fresh amidst the family of nations they were yet to realise that conflict was endemic to an international system divided into two camps and armed with nuclear weapons and extensive quantities of conventional arms. The Old World (i.e. nations that had been actively associated with the Second World War) was security-conscious and was bent on building 'alignment' for strength. The old 'balance of power theory' was after all still valid. Arms and nations are an integral part of such a system. The possibility of conventional disarmament was exceptionally remote. Yet the Third World talked of such a possibility. This was facilitated by the 'non-aligned' movement which tried to provide security through a diplomatic stance as also to reduce dependence on arms and conventional strategic thinking. This was also implicit in Nehruvian foreign policy. However, it is doubtful whether 'non-alignment' was floated by India as only a moral argument against the Cold War, though Gandhian ways of thinking would prefer such a stance by itself. Jawaharlal Nehru seems to have blended his own views of development, peace and security with the moral necessity of reducing tension which could escalate into a total disaster for humanity.[1] In fact in the early 1960s the Third World rhetoric was against defence spending and considered disarmament as an 'urgent and vital' problem.[2] Nehru was very emphatic and precise about the need for disarmament. He suggested a phased programme of disarmament, not affecting the world balance.[3] The inclusion of eight neutralist nations in the erstwhile Ten-Nation Disarmament Commission (which became the Eighteen-Nation Disarmament Committee) was largely due to the intense efforts of the non-aligned for the cause of disarmament negotiations. Non-alignment around that period implied a lessening of defence expenditure and an increase in security. This was conbined with a strong belief in the futility of the Cold War.[4]

It was not strange that in these circumstances non-alignment was perceived as a balanced security guarantee in a Cold War world. Complete and universal disarmament would then provide complete security and 'alignment' would lead to 'severe insecurity'. Neutralisation too would give 'balanced security' but would limit a nation's sovereignty and hence was a most unwelcome proposition to most of the newly independent nations. A 'nuclear umbrella' would guarantee security but would also equally invite a 'threat' from one of the superpowers and so would only provide a 'precarious security'. These early non-aligned perceptions of security can diagrammatically be shown more precisely as shown in Figure 1.

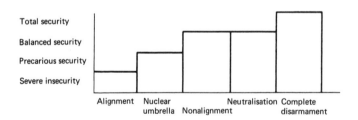

FIGURE 1

However, these initial perceptions of security received a rude shock later on as the Third World began to encounter real-life security problems. Nascent nationalism and disputed borders often brought frontier skirmishes and small-scale hostilities. Further, the Third World, despite the non-aligned movement, could not be thoroughly insulated from the covert influences of the great powers. These realities necessitated thinking on defence and other related topics. Arms, being an integral part of any defence system, very soon became trade commodities. Initial Third World defence programmes were nothing but trade agreements for the import of armaments and spares. India learnt the need of conventional security thinking from its war with China in 1962.[5] The Sino–Indian imbroglio exposed another important aspect of defence planning, namely the indigenisation of defence. Most of the Third World nations faced the problem of lack of foreign exchange reserves for arms purchases. This in effect meant their reliance on the manufacturers and also on long-term loans with possible political strings attached. This limited a nation's foreign policy options as also its scope for political manoeuvre. Hence, the emphasis on the indigenous manufacture of weapons.[6] This too would have been a difficult task if the earlier links with the ex-coloniser nations had not existed. India could get the patent for its Gnat aircraft from Great Britain as also for its frigates and other small arms. Indigenisation of arms manufacture can also be attributed to the growth of technical expertise within the Third World. This apart, the belief that security can be enhanced through arms production has also contributed to an increase in the expenditure on defence in the Third World nations. The perceptual possibility of the existence of a military threat aided by one of the two superpowers has often loomed large in the minds of Third World writers on defence subjects, justifying the need for an arms build-up.[7]

Given all these circumstances, arms control becomes a difficult proposition as far as the Third World is concerned. The Third World nations are impressed and are also overawed by the superpowers and nuclear weapons. They are also aware of the destructive potential of a nuclear war. To them, much more than to others, the existence of the nuclear bomb makes all conventional arms psychologically diminutive in character. Hence the justification for possessing and acquiring them. On a hypothetical 'security-measurement scale' they become a minimum-security need.[8]

Attempts to restrict supply of these minimum-security-need items would be unwelcome, both to the buyer and the seller. A case in point is the Americans' attempts in 1976 to reduce the supply of arms to Third World nations.[9] This alone, however, does not account for the alleged non-aligned softness towards the Soviet Union; rather American preference for 'aligned' Third World states accounts for this to an extent. This is particularly so because the other Western major suppliers like Great Britain, France and Sweden have been 'free' in their arms deals. The Soviets benefit diplomatically from arms aid and ideological arguments to justify the acquisition of conventional arms to protect 'national integrity' from the machinations of alleged 'imperialists'. This trend does not favour disarmament. Any proposal for a conventional arms reduction must necessarily imply a reduction of conventional arms production by the great powers. Meaningful arms control also is not possible without checks on production.

Much of the post-1945 effort at disarmament has in reality yielded nothing substantial. Arms control measures also have proved to be peripheral and of not much value.[10] The attempts at non-proliferation, too, fare no better, since vertical proliferation continues unaffected and the NPT remains to be signed and ratified by a large majority of Afro-Asian and Latin American states. In addition there is the explicit acceptance of the 'flimsiness' of the treaty itself.[11] It is in this global context that conventional arms as well as nuclear ones acquire legitimacy. So the world lives on happily under an 'arms-security' syndrome. Meanwhile the nuclear weapon has also become a symbol of 'status' since it has come to be an accepted idea that the permanent members of the UN Security Council must necessarily be those who possess nuclear weapons. A Japanese writer on international relations has suggested that a non-nuclear weapon nation must also be made a permanent member. This argument underscores the need for a perceptual underrating of nuclear-weapon status. Neville Brown, a British writer on strategy, does not agree with this. He considers that the capability of permanent members is not just merely nuclear but thermo-nuclear, thereby laying the emphasis on technological superiority involved in destructive capability. This is a thorough misunderstanding of technical expertise and competency and the argument is tenuous apart from being ethically indefensible.[12] The suggestion of the Japanese author is worth cool consideration.

Third World attitudes are thus conditioned by attitudes of the advanced nations, particularly the great powers, towards disarmament. It is not as if the non-aligned are not aware of the extreme unconcern of the superpowers about nuclear disarmament: the euphoria that did exist in the 1950s and early 1960s on that count has faded. The Third World paradigm of security has since the 1960s been one of seeking local balances of power and regional preponderance if possible. Within the parameters of this type of military thinking exists their attitude towards disarmament and arms control. Technology too acts as an 'auto-stimulus' for arms build-ups and nuclearisation among the Third World nations. However, demonstration of nuclear capacity cannot be equated with acquisition of nuclear capability. Much of the Third World nuclear demonstration and posturing is diplomatic manoeuvring to gain local preponderance or international influence or diplomatic leverage *vis-à-vis* both the superpowers. Hence, the Third World interest in peaceful nuclear explosions.[13]

Justifying disarmament and arms control in the light of global violence and strategic ideas, like the one that justifies 'short and quick' wars, becomes increasingly difficult. Calculated terror being the credo of any insurgency programme, countering it has become an essential state function today. At least such a need is felt .in multi-ethnic and multi-linguistic societies of the Third World. A minimum arms programme becomes necessary if one visualises the possibilities of any urban guerilla movement today. The manifold possibilities of such a movement can be gauged from Carlos Marighela's *Minimanual of the Urban Guerilla*. If states stop producing arms, the anarchists will not follow suit. The dilemma is painful, sad and real. Still, alternatives are necessary and it is a fact that arms breed violence.

The efforts at disarmament and arms control must necessarily continue both for the ethical value involved and as a practical way out of global disaster. The UN Special Session of 23 May 1978 was a milestone in disarmament efforts, in that it brought out certain new dimensions of the problem involved, like that of arms transfers and the vital need for conventional arms disarmament. The tragic irony of the whole drama of disarmament lies in the hypocrisy of the superpowers: such an attitude was displayed in the years between the wars, too, and the result is well-known history. Limitations on expenditure on nuclear weapons research, comprehensive limitations on vertical proliferation, de-nuclearisation of more zones, an intensive propaganda drive against nuclear arms, as also a massive public information programme (as once suggested by Nehru) educating the common man in the dangers and disaster involved in nuclear weapons, are all vital and necessary if disarmament and arms control are to progress. Unless the problem is urgently tackled even the forlorn hope of a disarmed world nurtured by some of us will slowly recede and would inevitably drive the very talk of a general and complete disarmament into the realms of fiction.

Notes

1. See R. V. R. Chandrasekhara Rao, 'Indian Strategic Thinking – Perspectives of the Seventies and Prospects for the Eighties', paper presented at Center for Strategic Studies Seminar, Australian National University, Canberra.
2. Cecil V. Crabb, Jr, *The Elephants and the Grass: A Study of Non-alignment* (New York, 1965) pp. 100–1.
3. See Nehru's speech to UN General Assembly, 3 Sept. 1960. See also Sisir Gupta, 'The Third World and the Great Powers', *The Annals of the American Academy of Political and Social Science*, 1969, pp. 62–3.
4. Crabb, op. cit. Kwame Nkrumah described great power rivalry as a 'senseless fratricidal struggle to destroy the very substance of humanity'.
5. K. Subrahmanyam, 'Nehru and the Indo-China Conflict of 1962' in B. R. Nanda (ed.), *Indian Foreign Policy: The Nehru Years* (Delhi, 1976). See also Emile Benoit, *Defense and Economic Growth in Developing Countries* (Lexington, Mass., 1973) p. 151; and G. S. Bhargava, *India's Security in the 1980s* (Adelphi Paper no. 125, London, 1976) p. 8.
6. Benoit feels that a combination of economic capabilities and the political doctrine of non-alignment has led India to opt for the 'home manufacture' of arms. See Benoit, op. cit., p. 150.
7. Bhargava, op. cit., p. 13. In fact Subrahmanyam feels that Pakistan will be aided by the United States in the future also.
8. William Gutteridge, 'Arms Control and Developing Countries', in David Carlton and Carlo Schaerf (eds.), *The Dynamics of the Arms Race* (London, 1975) p. 214.
9. Lawrence G. Franko, 'Restraining Arms Exports to the Third World: Will Europe Agree?', *Survival*, xxi (1979) 14.
10. See Neville Brown, *The Future Global Challenge: A Predictive Study of World Security, 1977–1990* (London, 1977) p. 3.
11. ibid., p. 371.
12. ibid., p. 376.
13. See Ciro E. Zoppo, 'Nuclear Technology, Weapons and the Third World', *The Annals of the American Academy of Political and Social Sciences*, 1969, p. 114. See also *Strategic Digest*, June 1974, pp. 58–9.

5 Arms Control: The Bankruptcy of the Strategist's Approach

Trevor Taylor

Arms Control's Uninspiring Past

Members of the public, hearing political leaders speak on special occasions, might be forgiven for thinking that the arms limitation efforts by East and West in the past two decades have borne considerable fruit. President Richard Nixon, on the signing of the SALT I Agreements, claimed that they marked 'a new era of mutually agreed restraint and arms limitation'. His successor, President Gerald Ford, said that the Vladivostok accords represented 'a real breakthrough that put a ceiling on the arms race'.[1] In the middle of 1980 the American delegation at the Second Review Conference of the NPT emphasised the significance of the (unratified) SALT II Treaty, speaking of it as a 'major step' towards the great power nuclear disarmament called for in the NPT.[2]

This chapter starts from the position that such statements are misleading, that arms limitation efforts by the United States and the Soviet Union have not significantly influenced either levels of defence spending in NATO and the Warsaw Pact or the rate and direction of technological change in weaponry. The many arms limitation negotiations which have taken place have tended at best to yield agreements of little significance, in that they restricted the parties not to do things they were not inclined to do anyway. Alternatively, talks have dragged on, without total breakdown, but with progress being minimal. The US Defense Department's Annual Report for Fiscal Year 1981 summarised effectively the history of arms control when it described it as 'neither a stirring record nor the basis for great encouragement about the future'.[3]

A major characteristic of arms limitation talks has been their slowness in making advances. The Mutual Balanced Force Reduction (MBFR) Talks, which began in 1973, constitute perhaps the most extreme case; but SALT has scarcely been a more encouraging forum. It is an interesting thought that since SALT I took 3 years to negotiate and SALT II took 7 years (i.e. 2.3 times as long), SALT III in turn might be expected to take 16 years (i.e. seven years times 2.3) to finalise, even with no allowance being made for ratification delays!

In trying to understand why lack of productivity should have been such a feature of arms limitation talks, it is clear that much time has been devoted to drafting agreements which supposedly incorporate objective and absolute standards of verifiability and symmetry of advantage. Almost absurd situations have occurred such as when the Soviet Union demanded in the Comprehensive Test Ban talks that Great Britain, with its limited territory, should have the same number (ten) of seismic testing stations as the Soviet Union and the United States.[4] Clearly both symmetry and verifiability rest not on objective truth but on subjective judgement and so states should not be treating them as absolutes in all negotiations. States should be seeking more generally agreements that make them feel better off, even if unequally so, and whose language is clear so that a violation will be unambiguous if discovered. The arrangements for verification should be reasonable and judged in the light of the subject-matter. Ideally, as both sides feel is the case with SALT II, there should be a very good chance that serious violations would be discovered. But lack of verifiability should not prevent agreements being reached, as thankfully it did not with the Biological Weapons Convention. A pragmatic approach to verification is needed and certainly the Soviet Union must be pressed further to accept intrusive inspection where it is appropriate and can be limited in scope. But the idea that only absolutely verifiable agreements are acceptable must be rejected, as it has been in the cases of biological weapons and even SALT II which was presented by the US administration as 'adequately verifiable'.[5] The Senate Select Committee investigating the verifiability of SALT II found that

. . . under current Soviet practices, most counting provisions can be monitored with high or high–moderate confidence. Monitoring qualitative limitations on weapons systems is a far more difficult task and is dependent on the collective capability of a large number of systems. In general, these qualitative limitations present some problems but can, on balance, be monitored with high to moderate confidence. There are some provisions of the treaty which can be monitored with only a low level of confidence.[6]

Nevertheless relatively crude formulations are still sometimes favoured by the British government in statements simply advocating 'realistic and verifiable agreements'.[7]

In explaining the poor record of arms control, the near obsession with symmetry and verification has certainly often had a negative impact. Two other factors, however, which are often presented as bearing considerable responsibility, can easily have their significance overstated.

The first of these is the claimed complexity of arms control matters which in turn makes agreements hard to reach. The present writer believes that arms control complexity is often overstated; warheads, throw-weight and delivery vehicles, so important in SALT, constitute only three variables. Certainly it is not the case that complexity alone requires that talks advance slowly. In industrial relations it is not uncommon for corporations, in reorganising their workforces, to negotiate simultaneously with four or five trade unions, with thousands of workers and hundreds of detailed and specified job types being involved. Not all such negotiations run smoothly but conclusion within a year is not unknown. Again, arms control talks are generally not nearly so complex as discussions on collaborative arms development projects, whose subject-matter includes mission needs, weapon performance, engineering standards, work-sharing and project management. In arms control, complexity is an excuse for failure, not a reason.

Similarly the often-mentioned speed of technological change in weaponry should not be held responsible for the setbacks of arms control. While a superpower is often reluctant to make legal commitments on technology which its rival possesses and it does not, or on unfinished technological developments, it is quite inaccurate to believe that technological change is proceeding so rapidly that arms control cannot keep up with it. A more accurate perception would be that, in the past two decades at least, technological advance in weaponry has been steady and almost predictable, if anything slower than might be anticipated from the often-quoted statistic that a quarter of the world's scientists and technologists work on military matters. In procurement sections of government it is widely appreciated that it takes between 10 and 15 years to get a major weapons system from the drawing board into service. Consequently the armed forces of the major powers are fairly confident of the main weapons systems which they will be operating in 1990. Once in service, weapons remain there, admittedly with modifications, often for many years. The B52 and Vulcan bombers, developed and introduced into the American and British air forces in the 1950s, were still operational in a strategic or strike/attack rôle in 1980. Technological breakthroughs can occur but they rarely come out of the blue. They come from areas where progress seems possible and where funds have been invested over a period of years. There is some evidence that thinkers on arms control, within and outside governments, have neglected to think ahead to any extent on technology. The neutron bomb has been seen as a technological possibility since the mid-1950s, and yet, when it was finally developed in the late 1970s, it came as an apparent surprise to many concerned with arms limitation. Only then were its implications and utility as a tank/people killer widely debated. Arms control thinkers cannot afford to wait until technologies are ready; they must try to come to terms with planned, predictable technological change. 'Coming to terms with' implies, moreover, other than just urging that developments should not occur. Asking arms control thinkers to have more foresight is, however, a diversion from the main argument (at this stage) which is that it is less that technological change is very rapid and more that arms control negotiations are very slow.

Reforms in Arms Control

The remainder of this chapter is devoted to suggesting changes which could improve the success rate of East–West arms limitation efforts. The first two points are of a general theoretical nature whereas the others address the nature and structure of negotiations.

An initial consideration related to the failure of arms control is that talks, insofar as they have been directed towards war-avoidance and insofar as they have been guided by intellectual ideas, have depended of necessity on deterrence theory, a set of ideas with considerable ambiguity and weakness. The faults of deterrence theory are least apparent at the highest levels of violence. There is general consensus that a massive nuclear attack by one superpower on the other would be deterred by the prospect of a substantial second strike from the victim which inflicted 'unacceptable damage', most obviously the destruction of cities. The United States more recently has been publicly envisaging retaliation against 'things the Soviet leaders appear to value most — political and military control, military force both nuclear and conventional, and the industrial capability to sustain a war'.[8] It is at lower levels of violence that the implementation of deterrence brings problems. How does NATO deter a Soviet conventional attack such as an effort to invade Federal Germany as far as the Rhine? To this old question NATO still has no completely coherent answer which could guide arms limitation eforts. NATO doctrine is that deterrence is effected by a commitment to respond at the same level of violence as the attack with forces strong enough to inflict heavy losses *and* by a threat to escalate if necessary to halt the attack.[9] It is a mixture of *certainty*, that NATO forces at all levels will be able to inflict great damage to the attacker, and *uncertainty*, that the initiator of violence cannot be sure at what level of destruction any violence might end up.

If nuclear weapons, that is the escalation option, are excluded from consideration, it is not clear what conventional force relationships are needed for mutual deterrence. Deterrence in conventional weapon terms is an area in which we have little expertise, although George Quester has argued that the distinction between offensive and defensive weapons should be given serious atention and Yair Evron has written with some insight on the rôle of arms control in the Middle East.[10] In many ways we are little further advanced than the traditional arguments among theorists of international relations about the relationship of the balance of power to peace. These arguments contain two contradictory schools of thought. The first says that equality of strength brings peace because neither side, considering an attack, can be sure of victory. The second claims that only blatant inequality leads to peace because the weaker will not dare attack and the stronger can get its way without having to.[11] Both schools consider only the totals of military strength, not its nature. These ideas provide no clear guidance for the arms control negotiator. There have been assertions in the West of the need to 'educate' Soviet decision-makers regarding arms control. The foregoing arguments indicate that the West has little to tell. It is not surprising that, when the issue of arms control in Long-Range Theatre Nuclear Forces (LRTNF) was raised in 1979, few ideas were forthcoming as to what a reasonable agreed arrangement might look like.

Consideration of deterrence at lower levels of violence should be intensified. As the present writer has suggested elsewhere, a promising avenue may be to design agreements which take away the capacity for a successful Blitzkrieg-type surprise attack through restrictions on deployment, demilitarised zones and information exchanges rather than by limiting weapons numbers or types.[12] Such ideas owe much to the 'mission' approach of Christoph Bertram[13] and they suggest that the sort of military negotiations held within the format of the Conference on Security and Co-operation in Europe (CSCE), designed to produce what are modestly designated as confidence-building measures, should be widened and strengthened.

Besides having to rely on deterrence theory, arms control also suffers from logical faults relating to its own accepted purposes. These have traditionally been seen to be threefold and all have been reflected in some way or other in negotiations. The three purposes – minimising the chances of war, reducing the horror of war should it occur and cutting the costs of deterrence and war-preparation – contain contradictions whose seriousness can easily be overlooked. The clash between the first two is particularly significant since reducing the horror of war almost invariably increases its feasibility as a tool of policy. Contemporary issues starkly illustrate this point. On horror-limitation grounds the West would be far more concerned to restrict the old, inaccurate SS-4 and SS-5 Soviet missiles rather than the SS-20. Evolving American targeting doctrine, involving increased emphasis on attacks against Soviet missile sites and other military targets, can be criticised as an effort to gain a first-strike capability. But it can also be commended as a humanitarian measure designed to minimise the horror of nuclear war should it occur and as a counter to the immoral logic of mutual assured destruction which requires civilian populations to serve as permanent hostages.

The clash in the arms controller's purposes hinders clear super-power communication and increases mutual suspicions. Many Soviet analysts would like most to remove the danger of nuclear war and some in the West share this priority, but the predominant Western response to any Soviet proposals for initial nuclear disarmament is that it would confer an unequal advantage on the Warsaw Pact with its more numerous conventional forces. It would thus make war more likely by weakening NATO's escalation option. This would suggest that the arms control intellectual community and negotiating governments should clarify their priorities regarding war-avoidance and limitation. The present writer believes that the former is the most significant, if only because any superpower war would be highly destructive and would involve unknown escalation risks whatever commitments about nuclear or other weapons had been made beforehand. There is, however, a need for coherence whichever priority is selected.

Turning to the structure of negotiations, we come to what is perhaps the major single suggestion in this chapter — that more explicit consideration should be paid to political considerations, to the nature of the East–West conflict. Political discussions should parallel arms control efforts dealing with military capabilities. The basis for this assertion is that arms control is about limitations on military capabilities and states will not agree to restrictions which are incompatible with their political goals, means and conflicts.

Arms control literature to date has paid comparatively little attention to the political relationships between negotiating parties. Three rather unsatisfactory arguments are often given but they constitute a rather inferior substitute for precise political analysis.

One is the reminder that arms control talks take place between 'adversaries'. This leaves much undisclosed on the nature and extent of the competition between them, neglecting to answer particularly how much is due to mutual (unjustified) fear and suspicion and how much to conflicting objectives. The term adversary is used, less to delineate the military limitations compatible with the intentions and objectives of the parties, and more to emphasise that states discussing arms control do not trust each other.

Second there is the perspective often applied to inter-state relations in general which says that states must defend against the capabilities of others, not their intentions. In the anarchic international system, states cannot be trusted not to exploit any advantage they may hold. Arms control thus becomes a matter of offsetting the capabilities of others regardless of their intentions. This perspective, however, obviously presents only a partial view of international life since states do not prepare defences against all others but only those whose intentions they fear. France no longer has defences against Britain. As K. W. Deutsch so clearly pointed out, security communities can be discerned within the state system in which states conduct their relations without even reference to the threat or use of force.[14] The idea that states should take into account only the capabilities of others is in itself damaging to arms control because one country, in trying to offset another's capability, can itself acquire might which others will fear. Undoubtedly there are many in the Soviet Union who see 'the relentless accumulation of Soviet military power over the past 15 years'[15] as necessary just to offset the NATO threat. Insofar as arms control negotiations to date have concentrated on military forces and, the CSCE negotiations apart, have excluded politics, this perspective appears to have dominated arms control. It would seem to be held also by Presidential Adviser Zbigniew Brzezinski who argued in August 1980 that arms control arrangements are needed 'whatever the state of US—Soviet relations' and that, despite the Soviet action in Afghanistan, which he defined as 'litmus test' of Soviet expansionist intentions, the United States hoped to move ahead on SALT II, MBFR and LRTNF in a SALT III framework.[16]

Thirdly, there is the line of thought of political realism as applied to the question of disarmament. Disarmament will not take place, it is asserted, while states' interests clash. Once these interests coincide, and once there is 'a mutually satisfactory settlement of the power contest',[17] disarmament will be feasible. In the words of John Foster Dulles, 'if limitation of armaments comes, it will be a result rather than a cause of peace'.[18] This final perspective is more promising but it is too simplistic. It does not take into account the possible harmony of interests between states on some issues or in some parts of the world alongside clashes of interest elsewhere. The power contest may be settled in some areas and not others, with the impact on arms control efforts being considerable.

At present the United States and the Soviet Union appear to

have no agreed idea of each other's political strategies, objectives and means. Both have spoken in favour of detente but there is no common or clear conception of what detente is. A major lesson to be stressed here is that, when uncertainty prevails states fall back on the second perspective described above; that is, they defend against capability. The Stanford Arms Control Group put it clearly:

> Unless a nation has clear and reliable information about its opponent's intentions, the nation will tend to use worst case analysis and to assume that its opponent intends to do all the harm it is capable of doing. The nation may respond with actions that suggest to its opponent that its intentions cannot be trusted either.[19]

Logically the United States and the Soviet Union should, therefore, work explicitly, if privately, on trying to agree on the rules of detente, on what forms and within what limitations their competition is to take place.

Their discussions could apply a regional approach, treating different areas as politically isolated from each other. The advantage of this is that it may offer considerable scope for arms control and even disarmament in Europe where we already have substantial evidence, ranging from the Western response to the invasions of Hungary in 1956 and Czechoslovakia in 1968 to the building of the Berlin Wall and the treaties concluded under West Germany's Ostpolitik, that neither seeks any major change in the *status quo*. Arms control measures, such as demilitarised zones and agreed reductions in force readiness levels, could help to confirm the accuracy of this impression. The disadvantages of the regional approach alone are twofold. First, it involves the dubious assumption that areas can be treated as politically separate even in crisis: in the scenario of a Soviet–American confrontation in the Middle East over oil, it seems at least possible that Europe would become involved. Secondly, and related to the first, states may be reluctant to conclude agreements on one area if the effect is to enable one state to divert resources and energy to causing problems in others areas, safe in the knowledge that a previously worrying area, most obviously Europe, is secure.

The Administration of Jimmy Carter acknowledged these points in arguing that Europe cannot be 'an island of detente'. (Some

Europeans would prefer it to be a bit more isolated from periodic stresses in Soviet–American relations.[20]) Any regional approach to politics and control is, moreover, quite incompatible with the 1980 Republican Party platform which called, in cases of Soviet aggression against Western weak points, for 'military action elsewhere at points of Soviet vulnerability – an expression of the classic doctrine of global maneuver'.[21] Although the Republican position is extreme, it seems sensible that any regional arrangements should be reinforced by discussions on global rules of behaviour designed, not to end Soviet–American competition or to freeze a world *status quo*, but to restrict and channel competition.

Two possible global rules are that the superpowers and their allies should not try to use force to induce change and that they should not seek to induce changes by peaceful means which would constitute such a threat to the interests of the other side that it would be willing to use force if necessary to resist them. Returning to the Gulf as a source of possible conflict scenarios, a Soviet effort to gain control by peaceful means of Middle East oil would not be compatible with any agreed offsetting of military capabilities in the area since the West would wish to retain the option of resisting such a change by force. The Soviet Union would feel similarly about Europe if it thought the West was actively, if peacefully, seeking to change the basic orientation of East European governments.

Of course it is not the case that all uses of force are incompatible with all arms control. Considerable use of arms supplies or even proxy forces may be allowed as within the rules. All that must be said is that the more violence is permitted, the less arms control will be possible and the greater the dangers that escalation will occur, perhaps unintentionally, should crises occur in which the superpowers are using force, even indirectly, against each other.

There remains the possibility that all this could go extremely wrong in that a more open and thorough political dialogue between the superpowers and between East and West would reveal deep and irreconcilable clashes of interest incompatible with any arms control arrangements other than those directed at avoiding the mutual suicide of all-out nuclear war. If so we could at least stop wasting time and energy seeking arms control and disarmament until such time as political intentions change. At the present we are uncertain regarding the real nature of the East–West conflict and the rôle of mutual fear in sustaining it. The optimistic view of course is that clarification of intentions would open up new opportunities for arms control arrangements which would add credibility to political commitments. Moreover it must be remembered that, in the arms race, pessimism serves as a source of self-fulfilling prophecies.

As the final reform in the arms limitation process, the present writer suggests a psychological and elusive change for arms control negotiators as well as for politicians and even the wider general public. In assessments of prospective arms limitation agreements, complacency about the present should be reduced. Today negotiations tend to be carried out on the assumption that deterrence is stable for the time being and that our military and governments are doing a good job in ensuring that war will not break out. This may be quite misleading. McGeorge Bundy argued recently that the avoidance of nuclear war over the past 25 years was due rather more to luck than wisdom.[22] Yet the risks of living daily with the possibility of nuclear war tend to be forgotten. In consequence, arms control suggestions tend to be evaluated, not in terms of whether they would replace existing dangers with something less, but in terms of whether they would exchange a satisfactory present for a perfect, risk-free future. The result, as F. C. Ikle has noted, is that 'we are disposed to reject suggestions for improvement by demanding perfection at the outset'.[23] In short, those concerned with arms limitation should acquire some of the urgency of those who have traditionally argued for general and complete disarmament. A system based on nuclear deterrence can mean war at any time, perhaps sooner rather than later.

Conclusion

Arms control has held the hopes of many for the past 20 years but has failed to make significant advance. This chapter has argued that this has not been because of the rate of technological change or the complexity of issues dealt with in negotiations, but because of unresolved issues about deterrence and a failure to set priorities about the purposes of arms control. Complacency about the present has also played a rôle, but perhaps most significant has been the failure to deal directly with the political intentions which are represented in some way in military capabilities.

To those who take a traditional view of arms control and who perhaps have been involved in the daily grind of trying to negotiate agreements, this chapter may appear provocative. But the record of the past two decades is not impressive; the negotiators have delivered little. Those NPT signatories who complained so bitterly at the 1980 Review Conference of the nuclear powers' failure to live up to their disarmament commitment in the treaty have a good case. Arms control negotiations have served as a long-term source of employment for diplomats and of copy for journalists and academics but they have had little military impact. There is thus a case for being provocative or, to use a kinder word, stimulating. If arms control does not get off its present road and on to a new one, there is little reason to hope for anything better in the next 20 years than in the last. The political discussions suggested here would face obvious problems. From a Soviet point of view, explicit even if private discussion of political means and objectives would be at least embarrassing, since it would link major arms control progress to restricting the promotion of the socialist system within agreed limits. Indirectly the Soviet Union's formal ideological belief in the inevitable eventual triumph of socialism may assist here. From the American perspective, the immorality of communism would need to be pushed further into the recesses of the mind and great attention devoted to persuading the Soviet Union that the crushing of communism is not an objective of the capitalist states.

Political talks would also be extremely hard to organise in terms of agendas, participation and so on. But they would provide a chance, albeit an elusive one, whereby arms control talks might become a reinforcer rather than a consumer of trust. It is just conceivable that they would become what they are formally envisaged to be − a means of expressing common interests, and not a technique by which an unwary enemy can be tricked into an unwise concession or an ill-informed public or concerned Third World states can be misled into thinking that meaningful arms limitations are being made. Arms control cannot flourish in an uncertain political environment; states will not restrict their military capabilities unless they are confident of the intentions of others. At present the political environment is occasionally unfavourable but fundamentally uncertain; there is dispute, not only about the fundamental objectives of the United States and the Soviet Union, but also about the behaviour compatible with detente. Until there is clarification, arms control will continue to flounder.

Notes

1. See Marek Thee, 'The SALT II Agreements and Disarmament', *Transnational Perspectives*, v (1979) no. 2, p. 9.
2. US delegate Ralph Earle speech of 12 Aug. 1980, published by US International Communications Agency (USICA), 14 Aug. 1980.
3. Published by USICA, 31 Jan. 1980.
4. Speech by Douglas Hurd, 27 Mar. 1980, published in 'Arms Control and Disarmament', Arms Control and Disarmament Research Unit of the Foreign and Commonwealth Office, 4 May 1980.
5. Harold Brown, Secretary of Defense to Senate Foreign Relations Committee, 10/11 Oct. 1980, published by USICA, 12 Oct. 1980.
6. Senate Select Committee on Intelligence, Report on Monitoring SALT II, published by USICA, 9 Oct. 1979.
7. See, for instance, speech by Hurd to UN General Assembly, 17 Oct. 1979.
8. Brown speech of 20 Aug. 1980, published by USICA, 22 Aug. 1980.
9. For an interesting discussion of the contemporary weakness of NATO's escalation threat, see F. C. Ikle, 'NATO's First Use, a Deepening Trap', *Strategic Review*, Winter 1980, pp. 18–23.
10. George Quester, *Offense and Defense in the International System* (New York, 1977); Yair Evron, *The Role of Arms Control in the Middle East* (Adelphi Paper no. 138, London, 1977) and his contribution in Jonathan Alford (ed.), *The Future of Arms Control:* Part III: *Confidence-Building Measures* (Adelphi Paper no. 149, London, 1979).
11. For this latter view, see particularly A. F. K. Organski, *World Politics* (2nd edition, New York, 1968) ch. 12, esp. pp. 293–4.
12. Trevor Taylor and D. J. Dunn, 'Arms Control and Conventional Weapons: Some Conceptual and Empirical Issues', paper written for the 36th Pugwash Symposium, London, 10–12 Dec. 1980.
13. Christoph Bertram, *Arms Control and Techological Change: Elements of a New Approach* (Adelphi Paper no. 146, London, 1978).
14. K. W. Deutsch *et al.*, *Political Community in the North Atlantic Area* (Princeton, NJ, 1957).
15. The words of General B. W. Rogers, statement to the US Senate Armed Services Committee, published by USICA, 20 Feb. 1980.
16. From a statement in *US News and World Report*, 25 Aug. 1980, published by USICA, 20 Aug. 1980.
17. Hans J. Morgenthau, *Politics Among Nations* (5th edition, New York, 1972) p. 403.
18. Quoted in N. D. Palmer and H. C. Perkins, *International Relations* (3rd edition, New York, 1969) p. 198.
19. J. H. Barton and L. D. Weiler (eds), *International Arms Control: Issues and Agreements* (Stanford, California, 1976) p. 311.
20. See, for instance, International Peace Research Association, Disarmament Study Group Workshop on Confidence Building Measures, 'Building Confidence in Europe', *Bulletin of Peace Proposals*, no. 2, 1980, p. 12.
21. Published by USICA, 18 July 1980. Interestingly at the CSCE Review Conference in Madrid in the autumn of 1980, the United States was anxious that security concerns should not become separated from human rights and

indicated that progress in the former area might depend on progress in the latter. See statement by State Department Counsellor R. L. Ridgway to the Sub-Committee on International Organisation of the House Foreign Affairs Committee, 16 Sept. 1980, published by USICA, 17 Sept. 1980.

22. In F. Griffiths and J. C. Polanyi (eds), *The Dangers of Nuclear War* (Toronto, 1980) p. 33.

23. See his chapter in P. J. Pranger (ed.), *Detente and Defense: a Reader* (Washington, DC, 1977).

6   Military Parity, Political and Military Detente

Max Schmidt

Introduction

The international situation has undergone palpable aggravation at the beginning of the 1980s. The results of the process of political detente, achieved in the 1970s to the benefit of all nations, primarily those of Europe, are now in danger. There may be a colourful variety of underlying reasons, but the main reason cannot be denied: it is the *quest of certain circles for military superiority, flanked by an enormous increase in armament, in their failure to back up political detente by military detente.*

The system of international relations is being jeopardised to an extreme degree by a discrepancy between apparent willingness to accept arms limitation and disarmament verbally expressed in statements and conventions, on the one hand, and precarious activities undertaken by leading NATO states, on the other, all aiming in an opposite direction, towards reinforcement of the arms race. The development, manufacture, and deployment of new nuclear and 'conventional' weapons of mass destruction are being advanced at a high rate, whereas negotiations on arms limitation are handled in a clumsy and ineffective manner. The enforcement of SALT II, a convention of such great potential importance to peace, is being blocked by non-ratification in the United States. Attempts are being made, at the same time, to set up tremendous stocks of additional nuclear weapons in the heart of Europe. To stave off that 'threatening cloud', as George F. Kennan put it, and to forestall the risk of limitless intensification of nuclear armament and the associated dissemination of nuclear weapons among a multiplicity of states is the cardinal challenge to mankind in the 1980s.

Parity of Forces, Equitable Security, Peaceful Coexistence

It appears to be essential to build on the foundations provided to mankind in the 1970s. The emergence, existence, coming into force, and preservation of approximate strategic military parity between the major forces of the two different social systems in the world and their groupings of states has been one of the most substantive results in that context. This is one of the most critical conditions for safeguarding and consolidating peace, for parity of forces, which came about in the 1960s and 1970s, has proved to be of major relevance for the following reasons: it became a decisive basis and prerequisite for the initiation of the process of political detente, owing to the efforts of the Socialist states and of leading reality-minded forces in the Western world, as well as for all political and economic results and forthcoming trends of that process which proved beneficial to all parties involved; it has so far provided one of the toughest obstacles against the outbreak of a third world war, a war which would be fought with nuclear missiles; it has turned out to be a major precondition for the remarkable fact that Europe, the flashpoint of two world wars, has passed through its longest period of peace in this century and begun to become a model of peaceful coexistence between states with different social systems; and it is a fundamental condition for successful negotiations on arms limitation and disarmament, as reaffirmed by SALT I and II.

The notion of parity as a prerequisite for peace is relatively new. Its first deliberate use has been by the Socialist states which have defined parity as one of the foundations and guarantees for peaceful coexistence between states with different social systems. This is far from meaning acceptance, still less idolisation of a 'parity of horror', but it simply means acceptance of one fact: with the present constellation of forces in the international arena, this military parity is the point of departure from which arms limitation and, eventually, reduction can be agreed, with unreduced security being maintained for all parties involved.

The member states of the Warsaw Treaty have repeatedly

claimed that at present 'military parity does exist in Europe and the rest of the world'.[1] Such an assessment has been derived from an analysis of all factors with relevance to the evaluation. Included are an overall comparison and estimate of nuclear and conventional weaponry systems, numerically and by fire-power, number of troops, the strategic situation, the consequences of possible surprise strikes, and the effectiveness of defence installations. Geographic, logistic, and other factors, including economic developments, have also to be borne in mind.

True, military parity is an extremely delicate phenomenon. Its analysis must be based on a multitude of quantitative and qualitative factors, both global and regional. Yet on a realistic assumption of the totality of military forces facing each other, this seems to be the crux of the matter. Any attempt to isolate for comparison individual weapons, countries or regions will, necessarily, give a distorted picture.

Strategic parity actually is a reflection of a situation in which neither side has a decisive first-strike capacity nor can obtain one. The existence of approximate parity between the Soviet Union and the United States, as well as between the Warsaw Pact and NATO countries, has been admitted repeatedly until very recently by Administration spokesmen in the United States and in other NATO states. It was reiterated by the President of the United States, Jimmy Carter, on signing SALT II in June 1979. The existence of parity has been repeatedly underlined, as well, by West European politicians.

There is another aspect of international relations which inevitably emanates from the existence of parity of forces: the principle of equitable security, defined to the effect that neither party should seek to outmatch the other nor to obtain military superiority nor a first-strike capacity and, what is even more important, that the concept of equitable security for all should be made the basis of all negotiations and agreements on arms limitation, arms reduction, and disarmament. It is in that context that the principle of equitable security has been accepted in multilateral conventions, such as the Final Document of the UN Special Session on Disarmament, as well as in bilateral conventions, including the Vienna Communiqué of 1979 signed by the Soviet Union and the United States and agreements between the Soviet Union and West Germany and between the Soviet Union and France.

However, against this background of present international

developments, the question arises as to the *real* attitudes taken towards that fundamental issue of peaceful coexistence. To this we now turn.

The Danger to Parity of Forces by the Drive for Military Superiority

An answer to the above question will depend on a more accurate analysis of intentions, doctrines, and actions. Are the trends towards recognition of parity, lowering of the degree of military confrontation, and achievement of arms limitation in line with the principle of equitable security or are those needs violated?

It cannot be ignored that government representatives and military leaders of certain Western states, in particular the United States, have recently tended to demand with blunt candour that war or military power should be made more practicable again or more effectively applicable as a tool of politics on the basis of superiority. Carter, on a visit in the Pentagon, said he would see that the United States remained the world's first military power.[2] This was an unmistakable orientation for American armament and military policies in the direction of achieving military superiority. Carter's Defense Secretary, Harold Brown, elaborating on the purpose of intensified armament efforts by the United States and NATO at large, told the US Senate's Foreign Relations Committee, on 19 September 1979, that there was a need for 'outbidding' the Warsaw Pact. He added, 'full implementation of our own defense programmes, after all, is a fundamental prerequisite for achieving unambiguous advantage'.[3] Addressing the Armed Services Committee of the US Senate, he called for an increase in the military budget, reasoning that 'we must decide now, whether we intend to remain the strongest nation in the world'.[4]

The attempt to obtain military superiority, again, was the main topic in speeches made by former US Secretary of State, Henry Kissinger and by former NATO Commander-in-Chief, retired General Alexander Haig, at a conference of 120 Western military experts held in Brussels early in September 1979, under the title of 'NATO in the Forthcoming 30 Years'. According to comments in the press, 'the conclusion may be drawn from their statements that they seek to obtain superiority rather than approximate parity'.[5]

Carter's 'State of the Nation' message of January 1980 contained specific tasks which had to be accomplished to end the approximate military parity between the Soviet Union and the United States, with a view to achieving American military superiority. Reinforcement of the United States's and its allies' military power has been declared the top priority objective of the United States for the 1980s. Military spending by the United States will go up by $20,000 million in the next fiscal year alone, and the entire military budget will exceed $200,000 million by the mid-1980s. Large-scale military preparations at all levels of troops and equipment are envisaged. Particular emphasis is being laid on the strengthening of nuclear missile forces. The development and manufacture of qualitatively new systems of strategic offensive weapons have been planned, among them MX, cruise, and Trident missiles. The setting up of a 'rapid deployment force' for intervention with a special fleet of floating naval bases and an air transport fleet designed to move large units to the remotest parts of the world was explicitly fixed in the Presidential Message of January 1980.

Voices to justify a policy of military strength and of using military power are becoming louder also among political scientists in Western countries. According to Robert Kennedy of the Strategic Studies Institute at the US Army College, 'the capability of a nation to negotiate with good success on affairs which provides an opportunity for using force is a function of that nation's military power and of its capability of threatening and, if necessary, of resorting to military power for the purpose of imposing upon the world order its own preferred views'. He added, 'military power quite often was an important bargaining chip in negotiations not primarily concerned with power factors'.[6] Just note: the drive for military superiority is to help in 'imposing upon the world order their own preferred views'!

The enforced arms race conducted by the senior power of NATO is motivated by a quest for world-wide expansion rather than by American security interests. Arthur M. Cox, a former US diplomat, wrote: 'Authors of the Brookings Institute feel that the defense budget should be cut by half, if we were oriented exclusively to defending the territory of the United States.'[7] The United States, however, is the only nation in the world which has under its control a world-wide system of military bases in 114 countries.[8]

Yet one of the most recent decisions taken by the United States on nuclear strategy must be considered a very particular challenge to the research community with its responsibilities and cause unrest among research workers. Special reference has to be made, in that context, to nuclear strategy. Carter, according to American reports, signed Directive No. 59 which is to modify the targets of American strategic nuclear missiles. The gist of that modification, according to the *New York Times*, is a threat to strike the first blow against military targets in the Soviet Union and to lower the nuclear threshold, in order to be capable of fighting a limited nuclear war.

The concept of a limited strategic nuclear war against the Soviet Union is not new. It had been drawn up by former US Secretary of Defense, James Schlesinger, as early as 1974 and even before. Basically, it had always been in conformity with the intentions of forces hostile to detente to encounter the Soviet Union from a position of strength and superiority.

However, when the Soviet Union's attainment of strategic parity foiled the United States's capability of striking a first destructive blow, consecutive US administrations found themselves forced to recognise that parity. That was reflected in the 1972 documents on limitation of strategic offensive weapons and of defensive missile systems, the 1973 Convention on Prevention of Nuclear War, and more recent documents. However, there have always been strong forces in the United States who refused to accept strategic parity. They continued to seek military superiority which they defined, above all, as the capability of striking a destructive first blow, using superior weapons. US Administrations have never given up the possibility of heading for such a first-strike capacity. Even their approaches to arms control agreements have always been influenced by the desire to retain a loophole permitting the re-attainment of military superiority. This line, again, has become visible from the debates on SALT II in the United States.[9]

Statements were issued to the public by the Carter Administration, according to which it was ready to preserve parity with the Soviet Union in the sphere of strategic nuclear weapons, allegedly being aware of the grave risk that might emanate from violation of such parity. Yet, in reality, a goal was set involving the ending of that parity, both physically and in terms of conceptualisation. This may be seen from steps leading to an acceleration of the qualitative strategic arms race and to continuous modernisation of all three components of strategic forces, the 'strategic triad'. It has also become apparent from current programmes for the development of new systems of strategic weapons.

As to the qualitative factor, emphasis is being laid on obtaining the capacity for a disarming first strike by speeding up improvement of warheads in terms of accuracy and explosive intensity. Resetting of 300 'Minuteman-3' missiles was begun as early as late 1977 by the incorporation of Type MK-12A nuclear warheads, a type twice as destructive and accurate as its predecessor. There is a third factor which may be defined as the quest for relative invulnerability of American systems accompanied by a reduction in the capacity of Warsaw Treaty states to defend against them.

The signing of Directive No. 59, above all, deals with the following new weaponry systems: first, the intercontinental mobile ballistic system of ground-launched nuclear MX missiles of which 200 will be available; secondly the development and deployment of sea-launched 'Trident-2' missiles with individually controllable and manoeuvrable warheads, with every single nuclear-powered submarine carrying 24 missiles and said to be capable of destroying at least 200 reinforced military targets. (In a report of the US Arms Control and Disarmament Agency, this missile has been defined as 'a first-strike weapon with a sizeable potential for the destruction of top-priority targets'); and thirdly, the development of what has been called, more recently, an invisible aircraft or other module claimed to be almost undetectable by radar.

Directive No. 59 and its re-evaluation of nuclear strategies, quite obviously, physically relates to the above systems. Against the background of Carter's decision, closer thought should also be given to the resolution providing for the development and deployment of new American nuclear missile systems (Pershing II and cruise missiles) in Western Europe which was adopted on 12 December 1979.

Since there is parity of strategic forces between the Soviet Union and the United States, the drive towards renewed superiority in the outlook of American political and military leaders has implications not only in terms of new strategic weapons systems, but a particular rôle is played, as well, by regional aspects, that is adjustment to the United States's benefit of 'regional balances of forces'. Highest priority, in the latter context, has been assigned to Europe which is considered a theatre of particular importance to military confrontation with the Soviet Union and the other member states of the Warsaw Treaty. Shifts in that direction were first envisaged in the so-called Schlesinger Report of 1975. Alleging Soviet intentions to commit aggression against Western Europe and stipulating

NATO's function of deterrence, he reasoned that 'the free space within which hostile activities may be staved off by strategic forces is likely to be limited by threats of mutual annihilation, and more emphasis should be laid on deterrence, using medium-range missiles and conventional forces'.[10]

Expansion of NATO's medium-range missile armament was given priority as early as 1975 in a long-term strategic programme. True, this was based on the assumption of military—strategic parity rather than military superiority over the Soviet Union. But it was nevertheless a programme aiming, at least, at overcoming the consequences of that parity. Meanwhile, the real objective was formulated much more clearly and more comprehensively by US Defense Secretary Brown in his report to Congress, commenting on the draft military budget for the Fiscal Year of 1980: 'NATO, in our view, needs to have its own strategic "triad", *different* from ours. . . . It must have at its own disposal nuclear strategic forces, nuclear theater weapons, and non-nuclear forces.'[11]

The United States is aiming at a military—strategic ratio of two to one. The nuclear—strategic forces of the Soviet Union, according to this concept, are to be confronted by the forces of the United States and by additional forces of NATO. The 'Eurostrategic' arms systems, as provided for by the NATO Council resolution of December 1979, would provide the primary basis. This also shows the close links between the intention of setting up 'separate' nuclear—strategic forces of NATO in addition to those of the United States and a more recently advocated concept of making a distinction between strategic Soviet—American parity and regional nuclear parity between Western Europe and the Soviet Union, all with a view to covering up efforts to establish superiority.

Let us return, once again, to the Schlesinger Report of 1975 which explained the need for more emphasis on medium-range missiles. First use of nuclear weapons was its explicit assumption. Albeit 'clearly delimited', the 'attack was to be launched with adequate thrust and determination, sufficient to modify effectively the views of the Warsaw Pact leaders and to create a situation conducive to talks'.[12] That was far from being a threatening gesture of a mere tactical nature. For, according to Miles Kahler of Princeton University, there are forces in the United States today 'to whom the doctrine of "inevitable mutual annihilation" seems to be obsolete and who, therefore, wish to have nuclear weapons rendered "applicable"'.[13]

Now let us make, in this context, an assessment of the NATO decision of December 1979 with regard to military parity. The decision provides for the manufacture and deployment in Western Europe of another 572 American nuclear weapons of enhanced quality, in addition to the 8000 nuclear weapons plus 3000 nuclear carriers already in Western Europe, and 1000 nuclear carrier devices on board naval units in the Atlantic and in the Mediterranean Sea. They are to be Pershing II and cruise missiles which need a few minutes of flying time to cover ranges between 1800 km and 2500 km. Their multiple warheads, higher in accuracy and more difficult for the defence to destroy, can strike at several targets at one and the same time. Early warning margins go down from 30 to about 4—6 minutes. This is not 'simply modernisation' of obsolete weapons for unaltered purposes, as is sometimes claimed, but it basically means the introduction of strategic weapons which could reach far into Soviet territory. The NATO decision, consequently, is aiming at a fundamental change of the strategic situation in Europe. This is to undercut SALT II.

G. Bastian, a Major-General in the Bundeswehr, spoke of a 'new situation' for Moscow, 'one in which the Soviet Union will not have equal possibilities at her disposal, that is ground-launched medium-range weapons which would be a nuclear threat to the USA'.[14]

The United States is also heading for the acquisition of a first-strike capacity in the European theatre.

The positions of NATO regarding plans to deploy new nuclear medium-range missiles in Europe are explained primarily by an alleged need for modernisation of armament. However, such positions are neither militarily, nor politically, nor historically in agreement with reality.

Historically, the point should be made that NATO's tactical policy decision to deploy new US missiles in Western Europe was not born in December 1979, but actually in autumn 1977, when the Nuclear Planning Group of NATO met in Bari. The decision to set aside funds for the development of Pershing II had been taken as early as 1974, according to the official 1980 Fiscal Year Report of the US Arms Control and Disarmament Agency.[15] The Soviet SS-20 missiles, now used as a pretext for the decision, were not discovered by US reconnaissance satellites until 1975.

The decision to fund the development of cruise missiles had been taken even earlier, back in 1972. And, once more, reference must be made to the long-term American concept for attaining military superiority. Relevant in this context was this comment by Lothar Ruehl, correspondent of the Second Television Programme of West Germany: 'The drive for the introduction of the new and long range theatre nuclear force systems of NATO in Western Europe was inevitable even without the deployment of SS-20 and the TU 22 AM bomber ('Backfire') in the Western part of the Soviet Union, if "flexible response" was to remain effective.'[16] Ruehl is sometimes well-informed.

Politically, it should be borne in mind that the Soviet Union had proposed the inclusion of medium-range weapons in the SALT negotiations, long before any decision had been taken on new nuclear medium-range systems for the United States and NATO and before the Soviets had begun modernisation of their own potential. Those weapons were left out by the United States. It is also known that silence was the response to the Soviet Union's proposals of 1979 to talk about the medium-range potential.

Militarily, reference should be made to a number of facts. First, unbiased calculations show approximate parity to exist also in the field of nuclear medium-range weapons, provided such parity is correctly related not only to the equality of means, but also to the equality of obtainable effects. In support of the modernisation-of-armament doctrine, many calculations have been made but the ulterior motives behind those calculations have quite often been obvious. A striking example of the manipulated comparison of the strength of missile systems can be seen in a study prepared for Peter Kurt Würzbach and Markus Berger, both members of the West German Bundestag. In that study the claim was made that 'Soviet superiority to NATO was 4.5:1 in the field of short-range missiles'.[17] Such manipulated calculations have been critically appraised by Dieter S. Ludz, who is engaged in peace research in Hamburg. He found 'that military inferiority of NATO was an assumption which could not be derived at all from the sphere of tactical nuclear forces'. 'On the contrary,' he continued, 'it could not be ruled out that the Warsaw Pact believed in the need for some rearmament in order to counter the improving quantitative and qualitative standards of NATO.'[18] A comparison of all stocks of NATO with those of the Warsaw Treaty would give a ratio of 1622 to 1637 systems, according to Ludz's calculations which were based on data supplied from the International Institute for Strategic Studies (IISS) and from the Stockholm International Peace Research Institute (SIPRI). Such a ratio, however, means approximate parity. The above calculations were made with due consideration of both the number of systems and their differentiated qualitative criteria. Some further elements were correctly included in those calculations, though they had often been excluded from many other Western analyses, such as the overall potential of both the United States and NATO ('forward-based systems'), US submarines with Poseidon missiles operating under European NATO Command in the Atlantic and in the Mediterranean Sea, carrier-launched US aircraft in the same region, and all NATO air force units with fighting ranges beyond 1500 km. The nuclear systems of France and Great Britain were included as well. Medium-range systems cannot be compared nor be the subject of any negotiations unless the 'forward-based systems' are also considered. They can reach into Soviet territory, and the potential of ground-launched Soviet missiles is actually a response to them.

Secondly, there are considerable differences in strategic combat use between Soviet SS-20 missiles, on the one hand, and the planned Pershing II as well as cruise missiles, on the other. The SS-20 actually replaces the former missile types SS-4 and SS-5 which had been put into service more than 10 years ago, and firing ranges are not increased. Gregory Treverton, Deputy Director of IISS, has said that the 'SS-20' does 'not constitute a qualitatively new danger', as compared to its obsolete predecessors.[19] The following assessment has been made in SIPRI's latest Yearbook: 'No quantitatively new menace will result from piecemeal replacement of the existing missiles by SS-20.' To define the Pershing II and cruise missiles as 'modernisation', on the other hand, is judged by SIPRI as an 'understatement', and reference is made, in that context, to 'qualitatively new capabilities' obtained by NATO over the Warsaw Treaty.

Thirdly, the number of Soviet medium-range missiles in the European part of the Soviet Union has not been increased over the last 10 years, nor has that of carrier aircraft. In addition, the Soviet Union has not based such weapons on the territories of its allies. The numbers of launching pads for medium-range missiles, nuclear explosive charges, and the number of medium-range bombers have even been somewhat reduced. Even the Ministerial Meeting of the Nuclear Planning Group of NATO, in its communiqué, issued in

The Hague on 14 November 1979, admitted 'that the overall number of Soviet missile launching devices, potentially pointed at European NATO territories, has been somewhat reduced, in recent years'.[20] Also, Carter's Defense Secretary Brown told staff at the Brookings Institute in February 1980 that the Soviet Union had reduced rather than increased the number of her medium-range weapons and warheads during the 1970s.[21]

The decision to develop, manufacture, and deploy new nuclear medium-range systems of NATO in Western Europe was not taken to meet a danger of military superiority of or threats by the member states of the Warsaw Treaty. It was taken to satisfy NATO's quest for its own military superiority and to get rid of the principle of equitable security as the foundation for relations and negotiations. This is an extremely dangerous concept, and its consequences may be summarised as follows:

1. The risk of general nuclear missile war is aggravated rather than mitigated, primarily by the erroneous view that limited nuclear war might be won. To believe in the possibility of a locally limited nuclear war is a view far from any realism. Any nuclear attack would proliferate into direct confrontation with retaliatory strikes very soon after its launching.
2. The risk of nuclear confrontation is aggravated by attempts at the creation of a first-strike capability, and this danger primarily threatens Europe. Deployment of new medium-range systems in the countries of Western Europe is likely to turn those countries into nuclear hostages of the United States, against the background of the new American strategy. In certain smaller NATO countries there have recently been official and unofficial voices rejecting, in deviation from the American position, any lowering of the nuclear threshold by the new American strategy. The two largest political parties of the Netherlands are examples.[22] They are becoming increasingly aware that the hazard of military conflict in Europe and, consequently, the dangers to all nations on the continent cannot be simply avoided by introduction of new weapons, but rather have to be staved off by military detente and arms reduction.
3. The arms race is continuously stepped up, and new rounds are initiated, as the Socialist states feel themselves compelled to meet the acute menace by ensuring for themselves a maximum amount of military security. History has shown that the Socialist

states do have all the capacities required for countering any
armament invention in advanced capitalist industrial countries by setting up new types of weapons of their own as well
as any system needed for their own defence. But another
round of the arms race is something the Socialist states wish to
avoid.

It is a somewhat widespread but erroneous assumption that
any round of the arms race will mean nothing but numerical
expansion of 'modernised' weaponry systems. A thoughtless
conclusion often drawn is that military parity will eventually re-
emerge with the *status quo* being, basically, restored and world
peace being reinsured. If one group of states decides to throw
more armament potential into its own 'scale', the 'international
scales' will be rebalanced as soon as the other side tips its own
'scale' by adding the same weight. The traditional parable of
scales to represent equilibrium is, admittedly, illustrative. But
it reveals the severe shortcomings of a mechanistic approach.
Those who believe in it should not ignore one extremely important condition: every balance has an ultimate load-bearing
capacity which can be surpassed only at the risk of breaking the
whole system. Any sober, candid assessment of the military–
strategic situation throughout the world (and, above all, in
Europe) must necessarily lead to this conclusion: quantity and
quality of armament have come dangerously close to the
ultimate load-bearing capacity of the military balance.
Strategic stability will be fundamentally endangered by any
further round of the arms race, particularly by the development, manufacture, and deployment of weapons of large-scale
annihilation and of carrier devices with substantively new
parameters. That is why one can really subscribe to Klaus von
Schubart's statement: 'The continued arms race together with
qualitative leaps actually foreshadows strategic destabilisation
in the eighties.'[23]

4. The principle of equal rights of states in the system of international relations is comprised by the arms race aimed at
attaining military advantage. Hegemonism is thus favoured.
The policy of relying on force, flanked by attempts to apply
military pressure and blackmail for turning negotiations into
Diktats, is on a rising trend. Tension and suspicion between
groups of states, no doubt, would get worse also at other levels
of international life. It is quite evident that such developments

would strongly jeopardise all existing and planned talks on arms limitation and disarmament.

5. Finally, brief mention at least should be made of the multitude of economic and social consequences for all countries directly or indirectly involved or affected, though those consequences cannot be discussed in detail here.

Arms Limitation on the Basis of Equitable Security

What is the general position taken by the Socialist states regarding continuation of detente and, more specifically, on the problem of parity? The Socialist states feel strongly that, with all the present tension and difficulties in the international situation, the process of detente and its results so far must continue to be the first priority in international relations. They are in favour of constructive steps to counter a further hardening of the situation in Europe and throughout the world. Effective steps towards prevention of another round of the arms race and genuine arms reduction: this is the key problem.

An evaluation of multilateral, bilateral, and unilateral statements made by Socialist states leads the present writer to define the policy positions held by them as follows:

1. The Socialist states do not seek to attain military superiority nor any change in their favour of the historically achieved military parity. This attitude applies fully to both levels of strategic balance, between the Soviet Union and the United States as well as between the Warsaw Treaty and NATO in Europe. The member governments of the Warsaw Treaty reiterated in May 1980 that they would never create for themselves a nuclear first-strike capability nor try to assume control over 'spheres of influence' or international transport routes.[24] Their policies, as a whole, are orientated towards reducing and, eventually, eliminating the rôle played by the military factor in world politics. Yet the military factor does continue to play an important rôle as long as no far-reaching steps can be taken towards general and complete disarmament. Maintenance of military parity, therefore, is one of the basic prerequisites for peaceful coexistence between states of different social systems. Military parity is not only militarily desirable but it is also a

point of departure for practicable potential steps towards arms control and disarmament.

2. Foreign and security policies of the Warsaw Treaty countries remain focused on reducing, on the basis of reciprocity, the level of military confrontation by agreed reduction of troops and equipment. The principle of equitable security, respect for the legitimate security interests of other states, and readiness to enter into negotiations on all types of weapons have continued to be the tenets of their policies. Guaranteed approximate parity is considered to be, and is, supported by them as an important stabilising factor in world affairs. Therefore, their proposals were and are aimed at preserving approximate military parity which, however, should be lowered on a step-by-step basis, for the purpose of obtaining effective and mutually acceptable cuts in military spending.

3. Many and varied efforts are being made by the member states of the Warsaw Treaty to foil any attempt aimed at destabilising the military–strategic balance and at attaining unilateral military advantage. But once the United States and other NATO members have embarked on an intensified arms race, the states of the Warsaw Treaty find themselves inescapably compelled to take measures to strengthen their own defence capability, with a view to preserving approximate parity. Those are measures which do not compromise the security of any other state. But the Socialist states are unable to accept any interference with military–strategic parity, since this would bring about a serious danger to their own security and to international peace.

4. Guidelines for implementing co-ordinated Socialist foreign policies, to the benefit of their own security and of international security interests at large, were laid down in a Declaration issued in May 1980 at a Meeting of the Political Consultative Committee of the Warsaw Treaty:

   (a) Agreement to the effect that from a specified deadline no state or group of states in Europe shall increase the numerical strength of its armed forces within the area specified in the Final Act of Helsinki.

   (b) Stringent compliance with all provisions of the Final Act of Helsinki, in particular with those fundamental principles to which the participating states have made a solemn commitment, such as abstention from threats or the use of force, inviolability of frontiers, peaceful settlement of disputes, non-interference in internal affairs, and fulfilment in good faith of all obligations under international law.

(c) Intensive bilateral and multilateral exchange of views in preparation for the CSCE meeting to achieve agreement, beforehand, on all issues regarding which practical steps might be taken for a more comprehensive implementation of the Final Act.

(d) Accelerated preparations for a conference on military detente and disarmament in Europe, with a view to deciding in the CSCE context such practical matters as the tasks of the conference, time, place, and procedures, and with a view to concentrating efforts, in the first phase, on confidence-building measures.

(e) Ratification of SALT II and the earliest possible conclusion of current or disrupted negotiations, including those on a ban of nuclear weapons testing, on radiological and chemical weapons and on non-use of nuclear weapons against non-nuclear countries.

(f) Immediate initiation of constructive negotiations on additional problems, such as a world treaty on the non-use of violence, the cessation of any manufacture of nuclear weapons, as well as a ban on the development of new types and systems of large-scale weapons of annihilation.

(g) Dicussions on the limitation and reduction of military presence and military activities in the Atlantic, Indian and Pacific Oceans as well as in the Mediterranean Sea and in the Gulf region.[25]

All efforts and proposals are primarily focused on further steps by which to mitigate the danger of nuclear war. This will require not only ratification of SALT II, but an urgent commitment to reopening the road towards negotiations on medium-range missiles. That road, as is well known, was blocked by the rejection of the Soviet proposal of 6 October 1979, and by the resolution on medium-range missiles passed by NATO in December 1979.

Extraordinary importance in terms of long-range policy and immediate action, therefore, should be attributed to the latest initiative taken by the Soviet leadership for the immediate initiation of talks on the best possible solutions for the problem of medium-range nuclear missiles. Those proposals were submitted to Helmut Schmidt, when he visited Moscow in June 1980, and they were conveyed also to the leaders of the United States. What is that intiative all about? Talks are proposed, at the earliest possible date, on the deployment of medium-range nuclear missiles in Europe, even before ratification of SALT II which so far has been prevented by the United States. Those talks should be 'organically linked' to the problem of so-called 'forward-based' American nuclear systems, including F-11 and Phantom combat aircraft based in Great Britain and missile-carrying American submarines cruising under NATO command in the Mediterranean Sea. The arms-limiting steps, agreed in such talks, may be put into practice *following* ratification of SALT II. No conditions are specified for the beginning of such talks, not even cancellation of the NATO resolution of 5 December 1979.

There has been some favourable reaction to several aspects of these proposals in a number of West European NATO countries, which seems to underline their importance. Their realisation would be conducive to getting out of the deadlock which has resulted from the aforementioned NATO resolution. Schmidt, for example, said that he considered it a 'really logical approach' that the forward-based systems should also be discussed. He also expressed 'understanding' for the position of the Soviet Union regarding SALT II.[26]

Alfons Pawelczyk, well-known disarmament expert of the West German Social Democratic Party, referring to the Soviet proposal, stressed the chance of buying time. He considered that this would be one of the aspects that would 'decide whether or not it will be possible to forestall in Europe an arms race in the context of nuclear medium-range systems'.[27]

On the other hand, regrettably enough, these and similar statements have not yet been matched by American action. A few official statements promising study and consultation have been accompanied, as in earlier instances, by negative arguments. For example, demands are made to the effect that the forward-based systems be excluded from forthcoming talks which should be confined to medium-range missiles. Yet not even NATO military officials deny that the deployment of Soviet medium-range missiles in the Western part of Soviet territory has come as a response to the existence of such forward-based systems which actually possess the function of medium-range nuclear missiles. An approach has to be taken to the totality of weapons with identical or similar functions. Any other position would be equivalent to trying to bring about a high-handed alteration, to one's own unilateral benefit, to the prevailing approximate military parity.

Pessimistic views are also being disseminated to the effect that such talks and negotiations would be extremely difficult. It might even take years to agree on a definition of the subject. Yet, the subjects of SALT I and SALT II were also extremely complex. Included were types of weapons, sites, ranges, striking potentials, and so forth. Nevertheless, results were obtained in conformity with well-defined mutual interests. There must be goodwill on either side, since this, after all, will be also an essential element of reciprocal confidence. Everyone knows about the impatience with which peoples are waiting and striving for negotiations.

We can all see in the world today increased tension and a complicated situation. This should encourage all of us to redouble our efforts for continuation of detente. The situation calls for utmost political readiness to enter into dialogues on disputed issues and to refrain from anything which might lead to a deterioration of the situation. A turn towards military detente is possible in the 1980s, provided that the existing approximate strategic parity and the principle of equitable security for all are made the points of departure for negotiations.

The military–strategic balance so far achieved between Socialism and Capitalism is of foremost historic importance. This seems to be increasingly understood by realistically minded politicians and by many scientists, not least in the United States. This was written by Paul Warnke:

> The Russians are in a position to repulse any threatening of strategic parity, just as we are capable of foiling any of their attempts to gain advantage. Sharpening competition will result in a situation comparable to the present one, but with higher levels of destruction potential and in a more restless political environment. . . . The best alternative, by which to guarantee non-occurrence of nuclear war, seems to be conventions on the control of strategic armament which should be conducive to minimising tension and to paving the road to far-reaching, effective disarmament, in the long run.[28]

And according to G. B. Kistiakowsky, former US Presidential

Scientific Adviser, 'In order to obtain an agreement [in the field of arms limitation] we should unambigously concede to the Soviet Union a status of equality and take her legitimate security interests into account'.[29]

These are positions from which hope may be derived. Confident in the chances of improving conditions for peace on the basis of equitable security, the present writer feels sincerely that to disseminate this message is one of the noble responsibilities of political science.

Notes

1. *Neues Deutschland* (Berlin, German Democratic Republic), 24 Nov. 1978.
2. *Süddeutsche Zeitung* (Munich), 8 March 1977.
3. *ICA Bulletin* (Washington and Bonn), 20 Sept. 1979.
4. *New York Times*, 14 Dec. 1979.
5. *Frankfurter Zeitung*, 8 Sept. 1979. Haig subsequently became Secretary of State in Reagan's Administration. The present article was completed before Reagan's inauguration.
6. Robert Kennedy, 'Das Messen des strategischen Gleichgewichts', in Robert S. Nichols *et. al.* (eds), *Die USA und das strategische Gleichgewicht* (Munich, 1980) p. 28.
7. A. M. Cox, *The Dynamics of Detente* (New York, 1976) p. 180.
8. *New Times* (Moscow) no. 4, 1979.
9. See J. Strelzow, 'Strategische Parität oder Strategische Überlegenheit? Die Entwicklung der Haltung der USA zur Begrenzung der Strategische Rüstungen', *Deutsche Aussenpolitik* (Berlin, German Democratic Republic) no. 8, 1980.
10. James Schlesinger, *The Theater Nuclear Forces Posture in Europe* (Washington, DC, 1975).
11. S. D. Fair, 'TNW und das strategische Gleichgewicht', in Nichols *et. al.*, op. cit., p. 38.
12. Schlesinger, op. cit., p. 15.
13. *Neues Deutschland*, 1 July 1980.
14. *Frankfurter Rundschau*, 13 Aug. 1980.
15. *Europa-Archiv* (Bonn) no. 2, 1980.
16. Lothar Ruehl, 'Europäer müssen die Lücke füllen', *Die Zeit* (Hamburg) no. 21, 1980.
17. H. Hoffmann and R. Steinrücke, *Rüstung und Abrüstung im Euronuclearen Bereich* (Washington and Bonn, 1979) p. 35.
18. D. S. Ludz, 'Das Militärische Kräftverhältnis im Bereich der Europäischen Waffensysteme', *IFSH-Forschungsberichte* (Hamburg) no. 12, 1979, pp. 31–2.
19. Gregory Treverton, 'Nuclear Weapons and the Gray Area', *Foreign Affairs* LVII (1978–9) 1080.

20. *Europa-Archiv*, no. 2, 1980.
21. *Frankfurter Rundschau*, 31 July 1980.
22. ibid., 12 Aug. 1980.
23. Klaus von Schubart, 'Bedingungen des Überlebens: Sicherheitspolitik und politische Moral zwischen Militärstrategie und Waffentechnik' in *Aus Politik und Zeitgeschichte: Beilage zu Das Parlament* (Bonn) no. 10, 1980, p. 25.
24. *Neues Deutschland*, 16 May 1980.
25. ibid.
26. *Der Spiegel* (Hamburg), 7 July 1980.
27. *Frankfurter Rundschau*, 21 July 1980.
28. P. Warnke and M. Krepton, 'The Awesome Fact behind the SALT Debate', *Across the Board* (New York) no. 3, 1979.
29. *The Defense Monitor*, March 1978.

7 Disarmament-supporting Measures: Conceptual Innovation and Institutional Reform of the National Arms Control and Disarmament Machineries

H. G. Brauch

Introduction

Are those assumptions and goals of arms control developed in the late 1950s and published in a special issue of *Daedalus* in 1960 still valid?[1] Have the traditional objectives of East–West arms control, namely to reduce the likelihood of war by increasing stability, to reduce the damage of war if deterrence should fail, and to reduce the economic burden of preparing for war, been implemented during the past two decades of arms control negotiations?[2]

Many arms control experts appear to agree today with Leslie Gelb's frank and gloomy assessment: 'Arms control has essentially failed. Three decades of US–Soviet negotiations to limit arms competition have done little more than to codify the arms race.'[3] Two decades of arms control negotiations did not lead to disarmament but rather stimulated qualitative arms competition. Besides a lack of determined political will for arms reduction on the part of both military alliances that spend 70 per cent of the global military burden of $500 billion in 1980,[4] we experienced since the mid-1970s a deterioration of mutual confidence between the two superpowers and a major decay of domestic support for arms control in the United States and in several other West European countries. Arms control, in the view of Christoph Bertram, 'consumes trust between East and West, but it does not produce it. The symbolic political value of successful arms control is lacking because "success" is being questioned by technological development'.[5] In comparing arms control theory and practice, Erhard Forndran concludes that 'stability cannot be achieved by these measures'.[6] Bernard T. Feld has written of the phenomenon of 'arms control negotiations generally having dealt with arms systems that were no longer of crucial significance in the ongoing technological arms competition'. He added: 'This tendency towards new technological destabilization continues. The latest example is the cruise missile.' He concluded: 'We are in grave danger of entering into a new phase of military competition, replete with prospects for conflict and confrontation. . . . What is important is for both sides to practice restraints in new weapons systems, or the upward spiral will continue indefinitely.'[7]

What conclusions can be drawn from these pessimistic statements? First, a basic reassessment of the theory, goals and achievements of arms control and disarmament is imperative.[8] Secondly, this conceptual re-evaluation should take into account the results of empirical studies on the determinants of the weapons-acquisition process and on armaments dynamics.[9] Third, a reassessment of the national governmental arms control and disarmament machinery and of the decision-making process is necessary. Fourth, a careful analysis of the international co-ordination and consultation processes on arms control and arms procurement matters in the alliances is needed. Fifth, a discussion of supplementary strategies of arms control and disarmament by either national initiatives[10] or negotiated agreement is required.

There exist at least four conditions for any successful effort at arms limitation and reduction: a favourable global or regional political climate; the need for confidence among the major parties to an international agreement; the political will of the political leadership; and the need for domestic support for these efforts. Without sufficient domestic support and mutual confidence any government of goodwill and of good intentions is going to fail or will be forced to adapt to the opposite trends in order to survive politically. Confidence-building measures[11] on the international level and disarmament-supporting measures[12] on the national level as supplementary elements to a new conceptualisation of arms control and disarmament and to a new double strategy of implementation may facilitate the process of arms reduction, provided there exists a political will by the responsible leadership and favourable domestic and international environments.

This chapter focuses primarily on a few national determinants of armaments dynamics – on the level of the political–administrative system and of society – and on some domestic obstacles for the initiation and implementation of an alternative arms control and disarmament policy. B. V. A. Röling has stressed:

> The need for a new approach which does not rely on qualitative or quantitative restrictions but considers instead not weapons but the missions or functions of national armed power. . . . Some capabilities should be forbidden – the capability of launching a pre-emptive first strike or a successful surprise attack. . . . A start might be made with the prohibition of the introduction of new offensive or de-stabilizing weapons systems.[13]

Are the governmental arms control and disarmament machineries capable of making such a fundamental conceptual reassessment? Can conceptual innovations be furthered by an upgrading of arms control within the national bureaucracies and international secretariats? Are the national arms control bureaucracies willing to reassess their past performance? These questions lead to the following working hypothesis: the initiation and implementation of a conceptual reassessment of arms control theory and practice requires an institutional reform within respective bureaucracies and a higher emphasis on arms control issues in the public domain.

Reasons for the Lack of Support for Arms Control and Disarmament

Both analyses of the determinants of armaments dynamics and suggestions for arms control and disarmament focused primarily on the international system until the early 1970s. National procurement measures and military activities were largely defined and legitimised in terms of necessary reactions to advantages of the other side. For example, more recently the introduction of new long-range theatre nuclear forces into Western Europe (Pershing II and ground-launched cruise missiles)[14] was legitimised with the deployment of Soviet SS-20 missiles. Action and reaction patterns provided a model for many interpretations of the arms race during the Cold War. These explanations have re-emerged both in political statements and in scientific analyses in the late 1970s. These traditionalist explanatory patterns were repeatedly questioned, especially during the Vietnam war. Domestic determinant factors of armament dynamics both for the United States and for the Soviet Union were increasingly stressed in studies dealing with the inputs of procurement policy and societal objections to arms limitation: societal processes and coalitions (for example, hypothesis of the military–industrial complex),[15] bureaucratic routines and politics,[16] economic factors (jobs, profits, structural and regional implications)[17] and rapid technological innovation.[18] Graham Allison and Frederic Morris, exploring the determinants of American strategic weapons programmes in the 1960s, concluded in their contribution to *Daedalus* in 1975: '. . . the weapons in the American and Soviet force postures are predominantly the result of factors internal to each nation. Not only are organizational goals and procedures domestically determined, but the resulting satisfactions of political officials are to be found overwhelmingly at home.'[19]

Any realistic strategy of arms limitation has to address both the international and the domestic determinants of armaments dynamics. It should not only focus on the number of weapons systems but it should increasingly problematise the qualitative features of the weapons modernisation process itself. Arms limitation talks should gradually be extended from the deliberation of hardware to software: military doctrines, the most likely military options, military missions and the discussion of global strategic issues other than weapons. Any longer-term arms control and disarmament strategy requires on the domestic level a supplementary strategy to deal with the domestic obstacles and on the international level political efforts to enhance mutual confidence and co-operative behaviour.

The Concept of Disarmament-Supporting Measures

Disarmament-supporting measures are intended to address on the national level the societal and domestic obstacles to arms control and disarmament. Their primary task is to create favourable domestic conditions both on the governmental and on the societal level for an innovative arms control policy and to create domestic political support for their implementation, as, for example, for the ratification process in legislative bodies. Disarmament-supporting measures aim at a higher degree of openness, transparency and legislative controllability as well as executive political leverage in planning and steering of the weapons of research, development and procurement process.

Disarmament-supporting measures should address the domestic determinants of armaments dynamics: by overcoming the economic obstacles to arms control agreements (such as the fear of loss of jobs, of falling profits, of closing of production lines, and of reduction of indirect support of regions); by conversion planning and conversion policies; by supplementing defence-oriented and defence-sponsored research (such as that of RAND and the Hudson Institute) with politically relevant and forward-looking research on peace, conflict and disarmament; by enhancing the political leverage to control and to contain the technological impulse (for example, by the introduction of arms control impact statements); by strengthening the position of arms control and disarmament units within the governmental decision-making process (for example, by the establishment of strong disarmament sections within foreign ministries, of independent disarmament agencies like the US Arms Control and Disarmament Agency (ACDA) or even of a separate department for security policy, arms control, disarmament and detente); and by overcoming ideological predispositions in pointing out that the major threat is not the rival social system but the danger of a nuclear war that may lead to the destruction of both systems.

In dealing with the fears about the consequences of arms reductions on the national level disarmament-supporting measures have to be implemented unilaterally. The achievement of more openness and transparency of the weapons research and development process, however, becomes at the same time a major confidence-building measure that should be reciprocated by the other side at an appropriate time.

Conceptual Innovation by Institutional Reform

Organisation does matter.[20] Various case-studies on arms control decision-making processes, conducted under the auspices of the Murphy Commission,[21] suggest a close relationship between organisation structure and decision outcome:

> Organizational patterns determine the probabilities that a decision will be taken at one level rather than another, or in one agency instead of another. And since perspectives differ from level to level in government, and from agency to agency, the resulting decisions will differ also.[22]

While scientific analyses can contribute to the recognition of present and future problems, societal groups and the media as well as legislative bodies may contribute to the definition of arms control and disarmament goals. However, for the development of innovative arms control programmes and for their implementation in the framework of competing bureaucratic interests within the executive, in the negotiation process on the international level and in the process of ratification on the national level both knowledgeable and influential arms control components are needed within the executive that are both willing and capable of conceptual innovation.

The greater the domestic pressure for arms control, the more severe the fiscal constraints for defence budgets, the more the readiness of the political leadership for a conceptual reassessment of past arms control performance and for new initiatives may increase. The problem of conceptual innovation by institutional reform has to be analysed in this broader political context.

The prospects for an institutional reform solely on the political–administrative level, given the absence of domestic pressure for arms control initiatives, may be dim. However, public pressure, the political will of the leadership and the readiness of the arms control bureaucracy for a conceptual reassessment and for a new arms control strategy will not suffice, if the capabilities of conceptual innovation are lacking. Conceptual innovation by institutional reform requires a broader definition of arms control in the context of national security policy, a direct involvement of arms control experts in the national military research, development and procurement process, a high degree of professionalisation to be able to compete with the military and the defence establishment, direct access to the political leadership in the department and an involvement in all planning and co-ordinating efforts at the highest political level dealing with issues of security and arms control.

The American Experience: Conceptual Innovation and Institutional Reform in Arms Control and Disarmament

The American experience in arms control and disarmament conceptualisation and organisation structure indicates a close relationship.[23] While in the early 1960s a conceptual reassessment (from disarmament to arms control) led to an institutional upgrading of arms control policy (the creation of ACDA in 1961), in the mid-1970s an institutional reform (introduction of arms control impact statements) created a potential for a conceptual reevaluation.

During the postwar period we may distinguish at least four approaches to arms limitation and disarmament policy: the efforts for international control of nuclear weapons (1945–46) largely influenced by the domestic campaigns of nuclear physicists;[24] the public diplomacy of general and complete disarmament (1947–61) that played a rôle in the psychological warfare between the superpowers during the Cold War;[25] the emergence of joint steering goals among the nuclear powers (prevention of nuclear proliferation, containment of the probability of accidental nuclear wars and the limitation of nuclear testing) which favoured the less ambitious, piecemeal approach of arms control; and the increasing disillusionment with the failure of arms control and with the inability to deal with weapons innovation among scientists and statesmen in the 1970s.

The public pressure of the nuclear physicists was partly canalised by the creation of the Atomic Energy Commission in 1947. During the Cold War suggestions for general and complete disarmament did not require major analytical or planning capabilities. Large public relations components for speech-writing and dissemination of material countering the Soviet peace campaigns were sufficient. But with the emergence of joint steering goals between the two superpowers in the mid-1950s and increasing domestic pressure for a test ban, President Eisenhower appointed a Special Assistant to the President for Disarmament in March 1955 with a seat both in the Cabinet and in the National Security Council (NSC).[26] After a conflict on the determination of

policy between John Foster Dulles and Harold Stassen, responsibility for arms control matters was transferred back to the State
Department to a newly created Office of the Special Assistant to
the Secretary of State for Disarmament and Atomic Energy. In
1961 ACDA was established as a semi-independent agency whose
Director was to advise both the President and the Secretary of
State. After two decades the experience with ACDA is mixed.[27]
Paul Walker concludes his analysis of ACDA with the following
observation:

> If an agency is to meet its goals, adequate amounts of appro-
> priations and personnel allocations . . . are a fundamental
> necessity. This should include monies sufficient to support
> strong public relations and external research programs, both
> meagre in this case of ACDA.
>
> If a newly created bureaucracy is to have a chance for strong
> advocacy and effectiveness in policymaking, the ACDA case
> illustrates seven fundamental building blocks, all interrelated:
> presidential or ministerial support, strong agency leadership,
> good organizational esprit, informational access, organizational
> participation, congressional or parliamentary support, and last
> but equally important, adequate financial and personnel
> resources.[28]

With the establishment of ACDA, arms control became a major
foreign policy issue for the United States. Undoubtedly its highly
professional personnel acquired both the capability and the
willingess for an innovative arms control policy in the period of the
limited Cold War (1963–68) and of detente (since 1969). The very
creation of ACDA stimulated a debate in various West European
countries suggesting an enlargement and institutional upgrading
of their arms control components within the executive branch.

After the purge of ACDA at the beginning of the second Nixon
Administration, the Murphy Commission concluded in June
1975 that ACDA had played a useful rôle. In order to strengthen
and upgrade ACDA the Commission suggested the following
reforms: expansion of ACDA's external research programme,
focusing on longer-term problems and possibilities for arms
control; enlargement of ACDA's capability to assess the arms
control implications of American security assistance policy and
arms sales; expansion of public information on arms control and

disarmament matters; and the establishment of the Director of ACDA as principal adviser to the NSC on arms control and disarmament matters.[29]

In 1975 the Congress enacted legislation that requires any government department requesting authorisation or appropriations for a wide variety of military programmes to accompany such requests with a statement detailing the programme's impact on arms control policy and negotiations. ACDA has primary responsibility for implementing the legislation. The introduction of the procedural requirement for the preparation of annual arms control impact statements involved ACDA for the first time in the weapons acquisition process. However, this procedural device has not been efficiently utilised.

ACDA as a Stimulant for Institutional Reform in Western Europe

Both the political and the institutional upgrading of arms control policy in the United States in the early 1960s stimulated several institutional reforms of arms control policy in Western Europe. In Great Britain in October 1964 Prime Minister Harold Wilson appointed Lord Chalfont 'Minister of State, responsible for disarmament', a position that was later downgraded to that of a Parliamentary Secretary. And in order to stimulate innovative thinking of operative relevance an Arms Control and Disarmament Research Unit was established in 1964 within the Foreign Office. In 1966 Alva Myrdal, the Swedish Resident Ambassador for Disarmament Questions in Geneva since 1962, was appointed as the first Minister of Disarmament without Portfolio but with Cabinet rank. In West Germany Fritz Erler, the leader of the Social Democratic Party in the Bundestag, suggested in 1963/64 the establishment of a disarmament agency in the context of the executive branch. As a result of this institutional initiative in the summer of 1965 Chancellor Ludwig Erhard appointed a Special Commissioner for Disarmament and Arms Control Matters of the Federal Government to be located in the Foreign Office. At the same time he established an independent research unit on strategy, disarmament and arms control within the Foundation of Science and Policy in Ebenhausen. Minor changes and institutional upgrading occurred in several other European countries in the 1960s. For example, in 1961 Arms Control and Disarmament Advisory Bodies were established in Denmark and Norway and in 1964 in the Netherlands and in Great Britain. The minor institutional reform relating to arms control and disarmament matters in Europe was to enable the respective governments to cope with the increase in arms control negotiations. Given the conceptual leadership rôle of the United States within NATO only limited innovative components were introduced.

The First United Nations Special Session on Disarmament and Institutional Reform

In order to enhance the preparation for the first Special Session on Disarmament in May and June of 1978 or to facilitate the development of new proposals tabled during the Special Session various institutional reforms occurred. In autumn 1978 Canada created the position of a Special Advisor for Disarmament and Arms Control in the Ministry of External Affairs (the title was changed in 1979 to Ambassador for Disarmament) and enlarged the staff working on these matters. Denmark appointed a Special Adviser on Arms Control Matters in its Foreign Office with the rank of Ambassador. Finland created a small disarmament section under the Under-Secretary in 1978. In April 1979 France created a Service des Affaires Statégiques et du Desarmement in the Quai d'Orsay and enlarged the staff working on arms control matters from four to about sixteen officers in three units working on disarmament, on NATO-related questions and on military aid.

The Final Document of the Special Session on Disarmament devoted a whole section to questions related to machinery. Various countries suggested institutional reforms in disarmament machinery both at the national and international level:

1. Memorandum from France concerning the establishment of an International Satellite Monitoring Agency.
2. Memorandum from France concerning the establishment of an International Institute for Disarmament Research.
3. Proposal by Uruguay on the possibility of establishing a Polemological Agency.
4. Memorandum from France concerning the establishment of an International Disarmament Fund for Development.

5. Proposal by Norway entitled 'Evaluation of the impact of new weapons on arms control and disarmament efforts'.
6. Proposal by the Netherlands for a study on the establishment of an International Disarmament Organization.[30]

As a consequence of the Norwegian proposal to the Special Session, the Norwegian Disarmament Commission financed a feasibility study on how to institutionalise arms control impact statements into the Norwegian foreign and defence decision-making process.[31] The institutionalisation of an arms control perspective into the military research, development, production and procurement process may create a political early warning system within the executive forcing the political leadership to get involved at an earlier stage of the weapons acquisition process.

A Comparison of Organisation Structures and of Decision-making Processes Dealing with Arms Control and Disarmament Policies in Several CSCE States

In our comparison of organisation structures and in our attempt to describe the decision-making processes on arms control and disarmament matters the following CSCE signatory states were surveyed: both superpowers, the United States and the Soviet Union; both European nuclear powers, Great Britain and France; eight NATO countries, namely Italy, Canada, the Netherlands, Belgium, Denmark, Norway, Italy and West Germany; three additional Warsaw Pact states – Poland, Romania and the German Democratic Republic; and four neutral and non-aligned nations – Sweden, Finland, Austria and Switzerland.

Here an evaluation of the effectiveness and of the innovative potential is hardly possible. This would require selected case-studies of each country focusing on the relationship between organisation structure and policy outcome during different periods. Such an analysis would require a multinational research effort. In this descriptive comparison it is intended to concentrate on the following factors:

1. political rank of the arms control unit and of its director;
2. organisation models in foreign ministries;
3. organisation models in defence departments;

4. co-ordination processes dealing with arms control matters;
5. level of professionalisation of the arms control experts;
6. support for arms control and disarmament research;
7. advisory bodies for arms control and disarmament;
8. arms control and legislative bodies – control and participation.[32]

1. Political Rank of the Arms Control Unit and its Director

No country of our sample has a separate department dealing with
arms control and disarmament matters. Sweden had a Disarmament Minister Without Portfolio but with Cabinet rank in the
person of Alva Myrdal (1966–73). Only the Americans have a
semi-independent arms control and disarmament agency in
ACDA, whose Director is an adviser both to the President and to
the Secretary of State. During Paul Warnke's tenure, the ACDA
Director was at the same time the head of the American SALT
delegation and a full member of the NSC. Great Britain appointed
a 'Minister of State for Disarmament' (1964), a position that was
later downgraded to that of a 'Parliamentary Under-Secretary of
State for Foreign and Commonwealth Affairs'. In 1965 West
Germany created the position of a Commissioner for Arms Control
and Disarmament of the Government in the Foreign Ministry who
became a member of the Federal Security Council in February
1979. The Netherlands during the term of the centre-left government from 1973 to 1977 established the position of an Under-
Secretary of State for problems of arms control and disarmament.
Canada, Denmark, Norway, Finland and France upgraded the
rank and enlarged the staff of their arms control units after the UN
Special Session devoted to Disarmament.

An upgrading of the rank of the person responsible for arms
control matters in the early and mid-1960s and in the late 1970s
does not automatically indicate an upgrading of arms control and
disarmament policies. Primarily, it was an act of symbolic politics
addressed to the domestic scene to please an element of the
electorate. A political upgrading of arms control policy units may
be of political consequence if its director is both knowledgeable in
the field and has a broad political backing, like Alva Myrdal or
Warnke.

The number of arms control experts in various government
positions is also no direct indication of the political will and readiness for a policy of arms reduction and restraint. The United States

with about 250 positions within ACDA and another 150 arms control experts in the State Department, the Defense Department and the Energy Department is at the same time the pacesetter of the qualitative arms race.

2. Organisation Structures in Foreign Ministries Relating to Arms Control

Besides the semi-independent ACDA, the US State Department has a separate Office of Disarmament and Arms Control within its Bureau of Politico-Military Affairs. While France, West Germany and Canada (since 1978) have organisational units that cover both global (UN-related issues) and regional (NATO-related issues such as SALT, MBFR and CSCE) arms control matters, Great Britain, the Netherlands, Denmark and Norway maintain a functional division between UN- and NATO-related matters which sometimes leads to a rivalry of both units. Not advisable appears to be the appointment of special disarmament advisers who are not organisationally linked with the arms control units and who only devote a part of their time to arms control matters.

3. Organisation Structures in Defence Departments

The size of the arms control units in defence departments reflects the military significance and sensitivity of arms control issues. The greater the military significance of arms control in defence planning (as in SALT), the greater the military resources devoted to arms control matters and the greater the potential veto power of the military.

In most defence departments arms control problems are being dealt with in two separate organisations: the military organisation of the armed forces (General Staff, Joint Chiefs of Staff and military staff units) and by civilian staff units, responsible for international questions, military planning and foreign-policy questions. In the United States both the Joint Chiefs of Staff and the Office of the Secretary of Defense (and particularly its division on International Security Affairs), as well as the Department of Energy and the Intelligence Agencies, are involved. In the Soviet Union besides the General Staff, the Department of Defence and the military—industrial departments appear also to be involved in the arms control decision-making process. In the British Ministry of Defence three different units consisting of six persons each deal with arms control matters located in the Secretariat Branch, in the

Defence Policy Council and in the Scientific Staff. In the Canadian Defence Department an arms control unit consists of about four officers. In the Dutch Defence Department about eight civilians and military people are working in the political division on arms control issues. Sweden has an Adviser to the Secretary of Defence on disarmament matters who has direct access to the Secretary of Defence. In West Germany six officers in an arms control unit within the Führungsstab der Streitkräfte, as well as two officers and one civilian on the Defence Department Planning Staff, deal with arms control matters.

4. Co-ordination Processes

Co-ordination among the leading foreign ministries, defence ministries, intelligence agencies and other government departments is highly formalised for the United States, for the Soviet Union and for West Germany. The American NSC has both planning (formulation of alternative options) and co-ordinative functions. Little is known about the co-ordination among the Defence Committee of the Politbureau, the *ad hoc* SALT committee of the Central Committee of the Communist Party, the Defence Council and the Military—Industrial Commission in the Soviet Union. West Germany has a separate Cabinet Committee, the Federal Security Council, with a tiny staff of less than five people. Informal co-ordination appears to be the practice in Great Britain, Canada, the Netherlands, Denmark, Norway, Sweden and Finland. Only in the United States does the co-ordination also relate to the arms control implications of emerging military technologies.

5. Level of Professionalisation of Arms Control Experts

In 1979, ACDA had about 251 positions, among them 18 officers and 34 diplomats. No other country had a higher level of professionalisation relating to arms control. This high level of professionalisation eased the personal exchange between ACDA and academic positions, lacking in most other states. In other countries arms control matters are usually the domain of generalists, of diplomats in foreign ministries and of officers in defence departments who ordinarily have an assignment of 2–3 years. The Arms Control Research Unit in the British Foreign and Commonwealth Office permits scientific experts to participate in the operative departments for a period of up to 3 years. It is questionable whether the dominance of generalists will be appropriate to deal with the sophisticated arms control and disarmament issues of the 1980s.

6. Arms Control and Disarmament Research

In fiscal year 1978 ACDA had a research budget of $3,635,000. The West German Foreign Ministry spent about DM240,000 for arms control-related research in 1977. In addition to research grants from various US departments and agencies, various private foundations, like the Ford Foundation, support arms control centres in several American universities. Since 1965 the British Foreign Office has had its own research component (Arms Control Research Unit) that employed between three and eight experts. While the British group is directly involved in operative matters, the West German arms control division within the Foundation on Science and Policy is both geographically and politically detached from the operative units.

In the Soviet Union at least two research institutes within the framework of the Academy of Science are involved in arms control matters: the Institute for the United States and Canada, and the Institute for World Economy and International Relations. The Soviet Academy of Science has a SALT study group and a commission for disarmament. In June of 1979 the Soviet Academy of Science established a research council for peace and disarmament.

Canada, the Netherlands and Norway support research studies on arms control and disarmament matters. Sweden and Finland support two peace research institutes that deal with arms control-related issues.

7. Advisory Bodies for Arms Control and Disarmament

Many countries have appointed advisory bodies for arms control and disarmament including scientists, members of parliament and representatives of societal groups. These advisory bodies perform major functions: to stimulate innovative conceptual inputs and to contribute to the legitimisation of official arms control policies. In the United States the General Advisory Committee on Arms Control and Disarmament of ACDA − consisting of 14 members, including scientists, representatives of social groups and businessmen − is intended to advise the US Government, to control ACDA and to educate the public. The British Advisory Council for Disarmament includes members of the House of Commons, of the House of Lords, former officials and representatives of social groups. Its purpose is to advise the Government and to initiate research. The Dutch Council on Disarmament, International Security and Peace includes members of political parties, the media, academia, the churches and action groups. Though its advisory function is rather limited, it primarily concentrates on educational efforts and on publications. The Danish Disarmament Committee comprises members of political parties, members of parliament, representatives of the foreign and defence departments and outside experts. The Norwegian Arms Control and Disarmament Committee appointed by the Government for a 4-year period consists of 15 members, five coming from Parliament, five from academia and five from social groups. The Swedish Disarmament Commission comprises members of parliament and of the foreign and defence departments. It is chaired by the Swedish Under-Secretary for Disarmament matters. In Finland the ten members of the Advisory Council on Disarmament Questions are appointed by the State Council. They can co-opt eight experts. The Finnish council meets once a month. It has four sections dealing with technical advice, co-ordination of research, educational efforts, and publications. In East Germany an inter-departmental group of governmental experts advises the respective government and party bodies. No advisory boards exist in France, West Germany, Belgium, Italy, Romania and Poland.

8. Arms Control and Legislative Bodies

In the Presidential system of the United States arms control problems have become a major issue of competition and conflict between Congress and the Executive Branch. In the Senate both the Foreign Relations and the Armed Services Committees have sub-committees dealing with arms control issues. In the House of Representatives in 1977 only the Foreign Affairs Committee had a separate sub-committee on international security and on scientific questions. West Germany has a sub-committee on arms control and disarmament matters whose members belong to either the Foreign or the Defence Committee of the Bundestag. No equivalent bodies exist in the other countries of our sample. Arms control issues until recently played only a minor rôle in European parliaments.

Compared with the scientific advisory bodies of the US Congress such as the Congressional Research Service, the General Accounting Office and the Congressional Budget Office, the scientific staff of the Bundestag employs two arms control experts, one on loan from the Defence Department. While the US Congressional committees and sub-committees regularly hold hearings on arms control matters, in Europe only the Dutch Parliament appears to have held hearings recently on arms control-related issues.

Are the Existing Organisation Structures in the Field of Arms Control and Disarmament Sufficient for the Problems of the 1980s?

One of the main reasons for the failure of arms control efforts during the past two decades has been the inability to restrain the weapons-modernisation process. As a result of the narrow definition of arms control, namely that focusing only on the international negotiation context, the weapons-innovation process has not been a concern for the arms control units in the foreign ministries. As generalists they often lack the expertise and the information about the ongoing military research and development programmes. Major deficiencies of the arms control machinery and decision-making processes in various countries of the CSCE-area appear to be the following:

1. The narrow definition of arms control focusing primarily on ongoing arms control negotiations is insufficient. Arms control has to include also the weapons-innovation and acquisition process and the social and economic consequences of arms control and disarmament steps. It should comprise all military-related issues including arms exports and exports of nuclear reactors and reprocessing facilities. The introduction of new routines, such as the annual preparation of arms control impact statements, will require additional administrative resources and new co-ordination structures.
2. The compartmentalisation both within the foreign ministries (in many countries there still exist two separate arms control bodies) and within the Government should be overcome by combining all arms control-related issues and administrative units either in a separate department for politico-military affairs in the foreign ministry or in separate arms control and disarmament agencies or offices within the executive branch of government.

3. Most countries lack an independent analysis and planning capability for arms control matters. If arms control is not to remain the victim of arms procurement and of the weapons innovation process then a synchronisation of planning perspectives is required. The introduction of arms control impact statements could stimulate and encourage longer-term integrated security and arms control planning.

4. The traditional goals of arms control, stability, reduction of damage in war and reduction of costs, have not been properly sought during the past two decades. A new arms control and disarmament strategy has to focus more on the determinants of armaments dynamics: uninhibited technological change, societal obstacles and international competition for the control of scarce raw materials.

5. The cognitive dilemma of many arms control experts in government has to be gradually overcome. Many governmental experts approach arms control issues as zero-sum games. The credibility of arms control rests on considerations of power politics. Bargaining chips are needed to induce the other side to serious negotiations and compromises. The institutionalisation of a rotation between governmental and scientific experts in the area of arms control may erode this cognitive dilemma.

6. Arms control has been largely an objective of political rhetoric and for speech-writing for many years. In the 1980s arms control will require a higher degree of professionalisation within government. Generalists with diplomatic and military skills have to co-operate more closely with specialists with scientific skills.

7. The negotiation approach has been partly dysfunctional. The requirement of a two-thirds majority for arms control treaties in the US Senate permitted small groups to get military compensations for their support of the ratification of arms control treaties. In order to overcome these deficiencies a double strategy linking national initiatives with negotiated agreements has become imperative.

General Suggestions for Further Research and for Policy Initiatives

This chapter started with a frank and gloomy assessment that two decades of arms control had not been able to achieve a higher level of stability, to reduce the defence burden and to reduce the damage if deterrence should fail and if war should occur. One central element in this failure has been the inability of arms control, and of arms control bureaucracies, to cope with the uninhibited weapons innovation and modernisation process. One other element has been the decrease in public support for disarmament efforts and the decay of mutual confidence among the two superpowers.

As supplementary elements to a new arms control strategy we have proposed on the international level confidence-building measures and on the national level disarmament-supporting measures. Both types of measures are to enhance the prospects for successful arms control and disarmament initiatives. Disarmament-supporting measures focus simultaneously on the societal and the governmental level. Addressing the political—administrative system, we suggest the following. The initiation and implementation of a conceptual reassessment of arms control theory and practice requires an institutional reform within respective bureaucracies in order to give a higher emphasis to arms control issues both within government and among the public. Such an institutional reform within the political—administrative system should be based on a broader definition of arms control. It should overcome the existing compartmentalisation, the lack of an independent analysis and planning capability and it should favour a higher professionalisation of the policy preparation and 'desophistication' in policy presentation to the public. One precondition for the reformulation of the traditional arms control goals is the overcoming of the cognitive dilemma of many governmental experts. The initiation of new governmental routines (such as the introduction of arms control impact statements) to assess the longer-term arms control and political implications of new weapons programmes oriented at greater openness, transparency and parliamentary controllability becomes at the same time a unilateral confidence-building measure and an important step to a new double strategy of arms control that links national initiatives at arms restraint with negotiated agreements on arms control and reduction. Both the concept of 'disarmament-supporting measures' and the working hypothesis 'conceptual innovation by institutional reform' have to be further clarified and specified. Their strategic relevance in terms of a new arms control, and disarmament strategy that inhibits the weapons-innovation process, have to be discussed. If the concept and working hypothesis are both of scientific relevance and of strategic–political importance a policy-oriented research strategy should be contemplated. Because arms control and disarmament is an international issue, institutional reform enabling conceptual innovation has to take place simultaneously in many CSCE states. In order to formulate specific institutional reform options for the national level an analysis of the specific deficiencies of the national arms control machinery is required. Various case-studies on the relationship between organisational structure and policy output in arms control are needed on the national level. The methodology of structured focused comparison developed by Alex George of Stanford University may provide an analytical framework for comparing the national case-studies and for locating the major shared deficiencies.[33]

The main research and policy questions may be:

1. How can governmental decision-making processes dealing with arms control and national security matters be reorganised in such a way as to enable the political leadership to cope with the de-stabilising effects of new weapons systems?
2. However, the best procedure, the highest level of expertise and professionalisation will not be sufficient, if the problems cannot be presented to the public in a 'desophisticated way' and if domestic support for these measures and the political will for their implementation are lacking.
3. Institutional reform on the top, and political pressure from the bottom, for a conceptual innovation of arms control thinking and for a new disarmament strategy have to coincide.

During the 29th Pugwash Conference in Mexico City the following disarmament-supporting measures to increase public awareness of the need for disarmament and to promote confidence and arms restraint were suggested:

1. The creation of national governmental disarmament agencies in order to promote the consideration and adoption of effective disarmament policies.
2. The establishment of national advisory boards and councils, which would include both governmental and non-governmental scientists and experts, to advise on disarmament policies and activities.

3. The creation of governmental agencies on policies and planning for conversion of military industries and production to peaceful civilian purposes.
4. The publication of arms limitation and disarmament impact statements in all cases of the proposed acquisition of new military weapons and systems.
5. The improvement of national education on disarmament and peace, including the establishment of chairs and study courses in these fields and the teaching of these and related subjects in schools.
6. The development of active co-operation with non-governmental organisations, especially those of an international character, involved in the promotion of disarmament and peace.[34]

They deserve most careful consideration.[35]

Notes

1. *Daedalus*, LXXXIX (1960).
2. Thomas C. Schelling, 'Reciprocal Measures for Arms Stabilization', *Daedalus*, LXXXIX (1960), pp. 892–914; and Franklin A. Long, 'Arms Control from the Perspective of the Nineteen-Seventies' in Franklin A. Long and Goerge W. Rathjens (eds), *Arms, Defense Policy and Arms Control* (New York, 1976) pp. 1–14.
3. Leslie Gelb, 'The Future of Arms Control: A Glass Half Full?' *Foreign Policy*, no. 36, fall 1979, p. 21.
4. SIPRI, *World Armaments and Disarmament: SIPRI Yearbook 1980* (London, 1980) p. 19.
5. Christoph Bertram, 'Neue Ansätze der Rüstungskontrolle', in Erhard Forndran and Paul J. Friedrich (eds), *Rüstungskontrolle und Sicherheit in Europa* (Bonn, 1979) pp. 337–46; and Christoph Bertram, '*The Future of Arms Control: Part II, Arms Control and Technological Change: Elements of a New Approach*' (Adelphi Paper no. 146, London 1978).
6. Erhard Forndran, 'Rüstungskontrolle − Theorie und Probleme' in Reiner Steinweg (ed.), *Das kontrollierte Chaos: Die Krise der Abrüstung* (Frankfurt, 1980) pp. 15–38.
7. B. T. Feld, 'New Technology and the Arms Race', *Proceedings of the 30th Pugwash Conference on Science and World Affairs* (Breukelen, Netherlands, 1980).
8. Hans Günter Brauch, 'The Failure of Arms Control in Coping with New Weapons Technologies and with Technological Change', paper prepared for the 36th Pugwash Symposium, London, Dec. 1980; Bertram, op. cit.; and Feld, op. cit.

9. Graham T. Allison and Frederic A. Morris, 'Armaments and Arms Control: Exploring the Determinants of Military Weapons', *Daedalus*, CIV (1975).
10. Charles Osgood, *An Alternative to War and Surrender* (Urbana, Illinois, 1962); and Herbert Scoville, Jr, 'A Different Approach to Arms Control — Reciprocal Unilateral Restraint', in David Carlton and Carlo Schaerf (eds), *Arms Control and Technological Innovation* (London, 1977) pp. 170–5.
11. Jonathan Alford (ed.), *The Future of Arms Control*: Part III, *Confidence-Building Measures* (Adelphi Papers, no. 149, London, 1979); Hans Günter Brauch, 'Confidence Building Measures and Disarmament Strategy', *Current Research on Peace and Violence*, 1979, no. 3–4, pp. 114–45; and Brauch, 'CBMs and the CSCE', *Arms Control Today*, Nov. 1980.
12. Hans Günter Brauch, 'Confidence Building and Disarmament Supporting Measures: Supplementary Elements of a New Disarmament Strategy', paper prepared for the Joint American–Canadian Pugwash International Symposium on New Directions in Disarmament, Wingspread, Wisconsin, June 1980.
13. *Proceedings of the 30th Pugwash Conference on Science and World Affairs* (Breukelen, Netherlands, 1980).
14. See note 8.
15. Steven Rosen (ed.), *Testing the Theory of the Military–Industrial Complex* (Lexington, Mass. and London, 1973); and Carroll W. Pursell, Jr (ed.), *The Military–Industrial Complex* (New York, 1972).
16. See note 9.
17. Seymour Melman, *The Permanent War Economy: American Capitalism in Decline* (New York, 1974); and Murray L. Weidenbaum, *The Economics of Peacetime Defense* (New York, 1974).
18. Raimo Väyrynen, 'Military R&D as an Aspect of the Arms Race', *Current Research on Peace and Violence*, 1978, no. 3–4.
19. Allison and Morris, loc. cit., p. 126.
20. Graham Allison and Peter Szanton, *Remaking Foreign Policy: The Organizational Connection* (New York, 1976).
21. Robert D. Murphy, *Report of the Commission on the Organization of the Government for the Conduct of Foreign Policy* (Washington, DC, 1975).
22. ibid., p. IX.
23. Duncan L. Clarke, *Politics of Arms Control: the Role and Effectiveness of the US Arms Control and Disarmament Agency* (New York, 1979).
24. Joseph I. Lieberman, *Scorpion and the Tarantula: The Struggle to Control Atomic Weapons, 1945–1949* (Boston, Massachusetts, 1970).
25. Robert Gilpin, *American Scientists and Nuclear Weapons Policy* (Princeton, New Jersey, 1962).
26. Saville Davis, 'Recent Policy Making in the United States Government' in *Daedalus*, LXXXIX (1960), pp. 951–66; and Hubert H. Humphrey, 'Governmental Organization for Arms Control', *Daedalus*, LXXXIV (1960), pp. 967–83.
27. See Clarke, op. cit.; Paul Walker, 'The US Arms Control and Disarmament Agency: Lessons from Past Experience' in Volker Rittberger, *Studien zur Abrüstungsplanung*, vol. III (Baden Baden, forthcoming).
28. Walker, loc. cit.
29. Murphy, Report, pp. 82–3.

30. SIPRI, *World Armaments and Disarmament: SIPRI Yearbook 1979* (London, 1979) pp. 524–47.
31. Anders Hellebust of the Nordic Journalist School in Oslo prepared this report.
32. For a detailed description and analysis see Hans Günter Brauch, *Abrüstungsamt oder Ministerium* (Frankfurt, 1981) pp. 143–247.
33. Alexander L. George, 'The Method of Structured, Focused Comparison: A Qualitative Approach to Theory-Building (unpublished manuscript); Dan Caldwell, 'American–Soviet Detente and the Nixon–Kissinger Grand Design and Grand Strategy', Ph.D. Dissertation, Stanford University, 1978; and Alexander L. George and Richard Smoke, *Deterrence in American Foreign Policy: Theory and Practice* (New York, 1974).
34. H. G. Brauch, W. Epstein, R. J. H. Kruisinga, Betty Lall and Sverre Lodgaard, 'Proposal for National Initiatives for More Effective Disarmament Efforts', *Proceedings of the 29th Pugwash Conference on Science and World Affairs* (Mexico City, 1979) p. 163.
35. For a more detailed and scholarly treatment of the themes of this paper see Hans Günter Brauch, *Abrüstungsamt oder Ministerium? Ausländische Modelle der Abrüstungsplanung: Materialien und Reformvorschläge* (Frankfurt, 1980).

8 The Maintenance of Peace is the Most Important Problem of Today

V. S. Emelyanov

The problem of how to preserve peace on earth is of increasing concern to the world community. Even the Second World War clearly indicated what our planet would turn into if a third world war, involving the use of modern arms, broke out. During the Second World War — the most sanguinary and devastating war in human history — a 5-megaton trinitrotoluol equivalent of explosives was expended. A present day 10-megaton bomb twice exceeds the yield of all the explosives used in the 4 years of the war. One should also remember that modern technology makes it possible to create nuclear bombs of 25-, 50- and even 100-megaton yields.

We can imagine what will happen if there is a war in which modern nuclear weapons are employed. The tragedies of Hiroshima and Nagasaki speak volumes. The very first atomic bombs, which had an explosive power of 20 kilotons each, destroyed two cities. Only one bomb was required for one city!

In the report on the effects of the possible use of nuclear weapons, prepared in 1967 in accordance with a decision of the 21st session of the UN General Assembly, it was shown convincingly what tragedy a nuclear war may lead to, in particular in densely populated Europe. Experts from 12 member countries of the UN cited in this report a great amount of evidence revealing what awaits mankind if a new war involving the employment of nuclear weapons breaks out. In it, specifically, they demonstrated what a terrible, incomparable catastrophe will happen if just two

15-20-megaton nuclear bombs are exploded over London and Hamburg. The zone of death and destruction in these cases will embrance vast territories from London to Paris, including Paris, and from Hamburg to Ulm, including Göttingen and Kassel.[1]

If all these weapons of mass slaughter are brought into action, the plague epidemic in the fourteenth century that took a quarter of the population of Europe to the grave will not look such a terrible calamity. At that time the survivors could bury the dead; and the tragedy took place over a period of years. In the event of a nuclear war everything will happen instantaneously. The survivors will not be able to inter the dead, and both the living and the dead — tens of millions of people — will be buried under the ruins of former cities.

In the wars that took place earlier, before the appearance of nuclear weapons, non-belligerent countries not only did not suffer from them, but even received certain advantages by supplying the belligerent nations with arms and strategic materials. Even those of the neutral countries which had common frontiers with the belligerents did not incur any losses from military operations.

The appearance of nuclear weapons has radically changed the situation not only of the closest neighbours of the belligerent countries, but even of those among them which, not having common frontiers, are linked with the areas where hostilities occur by such ties as would not in the past have been regarded as dangerous for states not involved. Here we can include rivers and water tables that serve as sources of water not for one, but for several states; seas with their currents washing the shores of several states; air flows passing from a country involved in a war to countries not participating in it; and many other links which earlier were not taken into account. In the event of a nuclear war, even a local one, even one that does not grow into a world war, many countries, and above all the belligerents' closest neighbours, will experience the destructive effects of nuclear explosions and their perilous consequences. To predict in advance what area will be struck by a blast wave is difficult, and sometimes even impossible. For Europe, with its high population density and the close proximity of its cities and inhabited areas to each other, the damage from a nuclear bombing will have particularly baneful consequences.

Adducing data on the wars of the past and forecasting a possible future, the British scientist Robin Clarke has drawn up a calculation on the number of wars that occurred in periods of 30–50 years since 1820 and information on the number of people killed in them.[2] From his calculation it emerges that in the course of 30 years from 1820 to 1849 there were 92 wars, in which 800,000 people were killed. Then in the 40 years from 1860 to 1899 mankind lived through 100 wars, which took a toll of 4.6 million. In the subsequent 50 years there were 117 wars, and the number killed in them amounted to 42.5 million or 2.1 per cent of the world's total population at that time. Extrapolating this process for the next two 50-year periods, the author shows what would be in store for mankind before 2000 and also in the first half of the twenty-first century. He assumes that mankind will go through 120 wars in each of the 50-year periods, but that the number of killed will strongly differ. During the second half of the twentieth century, in the 120 wars that may take place, the number of killed will reach 406 million, which will amount to 10.1 per cent of the world's entire population, and in the 120 wars of the first half of the twenty-first century the number of killed will amount to 4050 million or 40.5 per cent of the world's total. 1980 is the 35th year that the European continent has known no wars!

The credit for peace in Europe first of all goes to the states of the Socialist community and all the public movements and organisations working for peace. In a speech on American television on 24 June 1973 L. I. Brezhnev, General Secretary of the Communist Party of the Soviet Union Central Committee and President of the Presidium of the USSR Supreme Soviet, clearly and precisely defined the attitude of the Soviet people to the assessment of the importance of peace for them, and also the thoughts and plans of the Soviet people for the future:

The Soviet people, perhaps better than any other people, know what war is. In the Second World War we achieved a victory of worldwide historical importance. But more than 20 million Soviet citizens died in that war, 70,000 of our towns and villages were razed to the ground. One-third of our national wealth was destroyed.

Now the wounds of war have been healed. Today the Soviet Union is stronger and more prosperous than ever before. But we remember well the lessons of the war. And it is precisely for this reason that the people of the Soviet Union so highly value peace and wholeheartedly approve of the peace-oriented policy of our Party and Government.

To us peace is the supreme achievement, for which people must strive if they want their lives to be of any worth. We believe that reason must prevail and feel sure that this belief is shared also by the people of the United States of America and other countries. If this belief were to be lost, if it were to be replaced by a blind reliance on force alone, on the might of nuclear weapons, or some other weapon, then it would be a sorry outlook for human civilisation and for humanity itself.[3]

The postwar period saw the rise in a number of countries of mass public organisations actively working for peace. The Soviet Union also has several such organisations: the Peace Committee, the Committee for European Security and Cooperation, the Afro-Asian Solidarity Committee, the Peace Fund and a number of others.

The Soviet Peace Fund is a unique organisation: it incorporates 75 million people who have made and are making contributions to the Fund. Who are these contributors? They are Soviet people of all ages — from schoolchildren to pensioners. Workers in all the branches of industry and agriculture, people of science and arts, teachers, doctors and writers belong to this group. They voluntarily contribute a part of their earnings, and also bonuses and royalties from their printed works. Pensioners set aside some of their savings for the Fund, and children send the money they receive for paper and scrap metal collected by them. The contributions to the Fund are of different origin and vary in size, but they have one unifying motive — the deep belief by those who make them that they serve to maintain peace on earth. The Rules of the Soviet Peace Fund state:

Expressing the patriotism and internationalism of the Soviet people and guided by the goals and principles of the peaceloving foreign policy of the USSR, confirmed in the Soviet Constitution, the Soviet Peace Fund renders financial support to organizations, movements and people fighting for the strengthening of peace, national independence and freedom, greater friendship and cooperation among nations, a ban on all types of nuclear weapons and other instruments of mass destruction and the achievement of general and complete disarmament.

L. I. Brezhnev in his speech on 6 October 1979, at the formal meeting in Berlin dedicated to the 30th anniversary of the German Democratic Republic (GDR), stressed:

> . . . In Europe, just as in all other parts of our planet, we want peace, a lasting peace. . . . This is the fundamental basis of our foreign policy, its backbone. We are pursuing this policy consistently and undeviatingly. As Chairman of the Defence Council of the USSR, I am most definitely stating that the number of medium-range carriers of nuclear arms on the territory of the European part of the Soviet Union has not been increased *by a single missile, by a single plane* during the past 10 years. On the contrary, the number of launchers of medium-range missiles and also the yield of the nuclear charges of these missiles have even been *somewhat decreased*. The number of medium-range bombers, too, has diminished. As for the territory of other states, the Soviet Union *does not deploy* such means there *at all*. For a number of years now we have not increased the number of our troops stationed in Central Europe either.
>
> *I will say more. We are prepared to reduce* the number of medium-range nuclear means deployed in western areas of the Soviet Union *as compared to the present level*, but, of course, only if no additional medium-range nuclear means are deployed in Western Europe.
>
> I also want to confirm solemnly that the Soviet Union will never use nuclear arms against those states that renounce the production and acquisition of such arms and do not have them on their territory.
>
> Motivated by a sincere desire to take out of the impasse the efforts of many years to achieve military detente in Europe, to show an example of transition from words to real deeds, we *have decided*, in agreement with the leadership of the GDR and after consultations with other member states of the Warsaw Treaty, *to unilaterally reduce the number of Soviet troops in Central Europe. Up to 20,000 Soviet servicemen, a thousand tanks and also a certain amount of other military hardware will be withdrawn from the territory of the German Democratic Republic in the course of the next 12 months*.
>
> We are convinced that this new, concrete manifestation of the peaceableness and goodwill of the Soviet Union and its allies will be approved by the peoples of Europe and the whole world.

We call on the governments of NATO countries to properly
assess the initiatives of socialist states and to follow our good
example.[4]

One should only recall what happened in the middle of 1978.
What an unprecedented action was then committed by NATO
leaders! In May 1978 the UN General Assembly's Special Session
on Disarmament was at work in New York. For the first time those
attending it included not only the official representatives of individual countries, but also delegates from large mass organisations, representing millions of people on our planet. Their voices
had both a convincing and passionate ring. They appealed for an
end to the arms race, for efforts to bring about early disarmament
and the prohibition and destruction of all types of weapons, and,
above all, weapons of mass annihilation. And at the same time in
Washington a meeting of the NATO Council was convened to
consider a 15-year programme for arms build-up and a resulting
considerable increase in military expenditure. The meeting
approved this programme. The newspaper *Pravda* commented in
June 1978:

> Our people have seen too much and experienced too much to
> give in to pressure or to retreat before sabre-rattling. They have
> chosen the path of peace and will not allow anyone to push them
> off this path.
> We shall not accept an invitation to join the funeral of
> detente and the hopes of millions of people for a peaceful future
> and for the possibility of a life worthy of man for themselves and
> their children.
> The Soviet Union and the other countries of socialism are
> fully resolved to conduct a consistent and stubborn struggle for
> them along all directions and first of all along such a direction as
> the limitation and reduction of armaments.[5]

At the end of November 1978 Moscow hosted a conference of
the Political Consultative Committee of the Warsaw Treaty
member states. In the declaration they adopted, the participants
pointed out that in recent years the determination of the peoples
and of all the forces of progress and peace to put an end to the
aggressive and oppressive policy of imperialism, colonialism and
neo-colonialism has become ever stronger, and the struggle for

peace, for detente, for an end to the arms race, for freedom and social progress, for peaceful international co-operation on an equal footing, based on mutual respect for national independence and sovereignty, and non-interference in internal affairs, has been developing ever more widely.[6]

The conferees devoted considerable attention to the questions of strengthening security and promoting co-operation in Europe. In his evaluation of this conference General Secretary of the Communist Party of the Soviet Union (CPSU) Central Committee and President of the Presidium of the USSR Supreme Soviet L. I. Brezhnev said:

> We have had a broad exchange of opinions on questions which time and life have set our countries and we have approved an important political document which reflects our common views.
>
> I believe that our conference gives clear answers to at least three important questions.
>
> Firstly, concerning the essence of the time we are living through. What I mean is a joint, deep analysis of the international situation, an assessment of its pluses and minuses, its most important tendencies. Despite the increased activity of various forces coming out against detente, we are far from being pessimistic. . . .
>
> We also declared together what it is that we must do. The main thing is to build international security not on the basis of the arms race, but on disarmament, to press in deeds, not in words, for great respect for the sovereign rights of all states and peoples. New horizons will then open for peaceful cooperation on the continent of Europe and on an international scale, and the edifice of peace will stand firm.
>
> And finally, our conference gives the answer to the question as to how we must advance towards these goals. We must advance together, strengthening our cooperation with each other. We must always come out in solidarity with fighters for the freedom and independence of the nations. We must pool our efforts with all who wish to see peaceful skies over our planet and who want people to live happily.[7]

Two documents – two programmes. One was approved in May 1978 by the NATO Council, and the other in November 1978 by by the Warsaw Treaty member states. One, ignoring the hopes of millions of people, condemns them to further suffering and concern over their future, and subjects everything to the interests of a handful of profit-greedy arms manufacturers and the most reactionary elite who by these arms seek to maintain their privileged status and hold back the progress of mankind. The other holds out before people boundless opportunities for peaceful endeavour in accordance with their wishes and abilities without fear not only for their own future, but also for the future of their children.

The Declaration of the Warsaw Treaty Member Countries stated:

> The states taking part in the Conference consider it necessary to build up international efforts for the resolution of vital problems concerning the interests of all mankind, and especially of the younger generation, to press for the improvement of the living and working conditions of the masses of the people, the eradication of racialism and apartheid, and the propaganda of war, violence, immorality and hatred for humanity.

The Conference participants appealed to all European states and people of the world to

> resolutely set out on the road of firm allegiance to the policy of peace, detente, renunciation of the use or threat of force in international relations, peaceful settlement of all disputes, unconditional condemnation of aggressive wars, complete exclusion of war between states from the life of mankind, an end to the arms race, and the final eradication of the vestiges of the cold war.

They continued:

> The dream of millions of people on all continents about a world without military conflicts is not a utopia: it can be attained and can become a reality as a result of joint efforts by all those who are prepared to fight for it.[8]

Nothing unites people as firmly as does the awareness of a common danger. Modern instruments of war are so destructive and inhuman that they make people forget a great deal of what hindered their unification before the appearance of this danger.

The tendencies for unification of the most diverse public organisations in the struggle for peace and disarmament have been showing up ever more clearly. There is a growing, increasingly distinct awareness that only through the united efforts by public organisations and movements and their persistent struggle for peace and disarmament is it possible to remove the danger of a nuclear holocaust, thus opening up broad opportunities for the use of modern scientific and technological achievements by all countries and peoples.

The world public is a mighty force which no-one and nothing can resist, and the enlistment of this force in the struggle for peace and disarmament will undoubtedly lead to the triumph of the forces of peace over the forces of war. The United Nations Educational, Scientific and Cultural Organisation (UNESCO), as one of the largest and most prestigious bodies in the UN system called upon to serve the cause of peace by promoting mutually beneficial international co-operation in the fields of education, science, culture and communications, can and should make a more weighty contribution to the solving of this most important and most urgent problem of our time.

Notes

1. United Nations, *Effects of the Possible Use of Nuclear Weapons and the Economic Implications for States of the Acquisition and Further Development of Those Weapons* (New York, 1968) pp. 15–16.
2. Robin Clarke, *The Science of War and Peace* (London, 1971) p. 10.
3. L. I. Brezhnev, *Our Course: Peace and Socialism: A Collection of Speeches, January–December 1973* (Moscow, 1974) pp. 68–9.
4. *Pravda*, 7 Oct. 1979.
5. ibid., 17 June 1978.
6. ibid., 24 Nov. 1978.
7. ibid.
8. ibid.

9 Is the SALT Era Over?

Gloria Duffy

Shortly after the SALT I Agreement was signed in 1972, the American historian John Newhouse wrote that SALT was 'probably the most fascinating, episodic negotiation since the Congress of Vienna . . . likely to go on indefinitely'. SALT could, he said, 'develop a cumulative impact on the world system comparable to that of the Congress of Vienna, whose achievement was to spare Europe any major bloodletting for 100 years'.[1] But in mid-August of 1980 President Carter told an audience of the American Legion that, if necessary, the United States will compete in, and will win, a nuclear arms race with the Soviet Union.[2]

The purpose of the present chapter is to consider how SALT moved from being a central hope for moderating the strategic arms race to stalemate in 8 years; what exactly happened to the SALT II Treaty; whether the conditions which gave rise to the SALT negotiations in the late 1960s and sustained them through the 1970s are likely to be recreated in the near future; and, not least importantly, whether as a means of increasing the stability of the international environment, the SALT process is indeed worth saving.

The idea of negotiating about strategic arms originated inside the US Department of Defense in 1966, with a proposal to the Soviets to discuss limiting the defensive, anti-ballistic missile (ABM) systems then under development.[3] Secretary of Defense Robert McNamara's staff foresaw a competition in a technology which had already been tested by the Army and Air Force, but was still viewed as terribly costly and probably ineffectual for defending either populations or American forces from Soviet attack. Yet even the limited effectiveness of these systems was thought to create doubt in an adversary's mind about the damage his forces could actually do, and could thus spark a competition in offensive, as well as defensive, weapons.

At least five forces impelled the two sides to the negotiating table on SALT I, and encouraged an agreement setting limits on both defensive and offensive weapons. First, the leadership of both countries had reached a consensus that the military value of the ABM systems was not commensurate with their cost. The United States was under a great deal of economic pressure in 1966. At the height of its involvement, the United States saw its financial resources were bleeding into the Vietnam War. The Americans were also just tapering off investment in a major Intercontinental Ballistic Missile (ICBM) building programme. The Brezhnev regime in Moscow was simultaneously searching for funds both for conventional military expenditures, and increasingly for the concerted effort to strengthen the Soviet industrial and technological base, which eventually led towards detente and the turn to the West in the early 1970s.

Secondly, a sense of urgency prevailed on both sides. The 'smell of burning' still hung in the air from the Cuban Missile Crisis of 1962, creating the perception among leaders on both sides that nuclear weaponry might imperil rather than enhance national security.

Thirdly, a nexus had occurred between the technological superiority of the Americans − and thus their confidence to negotiate − and a Soviet technological lag, creating an incentive for the Soviets to forestall an arms race almost certain to leave them in a worse relative position. The United States seemed convinced that the Soviets were far behind in development of their *Galosh* ABM system, and would be pressed to negotiate out of the hope of gaining limits on the American *Safeguard/Sentinel* technology.

Fourthly, the political atmosphere on both sides was conducive to the act of will of beginning to negotiate. The initial policies of the Brezhnev regime in the Soviet Union had led to a decrease in Cold War rhetoric and a climate of greater optimism in the United States about the sobriety of the Soviet leadership.

Finally, a history of productive negotiations on arms issues in the recent past gave the new concept of strategic arms limitation the momentum of prior success. The conclusion of the Partial Test Ban Treaty in 1963 had left an important legacy of progress for the arms negotiation enterprise.

Less than a month after the American proposal, in January 1967, the Soviets agreed to talk, adding a proposal to discuss offensive as well as defensive weapons.[4] The United States accepted. More than a 2-year hiatus followed, as the Soviets built towards parity in ICBMs, as a new Nixon Administration got its bearings in Washington, and as the two sides navigated the crises of the 1967 Middle East War and the 1968 Soviet invasion of Czechoslovakia. The negotiations finally began in November 1969.

American diplomat George Kennan once called diplomacy and negotiations a 'cushion of safety for mankind'.[5] Yet it is remarkably difficult to judge, looking at history in retrospect, whether the SALT negotiations have prevented matters from being worse than they are, in terms of the arms race and international security, or indeed contributed to matters being as bad as they are now. Yet most of us would prefer to have lived the past 8 years with SALT I, and would feel more optimistic about the future under the premises of SALT II and continuing Soviet–American discussions about strategic arms.

SALT I simply precluded the deployment of a destabilising strategic system, and it set the stage for future talks. Despite the vociferous criticism from the right wing in the United States, the SALT II Treaty was not intrinsically flawed. The agreement had three important values. SALT II placed some ceilings on strategic weapons, achieved modest but not inconsequential restraints on technological modernisation, and it markedly facilitated the verification of both sides' compliance with the agreement.

The Treaty required an inventory of American and Soviet forces, to be updated semi-annually, which was a breakthrough into Soviet ambiguity and secrecy. Beyond the numerical ceilings SALT II set on ballistic missile launchers and strategic bombers, the ban in Article IV on flight-testing missiles with more warheads than had been tested to date would have made more predictable the extent of further proliferation of warheads. Article IV also closed off the way to more than one 'new type' of ICBM, and to significant modifications of existing missiles during the life of the Treaty. Continuing dialogue on military issues between the United States and the Soviet Union; removing the excuse of superpower nuclear competition sometimes used to mask other reasons non-weapons countries move towards nuclear weapons; rebuilding the impression abroad of American conviction and leadership; and guarding the hope that nuclear weapons might yet have been managed through statesmanship, would not have been reasons for the United States to ratify a bad treaty. But they should have compelled a disposition to accept an agreement like SALT II which made clear contributions to both American and international security.

SALT II, and indeed the entire SALT process, is politically moribund in the United States at present, and is likely to remain so for many months, and perhaps even years to come. To be very plain, the demise of the SALT II Treaty represented a political failure by the Carter Administration to communicate the value of a useful, well-negotiated agreement very much in the security interest of the United States and its allies. This fault was compounded and fed by continued crises in the broader Soviet–American relationship which penetrated negatively into the process of consideration of the Treaty in the United States.

Winston Churchill referred to the Soviet Union as a 'riddle, wrapped inside a mystery, wrapped inside an enigma'. But this may also be the feeling many non-Americans have about the workings of the American political system. So it may here be of value to indicate, in barest outline, some of the ingredients in Carter's failure to obtain what was for his Administration the highly valued goal of SALT II ratification. Like Woodrow Wilson 60 years before, Carter was elected in 1976 as an 'anti-Washington' President, supposedly not socialised to the prevailing political ways, and promising to infuse idealism into national policies. Now, the reverse side of the advantages a President with few connections to the national political and bureaucratic structure presents for fresh approaches to policy is that he may not have the political skill effectively to promote his goals. Carter's political naïveté was manifested in three ways which affected the fate of SALT II. First, his lack of experience and of a national political memory led to major political and procedural errors which hurt SALT II. By underestimating the growth of Senate authority over foreign policy, Carter made enemies in his dealings with Senators whose support for SALT was indispensable. Carter misjudged the seriousness and organisation of anti-SALT groups in the United States. Insensitive to the importance of timing in politics, Carter repeatedly dealt with issues, such as that of a Soviet brigade in Cuba in the fall of 1979, in ways which rebounded negatively onto SALT II. And he chose throughout to interpret public opinion in the United States as restrictive on SALT, when a better sense of history would have encouraged him to try to shape, rather than merely bow to, indications of public opinion on arms control. Secondly, competing foreign policy goals in the absence of the ability to establish a hierarchy of priorities caused the Administration's goal of completing and ratifying SALT II to be eroded almost by default by the precedence given to contrary objectives. The process of opening relations with the People's Republic of China, for instance, was repeatedly allowed to undercut the SALT enterprise. And finally, lacking central orchestration, the contradictory advice of contending personalities at the apex of the foreign policy structure in the United States pulled the Administration's behaviour about in ways which slowed and eventually stymied the SALT process.[6]

The gallows on which SALT was hung was thus under construction long before the Soviet invasion of Afghanistan in December 1979. The combination of a Soviet military build-up and adventuristic Soviet foreign policy in the Third World had been a trend disturbing to many in the United States. But the Carter Administration encouraged the alarm over the Soviet move in Afghanistan to stalemate a SALT process which had survived the American bombing of North Vietnam in 1972, the Soviet rôle in Angola in 1975, and other shocks. But for the deficiencies of the Carter leadership, the beginning of the post-post-Vietnam phase in American foreign policy need not have meant the end of SALT.

A consensus now seems to have formed in the United States around the thesis that the country must mount a modernisation programme directed towards superiority across a broad range of strategic systems, prior to engaging in any further negotiations with the Soviet Union. Agreement seems to stretch across both political parties that the only conditions that will produce a result acceptable to the Americans will be when they have an advantage creating the sense of security to negotiate, and when the Soviets have sufficient interest in forestalling further competition in areas of their strategic inferiority. Whether it is called bargaining chips or negotiting from a position of strength, this is by no means a new formulation in American diplomacy, even prior to the SALT era. Philip Mosely, a wartime negotiator for the United States, recommended at the height of the Cold War in 1951 a policy for dealing with the Soviet Union of building national strength while holding out the possibility of negotiation, the two 'going hand in hand'.[7]

Dmitri Simes, a leading American expert on the Soviet Union, phrased the new consensus this way: 'The US has a chance and indeed a responsibility to explore ways to influence Moscow's behavior by developing a strategy of being generous to the USSR from a position of strength rather than demonstrating hostility from a position of weakness.'[8]

At one end of the political spectrum, the Republican Party platform approved in the summer of 1980 listed three preconditions for engaging in further arms negotiations: the security of the United States is to be considered before the goal of arms control, and such security includes the capabilities to fight or win a nuclear war; arms negotiations must proceed on the basis of strict reciprocity; and arms control negotiations cannot be removed from their political and military context, and must be integrated with developments in these broader areas. The platform promised the United States the strategic superiority 'that the people demand', and rejected SALT II as it was negotiated.

On the Democratic side, the clearest articulation of the trend in policy was in the discussion surrounding the issuance of Presidential Directive 59. The new 'countervailing strategy' of the Carter Administration was not so new. Rather, it was an effort to get the maximum mileage both for enhancing deterrence and strengthening the American position in future negotiations, from the new strategic systems and the improvement of existing systems that is already under way in the United States. A 1979 Rand Corporation report, by the head of Rand's strategic studies programme, was entitled *Outlasting SALT II and Preparing for SALT III*. This essay was a full and public exposition which presented the countervailing strategy in precisely this light. The report pointed to ICBM vulnerability as the greatest dilemma for the United States, and to the necessity for obtaining lower ceilings on Soviet launchers and warheads in SALT II to address this problem. 'The prospects for achieving early agreement on SALT III on lower ceilings would be enhanced if US negotiators could point to additional leverage on and incentives for Soviet agreement', in the author's view.[9] Citing the Soviet momentum in ICBM deployment and accuracy enhancement, and the lack of comparable American programmes, the report concluded that 'this lack of deployment capabilities requires that we look to new R&D activities as sources of leverage and incentive'. The sources the author deemed necessary are the MX missile system; an accuracy-enhancement programme for sea-based systems; a hard-point ABM system for existing ICBMs, the MX or both; a new manned bomber; a ground-launched cruise missile of more than 600 miles range; and perhaps a launch-on warning targeting doctrine for existing ICBMs. The logical foundation for these, he continued, is the countervailing strategy.

Now, by attempting to re-create American nuclear superiority, is the United States likely successfully to pressure the Soviets into productive SALT negotiations in the future? It is possible, but seems unlikely that the experience of the ABM Treaty will be repeated. The range of pressures for fruitful negotiation are simply not present today to add to the leverage provided by active force modernisation, as they were in the late 1960s.

Of course, both countries do face economic challenges. The demand for capital investment in energy and other industrial sectors in the Soviet Union and the sentiment for tax-cutting and so-called 're-industrialisation' in the United States may unilaterally put brakes upon the impending military build-up.[10] The US MX system will likely prove a target for cost-reduction in the coming years. But for neither country are the pressures as acute as they were in the late 1960s.

There is little contemporary fear of nuclear war; security today is defined in terms of weaponry rather than arms control. The Soviet military production base is far more advanced and diversified today than it was a dozen years ago, which has significantly reduced lag times in developing strategic systems. Superiority has thus become more temporary and less clear in particular technologies, reducing the leverage value that any new American development might present. Political will to move ahead does not appear particularly strong.

The success of other arms negotiations is not exerting a positive spill-over effect onto SALT nowadays. Quite to the contrary, the Chemical and Biological Weapons Convention is now crossed by the shadow of alleged Soviet use of chemical weapons in Afghanistan and possible manufacture of biological agents at Sverdlovsk.[11] The ABM Treaty rests on ever more precarious foundations, as the United States contemplates abrogating the Treaty in favour of new ABM systems.[12] In addition, both countries are passing through a time of insecurity, the Soviet Union in coping with regional instability, the United States in contemplating how to respond to geopolitical changes, which disposes neither towards the certainty of purpose required for negotiation.

Yet the logic of the nuclear era which moved the superpowers towards negotiated security has not changed in the least. It is almost inevitable that the present paralysis will give way eventually to negotiation again. If a programme to expand American nuclear forces is indeed now a political inevitability, then the path towards creating a climate in which the SALT process can be resurrected is composed of those indirect means which will make the difference between an unbridled nuclear competition and the incentive to negotiate.

For Americans, there are many lessons of the SALT II debate and defeat to digest and turn to use the next time around. Institutionalisation of interest in arms control in the Senate, working on public education on defence issues, insuring the defence establishment's understanding of the security and predictability value of arms control for military planning, demanding minimum political skill of Presidents, addressing the underlying economic and leadership problems which have produced the sense of insecurity leading to the current swing in foreign policy — the menu is a full one.

The activities of countries besides the superpowers will also importantly affect the prospect for renewed negotiation. There is some historical precedent for leadership by non-superpowers when the United States and the Soviet Union seem locked into confrontation. Discussions on a Non-Proliferation Treaty were initiated by non-nuclear weapons countries concerned in the early 1960s about the nuclear activities of the superpowers. Whether in the United Nations, European force reduction talks or elsewhere, pressure can be applied towards bringing the superpowers back to the negotiating table.

The arms control community faces the challenge of creatively suggesting new procedural approaches to strategic arms negotiations which might address some of the perennial deficiencies of SALT. Beginning negotiations at the research and development stage of military technology to lessen the tenacity of attachment to already existing weapons, disaggregating negotiations into multiple tracks to reduce the lag-times during talks — many proposals have already been generated, as well as suggestions for the issues to be discussed.

But, finally, it all comes back to the United States and the

Soviet Union. The inability of these two countries to codify acceptable limits of behaviour and to place SALT within the context of
the overall competition allowed successive political crises to
penetrate negatively into the process of consideration of SALT II
in the United States. The most important document the superpowers signed in 1972 may not have been the SALT limits, but
rather the Basic Principles of Relations, which set the goal of
lessening tensions between the two countries. But the meaning in
practice of these statements has remained vague. As a result, the
American public and Carter built unrealistic expectations of
Soviet conduct, and the Soviets have engaged in often expansive
definitions of their national security, asserting the interpretation
that peaceful coexistence permits just about anything. Hence to
emerge from stalemate and create the circumstances in which
arms control is possible, the United States and the Soviet Union
must be attentive to the possibility of opening a broad dialogue,
seeking common ground in the two varying views of detente.

Notes

1. John Newhouse, *Cold Dawn: The Story of SALT* (New York, 1973) p. 1.
2. *The New York Times*, 22 Aug. 1980.
3. Raymond L. Garthoff, 'Salt I: An Evaluation', *World Politics*, xxxi
   (1978–9) 2–3.
4. ibid., p. 4.
5. Quoted in US Library of Congress, Congressional Research Service, *Soviet
   Diplomacy and Negotiating Behavior* (Washington, DC, 1979), p. xxxiii.
6. This is a telegraphic summary of a more detailed discussion to be found in
   the chapter 'What Happened to SALT II?' in Institut français des relations
   internationales, *European Security in the 80s* (Paris, 1980).
7. Philip E. Mosely, 'Some Soviet Techniques of Negotiation', in Raymond
   Dennett and Joseph E. Johnson (eds), *Negotiating with the Russians* (Boston,
   Massachusetts, 1951).
8. Dmitri K. Simes, 'The Death of Detente?', *International Security*, spring
   1980, p. 25.
9. William Hoehn, *Outlasting SALT II and Preparing for SALT III* (Santa
   Monica, California, 1979).
10. The normally pro-defence-spending *Fortune* magazine recently published
    an article which, while approving the 1981 US defence budget increases,
    warned:

    > At the same time, though, the country should insist on a great deal more
    > prudence and thoughtfulness as an essential prologue to any future
    > increases. Another decision to spend more, taken in careless haste, could
    > leave us worse off than we were before: it could set up a new wave of public

dismay as the decision begins to hurt us economically, while adding little of consequence — or the wrong things — to our military capability. Walter Guzzardi, Jr, 'The Mental Gap in the Defense Debate', *Fortune*, 8 Sept. 1980.

11. *The New York Times*, 25 Apr., 29 May 1980.
12. Among American discussions of the new ABM technology, see especially Stephen P. Rosen, 'Safeguarding Deterrence', *Foreign Policy*, no. 35 (summer 1979) pp. 109−23.

10 Technological Misinformation: Fission and Fusion Weapons

Alexander De Volpi

Introduction

The complexity of technology is sufficient to guarantee that misinformation about its applications will be rife. Well-meaning people can easily be confused by the wealth of data, the variety of claims and counterclaims, and the plethora of experts. In addition, specialists are being outshouted by people who have limited experience or who have other preoccupations. For years now those interested in arms control have been divided by perceptions regarding nuclear power's contribution to proliferation. The result is, of course, a loss of focused energy on the central problem: the nuclear arms race. Knowledgeable scientists who witness an irrational debate are 'turned off', and the public has remained confused.

This contribution represents an effort to rectify some of the erroneous information and perceptions regarding nuclear deterrence and the arms race. Much of the information in this chapter is supported in two books that deal with the technical and political aspects of fission and fusion weapon proliferation.[1] Only certain disputed topics have been selected for inclusion here.

New Instabilities in Deterrence

The foremost danger of nuclear weapons must be the vertical proliferation of the quantity and quality of weapons amongst existing nuclear-weapons states. Human beings have now the capability of instantly destroying not only cities, but entire countries, and in a short span the civilised world. This danger clearly overwhelms the risks associated with horizontal proliferation to new nuclear-weapons states.

It has been argued that, irrespective of the level of weaponry, nuclear deterrence is stable. This is an illusion. A world in which nuclear-weapons states, in the spasm of war, have the unstoppable capability of destroying entire nations must be much less secure than one in which they have the potential of obliterating a dozen cities. Neither situation is enviable.

Philosophical questions aside, such as the 'thinkability' of any nuclear war, we should make note of some new factors that have created a less stable worldwide nuclear equilibrium. Primarily, the nuclear balance instability arises from the uncertainties tied to the command and control of nuclear weapons. On the one hand, we do not have sufficient public knowledge to make fully informed judgements about the safety, security, and responsiveness of nuclear-weapons systems; on the other hand, what we do know is cause for alarm.

Press reports in the United States indicate that there have been at least three false alerts in 1979–80 in the NORAD strategic-weapons computerised control and communications system. Relatively minor failures of hardware components, coupled with software bugs, have led to 'scrambles' of some military forces. Despite human precautions, considerable uncertainty exists regarding the prospect of a computer-initiated false alert that is carried past the point of no return or provokes a premature response. Taken by itself, this risk of a computer-initiated war is not comforting. But add to this the growing tendency to incorporate a hair-trigger response to perceived threats. In fact, it is no longer truly deterrence, but a countervailing strategy that appears to be promoted. Carter's Policy Directive No. 59, calling for a more flexible response, with military targets as aim-points, tends to reduce the margin for call-back. The problem is not so much the doctrine, but what it implies in terms of developments in hardware and control systems to put into effect the doctrine of quick response.

Another serious aspect to the problem is the vulnerability of command, control, and communications (C^3) systems. Because these systems lack the classical elements of military hardware –

mobility, diversity, and disguise — they are less likely to endure and survive nuclear weapons' attacks. A particular problem receiving attention is their vulnerability to the effects of high-altitude nuclear blasts causing electromagnetic pulse-induced blackout and breakdown of the C^3 systems. The consequence of this is that a controlled, limited nuclear war would be impractical; thus massive mutual retaliation against population centres would be about the only option remaining after an attack on military targets.

Technological innovation has contributed to 'pin-point' accuracy in missile delivery. Military targets could then be selectively attacked, a targeting doctrine considered semantically to be less indiscriminate. But operationally, a perception of high accuracy provides an opportunity for 'counterforce' war-making capability, a temptation for military planners to consider a 'first strike'. The perception that dependable accuracy can be achieved, that a missile can travel from one continent to another and land within 100 metres of a target, is an unproven estimate. Such weapons have not and cannot be tested over a trajectory that includes the vagaries of the intercontinental flight paths that would be used in actual war. The idea of limiting damage in nuclear warfare by eliminating ballistic missiles in their silos is militarily unsound. The only effective use for ICBMs is against population and industrial centres.

Moreover, the search for an active or passive defence against nuclear weapon delivery systems has been unsuccessful. Only a few nuclear warheads need get through defences to wreak havoc. In the decades since nuclear weapons were used on Japan, no practicable civil defence has emerged, the life cost of atomic warfare being nearly total obliteration. Illusions based on the survival of a few are hardly the basis for a rational national security policy.

Finally, we come to the question of custody. Who has sole or joint custody of nuclear weapons stationed outside national boundaries. Is it possible for this custody to be circumvented or overcome? Is it possible for a weapon to be launched without official sanction? What about 'accidental' launches? Could nuclear warfare begin because of some act or event outside of government control?

How do we get candid answers to these questions? The higher the level of deterrence — more nuclear warheads and delivery systems, greater built-in accuracy, increased dependence upon rational and workable control − the greater becomes the degree of instability. Those truly interested in national security must recognise that technology has brought nuclear weaponry to a new and dangerous capacity that may defeat its defensive purpose. Deterrence has reached into an ambiguous regime of unstable equilibrium, with heightened risk to all.

Proliferation

Sometimes people tend to think only of one form of nuclear-weapons proliferation and one solution to it. But we know it has two facets: vertical and horizontal. While much attention has gone into *prevention* of the horizontal transfer of nuclear weapons and related materials and technology to other countries, only limited efforts have gone recently into curtailing the vertical growth in quantity and quality of nuclear warheads and delivery systems developed by the nuclear-weapons states. One reason for this disparity in effort is probably related to lack of past success in stopping the nuclear arms race. In over one-third of a century, six nations have shown they have independently achieved fission-explosive technology. In that same span of time, two nations have developed inventories of thousands of nuclear weapons of many types and yields. Clearly the barriers to vertical proliferation have been practically non-existent, while horizontal proliferation has proceeded at a slow pace.

Both horizontal and vertical proliferation are interlinked; there can be little doubt of that. The nuclear arms race can hardly be considered a source of inspiration and restraint to non-nuclear-weapons states. Furthermore, the fear that more nations will gain significant (strategic) capabilities in nuclear warfare is bound to affect policies of nuclear-weapons states. Perhaps, though, that fear is not sufficient to spotlight the threat of a multi-nation, multi-megaton world: a well-armed nuclear crowd.

Efforts to minimise proliferation thus must be directed to its vertical and horizontal forms with a variety of technological and political instruments. Some measures are more effective against one form − others are impediments to both, a ban on nuclear-weapon explosive testing being a good example. Table 1 summarizes the key features of a comprehensive anti-proliferation strategy, a strategy that does not ignore any facet of the problem.

Table 1   *Principal Independent Anti-proliferation Methods*

Removing motivations for proliferation
   Restraining strategic and tactical nuclear arms
   Restricting use and deployment of nuclear arms
   Limiting testing of nuclear weapons delivery systems

Impeding weapons technology transfer or advancement
   Banning nuclear-explosive testing
   Maintaining security over military nuclear weapons
   Controlling technology for alternative weapon routes

Strengthening non-proliferation incentives
   Assuring security of nations
   Resolving regional disputes
   Influencing economic determinants
   Providing opportunities for non-nuclear energy
   Assuring nuclear-power fuel supply and facilities

Reinforcing mutual anti-proliferation safeguards
   Consolidating the nuclear fuel cycle in proliferation-resistant zones
   Implementing less diversion-prone alternative reactors
   Imposing full-scope safeguards
   Establishing an international safeguards regime
   Denaturing fissile materials

Not enough recognition has been given to the wide variety of technological barriers that impede proliferation. First, it should be remembered that some safeguards techniques are designed primarily to cope with the possibility of unsanctioned non-governmental diversion (for example, terrorists). These safeguards are almost universally strong in making terrorist diversion extremely difficult. Safeguards are not as great an impediment to national diversion (nor do they apply to military facilities). Although helpful in providing mutual confidence, technical barriers will not and have not stopped nations from gaining fission-weapon capability (because nuclear weapons can and have been made by determined nations from special military fissile production facilities). In fact, horizontal proliferation is largely a problem of political perception, rather than one preventable exclusively by technology. The two anti-proliferation avenues — political and technological — strengthen each other symbiotically.

The making of nuclear weapons requires skilled people, adequate resources and facilities, a technological base, and weapons-usable fissionable materials. Many nations, having experienced industrial or technological research and development, are in a position to undertake fission-explosive design and fabrication, provided they have access to the requisite fissile material. It is widely known that the most dependable means of acquiring the fissile substance is through dedicated production facilities, that is uranium enrichment plants or weapons-grade plutonium reactors. Despite these alternatives, the proposition has been put forth by some that the nuclear-power fuel cycle is a signficant contributor to horizontal proliferation. One fear is that the government would cheat or take over civilian power reactors and facilities for military purposes. In order to assess the potential for making weapons after nationalisation of nuclear power reactors, we should ascertain whether fuel from a power reactor is accessible for weapons use. There are three basic technologies that aid in curtailing proliferation: isotopic denaturing, adulteration, and safeguards. Denaturing is the process of rendering a fissile isotope less suitable for fission explosive use. By taking advantage of natural isotopic diluants (U-238) or byproducts of fuel irradiation (even-isotopes of plutonium), it is possible to cause fissile materials to be progressively and irreversibly denatured. All of these technological options make it costly, if not worthless, to confiscate civilian facilities to make weapons. There is still some confusion about denaturing. The technical feasibility for isotopic denaturing of plutonium is sometimes labelled as 'misinformation'. Yet it is just as wrong to state categorically that plutonium cannot be denatured as to state the contrary without qualification. The truth is in between: all fissile isotopes can be rendered progressively unsuitable for nuclear-weapons purposes; there is no clear-cut composition threshold at which fissile materials become unambiguously of no use for destructive devices. More will be written on this later. For the moment, let us make note of the rôle of other adulterants that cause the fissile material to be less useful or more dangerous for diversion. These are chemically reversible techniques, such as dilution in the form of oxide (which is a common fuel form) and the addition or retention of radioactive 'spikes'.

In addition to, and independent of, both isotopic denaturing and adulteration are the technical and procedural safeguards in a broad category that includes the physical security (and recovery) of fissile materials. This array of techniques and procedures offers formidable barriers to governmentally unsanctioned diversion of fuel, as the many years of safeguarding already attest. Although nothing is absolute, the combined measures provide a very high statistical probability of public protection against unsanctioned diversion. Anti-proliferation technologies should not be conceived to be technical fixes to horizontal proliferation, only aids to create confidence in political agreements of nations to forgo nuclear weapons as long as others do so.

In order to provide a better understanding of the possible rôle of, and limits to, a strategy of isotopic denaturing, it is worthwhile to see what the possibilities are. There are certain major factors that determine the mass of fissile material necessary to make a nuclear weapon. They are: type of fissile material, chemical form, isotopic content, fuel density, device geometry, reflector composition, and chemical explosive. To obtain a significant explosive yield, additional factors that must be taken into account are weapon design, implosion timing, neutron background, arming sequence, neutron initiator, safety interlocks, triggering and firing sequence, and materials temperature. Isotopic denaturing directly affects the yield by increasing the mass and radius of a critical configuration, introduces extraneous sources of radiation and heat, and influences neutron interactions in the assembly.

In fact, there are at least eight physical phenomena, each capable of affecting the yield of a fission explosive: critical mass, metallurgical phase, radial compression, subcritical multiplication, predetonation, generation time, reactivity limit, and surface leakage. Each of these characteristics is influenced by the quality of the fissile material. Hence, the manufacture of a nuclear weapon is made more difficult whenever the fuel is less than weapons-grade. In addition, the explosive yield is diminished if the design cannot overcome the deleterious effects of low-quality fuel. Thus military strategists are extremely unlikely to plan a fission-explosive development programme based on poor fissile material, especially when there are more reasonable alternatives.

Some people have over-reacted to the observation that any isotopic form of plutonium can be made into a critical mass. Although a critical mass is necessary, it is not sufficient for a fission explosion. The real questions for military use are: what is the comparative explosive yield for dilute forms of plutonium? and: do some of these influences cause a weapon made with low-grade plutonium to be otherwise unsuited for weapons applications?

The point is illustrated in the first three figures. Figure 2, for example, indicates that the critical mass for reactor-grade plutonium is nearly an order of magnitude greater than for

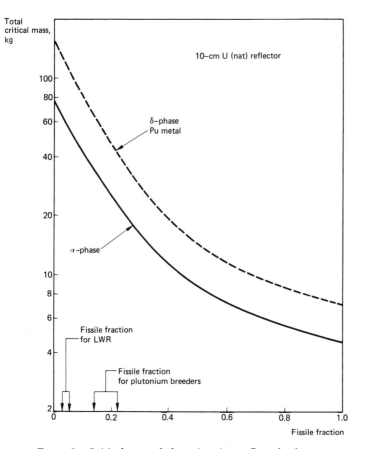

FIGURE 2   *Critical mass of plutonium in a reflected sphere*

weapons-grade. The critical mass for weapons-grade, which has a fissile fraction of 0.94 or more, is about 4.5 kg of plutonium metal in the high-density α metallurgical phase. On the other hand, plutonium used as fuel for reactors could be diluted to less than 20 per cent fissile fraction, which necessitates a practical (δ phase) mass requirement of over 40 kg. Thus, much more dilute plutonium would have to be produced or diverted to make a single weapon. Figure 3 shows that much heat and radiation is originated in the fissile material, which terribly complicates the design and feasibility of a weapon. As the critical mass requirement expands (due to decrease in fissile fraction), the amount of heat and radiation increases. Although the radiation level for denatured plutonium

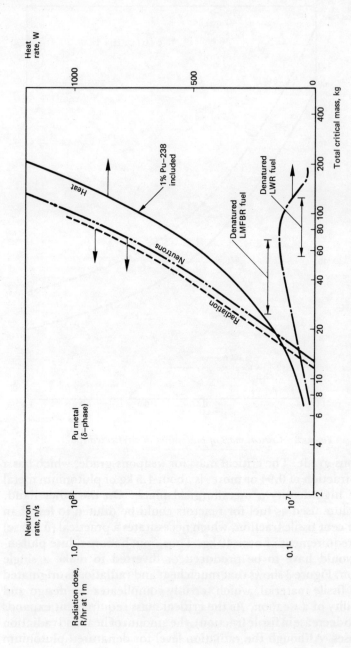

FIGURE 3   Heat and radiation emitted by plutonium

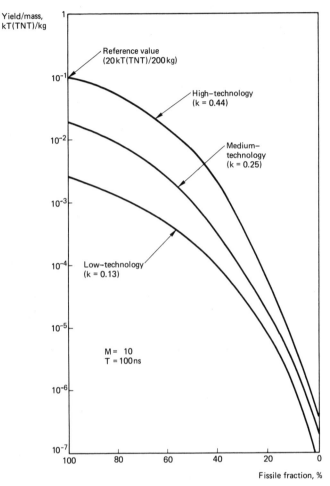

Yield/mass, kT(TNT)/kg

FIGURE 4   *Explosive yield of plutonium*

will not be lethal for short-term exposures, the neutron rate increases the probability of predetonation of weapons made of such material, and the heat imperils the stability of the plutonium and the conventional organic explosive. Figure 4 demonstrates that the average explosive yield diminishes rapidly as the plutonium is diluted by its even isotopes. As the fissile fraction decreases, the mass-normalised yield (which is a measure of weapons efficiency) drops dramatically. The three curves apply to different assumptions regarding technology capability. A high-technology nation, one that has already tested nuclear weapons, would be expected to milk the largest relative yield for a given fuel. However, an industrial nation lacking nuclear-explosive test facilities is likely to fall short of optimal performance. The low-technology case applies to poorly endowed governments or non-government entities that acquire fissile material but lack the resources of a prolonged government research and development effort; in such a case, the yield can be expected to be suboptimal on the average until a testing programme allows improvement of the design.

The upshot of all this is that denatured plutonium is a very poor choice for weapons; in fact, diluted plutonium is just as ineffective a fuel for weapons as is denatured uranium. Therefore, an unqualified statement that plutonium cannot be denatured is technically incorrect. Reactor-grade plutonium is not the material of choice in nuclear weapons, though as Table 2 summarises, it gives an unhealthy explosive yield under some situations. As the material is progressively diluted, the yield diminishes rapidly.

TABLE 2   *Estimated relative explosive yields from different grades of plutonium*

Fissile percentage	Grade	Yield kT (TNT)
100	Weapon	20
94	Weapon	18
70	Reactor	10
50	Reactor	2
20	Denatured	0.03
5	Denatured	0.007

The belief that plutonium cannot be denatured, the so-called 'misinformation' about denatured plutonium, is based on over-reaction to a straw man. In the late 1940s it was thought for a while that not even a critical mass could be formed if enough Pu-240 were added. It was some time before this expectation was recognised to be invalid. Ever since, a number of people have attempted to crucify the straw man, but never with the benefit of detailed evaluation of all the implications of isotopic denaturing. On the other hand, it would be an error to assume that denatured plutonium is a panacea or even an absolute barrier to proliferation. Although the quantity of such material that can be entered into the fuel cycle is limited by the production process, it has a possible practicable rôle in a comprehensive anti-proliferation strategy.[2]

Is the Nuclear-fuel Cycle the Link to Proliferation?

It is by now well known that nuclear weapons are best made through the use of dedicated facilities. Still, we hear from people that nuclear power reactors are the *sine qua non* of proliferation: do away with nuclear power and you will do away with proliferation.

Before getting into that, there is the general question of whether one or another fuel cycle (uranium, plutonium, or thorium) is less proliferation-prone. As a matter of fact, all nuclear-power fuel is unattractive for diversion to weapons purposes. Another technically inadequate idea that has worked its way into common lore is the suggestion that the thorium cycle is a better choice on non-proliferation grounds. That is not the case. In fact, a nation that wanted a power reactor for the purpose of hedging in terms of fissile material backup would do well to choose the thorium-cycle, even if denatured with U-238. The reason is three-fold: after dissolving the fuel elements, one could extract about one-third as much reactor-grade plutonium as would be possible from a uranium reactor; with sufficient time available (a few months) one could chemically separate the protoactinium at any time and allow it to decay (27.4 day half-life) to bomb-grade U-233; and one could, through centrifuge enrichment, isotopically separate the remaining U-233 from the U-238, a comparatively efficient process. The result can be the eventual build-up of a stockpile of fissionable material useful for weapons.

Of course, conversion of the fuel of any power reactor to weapons is a costly step, to be done only *in extremis*. If a nation were well advised in the first place, they would prepare for less visible, less expensive, and more suitable production through dedicated military facilities. In the time it takes to build a power reactor (nearly a decade), a small weapons-reactor or a centrifuge facility could turn out a large yield of weapons-grade fissile material. The cost would be about two orders of magnitude less than a power reactor, and the operation could be easily hidden by defence classification.

The connection between the nuclear power fuel cycle and nuclear weapons is tenuous. Although it is true that civilian nuclear power provides a stepping-stone for materials and technologies that might be used in making weapons, there are other routes that have proven to be more practicable. All existing nuclear weapons have been made under military direction.

Although many nuclear weapons have been produced, no 'civilian' power reactor route has ever been taken. So far, all known nuclear weapons have been made with fissile materials derived from isotope enrichment, military-production reactors, or a research reactor. The associated technologies for bomb-making were, in general, developed and applied specifically for that purpose. The historic development of nuclear power was unquestionably an aftermath of the military atom. Nuclear power did not exist when the first weapons were made.

The central argument tying together the nuclear fuel cycle and weapons is that weapons can be made from power reactor fuel (even though it is not known to have ever been done). Yet, the presence of nuclear reactors does not assure the necessary access to fuel, the means of processing, and the success in weapon-making that the naive would assume.

The last place to look for materials and technology is in the nuclear-power fuel cycle; the first place is in a deliberate, surreptitious military programme. To ignore this is to ignore the historical fact that all the nuclear-weapons states have developed their nuclear devices from dedicated military programmes. Even the plutonium for India's nuclear explosive was not created in a nuclear-power reactor: it was a byproduct of a dedicated research reactor and associated facilities. Granted that the research programme had operated under the 'cover' of peaceful applications, such a subterfuge is quite unnecessary, inasmuch as all nations keep secret their defence programmes and facilities.

Although it is possible, it is neither necessary nor sufficient that there be a technological carryover to nuclear weapons from the nuclear-power fuel cycle. Much modern technology contributes to weapons technology application. The production of nuclear warheads and delivery systems entails more than just the fissile materials and the means for their processing and fabrication. Most of modern physical science and technology is relevant, including electrical, electronic, communications, high-explosives, materials science and aerospace engineering — a long list indeed.

Would phasing out nuclear power and its supporting services be both a necessary and a sufficient condition for non-proliferation? The argument in favour is that, if nuclear power no longer existed, the whole panoply of goods and services that provide diverse routes to bombs would be unambiguously military in intent. The idea is that a world in which fissile materials were used only for weapons, because of its unambiguous nature, would be safer than one in which nuclear power coexisted. Nonsense! We all know that at least five nations are now making bombs. They have not been deterred by any international measures. Why should one believe that, in the future, determined bomb-making efforts will be deterred simply by the absence of power reactors?

No doubt there is value in being able to detect a military nuclear programme and there is a simple criterion that would be relatively unambiguous: any (nuclear) facility that is not open to international inspection should be assumed to be military, subject to whatever sanctions nations can be convinced to invoke. But detection of a military nuclear activity with high probability is unrealistic. Also, effective international reaction is not assured, judging from more than three decades in the atomic era. Historical fact cannot be forever ignored. Six nations with unambiguously military programmes have already demonstrated their ability to make nuclear weapons without nuclear-power reactors, and nothing and nobody stopped them. The first nuclear-power reactors were not operational until the 1950s, after two or three nations had already tested fission and fusion weapons. We have to conclude that phasing out nuclear power in order to avoid proliferation is a useless prescription – neither necessary nor sufficient.

Overemphasis on the linkage between nuclear power and nuclear bombs has distracted from more productive and less divisive efforts in the struggle against an uncontrolled nuclear arms race.

Thermonuclear Weapons Proliferation

Most of the preceding discussion has been in the context of fission-weapon proliferation. As a result of the attention partly given to it by a legal dispute in the United States, concern about horizontal proliferation of fusion weapons has surfaced. This is nothing more than another dimension to an old problem. The *Progressive* magazine was temporarily restrained from publication of an article containing conceptual information about H-bomb arrangements.[3]

There are actually three types of nuclear weapons: fission, fusion-boosted fission, and multistage fusion (See Figure 5).

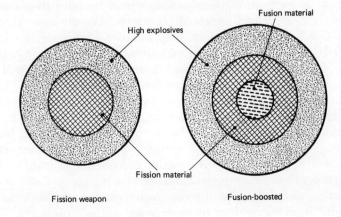

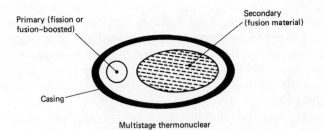

FIGURE 5   *Major conceptual aspects of nuclear weapons: fission;
fusion-boosted; and multistage thermonuclear*

Fission devices may be made either in the gun-barrel or implosion
mode, depending chiefly on the type of material (uranium for the
gun-barrel, plutonium for implosion). Yields range typically from
the nominal values of those dropped over Japan (10–20 kT) to as
much as 500 kT.

Fusion-boosted fission is understood to be essentially a fission
weapon with a core of material that can be ignited by the fission
burst, thereby augmenting the energy output. These are more
efficient than pure fission weapons, and they can be tuned for
larger or smaller outputs.

Multistage H-bombs, the type that were central to the *Progressive* case, have yields in the order of megatons. This is their dis-
tinguishing feature. By observing that there are limits to how
much fusion material can be put into a fusion-boosted weapon

(Figure 5b), one can immediately arrive at some of the underlying concepts associated with the once-secret Teller–Ulam principle. As revealed in the *Progressive* case, the principle included the separation of stages (Figure 5c) in order to gain a larger explosive yield. One must then ask: how should the energy from the primary (fission trigger) be transferred to the secondary (fusion material) to cause the requisite compression? The answer appears to have been to make use of the soft X-rays that occur during the fission explosion. This radiation is 'coupled' to the fusion material, which then is compressed and ignited. In principle, this can lead to almost unlimited explosive capability, the Soviets apparently having tested a (fission–fusion–fission) weapon to about 60 MT.

Although the United States Government resisted strongly in the American judicial courts the right of the magazine to publish the conceptual information outlined above, the case reveals more about the futility of depending upon secrecy as a barrier to thermonuclear weapons proliferation than it does about making an H-bomb. Clearly there are many details about materials, design, processes, etc., that have not been revealed. In fact on the average, the thermonuclear powers, after they had already tested fission-explosives, required about 5 more years to develop hydrogen bombs, which implies that a major national effort is required.

Somewhat peripherally, the question of proliferation risk arising from laser fusion has surfaced. In view of the remoteness of the techniques and their technology to weapons applications, and in view of the specific weapons engineering that must anyway be done, it is quite unlikely that laser fusion research is a short cut to thermonuclear proliferation.

Countermeasures to Proliferation

The foregoing technical review of certain key aspects of nuclear reactor and weapons technology is sufficient to suggest appropriate countermeasures to proliferation. Clearly a combination of measures are justified, but of all that have been suggested, at the moment the strongest weight — from the technology viewpoint — should be placed on a universal ban against nuclear-explosive testing.

Let us first examine the historic rôle of nuclear-explosive tests.

Why have nations carried them out? Can a ban be verified? What are the benefits and impact of test bans? There are some revealing facts about nuclear-explosive testing that cannot be ignored. One is that all states that have nuclear weapons have undertaken such tests, two nations having conducted hundreds apiece. Over a 35-year span, six nations have tested fission-explosive devices. And the unavoidable lag between the first fission test and the first fusion test of the five thermonuclear-weapons states has already been noted.

Although relatively simple weapons made of uranium fissile material apparently do not necessarily need testing, complex warheads probably do. Fission explosives made of weapons-grade plutonium (about 6 per cent or less even-plutonium isotopes) evidently need to be tested (as was done by India). To settle the technical question about usability of reactor-grade plutonium, the United States tested such a device, but the government did not release sufficient public information to allow deductions about its usefulness as a nuclear weapon.

Many tests have been conducted for the development of warhead configurations, including fission weapons, fission triggers for H-bombs, fusion-boosted fission devices, multistage thermonuclear weapons, mininukes, neutron warheads, and 'clean' bombs. Other testing has been for the purpose of studying explosive effects and countermeasures.

According to historical evidence, nuclear-weapons testing is critical to their development and effectiveness. Thus, a universal ban on testing would have wide-ranging impact on proliferation. It would limit the scope of additional vertical proliferation and also curtail new horizontal proliferation. Testing, in fact, is probably absolutely necessary if poor fuel grades (from power reactors) were to be used in weapons. Because of the lag between fission and fusion development, additional horizontal thermonuclear proliferation can be postponed. Furthermore, without an extensive programme of fission trigger development, the thermonuclear devices, especially multistage units, probably cannot be made dependable. If we had had a test ban in the early 1960s, for example, there would now be no MIRV, neutron bomb or Mark 12A warhead. In short, much of the nuclear arms race could not have taken off.

There are additional reasons why a prohibition on nuclear-explosive testing should be the foremost arms limitation measure being promoted. One of these is that a ban is, for the most part, subject to national means of verification. This would include expanded satellite, seismic, and radioactivity monitoring. If supplemented with episodic inspections, the prospects for any circumvention would be small, and the possibility of significant cheating would be negligible. Because clear warning would be received of any series of violations, there would be lead-time for a party to the treaty to take offsetting measures. A nation does not suddenly become a threatening nuclear-weapons state immediately after successful completion of a test (cf. India). It takes time to develop an arsenal of deployable weapons.

As a consequence of its critical position at the juncture of horizontal and vertical proliferation and because of its verifiability, a test ban is not merely one of many confidence-building measures; a universal ban on nuclear-explosive testing is one of the key political instruments, bolstered by technological support, that can now be enlisted in limiting the world-wide nuclear arms race. It is this type of anti-proliferation measure — a halt in nuclear-weapons testing — that has lost attention because of the misinformation and internecine disputes over nuclear power that have reigned in the last decade.

Notes

1. Alexander De Volpi, *Proliferation, Plutonium, and Policy: Technological and Institutional Impediments to Nuclear Weapons Propagation* (Oxford and New York, 1979); and Alexander De Volpi, G. E. Marsh, T. A. Postol, and G. S. Stanford, *Born SECRET: The H-Bomb, the Progressive Case, and National Security* (Oxford and New York, 1981).
2. De Volpi, *Proliferation, Plutonium, and Policy.*
3. De Volpi *et al.*, *Born SECRET.*

After this chapter was written, the United States tacitly confirmed the unsuitability of reactor-grade plutonium for direct use in military-quality nuclear weapons. Before using reactor-grade plutonium, the denaturant even-isotopes (Pu-238 and Pu-240) must be removed by means of laser isotope separation, a new technology that is very expensive and unproven. This declassified information increases confidence in the inhibiting effects of denaturants.

PART II

THE PROBLEM OF PROLIFERATION

11 International Strategies for Managing the Nuclear Fuel Cycle

Ian Smart

In one way or another, nuclear power is seen almost everywhere to be in trouble. The predictions of cheap and plentiful nuclear electricity so dramatically presented in the 1950s have apparently turned to ashes. The carefully reasoned forecasts of the 1960s and early 1970s, asserting the rate at which the use of nuclear fission to generate power would expand and spread internationally, have proved to be grossly – sometimes grotesquely – optimistic. The industries established in North America and Western Europe to manufacture the power reactors which the world was expected to need are hard-pressed to keep their skilled labour forces at work. Especially in many of the developed countries of the Organisation for Economic Co-operation and Development (OECD), public criticism and suspicion of nuclear power have become steadily more obtrusive, not least in the aftermath of accidents such as that at Three Mile Island in the United States. Fears about the possible connection between civil nuclear development and the proliferation of nuclear weapons have similarly been heightened by the Indian nuclear explosion in 1974 and by more or less well-founded rumours of preparations to emulate that achievement by governments in Asia, Africa and Latin America. At the same time, the spectre of terrorists or criminals preying upon a so-called 'plutonium economy' has seemed to many to loom ever larger. All in all, the first two decades of the civil nuclear era appear to be littered with the corpses of hopes and expectations, leaving a present populated only by disappointment and apprehension.

In such an atmosphere it is paradoxically difficult to avoid, or even perhaps recognise, some of the errors of the past. In particular it is difficult not to be trapped yet again into the unrealistic extrapolation of short-run trends, coupled with the substitution of personal preference or prejudice for clear-sighted analysis. Nuclear power programmes in many countries have admittedly faltered in the face of unanticipated obstacles, notably including slower growth in electricity demand, and more power reactors have recently been cancelled than ordered. The fact remains that nuclear fission *will* be used during the next 20 years to provide both an increasing amount and an increasing proportion of the world's electricity. At present, it contributes little more than 2 per cent to our total primary energy supply and generates only about 7 per cent of our electricity. Even now, however, it produces some 20 per cent of the electricity in particular industrial countries such as Sweden, Switzerland or Belgium, and over 10 per cent of electricity in the OECD as a whole (Table 3). And the completion of reactors already under construction will ensure that, by 1985, nuclear power represents about 5 per cent of global primary energy supply and about 17 per cent of the world's electricity. That growth will equally certainly continue thereafter, if only on the basis of investments already made, and, although it would be foolish now to predict a specific rate of increase for the 1990s and beyond, it is entirely realistic to suppose that nuclear power, despite all the problems already and yet to be encountered, may provide anything up to 20 per cent of our primary energy by 2020. There is every reason to be sceptical about particular forecasts of future nuclear power growth; the uncertainty and the margin of error, even for 2000, are enormous. The fact is, however, that, whatever happens in individual countries, nuclear power will continue to be used on a global level, and the rate at which it is used will continue for many years to increase.

It is particularly important that any international strategy to contain the risk and fear of nuclear weapons proliferation should come to terms with that current and future reality. As individuals or as citizens of individual countries, some may wish that the facts were otherwise, but wishing will not make them so. Whatever our personal preferences, the civil use of nuclear energy will not be abandoned in our lifetimes. Even if it were abandoned, that would

TABLE 3   *Nuclear power in the OECD, 1978*

	Percentage of total primary energy	Percentage of total electricity
Canada	3.72	9.13
United States	3.82	12.21
Japan	4.07	10.52
Belgium	5.71	24.61
Finland	3.41	9.27
France	3.70	13.45
West Germany	2.98	10.17
Italy	0.71	2.53
Netherlands	1.32	6.59
Spain	2.51	7.68
Sweden	11.37	25.69
Switzerland	8.14	19.43
Great Britain	4.29	12.99
OECD Total	3.54	10.92

Source: OECD: *Energy Statistics 1974/1978; Energy Balances of OECD Countries 1974/1978.*

not, of course, eliminate the problem of nuclear proliferation. The fact that no existing nuclear-weapons force has depended for its existence on a civil nuclear power programme serves to demonstrate that other forms of nuclear activity, involving facilities committed to military use or to general research, offer separate and, in many ways, more attractive routes to the acquisition of nuclear armament. The abandonment of nuclear electricity generation would do nothing in itself to close those well-trodden paths. Conversely, even if nuclear power programmes could make it easier to produce nuclear weapons – as, in certain circumstances, they may – it has to be recognised that such programmes will continue, expand and themselves proliferate internationally. Nothing could be more pointless or largely irrelevant, therefore, than to base any part of a non-proliferation strategy on an expectation that the use of nuclear energy for civil purposes can be made to diminish or disappear.

There are, in any case, good moral and political reasons for hesitating to suggest that the exploitation of nuclear power should be either 'frozen' or abandoned, exactly because either course would be widely seen as discriminating against poorer or less-developed societies. To decree that those countries which already use nuclear power should be free to do so in future, but that their number should not increase, would palpably be discriminatory in political terms, not only between North and South but also within the industrial world. On what conceivable grounds should India, say, have nuclear power when Mexico cannot have it, or Finland but not Denmark be permitted to exploit it? But a more subtle and dangerous form of discrimination would also be involved: a discrimination which would actually be maximised if all countries were to abandon or eschew nuclear power. It would occur simply because the burden of making good the resulting deficit in energy supply could not, in practice, be spread evenly or equitably. The industrial countries of the OECD currently use well over 200 million tonnes of oil and oil products a year to generate base-load electricity. Deprived of nuclear power already equivalent to another 130 million tonnes a year of crude oil, their consumption of petroleum for that purpose, among other fuels, would inevitably tend to increase. Higher world demand for oil would in turn mean higher world oil prices, which richer or more industrialised countries would, as always, find it less difficult than others to pay. As a result poorer countries, with only limited use for central electricity generation but crucially dependent on petroleum for heating, cooking, transport and agriculture, would be more and more painfully squeezed by the efforts of their wealthier neighbours to maintain electricity supplies without nuclear power. It is not too fanciful to suggest that the associated international friction might ultimately generate stronger pressures for nuclear weapons proliferation than any emerging from the civil use of nuclear power itself. The consequence is by no means inevitable, but the danger is too obvious to be ignored.

If the first thing to acknowledge is that civil nuclear power is here to stay — and that the risk of nuclear proliferation might be even greater if it were not — the second thing in danger of being forgotten is the existence of a wide, albeit not universal, international consensus in regard to the reality of that risk. In the recent plethora of dissent and distrust concerning non-proliferation policies, it is easy to overlook the continued prevalence of the conviction that a world in which more countries control nuclear weapons, or in which still more nuclear weapons are deployed, must be even less secure and even more dangerous, and that nuclear weapons proliferation, in all its forms, should therefore be halted. With remarkably few exceptions, contemporary quarrels between governments about non-proliferation are traceable not to differences over the importance of that goal but to disagreements about how it should be pursued. There are, of course, exceptions. The international consensus on the basic issue nevertheless stretches well beyond even the impressive participation in the NPT.

One reason for the persistent difficulty in expressing that consensus in the form of agreed and effective policies is that many efforts to address the issue of proliferation, and especially of 'horizontal' proliferation, have failed to appreciate that international security and stability have commonly been even more seriously disrupted by the subjective fear of future proliferation than by the reality or objective probability of such an event. The NPT and the safeguards system of the IAEA, arguably buttressed by such restrictive codes as the 1978 'guidelines' of the Nuclear Suppliers Group, go a long way towards providing a general framework of agreed arrangements to define and detect or deter deliberate attempts to convert civil nuclear activity to military ends. Inevitably, however, they do much less to inhibit activities which are germane to civil nuclear development and may well be completely innocent but which, because of their inherent ambiguity, may nevertheless provoke subjective fears of future weapons proliferation. That is not a criticism of existing formal agreements or arrangements. It is hardly conceivable that any formal international instrument could directly preclude an indeterminate range of actions which, though innocent in themselves, might inspire fear about their possible ramifications in future. It is, however, an indication that, if internationally disruptive fears of proliferation are to be held within reasonable limits, much will depend on supplementing the general framework of non-proliferation measures already available by less direct and essentially unrestrictive techniques of international nuclear management.

There is an undeniable connection between the global expansion of nuclear power and the emergence of subjective fears of nuclear proliferation – whatever the real relationship between the two processes. The connection is not, however, with the wider use of nuclear fission to generate electricity – a process which has nothing in common with the manufacture of weapons. Instead, it exists because the wider and larger use of nuclear power is bound to bring with it a range of pressures to extend access to those 'sensitive' components of the nuclear fuel cycle which might indeed contribute to weapons production. Although some countries wishing to exploit nuclear power will still be content only to operate reactors – drawing all their fuel materials from, and returning them to, foreign suppliers – nuclear power expansion as a whole will clearly tend, in one way or another, to increase also the number of countries with potential access to 'sensitive' materials – highly enriched uranium or separated plutonium – or with actual access to 'sensitive' technologies or facilities – plants for enriching uranium or reprocessing and separating plutonium from spent fuel. And it is exactly such access to 'sensitive' materials or facilities on the part of additional countries which, despite the innocent civil reasons readily to be found for it, may arouse or exacerbate fears of future weapons proliferation.

Just because there may well be good reasons on civil energy grounds for additional countries to obtain access to 'sensitive' components of the nuclear fuel cycle, any international strategy to avoid or limit consequential fear must be seen to serve not only non-proliferation objectives but energy objectives as well. Enrichment and reprocessing services, with their products, are available in the international market. Any country embarking on a nuclear power programme can therefore, in principle, look for those services to the small group of highly industrialised countries, clustered around the nuclear-weapon states, which supplies them. Another country may well, however, decide that its national interest, without regard to nuclear weapons, would be better served by performing those functions of enrichment and/or reprocessing itself or by having independent access to their products – because it believes it will be cheaper to do so, because the security of national energy supplies may thus be better assured, or because the purpose of national development will otherwise benefit. Even if it subscribes fully to the goal of preventing further weapons proliferation, and is prepared to pay an equitable price for achieving it, it cannot always be expected in those circumstances to give up the opportunity of such benefits without some return in kind – whether it has, in fact, identified the benefits accurately or not. If it is to accept any proposal for managing 'sensitive' aspects of the nuclear fuel cycle internationally, in order to minimise proliferation fears, it must thus be satisfied that the proposal will also serve its energy and development interests to an extent not wholly incommensurate with an independent national programme.

With that in mind, it is easy to understand why some strategies for reducing proliferation fears are doomed to failure. In theory, for example, one possible response to the prospect of those fears would be to restrict access to 'sensitive' nuclear materials and processes to those countries which already control them. Alternatively, access might be permitted only to those states with what have sometimes been called 'good non-proliferation credentials'. In practice, however, neither approach has much to commend it. The basic technology of reprocessing has been widely published since the 1950s, and comparable details of several of the numerous enrichment technologies are now more or less widely disseminated as well. As to the industrial exploitation of such technologies, several additional countries, including several non-parties to the NPT, have already embarked upon it or are expected to do so within the current decade (Table 4). There is no clear dividing line now to be drawn, therefore, between those who can and will use 'sensitive' technologies, capable of yielding 'sensitive' materials, and the rest. Nor is there any rational boundary to the former category in terms of political character or performance. Ultimately, therefore, a non-proliferation strategy based only on the enforced restriction of access to 'sensitive' fuel cycle activities or materials is neither feasible technically nor defensible in terms of international politics or equity.

TABLE 4   Operators of 'sensitive' nuclear facilities[1]

1980		1990	
Enrichment	Reprocessing	Enrichment	Reprocessing
United States	France	United States	France
Soviet Union	Great Britain	Soviet Union	Great Britain
France	India	France	India
Great Britain		Great Britain	Japan
Netherlands		Netherlands	Belgium
		West Germany	Brazil
		Japan	Argentina
		Brazil	West Germany
		South Africa	Spain
			Italy

That is not to say that policies of enforced restriction applied to 'sensitive' technologies or materials are completely ineffective. Those countries which now control such components of the nuclear fuel cycle could certainly make it more difficult for others to imitate them, by steadfastly withholding access to their technologies or 'sensitive' facilities and by administering that restriction with collective determination. At most, however, that policy could only retard the rate at which technical capability, and thus potential access to 'sensitive' materials, diffused internationally. The delays obtainable would be limited, and might sometimes be very short indeed. If the benefit of delay, from the non-proliferation point of view, were clearly seen to exceed the cost of obtaining it, a strong case might nevertheless be made for a purely restrictive approach. There is a good deal to be said, after all, for buying time, provided that the price is not excessive and that effective use is made of the time purchased. In the case of 'sensitive' nuclear fuel cycle activities, however, it is all too likely that the non-proliferation cost of delaying by that means would be greater than the benefit. For a policy on the part of the few supplier countries which consisted only of withholding 'sensitive' materials, equipment and technology would both arouse widespread resentment and greatly increase existing fears concerning the reliability of international nuclear suppliers. Given that the diffusion of technical capability cannot ultimately be prevented, the result could only be that a larger number of countries, determined to escape from dependence on an exclusive group of exigent and obdurate suppliers, would insist on building and operating their own enrichment or reprocessing plants, and would thenceforward pursue their national programmes of nuclear development not only on an autarkic basis but also in a bitterly adversarial manner. The eventual outcome would then be a world in which the maximum number of states had separate access to 'sensitive' nuclear materials while feeling and acting as thoroughly alienated from their previous suppliers. That would hardly seem to be a prescription for reducing fears of proliferation in the longer term.

The question is not whether governments have a right, individually or in concert, to adopt policies of pure restriction in regard to nuclear materials or technology within their control. Although one would normally expect the exercise of such a right to be constrained by existing commitments or contracts, and although arguments of international equity may also weigh politically, the sovereign right to supply or withhold clearly exists. The real question, against the background of the foregoing argument, is whether a non-proliferation strategy based only on exploiting that right, by restricting access to 'sensitive' fuel cycle components to a few countries, is likely to be effective. And the answer, given the probable impact on the way in which other countries apprehend their legitimate energy and development needs, seems to be a negative one. That, above all, is the reason for the recent re-emergence of interest in alternative strategies, based in part on maintaining and reinforcing the existing framework of non-proliferation commitments and safeguards, but including also proposals for managing and providing wider access to 'sensitive' components of the fuel cycle under international or multinational auspices, in ways which serve energy as well as non-proliferation interests on a non-discriminatory basis.

A number of more or less detailed and specific discussions of possible multinational nuclear fuel cycle arrangements have been published in recent years.[2] Their largely unheralded appearance in that short space of time, together with a succession of references to the concept in governmental statements from 1975 onwards, has given an impression that the idea of multinational management in such a context is a novel and exotic one. Nothing could be further from the truth. As the present writer has previously argued:

> The function of developing and using nuclear energy is a matter of state interest. To an extent that few seem yet to realise, functional as well as political aspects of inter-state relations have been increasingly influenced during the last half-century by the emergence of multinational institutions. Transport, communications, banking, commodity markets, trade in manufactured goods, 'high technology' research: all have bred a crop of multinational institutions, charged with regulation, co-ordination or actual collaboration. But nuclear energy is also an industry, or rather a network of industries. And the vigour and success with which the world's industries have engaged in multinational development and conjunction during recent years have been universally impressive.[3]

Nor is there any novelty in multinational nuclear institutions themselves. The IAEA safeguards system is a multinational arrangement between governments for inspection and regulation, as is the safegurds system of Euratom. More specifically, several arrangements have already been made, by both government agencies and private industries, to manage portions of the nuclear fuel cycle multinationally. Eurochemic was an early case, set up by the member states of the European Nuclear Energy Agency to establish and run the reprocessing plant at Mol in Belgium. United Reprocessors brings together, in technical and commercial co-operation, the reprocessing industries in France, Britain and West Germany. Eurodif provides multinational investment and commercial participation in the French gaseous diffusion enrichment plant at Tricastin. Urenco is a multinational consortium in which those responsible for centrifuge enrichment in Britain, the Netherlands and West Germany have combined to build, own and operate plants in those three countries and to market their product. Working experience of nuclear multinationalisation already stretches, therefore, over more than 20 years.

None of the existing multinational fuel cycle arrangements has non-proliferation as its primary object – although limiting its probability or the fear of it may well be among their side-effects. Their successful establishment and achievements nevertheless underline the feasibility of multinational collaboration in this field, given appropriate circumstances, while also indicating that multinationalisation may be seen by both government and industry to offer commercial energy benefits. That last consideration is important, since the earlier argument has demonstrated that no new proposal for managing 'sensitive' fuel cycle components multinationally can hope to succeed if it is seen to serve non-proliferation interests alone. The function of reducing the probability and fear of weapons proliferation must be visibly balanced by energy and development advantages if the proposal is to command sufficiently wide international support.

The ways in which multinational fuel cycle arrangements can help to restrict the probability or fear that civil nuclear activities may be converted to military use are various and, in most cases, reasonably obvious. Clearly, for example, involving several different nationalities in running a 'sensitive' facility or controlling 'sensitive' material tends directly to reduce the chances of any one country diverting some of the material concerned to make weapons. In the first place, provided that multinationalisation extends to all stages of the activity and that the interests of the countries involved are diverse enough to rule out collusion, it is unlikely that any one participant could divert material without detection. In the second place, the fact that the arrangement entails mutual and formal non-proliferation commitments on the part of several governments, and that for any one of them to violate those commitments would mean trampling directly on its specific undertakings to the others, argues that the arrangement can serve as an even stronger political deterrent to the diversion or seizure of 'sensitive' material than subscription to a more general treaty such as the NPT.

Those are only some of the non-proliferation benefits to be expected. To the extent that multinationalisation results in fewer separate 'sensitive' facilities or storage points for 'sensitive' material than would be needed if the participants worked independently, it may also, for instance, ease the problem of international safeguards and verification by diminishing the total number of sites to be inspected. More important politically, however, is the fact that multinational fuel cycle arrangements can offer an opportunity for countries which are directly handicapped by the apparent possibility of nuclear proliferation to reduce the internationally disruptive fear of that event. On the one hand, by entering into such an arrangement themselves, and submitting their access to 'sensitive' material or technology to its obvious discipline, they can demonstrate the exclusively civil nature of their purpose more credibly than by making an abstract commitment or accepting international safeguards alone. On the other hand, by securing participation in an appropriate multinational arrangement on the part of any other country of whose intentions they may themselves be fearful, they can help to reduce their own fears. From the overall non-proliferation point of view, and with international security, broadly conceived, in mind, those psychological benefits may be even more significant than the mechanical effects of multinationalisation on the management of 'sensitive' activities.

Some of the energy benefits which well-designed multinational fuel cycle arrangements can confer are also obvious, not least because they can already be seen as motives for setting up existing consortia such as Urenco or Eurodif. The first, for example, is that of economy. Although the empirical evidence, given the small number of plants in commercial operation, is inevitably scanty, there is no reason to doubt that economies of scale apply to enrichment and reprocessing plants. Their importance varies with technical and circumstantial factors. The capital cost of an enrichment plant, for instance, is much less sensitive to its size in the case of centrifuge technology than in that of gaseous diffusion. Conversely, the cost of building a reprocessing plant in a place where both labour and money are expensive − as in most OECD countries − may be quite a lot higher than the capital cost of a similar plant in another and 'cheaper' location. Overall, however, the unit cost of both enrichment and reprocessing certainly tends to reflect both the size of the plant and the extent to which its capacity is used. In the numerous cases where multinational collaboration would justify building a larger plant, or using its capacity more intensively, than would be possible for any one national participant, multinationalisation could therefore offer real and immediate economic advantages to the managers of national energy budgets. Those advantages are all the more attractive when the initial capital cost of enrichment or reprocessing facilities is so large in relation to the resources of many individual countries as, in any case, to argue the merits of multinational investment.

A second economic advantage potentially available through multinational arrangements, although one which it is more difficult to cost accurately, is the greater security of nuclear supply. Whereas the attraction of scale economies is likely to be greatest in comparison with building a smaller national plant, that of supply security is rather in relation to depending on foreign exporters of nuclear goods or services. The latter may nevertheless be an influential consideration. A multinational arrangement would normally include a provision for access by all the participants to the products of whatever fuel cycle process is involved: enriched uranium, plutonium and uranium separated by reprocessing, or reactor fuels based on those materials. A participant thus enjoys a firmer and more widely guaranteed right to that benefit than can be provided by any set of bilateral commercial contracts with foreign suppliers. At the same time, the ability of any one participant to withhold or suspend supply, or to demand some retroactive modification of contract terms, is much reduced: by the formal provisions of the multinational agreement itself, but probably also by the fact that a multinational consortium will be operating parallel processing or storage facilities in more than one country. Multinational arrangements can thus offer an unusually credible insurance against a political decision by a single government to interrupt supply.

One of the most contentious issues in the recent international debate about non-proliferation policy has been that of access not directly to 'sensitive' materials but to 'sensitive' nuclear technology, and especially, therefore, to technologies of enrichment and reprocessing in a more detailed form than is yet publicly available. Multinationalisation cannot resolve that issue, but it might considerably ease its resolution by offering the basis for a reasonable compromise. The nature of that compromise must vary from case to case. In Eurodif, for example, the other investor countries have been willing to leave 'sensitive' aspects of enrichment technology in the hands of France alone, in return for assured access to enrichment services. Within Urenco, however, all technology is, in principle, pooled. Arrangements for sharing technology in any future multinational enrichment or reprocessing consortium might tend towards either of those extremes, depending on circumstances and on the collective will of the participants. In most cases, however, some measure of technology-sharing is likely to be a precondition of agreement, for political if not commercial reasons. In general, therefore, it is fair to see that kind of multinationalisation as a probable mechanism for diffusing at least some 'sensitive' technology internationally. What is unreasonable is to reject it on that account. As has already been seen, there is no conceivable means by which the spread of 'sensitive' technology can be prevented or indefinitely retarded. The question is only the pace at which it is to spread and the terms on which it is thereafter to be exploited. Multinationalisation may entail transferring some elements of 'sensitive' technology more quickly than would otherwise be the case. But it will certainly also mean accepting a particularly strong and well-monitored commitment to use such technology only under multinational auspices and surveillance and, by definition, for demonstrably peaceful purposes. Although the balance must be struck in each case as a result of separate negotiation and compromise, that ordered outcome may well be preferable, from the non-proliferation point of view, to one in which 'sensitive' technology spreads somewhat more slowly and erratically but is then exploited in a larger number of completely independent national programmes without benefit of multinational regulation. At the same time, from the point of view of national development, national technical education and a sense of national energy security, the readier access to technology which multinationalisation can thus provide and justify may rank as a significant benefit in its own right.

One further reason why obtaining nuclear technology through multinational arrangements may be preferred by a national energy planner to a less ordered form of diffusion is that the process will then be openly legitimised by other governments. That might well be of real utility in the context of a national policy debate. Indeed, the legitimising effect of multinationalisation may have wider significance in that connection. In many countries, engaging nationally in 'sensitive' fuel cycle activities such as enrichment or reprocessing — or even holding 'sensitive' materials such as plutonium or highly enriched uranium — is calculated to provoke a good deal of domestic argument and dissent, on non-proliferation grounds as well as for reasons of cost, safety or environmental effect. Undertaking the same activity on a multinational basis may be a way of setting some of those domestic apprehensions at rest. At best, it may mean that 'sensitive' activities take place in another country. At worst, multinationalisation will greatly diminish the fear of future proliferation, will offer a way of spreading costs, and may also provide a source of expert advice on safety and environmental aspects.

If multinational fuel cycle arrangements are indeed to convey other non-proliferation and energy benefits to their participants, they cannot be multinational in name alone but must also be multinational in substance. Demonstrably reducing the risk and fear of proliferation depends on having the several participating states jointly involved in management and control functions at all levels, so that no one participant may divert 'sensitive' facilities or materials to its own illicit use. Equally, provisions for supply security, cost-sharing or technology transfer will only work if all the participating governments are really as well as formally involved together in managing the arrangement. Most importantly of all, however, the chances of recruiting many of the most significant governments as participants in multinational fuel cycle arrangements will be non-existent unless they are convinced that policy decisions will be made collectively and that they will have an appropriate part to play in both formulating and implementing them. There is no doubt that other states have come increasingly to resent real or imagined signs of an assumption by nuclear-weapon states, nuclear suppliers or developed nuclear countries in general that they have some exclusive right to determine policy at the international level on the use of nuclear power. Such states will not subscribe to any multinational fuel cycle arrangement which appears to recognise or perpetuate such a right. Against that, they will, however, be inclined to find particular attraction in an arrangement which implicitly rebuts the assumption of a resented and unacceptable prerogative, by providing for full participation in multinational policy-making by all its member states. Since that degree of participation is also important to the credibility of a multinational fuel cycle arrangement in the non-proliferation context, this is one point at which international security and national energy interests converge.

When the various non-proliferation and energy benefits are balanced together, it becomes clear that specific multinational fuel cycle arrangements are likely to vary considerably in their focus and form, but that all of them, if they are to be effective and durable, will have to satisfy four general principles. The first is a principle of *restraint*, which means that the arrangement must demonstrably limit the fear that any participating country will convert the relevant part of a civil nuclear programme to military ends. The second is a principle of *viability*, which means that the arrangement must offer its participants economic, commercial and/or technical benefits at least as attractive as those available through an analogous but independent national programme. The third is a principle of *symmetry*, which means that the non-proliferation (restraint) and energy (viability) effects of entering into the arrangement must be seen to be comparable in scale. The fourth is a principle of *parsimony*, which means that, given the inevitable difficulty of setting up and operating multinational arrangements, the operational scope of any of them should be as narrow as satisfying the other principles will permit. On reflection, those principles will be found to embrace all that has been said earlier.

It can also be seen that, in the present connection, multinational fuel cycle arrangements have two possible kinds of focus. On the one hand, there are 'sensitive' materials: highly enriched uranium, separated plutonium and fresh or spent fuel containing either of those in readily available form. On the other hand, there are 'sensitive' technologies and processes: enrichment, reprocessing and the handling or fabrication of 'sensitive' fuel materials. In each case, the purpose of multinationalisation is, in summary form, two-fold: from the non-proliferation point of view, to exert multinational control over 'sensitive' materials or processes; from the energy and development point of view, to secure dependable multinational access to them. Both the distinction between materials and processes and that between control and access are worth bearing in mind.

A start has already been made towards the multinational management and control of 'sensitive' nuclear materials. The safeguards systems of Euratom and, above all, the IAEA represent a crucial part of the international background. More specifically, an expert group has been meeting since December 1978 under IAEA auspices in an effort to design an acceptable scheme for international plutonium storage. The idea is that, as the reprocessing of spent reactor fuel gathers momentum, any of the plutonium which is separated but not immediately needed in national civil energy programmes should be placed in international custody, and released again, when the time comes, only for specified and agreed national use under full safeguards. Meanwhile, a parallel but separate effort at the IAEA by another group of national experts to design a scheme for international management of spent reactor fuel is at an earlier stage of development. Nor is either group concerned as much with multinational control, in the strict sense, as with supervision by the IAEA as an international agency. The discussions which have been going on in both groups illustrate, however, the continuing interest of numerous governments in the broad area of multinational fuel cycle activity, at least with regard to materials. Unfortunately, they also illustrate some of the difficulties likely to be encountered.

One difficulty, from the outset, has been an almost ideological tension between the concepts of international plutonium storage and international spent-fuel management. Plutonium storage implies plutonium separation, which implies reprocessing; and reprocessing for civil purposes has recently been regarded in some governmental quarters, especially in the United States, as anathema. Spent-fuel management has no such implication, and may even be regarded as a conscious alternative to reprocessing. Initially, therefore, there was a tendency for the proponents or opponents of civil reprocessing to line up behind one of the concepts, to the exclusion of the other. Fortunately, that simplistic dichotomy has become less obtrusive with time. What has remained, however, is a deep disagreement over what constitute legitimate uses for plutonium, and thus acceptable grounds for releasing it from international custody — essentially between those who argue that plutonium should only be used in fast-breeder reactors and those who maintain that it should also be available to fuel thermal reactors. There have also emerged all the more clearly some equally intractable differences over the scope and purpose of international control or management: for example, over whether national or international agencies should actually operate storage facilities. At the same time, what has been evident throughout is that the debate on both fronts, separated plutonium and spent fuel, has been more or less exclusively about non-proliferation costs and benefits, with only passing reference to the ways in which international or multinational management of 'sensitive' materials might be made to serve energy purposes as well. Indeed, it is one of the oddities of the present situation that interest in multinationalising 'sensitive' materials has so far been focused more or less completely on non-proliferation effects, to the almost total exclusion of energy benefits, whereas multinational exercises, such as Urenco or Eurodif, which deal with 'sensitive' processes, have been predominantly focused on energy objectives, with little regard for non-proliferation.

Without going into more detail than would be appropriate here, the present writer's view is that separate efforts to agree on arrangements for the international custody of plutonium and spent fuel are likely to be unsuccessful or of trivial effect while the two themes remain divorced and while the debate continues to focus on non-proliferation objectives alone. Bringing 'sensitive' materials under effective international or multinational control will only be possible if governments, by taking a wider view of a larger context, create a basis for offering real energy benefits as well. To be specific, that is likely to require a single arrangement covering both separated plutonium and unreprocessed spent fuel – and possibly highly enriched uranium as well – the parallel purpose of which would be to offer an economic incentive to place 'sensitive' material in international custody whether it is separated or still contained in fuel elements. That will probably entail creating a system of 'credits' for the fissile material contained in spent reactor fuel, as a basis for what might be regarded as a banking operation in which plutonium, separated or not, can be exchanged for fresh uranium-based fuel material or uranium enrichment services. The details of such an arrangement must obviously be more complex than that brief account can indicate.[4] The main point, however, is simple enough. The non-proliferation purpose of multinational control can only be served in practice by an arrangement which equally serves the purpose of multinational access to resources of value to national energy programmes.

Whether an arrangement covering 'sensitive' nuclear materials is formally under the multinational auspices of a group of governments or the international auspices of a single agency such as the IAEA is a point of secondary importance. What is essential is that the relevant governments should be seen to have committed themselves, in substance, to its objectives and success. In the final analysis it is, after all, national governments which control the production and use of 'sensitive' materials. The ultimate object of any arrangement, whatever its form, must thus be to convince each government taking part that other governments will, without fail, play their designated rôles in providing, storing, releasing and exploiting 'sensitive' material in a manner which serves both the non-proliferation and the energy purposes of the arrangement itself. The key, in fact, is a sense of confidence in the performance of all the states involved. That sense is no less important, of course, to the network of bilateral nuclear relations in the commercial and technical fields: a fact reflected in current efforts to restore some of the confidence recently eroded in that context, such as by the establishment of a Committee on Assurances of Supply within the IAEA. In the multinational context, however, and especially in the multinational control of 'sensitive' material stocks, creating and maintaining confidence is an even more demanding task, since each participant must be able to rely on the performance of several other governments at once. Partly for that reason, it is likely that, if progress is to be made in that direction, it will take the form of movement towards establishing a single multinational or international entity, having something of the character of a bank owned by its depositors, within which all governments concerned with the management or use of 'sensitive' materials can feel that they have an equitable measure of influence and to which each can see that all the others are fully committed.

The case of 'sensitive' fuel cycle processes is rather different. In that case there are strong and possibly more obvious economic and technical, as well as non-proliferation, reasons for adopting a multinational approach. Scale economy, as we have seen, is likely to be of considerable importance. So is the diffusion of technology. And assured access to a wider international market for the products of enrichment or reprocessing may also be a commercially significant consideration. At the same time, however, any multinational arrangement involved in offering enrichment or reprocessing services is bound to be more deeply embroiled in market activities than an arrangement covering only the custody of materials. The desire of participating governments for enhanced commercial and energy security will be as strong in one case as in the other. But the means by which a sense of security can best be conveyed are likely to be rather different. Where the issue is the deposit, release or exchange of materials, governments will be looking for the sort of security afforded by a bank, and will plausibly be able to find it in a single institution with the widest possible membership. Where, however, the issue is one which includes the commercial terms for services such as enrichment or reprocessing, it may be necessary to create that sense of security which comes only from being able to buy and sell in a competitive market. That would, in any case, tend to argue against trying to gather all the states involved in, say, enrichment into a single multinational syndicate (which might too easily be seen as a single multinational cartel). As it is, the real circumstances of international politics make such a single syndicate improbable: a fact already illustrated by the existence of two enrichment consortia in Western Europe. Prudence and realism combine, therefore, to point in the cases of enrichment and reprocessing towards a diversity of separate multinational consortia, possibly operating in parallel (and in competition) with those national suppliers which insist on continued independence.

Again, the detailed arrangements for establishing and sustaining a variety of multinational enrichment or reprocessing consortia need a fuller discussion than can be presented here.[5] The four principles of restraint, viability, symmetry and parsimony remain valid. In particular, given the inevitably commercial character of its work, that of economic viability has a special importance. Issues of plant size and location, of market access and of marketing behaviour thus arise and have to be resolved. So, of course, do difficult issues of technology transfer and diffusion. In addition, for commercial as well as non-proliferation reasons, participation in such a multinational consortium is likely always to involve a commitment not to exploit the techniques in question on a separate and independent national basis. It goes without saying, therefore, that establishing such a consortium is bound to require long and difficult negotiations between the prospective partners, and that the detailed form of the outcome is likely to depend heavily in each case on the circumstances of the particular participants. Multi-national enrichment or reprocessing consortia will, in fact, have to be tailor-made to fit different patterns of membership, and the tailoring will have to reflect the political as well as economic priorities of the individual governments involved. Partly for that reason, it is by no means clear that participation in each such consortium can necessarily be drawn from a single geographical region; in many cases, transregional membership may be a precondition for achieving an acceptable commercial, technical and political balance.

The fact that political, commercial and technical considerations are bound to be intertwined in negotiating and implementing any agreement on multinational fuel cycle collaboration poses a real problem of institutional structure. Governments must clearly be concerned at the political level and must retain overall political control, not least in order to substantiate their associated non-proliferation commitments. Equally clearly, however, industrial and commercial management, whether drawn from the public or private sectors in participating countries, needs to be separated somewhat from the political arena. One thing which stands out, therefore, is that there will almost certainly have to be a two-tier system of direction and supervision, with a political council of some sort clearly distinguished from the supervisory board which is responsible for the day-to-day management of the collaborative enterprise. The proper allocation of authority between those two levels, especially in regard to such matters as the siting of facilities or the transfer of technology, is an obviously complicated and difficult issue, demanding a more detailed analysis and explanation.[6] Much, in any case, will depend on negotiation. What can be said, however, is that it is likely to be the care and skill devoted to institutional design which, more than any other single factor, will determine the fate of any attempt to match a multinational fuel cycle arrangement to specific international circumstances.

The probable diversity of multinational arrangements to handle 'sensitive' fuel cycle processes, together with the probable separation of such arrangements from any single institution to control 'sensitive' materials, underlines the importance of a final consideration. Future multinational fuel cycle arrangements, as with those which already exist, will emerge from a process of detailed bargaining between particular national governments.

Because the political and commercial circumstances to be addressed in the real world are so various, and the patterns of complementary interest to be reflected so idiosyncratic, the institutional arrangements needed will also vary widely. To take only one example, different governments will certainly take different views on the extent to which private sector enterprises should be involved. Institutional criteria for multinational fuel cycle arrangements must be flexible enough to accommodate that sort of variety. At the same time, however, it is absolutely essential that all such arrangements should be seen to conform to an agreed common code, covering basic principles of both non-proliferation and commercial practice. Apart from anything else, there would otherwise be too high a risk that multinationalisation would come to be seen as no more than an exercise in international discrimination − and potentially destructive competition − elevated to a higher level. Drawing up and agreeing upon such a common code ranks, therefore, as the first and most urgent task. Indeed, if governments, in pursuit of both non-proliferation and energy benefits, are to make a serious attempt to explore the potential merits of fuel cycle multinationalisation more thoroughly, an effort to draw up the main elements of such a simple common code would be their logical starting point.

No-one with the slightest sense of realism can imagine that establishing or operating multinational arrangements for the nuclear fuel cycle will be an easy task. All our experience shows that multinational institutions, and especially those which involve governments in such a highly political context, are extremely difficult to negotiate and administer. Indeed, the difficulty is obviously so great that it would always be foolish to attempt multinationalisation unless there appeared to be no sufficiently effective way to serve the essential interests of those concerned by other means. That said, the recent history of bilateral international relations in regard to nuclear power has been so disturbing − marked as it is with a rising tide of dissent, suspicion, fear and misunderstanding − that an alternative multinational approach to some of the outstanding issues would seem to deserve at least a thorough examination.

If such an examination is to be attempted, it is vital that it should start from a clear understanding of the choice which we now face internationally in connection with nuclear materials and processes. The choice is not between a future world in which a few governments control all 'sensitive' materials and technologies and one in which many do so — because the latter world is an inevitable part of future reality. The real choice is quite different. On the one hand is the prospect of a world in which many states — having access to plutonium, highly enriched uranium, enrichment and reprocessing — are impelled to exploit that access nationally, in a fragmented, embittered, adversarial and reciprocally suspicious manner — as one result of which the fear, and possibly the reality, of nuclear proliferation will ineluctably increase. On the other hand there is the possibility of a world in which as many states have at least an equal degree of access to 'sensitive' components of the nuclear fuel cycle, but in which they are disposed, institutionally, psychologically and by self-interest, to exploit it in co-operation rather than conflict, partly by the presence of a wider range of credible constraints on the independent or covert diversion of nuclear programmes to military purposes. The latter world is clearly to be preferred, from the point of view of human welfare as well as from that of international security. Without building excessive hopes or making extravagant claims, it is not unrealistic to suppose that multinational arrangements for managing certain parts and products of the nuclear fuel cycle may have something to contribute to shaping that preferred world. At the very least that possibility, which international debate has hardly begun to explore, is worth serious attention by governments concerned with either non-proliferation or energy security. The difficulty and complexity of fuel cycle multinationalisation are undoubted, but that is hardly a sufficient reason for shying away from a serious international effort to capture its potentially unique benefits.

Notes

1. The list includes only 'technology-holders' (i.e. states with autonomous access to the 'sensitive' technology concerned) which are undertaking, or have announced plans to undertake, commercial-scale enrichment or reprocessing for civil purposes at the date in question.
2. Ian Smart, *Multinational Arrangements for the Nuclear Fuel Cycle* (Energy Paper no. 43, London, 1980). See also Abram Chayes and W. B. Lewis, *International Arrangements for Nuclear Fuel Reprocessing* (Cambridge, Massachusetts, 1977); Stockholm International Peace Research Institute, *Internationalization to Prevent the Spread of Nuclear Weapons* (London,

1980); and G. I. Rochlin, *Plutonium, Power, and Politics* (Berkeley, California, 1979).
3. Smart, op. cit., p. 76.
4. ibid., pp. 46–8, 58–62.
5. ibid., pp. 38–46, 54–8.
6. ibid., pp. 51–62.

12   Non-proliferation of Nuclear Weapons as an Essential Step towards Nuclear Disarmament

V. S. Emelyanov

From the first days of nuclear weapons a number of statesmen and politicians were under the impression that at last a weapon had been made which provided the means for solving all the most complicated world problems. They imagined that the possession of this weapon makes a country so strong that no other country could face it. These ideas were especially strongly articulated by a number of statesmen, politicians, military men and even 'scientists' of the United States. Recently, in January 1979, a classified document written by Winston Churchill in 1948 was made public. In it he *proposed to start an atomic attack on the Soviet Union before she had made her own atomic weapons and consequently would be unable to make a retaliatory atomic blow.*

The formation of NATO in 1949 began a broad involvement of the Western European countries in an arms race. In 1952 the ground forces of the United States deployed in the territory of the member countries of the North Atlantic bloc began to be armed with the nuclear weapons. In the following years the deployment of American atomic weapons in foreign territories, mostly in Western Europe, was extended on an even greater scale. In accordance with the 'new line' in military policy and the 'massive retaliation' doctrine, particular emphasis was placed upon increasing strategic offensive forces and a first atomic strike capability.

At the NATO Council session which took place in Paris on 14–16 February 1953, the US representative said his Government had prepared amendments to the Atomic Energy Act and considered getting authority from the Congress to transfer information on atomic weapons to the member countries of NATO 'for the purpose of making plans'.

On 30 August 1954 the US Congress accepted an amendment to the Atomic Energy Act which permitted the transfer of information on atomic weapons, which was necessary for making defence plans, personnel training in the use of atomic weapons by the NATO countries and the military organisation of the bloc. The transfer of information concerning the exterior characteristics of atomic weapons as well as delivery systems and the methods of their use was permitted. The information did not include data about which the Joint Congressional Committee on Atomic Energy and the Defense Department were not in agreement as to its not revealing important information on the construction and the preparation of the nuclear parts of the atomic weapon.[1]

On 16 July 1957 the US Secretary of State, J. Foster Dulles, said at a press conference: 'We act on the prerequisite that if war comes our allies may use atomic weapons and that perhaps it may be used by them.'[2]

Within a decade after the first test atomic bombs had been made in the Soviet Union (in 1949) and in Great Britain (in 1952). Later in 1960 France became a nuclear power and in 1964 the People's Republic of China carried out a nuclear explosion.

'At least ten, perhaps twenty countries are capable of making nuclear weapons within three years', said Robert Kennedy on 23 July 1965. 'Two of them, Israel and India, already have fissionable materials which may [allow] an atomic construction within several months.'[3]

The process of proliferation of nuclear weapons all over the planet caused great concern among public opinion in many countries of the world. Considerable attention was focused on the nuclear tests conducted by France in the Sahara. The press published reports on work connected with nuclear weapons production in China. The striving of West German militarists to get access to the American nuclear arsenals through the multilateral nuclear force of NATO was a cause for a great concern. Public opinion in the United States also expressed anxiety because of the process of nuclear weapons proliferation. It caused the US President John F. Kennedy to speak in support of the solution of this problem: 'I ask you', he said, addressing the members of the US Congress, 'to stop and think what the presence of nuclear weapons in so many hands could mean, in the hands of big and small countries, stable and unstable, responsible and irresponsible, scattered all over the world. You would have lost calm, there would be no stability, no real security and no hope for effective disarmament.'[4]

In Autumn 1964 in Cairo a non-aligned Summit Conference was convened. Its participants called on the nuclear powers to refrain from proliferation of nuclear weapons. They declared their readiness not to produce, not to acquire and not to test nuclear weapons.[5]

Since the emergence of the problem of proliferation of nuclear weapons the Soviet Union has taken a quite definite stand, considering that the achievement of agreement on this problem will considerably facilitate the solution of other problems in the field of disarmament; namely the cessation of nuclear weapon tests, the limitation of nuclear armaments and armed forces and other questions. Already in the middle of the 1950s the Soviet Union was an initiator of proposals directed against the proliferation of nuclear weapons.

Ireland was very active in the area of nuclear non-proliferation. In 1958 at the 13th session of the UN General Assembly Ireland introduced this question onto the agenda, and then again introduced it the following year. The 15th session of the UN General Assembly accepted a resolution on the question introduced by Ireland. This resolution called upon 'all governments to apply all efforts possible for the achievement of a permanent agreement to prevent widespread proliferation of nuclear weapons'.[6] The Soviet Union supported this resolution and the United States abstained during the vote, asserting that 'one cannot rely upon other countries abstaining from acquiring nuclear weapons for an indefinite period of time'.[7]

After the explosion of an atomic bomb in China in 1964, the desire to find a solution to the problem of non-proliferation of nuclear weapons increased considerably in the United States. Robert Kennedy, in his speech in the US Senate in 1965, recalling the above-mentioned words of John Kennedy from 1963, declared: 'The United States and the whole world are vitally interested in preventing the spread of nuclear weapons. In the success of these efforts the future of our people will depend. The necessity to stop the spread of nuclear weapons must become the main and first goal of American policy.'[8] The recognition in the United States of a dangerous further spread of nuclear cancer all over the planet created the necessary prerequisites for serious discussion of the problem of non-proliferation and the working out of the international measures to stop this harmful process.

The concrete negotiations on working out the draft of the Nuclear Weapons Non-Proliferation Treaty were conducted in 1966–67 in Geneva within the framework of the 18-Nation Committee on Disarmament. The negotiations were very complicated and often were intense in character.[9] Among the most complicated questions which emerged during the discussion were, for example, the extent of the ban on the non-proliferation of such a weapon, control over the fulfilment of the obligations of the treaty, security guarantees to non-nuclear-weapon nations which ratified the treaty, and the problem of peaceful use of nuclear energy by non-nuclear nations, including making nuclear explosions for peaceful purposes.[10]

During the negotiations the US representatives tried to ensure that the Non-Proliferation Treaty did not prevent countries belonging to the military blocs, above all to NATO, from getting access to nuclear weapons. The Soviet Union decisively stopped all such attempts and exerted great efforts to close all gaps permitting the spread of nuclear weapons.

As a result of lengthy negotiations between the Soviet Union and the United States a basic obligation of the Non-Proliferation Treaty was arrived at:

Not to transfer to anyone nuclear weapons or any nuclear installations or control over such weapons or explosive installations neither directly nor indirectly; similarly not in any way to help to promote or to incite any nation which does not have nuclear weapons to produce or acquire by any means nuclear weapons or any other nuclear explosive installations, or control over such weapons or explosive installations.[11]

After the 18-Nation Committee by the end of 1967 had reached agreement on questions in dispute, primarily the questions relating to the control over non-proliferation of nuclear weapons and measures for promoting the peaceful use of nuclear energy, the draft of the treaty was transferred to the UN General Assembly.[12]

The 22nd UN General Assembly approved the Treaty and asked the Governments in the countries where the Treaty was to be deposited (the Soviet Union, the United States and Great Britain) to open the Treaty for ratification as soon as possible. On 1 July 1968 the Treaty was opened for signing in Moscow, Washington and London. In March 1970 the Treaty became operational.[13] At present 114 nations have signed.

After the signing and enactment of the Treaty the most serious question has become the question of its universal character, that is the participation in the Treaty of a maximum number of nations, and above all of all nuclear and near-nuclear nations. France and China have not signed the Treaty. However, France has declared that, while not taking part in the Treaty, she will take into account its provisions and abide by them. This was confirmed in the Soviet–French declaration on nuclear non-proliferation of 22 January 1977 in which it was stated that the Soviet Union and France 'conscious of the responsibility which is upon them as nuclear nations and motivated by the eagerness to escape the dangers, caused by proliferation of nuclear weapons, confirm their joint decision to exert all efforts directed at the prevention of the spread of such weapons'.[14]

How does the Treaty work? In accordance with article VIII 3, in May 1975, 5 years after the enactment of this Treaty, a conference of the Treaty participants was held to consider how the Treaty was operating to be sure that the goals expressed in its preamble and its terms were being observed. In the final declaration accepted by the conference it was said that the participants of the Treaty were fulfilling their obligations on non-proliferation of nuclear weapons. At the same time, recognition was given to the necessity of further strengthening and perfecting the system of guarantees against the use of nuclear technology for military purposes and also the necessity to extend the number of the Treaty adherents.[15] Among the non-signatories are Israel, South Africa, Argentina, Pakistan and Egypt.

The President of the World Federation of Scientific Workers, Eric Burhop, made a convincing case in the press about the danger of the spread and use of nuclear weapons particularly in connection with South Africa. In an article published not long before his death in the magazine *The World of Science* he wrote with alarm:

Many British scientists and engineers, experts in the field of nuclear physics, well versed in the newest achievements of nuclear energy, began to work in South Africa, using special scientific information that they have. The aid to South Africa in the making of its own nuclear industry is seen as a compensation for the access to the deposits of nuclear ore. The construction of huge plant producing UF_6 out of U_3O_8 is a necessary step in construction of an enrichment installation. South Africa is being helped considerably by Great Britain and the USA.[16]

Further Burhop wrote:

In connection with the growth of commercial interest of many countries in nuclear energy, technical contacts of South Africa with other countries, especially with the Federal Republic of Germany, increased considerably. There is a suspicion that the cooperation with the FRG is not limited by commercial interests only. The West German military circles rely on the possibility of getting nuclear weapons with the help of South Africa. Evidently, close technical cooperation with Israel in this area is also organized. It is commonly known that Israel is capable of making nuclear weapons or is close to it.[17]

Thus a new nuclear country is emerging, namely South Africa, which organises or has already created production of nuclear explosives out of U-235.

Burhop concluded his extremely alarming article with the quite correct recommendation that 'urgent measures are necessary which include a threat to use effective sanctions by the basic trading partners of South Africa, in order to exclude a possibility of nuclear weapons proliferation, which in the existing political situation presents a serious threat to peace in one of the most unstable areas of the globe'.[18]

All nations − nuclear and non-nuclear alike − are interested in strengthening the Non-Proliferation Treaty. Efforts must accordingly be made to find ways and means of strengthening this extremely important international document and thus weaken the danger of nuclear war.

Notes

1. Cited in *The Strategy of Imperialism and the USSR Struggle for Peace and Disarmament* (in Russian) (Moscow, 1974) pp. 203–4.

2. Cited in ibid., pp. 205–6.
3. *Congressional Record*, 1965, vol. III, no. 113, p. 14050.
4. ibid.
5. *International Life* (in Russian), 1964, no. 11, p. 156.
6. UN General Assembly Resolution 1576 (xv), 20 Dec. 1960.
7. A. A. Roshchin, *International Security and Nuclear Weapons* (in Russian) (Moscow, 1980) p. 172.
8. *Congressional Record*, 1965, vol. III, no. 113, p. 14050.
9. Rochchin, op. cit., p. 181.
10. ibid., p. 182.
11. *The Soviet Union in the Struggle for Disarmament* (in Russian) (Moscow, 1977) p. 31.
12. Roshchin, op. cit., p. 187.
13. ibid.
14. *The Soviet Union in the Struggle for Disarmament*, p. 187.
15. Roshchin, op. cit., p. 193.
16. Eric Burhop, 'Estimating the Danger of the Spread and Use of Nuclear Weapons, with Reference to the Possibility of their Production in the South African Republic', *The World of Science* (in Russian), 1980, no. 1, p. 14.
17. ibid.
18. ibid.

13 The Dilemmas of Non-proliferation Policy: the Supplier Countries

Pierre Lellouche

Introduction

To a certain extent, writing about non-proliferation issues at the beginning of the 1980s may seem largely irrelevant as compared with the urgency and gravity of the current international situation. The Soviet occupation of Afghanistan, since December 1979, the Iran–Iraq war, the troubles in Poland and the resulting threats of Soviet intervention in that country have dramatically altered the climate of East–West relations. A new phase of super-power confrontation, both in Europe and in key Third World regions, seems to be taking place, thereby bringing to an end the era of detente and arms control which started in the late 1960s. In addition, the current East–West crisis is paralleled by a profound rift in European–American relations, both sides having different perceptions and interests with respect to the future of detente, arms control and defence policies.

Given this background, non-proliferation has definitely fallen out of fashion, as the centre of attention has shifted back to the more traditional East–West security issues. This is particularly true of the United States, which presented itself as the champion of non-proliferation policy since the mid-1970s. It is symptomatic, for example, that despite its earlier emphasis on non-proliferation, as a top priority concern in its foreign policy, the Carter Administration apparently made a 180 degree turn in its attitude, by reversing its embargo decision towards both Pakistan and India in the aftermath of the Soviet invasion of Afghanistan.[1] Similarly, in sharp contrast with the 1976 election, proliferation played virtually no rôle in the American Presidential campaign of 1980. Finally, the conclusions of the International Nuclear Fuel Cycle Evaluation (INFCE) in February 1980, and the convening of the second NPT Review Conference in August 1980 attracted scarcely any public attention.

Yet the problem of checking the spread of nuclear weapons remains. Technology, equipment and fissionable materials are being transferred to many nations, some of which are known to be actively seeking nuclear weapons more or less openly, especially in the Near-East, in South-West Asia and in Latin America, thus adding to the already dangerous instability of key regions in the world. Similarly, the nuclear issues which divided supplier countries of the industrialised 'North' and recipients of the 'South', as well as the United States and its European allies, over the past decade have yet to be resolved. Non-proliferation problems may therefore attract less attention today, but they remain of fundamental importance to international security in the years to come. Furthermore, given the new tensions at work in today's international situation, non-proliferation in the 1980s will evolve in an environment much less favourable to international negotiation and compromise, one where other problems will demand priority and where the general insecurity of the world will add many more incentives for nations which do not possess nuclear weapons today to acquire them. In short, the 1980s may well turn out to be a much more dangerous era in terms of proliferation trends, and at the same time one where non-proliferation policy will be much more difficult to conduct.

For these reasons it is perhaps useful to reflect on the events of the past decade from the perspective of the key supplier countries, namely the United States, France and West Germany, and to analyse how their nuclear policies have interacted. Such an analysis may then help us to evaluate the trends likely to emerge in these countries and their influence in future international nuclear politics.

This chapter is not, however, intended to provide yet 'another account of the various events that took place over the past decade, in particular since the Indian nuclear detonation of May 1974. For an impressive literature has already been devoted to most of these events, ranging from the 'sensitive' contracts signed by France and West Germany in the early 1970s to the London Suppliers Group, the Carter policy, the Nuclear Non-Proliferation Act of 1978 (NNPA) as well as INFCE.[2] Rather, it is intended here to assess the extent to which European attitudes towards non-proliferation have evolved as a result of American policies, in order to provide some guidelines as to what needs to be done to reach a settlement in the still unresolved transatlantic non-proliferation controversy.

The Transatlantic Non-proliferation Quarrels in Perspective

One of the most striking paradoxes of the non-proliferation controversy of the last 7 years is that while the target of proliferation concerns was clearly centred on a series of unstable Third World countries, the main battle was fought between the allied Western nations of Europe and the United States. It may be too early to assess whether this transatlantic quarrel will eventually make a positive contribution to non-proliferation. But one thing is sure: the quarrel over non-proliferation and nuclear energy has certainly helped to create very profound and long-term damage to the overall climate of European–American relations and particularly of relations between Washington and Bonn.

The Carter Administration's non-proliferation policy gave rise to the first major quarrel with the Europeans (and West Germany in particular) in a series of transatlantic troubles which, over the past 4 years, gradually included economic and energy issues, strategic problems (including the neutron bomb episode, the handling of the SALT II Treaty ratification process and the Theatre Nuclear Force modernisation programme) as well as political issues (Iran, the Middle East and the policy towards the Soviet Union in the aftermath of Afghanistan).

Looking back at this distressingly long list of troubles, it is clear that the nuclear non-proliferation quarrel did play an important rôle in shaping what was going to become the standard European perception of the Carter Administration's record in foreign policy: namely a mixture of incoherence, reversals, poor management of the Alliance, misplaced priorities coupled with an overreliance on quasi-religious principles.

This having been said, the recent transatlantic quarrel over non-proliferation cannot be fully understood without reference to earlier events. It is well known that European–American relations in the field of nuclear energy and non-proliferation have never been altogether smooth. Indeed, when looking at the history of international nuclear relations since the Second World War, one finds that non-proliferation has been a constant source of strain in transatlantic politics.[3] The 1940s was the decade of aborted co-operation among the Allies in respect to the Manhattan Project. In that decade the United States breached the 1943 Tripartite Quebec Agreement signed with Great Britain and Canada and later sealed off its nuclear know-how from the rest of the world behind the walls of secrecy of the McMahon Act of 1946. Similarly, the 1950s created new strains between the United States and continental Europe, and particularly France, over the extent of American assistance to the newly-formed EURATOM and the birth of the French military nuclear programme. During the 1960s, while progress was made towards the establishment of an international nuclear safeguards regime, Europe and the United States were again at odds in respect to both the relationship between EURATOM and the IAEA–NPT safeguards and the issue of nuclear sharing within NATO (the Multilateral Force plan).

All of these issues and strains in one way or another revolved around the risks of proliferation and the policies which the United States was trying to implement at the time. Though often overlooked in the United States, this historical background played an important rôle in shaping European reactions to American policies in the 1970s. From a European standpoint, the non-proliferation debate of the 1970s constitutes the latest episode in a Euro–American rivalry which has lasted some 40 years! There were, however, some crucial differences, which go a long way to explaining the intensity and duration of the current quarrel. First, the Europeans in the 1970s, in contrast to earlier periods, committed themselves on a very large scale to nuclear power programmes, in the hope of reducing their very great dependence on imported fossil fuels. For the Europeans, therefore, non-proliferation was no longer a cost-free objective (as it was in the 1950s and 1960s), but one that entailed a great deal of sacrifice both in economic and energy terms as well as — though to a lesser degree — in foreign policy objectives. The second major change involved the 'balance of power' between American and European industrial and technological capabilities in the field of nuclear energy. In effect, the 1970s saw world leadership of the nuclear industry shifting from the United States to Europe, as well as the end of the long-held American monopoly in reactor manufacturing and in fuel cycle services.[4] Early in this decade at least two major suppliers of nuclear reactors had fully emerged on the international market (in West Germany and in France); moreover, Europeans managed to free themselves to a large extent from the dependence on American enriched uranium fuel, after the Urenco facilities and the Eurodif plant at Tricastin became operational. Finally, the Europeans even developed an impressive technological edge over the United States in reprocessing and in fast-breeder technology.

The results of this new situation have been of fundamental importance in shaping both the substance of the non-proliferation quarrel and its outcome. For their part, the Europeans discovered very early in the debate that their own energy-security interests and − to a lesser extent − their foreign policy objectives were directly threatened by the new policies put forward by the United States. But while in a defensive position, they also realised that, in contrast to earlier periods, they then held the technological and industrial means necessary to defend these interests and effectively to resist American pressures. At the same time these industrial achievements brought new problems. The Europeans having established themselves because of the very success of their industries as key actors in international nuclear relations, also had to learn − often reluctantly − to live with the political responsibilities that came with the new rôle. This has been a slow and somewhat difficult realisation and it is still unclear − as will be shown later − whether the Europeans are willing to pay the political and economic price which is inherent in a non-proliferation policy.

Similarly the United States, which was accustomed to treating non-proliferation unilaterally, as its own 'special responsibility' (to be shared at best with the other superpower) also took a very long time before realising the magnitude of the changes that had taken place in international nuclear relations. Not only did the United States have trouble recognising the legitimate energy preoccupations of the Europeans, but it discovered very late in the game that henceforth, non-proliferation had to be negotiated with − rather than imposed upon − the European allies, and that in any case such a policy could not succeed without the full cooperation of the European suppliers.[5]

In essence, therefore, the Euro-American non-proliferation quarrel of the 1970s constitutes one particular aspect of a wider ongoing structural transformation of transatlantic relations, which is characterised by a sharp decline in the ability of the United States directly to shape events and policies in Europe in accordance with American objectives and by an increasing ability on the part of the Europeans to assert and defend their own interests against those of the United States.

What renders this structural problem even more difficult and apparent in the case of non-proliferation is that both sides are in essence condemned to co-operate. Not only does Third World proliferation constitute an objective security threat to both the United States and Western Europe, but the continued development of nuclear power in the industrialised world also requires the restoration of a stable climate in international nuclear politics. This entails the need to reconcile the respective energy and military security concerns of Europe and America into mutually agreed policies; this also means that a more balanced form of co-operation has to replace the unilateral American policies of the past. In essence, the painful quarrel of the past decade reflects precisely this evolution, from an initial situation of open conflict, to one in which both sides increasingly realise the need to establish a new co-operative relationship aimed at jointly managing proliferation in the future.

Viewed from a European perspective, recent American non-proliferation policies have confronted European suppliers with two separate, though interconnected issues. First, they face the problem of nuclear transfers to the Third World and its impact on European exports policy. Secondly, they must consider the future of the 'plutonium economy' and its consequences on European breeder and reprocessing programmes. Each of these aspects will be addressed separately in the following two sections of this chapter.

Nuclear Exports and Safeguards: Impact of American Policy on European Suppliers

In retrospect, perhaps the single most important achievement of the Ford and Carter Administrations' foreign nuclear policies has been the triggering of an awareness in Europe of the fact that the exporting of nuclear materials and equipment is a special business and that non-proliferation is a policy for which Europe should be responsible as well. Although European policy has evolved considerably in this direction since the mid-1970s, disagreement persists with the United States in at least two areas: (1) the type of export controls and safeguards which should be established to deal with Third World proliferation from commercial fuel cycles; and (2) the economic and political price that Europe should pay in order to implement such a policy.

1. Non-Proliferation and Nuclear Exports as a European Responsibility

Until the mid-1970s, when the controversy erupted with the United States, Europeans scarcely thought of themselves as responsible for — or indeed involved in — implementing non-proliferation policy. The latter was typically seen as 'superpower business' which one should either oppose (as France did when it sought to acquire nuclear weapons against the wishes of both the superpowers), or submit to, more or less reluctantly (as West Germany did when it signed the NPT in 1968). From a West German perspective, non-proliferation had been settled, as far as West Germany was concerned, with the Treaty of Paris in 1954. As a result the question was seen from a purely economic angle, that is in terms of non-discriminatory access of West Germany to fuel cycle technology and to the international market. This preoccupation was central in delaying West German ratification of the NPT until 1975.

The French, on the other hand, viewed the problem from a purely political angle. Having themselves 'proliferated' under President Charles de Gaulle, they conveniently chose an ambigious position. On the one hand, they refused to oppose the right of every nation to acquire atomic weapons with its own means; hence, France's refusal to join the NPT. But on the other hand, France announced that it would conduct itself as if it were a party to the Treaty.[6]

Another important element explaining this general attitude of aloofness with respect to non-proliferation policy, was that France and West Germany only achieved a large-scale industrial capability in the nuclear area in the early 1970s. During the 1960s both nations had played a very marginal rôle as exporters of nuclear reactors in a market totally dominated by the United States,[7] where in addition, safeguard rules were either purely bilateral or non-existent. As a result neither France nor West Germany had felt the need to set up a procedure for the political control of nuclear exports, though West Germany (but not France) did participate in the early 1970s in the discussions of the Zangger Committee.

The irony of this situation was that France and West Germany were drawn into the non-proliferation issue, not because they intended to politically – indeed they were caught totally unprepared by the new American policies set forth in 1974–77 – but because they emerged as alternative nuclear suppliers to the United States precisely at the time when Washington was having second thoughts about the efficiency of the NPT–IAEA system (which the United States had been instrumental in creating only a few years earlier).

In essence the Europeans soon found themselves caught between three conflicting forces: pressures from the United States – which had 'discovered' the loopholes in the NPT–IAEA regime after the Indian nuclear test of 1974 and was demanding stronger non-proliferation rules; a series of demands for nuclear assistance from developing countries triggered in part by the 1973 oil shock; and the pressures from their domestic nuclear industries which needed export outlets in order to minimise the cost of the large domestic nuclear programmes which were being launched at the same time in Europe.

Nuclear and industrial bureaucracies in both France and West Germany, which at the time enjoyed full control over exports, simply decided to treat their expanding business on a 'business as usual' basis, that is according to the international rules in force at the time. And in fact, none of these rules prevented the transfer of 'sensitive' fuel cycle technologies (i.e. enrichment and reprocessing). Indeed, the general assumption then, as derived from the NPT, repeated statements by US officials, as well as from the Zangger Committee's trigger list, was that 'the whole field of nuclear science associated with electrical power is accessible now . . . including not only the present generation of power reactors, but also that advanced technology . . . of fast breeder power reactors'.[8] When combined with the other provisions of the NPT relating to nuclear exports to non-weapons states remaining outside the Treaty, the 'normal' rules at the time were that national access to the entire fuel cycle was implicitly guaranteed to non-nuclear weapon states party to the Treaty (as per Article IV), while even non-parties could also benefit from this liberal regime to the extent that they accepted limited safeguards when dealing with a supplier nation party to the NPT.

In effect, several nations in the early 1970s had already used their (then) legitimate right to acquire sensitive technologies. This was the case in Europe with the establishment of Urenco and the construction of a centrifuge enrichment plant in Almelo (The Netherlands); this was also the case in Japan which obtained a demonstration-size reprocessing plant (Tokai Mura) from France. Similarly, nothing prevented Korea (a party to NPT) and Pakistan (a non-party) from obtaining French co-operation in the reprocessing field, or Brazil from asking for similar assistance from the United States and West Germany.

In the meantime, however, the United States had changed its mind about the viability of such a liberal system (which, it must be emphasised again, the United States itself had established). Several events occurring in 1974–75 caused that change and triggered a true 'proliferation scare' in the United States. The first was of course the Indian explosion of May 1974. The fact that India managed to build its first 'bomb' from the plutonium produced in a Canadian-imported reactor (although reprocessing was carried out in a locally built facility and that there was no technical violation of safeguards in force in India at the time) gave rise to new concerns in the United States, about the proliferation potential of the *commercial* fuel cycle as well as about the true value of the international safeguards regime. Moreover, the fact that the Indian detonation occurred in the aftermath of the 1973 oil shock, at a time when nuclear energy was expected to grow extremely rapidly throughout the world (as seemed to be indicated by a series of large nuclear contracts signed by key nuclear states such as Brazil, Iran, Pakistan and Korea), caused the Americans to react very strongly to a situation which seemed to be getting out of control. As a result, non-proliferation policy took on a new sense of urgency, and this led many in the United States to tend to forget the basically political nature of proliferation, and to focus on the possible economic and technical 'fixes' which could be erected quickly in order to check what was perceived to be a new 'phase' in proliferation.

This succession of events, and the resulting proliferation scare in the United States, produced two major changes in American policy, which came to be implemented from 1975 onwards, first under the Ford Administration, and in particular under the Carter Administration (after January 1977). According to the new American approach, the non-universal, non-compulsory safeguards regime valid under NTP–IAEA norms had to be 'improved' in order to prevent countries from coming 'three months away' from the bomb and getting it 'without quite breaking the rules'.[9] Thus, the traditional deterrence function of safeguards through *detection* was no longer thought to be fulfilled under the 'old' regime: safeguards should now be made *compulsory* and *universal* in order to ensure effective *prevention*. The second major change in American thinking was that certain fuel cycle activities (namely, enrichment, and in particular, plutonium reprocessing) were now considered to be too dangerous to be exported, *even* under safeguards. After having promoted full nuclear co-operation under its Atoms for Peace Plan of 1953, the United States was thus reverting 20 years later to the policy of denial of the immediate post-war period.

From a European perspective, these changes were seen as an attempt to rewrite valid international norms and agreements. Implied in this criticism was the notion that the 'old' IAEA–NPT regime had been 'good enough' as long as the United States was the dominant factor on the world market. The prevailing view in Europe then was that the United States was simply trying to eliminate its European competitors by changing the political rules of nuclear trade. (Ironically, Americans were convinced of exactly the same thing on the part of the Europeans when they looked at the technological 'sweeteners' willingly sold by Europeans in order to eliminate American firms from Third World Markets.)[10]

While perhaps partly founded and certainly understandable given the history of American–European rivalry in this field since the 1950s, these suspicions about American commercial objectives were also in part self-serving. There can be no doubt that both the French and West German nuclear-industrial 'complexes' (or bureaucracies) were fully aware of the loopholes in the NPT–IAEA regime in force at the time and that they used them in order to establish their respective industries on the world market. Hence, the tendency on the part of European suppliers to respond to American political pressures by overplaying legal arguments, particularly by insisting that all the controversial nuclear deals signed in the mid-1970s were fully consistent with established international norms.[11] One should note, however, that these practices were not new as such. After all, the United States had employed similar 'carrots' in the 1950s and 1960s, particularly in the safeguards area when it sought to establish its own industry in the European market.[12]

Beyond these immediate commercial objectives, the behaviour of both European suppliers revealed an analysis of proliferation risks different from that of the United States. Europeans tended (and still do) to view proliferation as a purely political problem. To a large extent, therefore, the connection with the commercial fuel cycle, including sensitive facilities, is considered irrelevant, for if a state really wants to acquire nuclear weapons, it will do so with or without safeguards or other technical obstacles.[13] In this context, embargoes and denial policies, while perhaps useful in delaying proliferation in certain countries, will also reinforce tendencies of nuclear autarchy, thereby depriving the supplier states of any form of control over such national programmes.[14]

In spite of these suspicions about American objectives, in spite also of the Europeans' own commercial motivations and their different views of proliferation risks, the European suppliers did gradually evolve towards the recognition of their own responsibilities in the non-proliferation area. A first step was made with the participation of France in the London Suppliers Group following the Martinique Summit between Presidents Ford and Valery Giscard d'Estaing. France, it is important to recall, had previously boycotted the Zangger Committee meetings. Moreover, its participation in what could appear as a suppliers' 'cartel' was not without political cost as France claimed to promote a 'mondialiste' policy where it intended to be a link between North and South. A second important step was made with the agreement on the Suppliers Group's Guidelines in September 1975. Though both France and West Germany had opposed the American concept of 'full-scope safeguards' as well as the notion of denying exports of 'sensitive' technologies as contrary to the sovereign rights of nations, the two European suppliers did agree upon a set of international rules aimed at strengthening the non-proliferation regime, including one providing for suppliers' 'restraint' in exporting sensitive facilities. While in the United States this evolution was not considered to be sufficient (particularly during the 1976 Presidential campaign), in both France and West Germany it was interpreted as a major step towards the American position. Indeed, in France, this 'concession' to American pressures gave rise to a series of political attacks from the Gaullists against Giscard d'Estaing's foreign nuclear policy, which they felt was too 'close' to that of the United States.

Another positive sign of a greater awareness of proliferation issues came in September 1976 when France decided to establish a high-level political organ entrusted with the task of elaborating and implementing French non-proliferation policy, the Conseil de Politique Nucléaire Extérieure. This was the first time France announced such a policy and imposed a direct presidential control over nuclear exports. In December 1976 this decision was followed by the announcement of an embargo on further sales of plutonium-reprocessing facilities. Although the plant promised to Pakistan was implicitly excluded from the decision, the latter still represented a further rapprochement between France and the United States.

One interesting result of the French embargo was that West Germany remained totally isolated in the nuclear exports controversy as the only country still willing to export reprocessing facilities. As a result, Bonn was now perceived by the Americans as the chief obstacle to the development of a common non-proliferation policy by all supplier nations. In fact, partly to offset additional pressures from the newly elected Carter Administration, West Germany did modify its policy 6 months later, by adopting, in June 1977, an export embargo phrased exactly like France's.

2. Evolution of European Attitudes During the Carter Administration

Looking back at the experience of the past 4 years, it is somewhat difficult to evaluate precisely the influence of the Carter Administration's non-proliferation policy on the behaviour of European suppliers. Part of this difficulty stems from the reason which was just discussed; namely that the Europeans had already evolved considerably since 1974, *before* Carter was elected: this is particularly true in the case of France which joined the London Group and adopted in late 1976 a much more restrictive nuclear export policy. But the major part of the difficulty is due to the Carter Administration itself, or rather to the way in which it chose to handle the non-proliferation question. Though not substantially different from that of its predecessor, Carter's nuclear

THE DILEMMAS OF NON-PROLIFERATION POLICY

export policy was considerably more confused, and its 'style' was quite different. The confusion was due above all to internal factors: the Administration took many months (if not years) before it only *began* to control the various centres of authority in the nuclear exports area, which included a whole series of organs in the Executive and regulatory branch (not to mention various conflicting offices in the State Department, the White House and the newly created Department of Energy) and an equally large number of decision-makers in the Congress. To any foreign government, the Administration spoke with many voices, all different and at times openly contradictory, a situation which goes a long way towards explaining many of the misunderstandings and quarrels of that period. To a certain extent, this regulatory mess or 'meltdown' was somewhat dealt with by the 1978 Nuclear Non-Proliferation Act (NNPA) but the sheer complexity of that legislation, coupled with the severity of its provisions, largely offset this benefit. To this administrative confusion, the Carter Administration added a confusion of substance, as Carter diffused the export issue as such − though central to Third World proliferation − by opening a new debate on the 'plutonium economy' which in turn raised an entirely new set of problems.[15]

Another characteristic of the new Carter policy, which also contributed to intensifying the quarrel with the Europeans, was the way in which the Administration chose to deal with some of the outstanding issues left over from the Ford Administration and in particular the 1974 West German−Brazilian Agreement. While the Ford Administration proved effective in working through discreet multilateral channels (the London Suppliers Group), the Carter Administration chose a 'high visibility' posture which proved totally counterproductive. Instead of obtaining the 'cancellation' of the Agreement, the Carter Administration simply antagonised both Brazil and West Germany, and in fact made any compromise on the part of the West Germans even more politically difficult as a result of the publicity given to the affair.

On the whole, the successes of the Carter Administration in the nuclear exports area are not altogether obvious. Not only did it fail to persuade West Germany to renounce its controversial deal with Brazil (or the 'sensitive' parts of it) but Carter also failed to prevent West Germany from signing in 1979−80 another contract with Argentina which includes the transfer of a 'Swiss'-made large-scale heavy water plant. As to the other outstanding cases left over from the mid-1970s, the French–South Korean contract had been cancelled before Carter was elected and the French–Pakistani contract was cancelled by France in 1978 as a result of various internal events in Pakistan (the execution of Prime Minister Z. A. Bhutto, and the accumulation of evidence showing that his successor, General Mohammed Zia, clearly intended to produce nuclear weapons by all available means). Moreover, American pressures failed to prevent certain oil-starved European suppliers from intensifying their nuclear co-operation with Arab oil producers (notably France and Italy with Iraq).[16]

Moreover, disagreements still persist on the full-scope safeguards issues, despite the inclusion of this requirement in the NNPA of 1978 and the discussion of the concept in INFCE. The Carter Administration insisted on a formal acceptance of the concept by both France and West Germany. By contrast, the latter argue that *de facto* full-scope safeguards are already in force in all but five non-weapons states, and that a formal inclusion of the full-scope concept in an international document (i.e. in the IAEA safeguards regulations) could only worsen the emerging North–South controversy about nuclear transfers.

Given this background, when looking back at the record of European behaviour in the nuclear exports area during the Carter era, it is interesting to note that this behaviour seems to have been less influenced by the Carter policy *per se*, than by the respective situations of the world nuclear market and of the European industries. The dominant factor here is the virtual paralysis of nuclear growth throughout the world since the mid-1970s as a result of a combination of societal, economic, technical and political reasons.[17]

Interestingly enough, the impact of this situation has been substantially different in the case of France in comparison with that of West Germany, as well as that of the lesser European suppliers. So far, France has managed to maintain and even increase its domestic nuclear programme. As a result, French nuclear industry is for the moment less dependent than its West German counterpart on nuclear exports, with plans aiming at 50 per cent of total electricity production in 1985 to be produced by nuclear plants (and 75 per cent by 1990). Framatome's order books are filled for many years to come by Electricité de France's (EDF)'s domestic contracts, a fact which considerably reduces exports incentives and the willingness to transfer sensitive 'sweeteners'.[18] As for the latter, the French have discovered that it is financially much more lucrative to provide reprocessing and enrichment *services* from large plants located in France (La Hague and Tricastin) than to export small-scale facilities at relatively low prices with the additional drawback of weakening the French situation on the world nuclear fuel market.[19] For the time being, therefore, France enjoys a unique position among Western nations: its non-proliferation policy coincides with the economic interests of its nuclear industry. History has shown that such a coincidence of interests is crucial to the successful implementation of a state's foreign nuclear policy.

The one exception to this situation is the case of the Osirak research reactor sold to Iraq in 1975. Following a long series of events, including the sabotage of the initial reactor core and many diplomatic exchanges with Baghdad, the French government confirmed in spring 1980 that it would sell Osirak according to the original terms of the contract (i.e. with a fuel core using 93 per cent enriched uranium) rather than with the new low-enriched 'caramel' fuel developed by the Commissariat Énergie Atomique (CEA). So far, this commitment has not been affected by the Iran–Iraq war, even though the reactor has been bombed by the Iranian Air Force, and that the war has hampered the implementation of IAEA safeguards.[20] While French officials insist that all the necessary precautions will be taken in order to prevent diversion of the highly enriched uranium (HEU) (through a variety of technical means), some lingering suspicions persist as to the proliferation potential of the Osirak reactor.[21] However, France's enormous dependence on Iraqi oil[22] would make the price of cancellation in this case too exorbitant to be contemplated. Moreover, following the events in Afghanistan, Iraq has become a key strategic asset for the West as a whole which is to be treated nicely: this perhaps explains why the United States has apparently recently stopped complaining about various Iraqi deals.

The situation in West Germany is profoundly different. While highly successful in the booming nuclear market of the early 1970s, Kraft Werke-Union (KWU) has suffered considerably from the depression of the world market in recent years, and more importantly, from the paralysis of the domestic nuclear programme. Until the recent Argentinian contract, West German industry had not had an order since 1975; by contrast, during the same period

Framatome has signed contracts for some 21 plants, 17 of them for the French domestic programme. Although KWU's production capability is in the order of eight reactors a year, the firm now has work on six contracts (not including the Argentinian one). By comparison, more than 33 reactors are currently being built in France. Given the situation of the domestic nuclear programme, exports have therefore become a matter of survival for the West German nuclear industry. This is fully understood by the West German Government which remains committed to atomic energy, despite the current environmental problems, and is thus determined to keep its industry alive until domestic conditions eventually allow a re-launching of the domestic programme. In such a context, the recent contracts signed with Argentina provides another illustration of the price that European suppliers are *not* willing to pay for non-proliferation. Although the West German bid was considerably higher than that of Atomic Energy of Canada Ltd (AECL) (in the range of $300 million), KWU did secure the contract because Bonn did not insist on full-scope safeguards while Ottawa did and because KWU's contract was linked to a separate deal signed with a 'Swiss' firm providing for the transfer of a heavy water production plant to Argentina.[23] While technically not a violation of the London Suppliers Group Guidelines, the Argentinian deal offers a disturbing sign of what could become a new phase of savage competition among suppliers, one that could turn out to be even more dangerous than that of the early 1970s, given the desperate situation of some nuclear industries.

In this connection, one should recall similar disturbing signs in Italy's behaviour[24] as well as the case of Switzerland which is involved in the West German–Argentinian deal. Similar pressures could also appear in Great Britain, should that country decide to go ahead with its plan to introduce a light water reactor (LWR) into its domestic programme. In such a case, a new British industry would have to be established, which might in turn require export outlays in order to be cost-effective. Such trends might even worsen in the future as other suppliers (Japan), as well as smaller European suppliers, emerge in an already highly competitive world market: this is the case in particular of Sweden, Finland (which is becoming active in Libya in connection with the Soviets) and perhaps at a later date Czechoslovakia which also is becoming involved in Soviet nuclear exports.

Thus after years of a bitter non-proliferation quarrel with the Carter Administration, the behaviour of European suppliers does display some disturbing trends. The record of the Carter policy points to much incoherence and confusion and certainly to a series of failures in changing European behaviour; many of the outstanding issues left over from the Ford Administration remain open and new ones have been added.

Disagreement still persists as to the definition and substance of non-proliferation policy and, more fundamentally, as to the price that Europeans are willing or able to pay in the name of such a policy. In this respect the cases of Iraq and Argentina are extremely revealing. Both point to the enormous vulnerability of Europeans to their particular energy status and to the link between the situation of their respective domestic nuclear programmes and their behaviour on the export market. In the final analysis, this means that, contrary to a belief widely held within environmental movements, anti-nuclear objectives and anti-proliferation ones are in fact mutually exclusive, rather than complementary. For the most effective way to promote a more responsible behaviour on the part of the European suppliers is to facilitate the growth of their domestic programmes, rather than the opposite. To a large extent, this lesson was not learned by the Carter Administration, whose policy in fact helped indirectly − if not willingly − European anti-nuclear groups (in particular in Germany), thereby making matters even worse in the non-proliferation area.

Despite these failures, the balance sheet of the Carter policy in the nuclear exports area should not be seen as entirely negative. A positive note deserves to be introduced in this otherwise sombre assessment in that the Carter Administration, by making non-proliferation a top-priority item in its foreign policy (at least until 1978−79), did help to generate in Europe a new awareness of the political and strategic risks associated with hasty nuclear exports.

To be sure, this awareness has not always had much effect, and it is somewhat difficult to predict how long such a constraint will remain active in Europe, particularly when the United States itself seems to be shifting its priorities once more, and giving much less importance to non-proliferation. This is all the more true when the European suppliers involved, in trying to save their nuclear programmes, have to compete for a very tight export market, and as a result, have to pay a high economic and political price for the sake of non-proliferation.

The Plutonium Controversy: European Energy Interests versus American Non-proliferation Policy

As seen from Europe, the decision by the Carter Administration to launch a major offensive against the 'plutonium economy', in April 1977, opened a *second* proliferation issue, distinct from the earlier controversy about nuclear exports. In essence, the new American anti-plutonium crusade represented a much more direct threat to European energy policies than did the earlier Ford policy on nuclear exports.

In the first place the Carter policy threatened the fast-growing and very costly breeder and reprocessing programmes under way in Europe, and particularly in France, which held a leading position in the world in both technologies. This European commitment to the breeder was in part based on economic considerations, namely the fear that uranium resources were becoming very scarce,[25] but also on political reasons; of all energy technologies, the fast breeder reactor (FBR) was seen as the one 'miraculous' source of autonomous energy for the future, the single most effective solution to the problem of Europe's tragic dependence on imported fuel. For the United States to go against this technology was therefore perceived not only as a selfish and irresponsible 'luxury' which only the Americans could afford, given its large domestic energy resources, but also as a political attempt to maintain Europe in its current state of vulnerability *vis-à-vis* foreign supply sources.

But more importantly perhaps, the Carter policy seemed to run counter to the very logic of nuclear power development *per se*, thereby encouraging a logic which, ironically, had first been promoted by the United States in the 1960s and which later became the Bible of European energy planners. It held that the present generation of thermal reactors simply constituted a transitory phase in the development of atomic power, to be followed by an era of 'plentiful self-generated energy produced by second generation breeder reactors using reprocessed fuel'.[26] Thus, to oppose that transition, as Carter did in April 1977, was to undermine the very rationale of the long-term nuclear programmes launched in Europe in the aftermath of the 1973 oil crisis.

In this context it is therefore not surprising that the Europeans perceived the Carter approach as fundamentally anti-nuclear and that they opposed it even more firmly than the earlier Ford policy on nuclear exports. The fundamental disagreement then, was less one of proliferation risks *per se*, than one about the true contribution of nuclear power to solving world energy problems. Is it a short-term parenthesis in the history of mankind or a major long-term energy source for the planet?

What lessons can be derived from this quarrel? Although the plutonium controversy is still without a solution, the interactions between the main actors (essentially the United States, France and West Germany) have brought to light many interesting — if not altogether positive — results. Two of these results merit some attention here. First, in reacting to the American policy, France and West Germany have tended to defend their own national interests rather than 'European' interests. Given the differences between the two states (both in weapons status and in the industrial level achieved in the breeder and reprocessing areas), this has led to a great deal of tension rather than to a united policy against the American anti-plutonium stand. Secondly, while the Europeans were partly successful in bringing about a gradual modification of the original Carter Administration policy, making it more compatible with European interests, this success is largely offset by the many uncertainties surrounding the future development of nuclear power.

1. European Behaviour: National Interests versus European Co-operation

One of the most interesting aspects of this transatlantic plutonium controversy has been the amount of tension which it has generated in intra-European nuclear relations. The main reason for this lies in the differences between France and West Germany in respect to nuclear weapons as well as the situation of their respective nuclear programmes (particularly in the breeder and reprocessing areas). These tensions, however, have emerged only gradually, in parallel with the evolution of American policy.

During the period immediately following the announcement of the Carter anti-plutonium policy, European reactions pointed to unity and cohesion against what was perceived as an unprecedented threat to European energy programmes. Political unity was evidenced first during the London summit meeting of May 1977. It was soon followed by a demonstration of technological and industrial unity in the breeder area — one that was most threatened by the American policy — with the signing of the

SERENA Agreement in July 1977 between France and West Germany with the participation of Italy, Belgium and the Netherlands.[27] A further example of European unity was given in the period immediately following the enactment of the NNPA in March 1978. Under French leadership, EURATOM as a whole decided not to comply with the requirement of the Act whereby a 'renegotiation' of the 1958 American–EURATOM Agreement had to be initiated within 1 month from the enactment of the NNPA.

These demonstrations of unity were not without 'arrière pensées', however, from the main European actors. France, in particular, promoted the SERENA Agreement because it reinforced French leadership in breeder technology. The Agreement also had the advantage of turning the French breeder programme into a 'European' one, thereby increasing its defences against further American aggressions. Similarly, although France had never been particularly eager to co-operate with EURATOM in the past, it found it very useful to encourage a joint response to the NNPA as a means to protest against the unilateral revision by the US Senate of a valid international agreement. But the main French motivation in this case was not only 'European'. Rather, the French feared that the inclusion of the right of *'prior consent'* for reprocessing in the 1958 American–EURATOM Agreement would jeopardise the expanding and very lucrative reprocessing business of the COGEMA facilities at La Hague.

However, when it became clear to the French, in the course of bilateral consultations with the United States in the summer and autumn of 1978, that the Americans had evolved in the meantime towards a more pragmatic and less dogmatic approach,[28] that the NNPA had 'grandfathered' La Hague, and that, as a result, the French breeder programme was not directly threatened by the American legislation, then the French tended to look for a separate arrangement with the United States in order to prepare for the post-INFCE world. Suddenly, several areas of convergence appeared between the two countries: co-operation was established in R&D work in the area of proliferation-resistant fuel for research reactors; the United States also showed interest in the French chemical exchange enrichment process while the French reacted favourably to President Carter's concept of an international fuel bank, as well as to the possibility of a plutonium repository scheme. Moreover, the French offered more conciliatory gestures when they cancelled the Pakistani reprocessing deal (in July 1978) and when they announced their opposition to thermal recycling.

This Franco—American rapprochement triggered a great deal of anxiety in West Germany and finally caused a very serious strain in the French—German 'couple', for several months in late 1978—79. The greatest West German fear was that this Franco—American 'détente' in the non-proliferation area would lead to a post-INFCE 'deal' concluded between the Western nuclear weapons states (the United States, Great Britain and France) at the expense of the non-weapons states in the industrialised world, with the latter being deprived of the right to own commercial reprocessing plants. In particular, the West Germans worried about the future of their planned Gorleben reprocessing centre, which, in contrast to La Hague, did not benefit from the 'grandfather' clause of the NNPA. In addition, West Germany opposed both France and the United States by insisting on its need for thermal recycling, and by rejecting the concept of an international fuel bank. Finally, in firmly maintaining the agreement signed with Brazil, West Germany added to the tension with Washington and further isolated itself from France. These tensions between France and West Germany culminated in late 1978 and early in 1979 during the highly secret bilateral negotiations on the status of the plutonium obtained after reprocessing of West German fuel at La Hague. The West Germans, fearing 'discrimination' by France, demanded immediate return of the plutonium to West Germany (presumably for recycling purposes). The French, on the other hand, insisted that the plutonium should be kept in France until West Germany could use it in breeder reactors. The dispute revived old fears of West German proliferation (in France) and of French domination and discrimination (in West Germany) and was actively exploited in both countries. Gaullist and Communist spokesmen in France accused Germany of making a bomb 'with the help of Giscard' (the latter having agreed to return the plutonium). Meanwhile, the West German press accused the French of taking advantage of their quasi-monopolistic situation in the reprocessing market in order to extract political concessions from Bonn. Further differences between the two countries surfaced after the European Court of Justice ruled in November 1978 that the EURATOM Treaty had to be applied fully by all members and without discrimination, which meant the revival of the supranational provisions of Chapter VI of the Treaty to which France, as a nuclear weapons state, had always refused to comply. One of the consequences of this ruling was that the EURATOM Supply Agency was henceforth entitled to exert direct control over the plutonium reprocessed at La Hague. While satisfying the West German 'non-discrimination' doctrine, this possibility was obviously unacceptable to the French and, as a result, France announced in 1979 its intention to ask for a revision of the EURATOM Treaty. Thus, while presumably allied against the American policy, France and West Germany spent the better part of 3 years fighting *their* internal plutonium battle.

2. *Après la bataille*

Although in the aftermath of INFCE's final conference in February 1980 neither of the two sides claimed 'victory' as to the outcome of the Evaluation, it is fair to say that, on balance, the Carter Administration has been unable to convince the Europeans (as well as the rest of the world) to forgo the 'plutonium economy'. Essentially, the key European actors maintained exactly the same policies in the reprocessing and breeder areas that they had established prior to 7 April 1977. To be sure, the European suppliers have developed an awareness of the special proliferation risks attached to plutonium, and some consensus has been reached on the notion that breeders should not be exported 'prematurely'. But, given the depressed state of the world nuclear market, the question of 'premature' exports of breeder reactors has become somewhat academic.

By contrast, when looking back at recent events, it is clear that the Europeans were quite successful in bringing about a gradual change in the original Carter policy. Interestingly enough, most of the changes in the original American policy were obtained in the very early stages of the controversy, when the Europeans reacted as a 'bloc' to Carter's speech and the NNPA. However, as soon as the Americans started to shift (essentially to the advantage of France) the situation became deadlocked again, as France and West Germany were now split, and as the controversy was deliberately frozen in the INFCE 'truce' as well as in bilateral consultations. Though this is not readily acknowledged by US officials (or ex-officials of the Carter Administration) the United States did gradually move from a position where breeders and reprocessing were simply ruled out, to one where the Americans recognised the 'special needs' of the developed nations from Europe and Japan, and merely asked (in 1978) 'those who bet on breeders' to behave responsibly in marketing these reactors.

Confirming this gradual evolution towards the recognition of the breeder, the Carter Administration went so far as to launch in August 1978 a $1.5 billion R&D breeder programme. In essence, by 1978–79 when efforts were being made within INFCE to restore some consensus between Europe and the United States on the post-INFCE nuclear regime, the Carter policy had shifted from an original universal 'no' to the plutonium economy to a more subtle question on 'where the line should be drawn between those States which can have breeders and reprocessing plants and those which cannot'. The irony, of course, is that by moving from this plain 'no', which was unacceptable to all of the Europeans, to this more subtle question, the Americans triggered a major quarrel among the Europeans themselves. For the question 'where do you draw the line' really raised the old problem of discrimination against West Germany and Japan. So far, no answer has been found to this question, though as noted earlier, the question alone has caused many tensions between West Germany and France, as well as between West Germany and the United States. In this connection, the conclusions of INFCE, as reflected in the Summary Report published in February 1980, are not very enlightening. On the whole, the Report largely contradicts the original Carter policy, by emphasising the resource limitations of the 'once-through' reactor system advocated by the Americans, and by stressing the economic advantages of plutonium recycle and fast breeder reactors.[29] Similarly, INFCE's Summary Report comes out in favour of reprocessing, and insists that safeguarding of reprocessing activities and plutonium (either in storage or in transport) 'can be readily carried out'. In addition, safeguards techniques for FBR cycles 'now being developed should enable effective safeguarding to be applied to future commercial FBRs, reprocessing and fuel fabrication plants at an acceptable cost'. The Report also mentions that 'development of a significant number of fast breeder reactors using current technology would be feasible by the year 2000'. The point, however, is that the conclusions of INFCE are far from providing a solid basis from which a new non-proliferation regime could be built in the future. In the first place, the conclusions of the Evaluation reflect the sum of various points of view from a variety of countries (industrialised, developing, suppliers and recipients of uranium and technology), rather than a true consensus among these nations.

This means that the key disagreements — between suppliers as well as between suppliers and recipients — still remain. As noted earlier, one of these disagreements involves the concept of full-scope safeguards which is not mentioned in the Summary Report, but which still remains a key provision of the NNPA of 1978. Another of such areas, where international consensus is still missing, is the whole issue of the future of the 'plutonium economy'. Here, although the Report comes out in favour of reprocessing and fast reactors, American policy in this area is still one of self-denial as well as direct or indirect denial of other nations' plutonium economy via the various provisions of the NNPA (right of 'prior consent' in particular). This entails that the problems which have plagued American–European and American–Japanese relations since the enactment of the NNPA in 1978 (i.e. renegotiation of the American–Euratom Agreement of 1958 and American right of prior approval of reprocessing by Japan, Sweden and other nations) still have to be resolved.

Secondly, despite certain proposals made in this direction during the final months of INFCE, no international mechanism has been established to deal, in the post-INFCE period, with countries deciding to acquire breeder and/or reprocessing facilities. Thus, the question of 'where to draw the line' remains open and can be expected to create more problems in the future both between industrialised nations and between 'North' and 'South'.

Finally, despite its generally pro-nuclear and pro-breeder tone, INFCE's final Report simply does not correspond to today's reality, namely to the stagnation of nuclear energy programmes in most countries, be they industrialised or developing. In a sense therefore, the 'non-proliferation battle' launched by Carter in April 1977 has ended in a draw. To be sure, the international community as a whole has rejected the denial policy proposed by the United States in respect to the 'plutonium economy'. But, on the other hand, as most nuclear programmes remain frozen in a state of deep depression, the commercialisation of breeder reactors in a significant number of countries has been postponed for a long time indeed. Despite a growing scarcity and insecurity of oil supplies, nuclear reactor orders remain extremely low: for a third consecutive year the number of reactor cancellations in the Western world exceeded that of new orders. (In 1980 the figures were 13 cancellations and 9 orders.)[30] As a result, it is becoming clear, even in those nations (such as France) which are heavily committed to the breeder, that the depressed market for nuclear power in the 1970s has probably postponed for a decade, perhaps longer, the time when fast reactors become commercially competitive because of the growing scarcity and rising price of uranium. Only at a much higher figure than today's uranium price can the electricity supply industry hope to offset a capital cost for the fast reactor currently expected to lie somewhere between 1.25 and 2 times the cost of equivalent pressurised water reactor (PWR) capacity.

Given this background, the fate of non-proliferation policy in the 1980s in the area of the 'plutonium economy' will in fact depend less on the (unlikely) settlement of the outstanding political issues among the various governments involved, than on the duration of the current cycle of nuclear depression. To be sure, the election of Reagan in the United States — who is considered to be much more pro-nuclear than his predecessor — may help a new start of nuclear power development in the United States; and this in turn would influence the situation elsewhere.[31]

Nonetheless, it is clear that the development of a new cycle of growth for nuclear power in the 1980s will be a function of a series of societal, economic and technical parameters, many of which are beyond the control of any government. In this connection, the case of West Germany is extremely enlightening: after fighting for 4 years against the United States (and France as well) in order to assert its right to own a large-scale reprocessing plant, Bonn has had to cancel its plans for the Gorleben facility, as a result of domestic pressures from local environmentalist groups. Thus, ironically, what the United States could not enforce upon West Germany by coercion (NNPA) or persuasion (INFCE) was self-inflicted by the West Germans themselves.

Lessons and Prospects

The above analysis points to the somewhat academic and unrealistic character of the nuclear controversy of the 1970s. In essence, the United States has been fighting to prevent a spread of breeder and reprocessing plants which in fact never took place. Meanwhile, the Europeans have been struggling to assert their rights to own such facilities, while most of these countries have been unable to keep their domestic programme active when confronted with increasing societal and economic pressures. The distressing aspect of this otherwise ironic situation is that while

Europeans and Americans were busily quarrelling over the future of the plutonium economy — which, in any case, they alone are technically and economically able to develop — clandestine proliferation by Third World countries using small-scale facilities has managed to proceed unhindered. A further distressing fact is that while a few of the non-proliferation objectives have been obtained, the plutonium controversy has greatly damaged the overall climate of European—American relations at a particularly inappropriate time, given the gravity of the current East—West crisis and the fragility of transatlantic relations in the present period.

If one lesson should be learned from the experience of the past decade, it is that non-proliferation policy is too complex an issue to be derived only from a series of abstract principles which can be written and rewritten according to the dominant fears of a given period. Similarly, non-proliferation simply cannot be based on apparently attractive technical or institutional 'fixes', which do not exist in practice. To do so can only jeopardise further the fragile non-proliferation system which was laboriously established since the 1950s.

In the future, the principal effort should concentrate on the tailoring of non-proliferation policy to the actual development of nuclear energy throughout the world. Had this been done in 1976, Europe and America would have been saved from fighting a largely irrelevant battle on the 'plutonium economy' and could have instead worked jointly towards managing the most pressing proliferation issues in the Third World, which have very little to do with the 'plutonium economy' and breeder reactors.

A further lesson to be learned from the experience of the 1970s is that, given the new realities of the international nuclear industry, the United States alone can no longer impose the 'rules of the game' of the world nuclear regime. Such a regime can only be based upon a new consensus between American and European suppliers as well as between suppliers and recipients. In this connection, one can only hope that the post-INFCE discussions now being conducted within a new organ of the IAEA — the so-called Committee for the Assurance of Supplies — will help to establish a more positive climate both for non-proliferation and for the development of nuclear energy in an oil-starved world. Here INFCE has perhaps defined what the guidelines of the new regime should be: namely, a trade-off between stable guarantees of supplies on the side of supplier nations, in exchange for guarantees of non-proliferation on the part of recipients.

However, one should caution against overly optimistic expectations. The 1980s will be an unfavourable period for non-proliferation policy. Given the deterioration of East—West relations, arms control in general will be more difficult to achieve in the coming decade. Indeed, as American—Soviet competition in the Third World intensifies, non-proliferation will most likely be sacrificed to short-term geostrategic objectives, with each side trying to preserve political and military links with key allies or client states in the Third World even at the cost of long-term non-proliferation objectives. Signs of such an evolution are already evident, such as American policy towards Pakistan and India since the Afghanistan crisis, as well as recent Soviet policy towards India, Libya and even Argentina.

Adding to the difficulties of conducting non-proliferation policy in such an environment, the process of proliferation is also likely to accelerate in the 1980s, as insecurity grows and as technology spreads further. Moreover, proliferation will also take on new characteristics, all of which will be more difficult to control by supplier nations. Some of these new factors are already evident; for example the emergence of new nuclear suppliers in the Third World, such as India and Argentina, the intensification of co-operation among Third World nations outside the controlled markets of Western nuclear suppliers, as well as the tendency on the part of certain Third World nations to move more and more openly towards a dedicated military nuclear programme by acquiring − often through clandestine or semi-clandestine channels − small-scale technology and facilities directly usable for military programmes (as was the case in the past of Taiwan, and South Korea, and today of Libya, Iraq, Pakistan and even Nigeria, among others).

Given this background, the task of the industrialised nuclear suppliers in the 1980s (both from the West and the East) will be formidable indeed. One can only hope, therefore, that the mistakes and the unnecessary quarrels of the 1970s will not be repeated as we enter a period which will most likely be more dangerous on the proliferation front as well as in other security areas. Decidedly, the 'nasty 1980s' already seem to deserve their name.[32]

Notes

1. Evidence that Pakistan was trying to build an enrichment plant to produce weapons-grade uranium caused the United States to cut off certain military

and economic aid in April 1979, as required by the 1977 Symington Amendment. That decision was reversed after the Soviet invasion of Afghanistan in December 1979, when the Americans renewed offers of military assistance to Pakistan. Similarly, India's refusal to accept full-scope safeguards on all its nuclear facilities, in accordance with the 1978 Non-Proliferation Act, should have entailed a total American embargo on nuclear deliveries to India (in particular nuclear fuel for the American-built Tarapur power station). However, despite the opposition of the Nuclear Regulatory Commission, and some resistance in the Congress, the Carter Administration decided, in summer 1979, to reverse its earlier embargo and to ship nuclear fuel to India, in order to salvage political relations between the two countries.

2. A good summary of all these events is to be found in Bertrand Goldschmidt, *Le Complexe Atomique* (Paris, 1980) pp. 411–80.
3. ibid.
4. Thomas Neff and Henry D. Jacoby, 'Non-Proliferation Strategy in a Changing Nuclear Fuel Market', *Foreign Affairs*, LVII (1978–79); Paul L. Joskow 'The International Nuclear Industry Today: The End of the American Monopoly', *Foreign Affairs*, LIV (1975–76); David Fishlock, 'A Year to Grasp the Nettle', *Financial Times* (Survey), 5 December 1980.
5. See Pierre Lellouche, 'International Nuclear Politics', *Foreign Affairs*, LVII (1978–79).
6. See Pierre Lellouche, 'France in the International Nuclear Energy Controversy: A New Policy under Giscard d'Estaing', *Orbis*, XXII (1978–79).
7. France sold a single power gas graphite to Spain, in addition to the Dimona research reactor exported to Israel; West Germany had managed to export only one PHWR to Argentina.
8. Statement by Arthur Goldberg, American Ambassador to the United Nations in May 1968, quoted in Karl Kaiser, 'The Great Nuclear Debate – German–American Disagreements', *Foreign Policy*, no. 30, spring 1978.
9. See Albert Wohlstetter, 'Spreading the Bomb without Quite Breaking the Rules', *Foreign Policy*, no. 25, winter 1976–77.
10. Parenthetically, it is important to note that this situation of mutual suspicion about the other side's commercial motivations runs throughout the entire controversy: as noted above such suspicion was evident in the mid-1970s with respect to nuclear exports to the Third World, but they also appeared later in the plutonium controversy which we shall analyse in the following section.
11. Kaiser, loc. cit., p. 89.
12. In this connection, it is useful to recall that the United States did conclude in the 1950s an unusually liberal safeguards agreements with EURATOM (as compared with its overall policy at the time) in order to promote the 'penetration' of the American nuclear industry in Europe in the late 1950s. See Warren J. Donnelly, 'Commercial Nuclear Power in Europe: The Interaction of American Diplomacy with a New Technology', US House of Representatives, *Science Technology and American Diplomacy* (Washington, DC, 1977).
13. See Horst Mendershausen, 'International Cooperation in Nuclear Fuel Services: European and American Approaches' (Santa Monica, California, 1978).

14. While this reasoning is often perceived in the United States as a convenient justification for European nuclear exports in the Third World, it is important to note that such reasoning is widely shared in Europe and that it has been proved correct by history as for example, by the failure of American attempts to prevent the Europeans from acquiring an autonomous enrichment industry.

15. See below, pp. 192–9.

16. See below, p. 189.

17. Pierre Lellouche and Richard Lester, 'The Crisis of Nuclear Energy', *The Washington Quarterly*, summer 1979.

18. In addition to 34 power stations currently under construction in France, Framatome holds orders from South Africa (two units), Korea (two units), and possibly more from China. The two units ordered by Iran in 1975 have been cancelled by the Islamic Government.

19. This economic element has played an important part in the decision, announced in September 1978, to cancel the contract signed with Pakistan. Politically this cancellation was also useful in terms of American–French relations: by behaving in a 'responsible' manner in the exports area, the French could demand in return more consideration on the part of the United States for France's plutonium programme.

20. The Iraqi Government has argued that the state of war with Iran made it 'unsafe' for IAEA inspectors to effectively control Iraqi nuclear facilities. [This was written before the Israeli strike of June 1981 – editors.]

21. Interestingly enough, these proliferation risks are not limited to the HEU itself, but to the plutonium to be produced by Osirak. Here the matter is further complicated by the interference of another European supplier, namely Italy, which is currently building a large plutonium 'hot cell' in Iraq and is training a large number of Iraqi technicians in Italian facilities in reprocessing technology. In so doing, Italy also hopes to sell a large commercial reactor to Iraq and to secure stable oil deliveries.

22. Prior to the Iran–Iraq war, Iraqi oil represented 20 per cent of total French oil imports, ranking second behind imports from Saudi Arabia.

23. See *Nucleonics Week*, 31 May and 27 September 1979.

24. See for example, Amory B. Lovins, L. Hunter Lovins and Leonard Ross, 'Nuclear Power and Nuclear Bombs', *Foreign Affairs*, LVIII (1979–80).

25. For example, André Giraud (then head of the French CEA) assessed the breeder's contribution to the uranium issue in 1978 in the following terms: 'France owns estimated natural uranium reserves of 100,000 tons. While these reserves are large, consumed in light water reactor, they nonetheless represent 800 Mtoe or one third of the North Sea oil reserves. Through the use of breeder reactors this uranium can produce 50,000 Mtoe, the equivalent of all the Middle-East oil reserves'.

   A speech before the Conference of the Japanese Atomic Industrial Forum, 8 May 1978, CEA *Notes d'Information*, no. 4, Apr. 1978.

26. Alvin M. Weinberg, 'Nuclear Energy; A Prelude to H. G. Wells' Dream', *Foreign Affairs*, IL (1970–71).

27. For an analysis of the SERENA agreement, see Pierre Lellouche, *Internationalization of the Nuclear Fuel Cycle and Non-Proliferation Strategy* (New York, forthcoming).

28. In this respect, the turning point was the Uranium Institute speech by Joseph Nye in July 1978 in London.
29. For a useful analysis of INFCE's Summary Report as compared with American Non-Proliferation policy, see Warren H. Donnelly, 'Conclusions and Observations in the Summary Report of INFCE which relate to US Non-Proliferation Policies', in US Congress, *Nuclear Proliferation Factbook*, (Washington, DC, 1980 edn) pp. 446–57.
30. Fishlock, loc. cit.
31. It is unclear, however, at this point, how much of an effect the Reagan Administration will have in resolving the social and economic obstacles which have plagued nuclear power growth in the United States during the 1970s. See Llewellyn King, 'Reagan Unlikely to Reverse Decline', *Financial Times* (Survey), 5 December 1980.
32. This chapter is a revised version of an article originally published in *International Organization*, xxxv (1981). Permission to republish is gratefully acknowledged.

14 Non-proliferation and Developing Countries

Olga Šuković

Introduction

The problem of preventing the proliferation of nuclear weapons and the commitments of nuclear-weapon states (NWSs) towards non-nuclear-weapon states (NNWSs) has become even more urgent during the past few years for mainly two reasons: first, the continuation of the nuclear arms race and, secondly, because of the energy crisis in 1973.

The efforts of the international community to end the arms race, and especially the nuclear arms race, have not resulted in an undertaking of such measures as would constitute genuine disarmament measures. The results achieved in this area are very modest, to say the least. Instead of reducing the stockpiles of nuclear weapons we have been witnessing daily a growing accumulation of nuclear weapons and their qualitative improvement. It is presumed that today the two leading nuclear powers have at their disposal huge stocks of these weapons. According to the Stockholm International Peace Research Institute (SIPRI), the number of vehicles deployed in the United States for delivery of strategic nuclear weapons has reached 2002, with the total number of warheads reaching 9200, while the Soviet Union has 2504 vehicles with 6000 nuclear warheads.[1] In addition to strategic weapons, the two superpowers also possess an enormous number of so-called tactical nuclear weapons. For example, it is considered that the total number of American tactical nuclear warheads amounts to 22,000, of which 7173 are located in Europe. As far as the Soviets are concerned, it is believed that they have 3500 tactical nuclear warheads in the European area.

Parallel with the nuclear arms race there has evolved a process of greater use of nuclear energy for peaceful purposes. The tendency became even more apparent following the 1973 energy crisis when it became clear that a large number of countries, in securing their alternative sources of energy, had to rely on nuclear energy. This trend, however, involves the inherent danger of having nuclear energy intended for peaceful purposes used for military purposes. The number of states using nuclear energy for peaceful purposes has been registering a constant growth, as has the number of nuclear reactors and power plants. For example, the first nuclear power plant of 5 megawatts was constructed and set in operation in 1954. In 1968 nuclear power stations having capacity of 9000 megawatts were already in operation, while at the end of 1979 their capacity, in 22 countries, increased to 128,000 megawatts. It has been estimated that the capacity of nuclear power plants will double by 1985, though this estimate probably will not be realised due to the latest development in the export policy of major nuclear supplier countries and anti-nuclear movements in some developed countries.

Although these data do not prove a direct link between nuclear power plants and the proliferation of nuclear weapons, one should not discount the link between the effects of using nuclear energy for peaceful purposes and the enlargement of the circle of countries acquiring nuclear weapons. Although peaceful and military aspects of nuclear energy are intrinsically linked and it is impossible to separate them, one should, however, bear in mind that in fact the first nuclear reactors in the United States, the Soviet Union and Great Britain were built not to generate electricity but to manufacture plutonium for nuclear weapons. At the same time, to this day it is impossible to generate electricity in a peaceful reactor without at the same time using or manufacturing materials that could be used for nuclear weapons. As a result any nation which acquires a nuclear reactor for peaceful purposes will have personnel trained in nuclear technology, from which it is only a short step to the acquisition of nuclear-weapon technology. If the materials for making nuclear weapons were also available, such a nation would become a potential NWS. Thus, the widespread use of nuclear energy for peaceful purposes is likely to lead to 'horizontal' proliferation, that is an increase in the number of

NWSs. Such proliferation would constitute a great threat to the security of mankind, as it greatly increases the probability of the outbreak of nuclear war.

However, the present level in the development of nuclear technology and techniques, the limited resources of conventional fuels, the energy crisis and the ever-growing price of oil have increased global interest in the broadest possible use of nuclear energy for peaceful purposes. The economic importance of nuclear energy is derived from the need to introduce new scientific achievement, especially for developing countries.

The danger inherent in the international spread of nuclear energy has been universally recognised from the beginning of the nuclear age. As a result, the international community has sought to deal with this problem in two interrelated ways: first, through international instruments to prevent further spread of nuclear weapons, and secondly, to make available through international instruments − bilateral or multilateral − to all countries, on the basis of equality, the benefits of nuclear energy for peaceful purposes. Ignoring either of these two components of so-called 'nuclear dilemma' could be only to the detriment of international peace and security.

Having in mind these general remarks, this chapter will deal with three main issues: efforts to halt nuclear weapon proliferation; the non-proliferation regime under the NPT; and non-proliferation and developing countries.

Efforts to halt Nuclear Weapon Proliferation

Efforts to prevent the use of nuclear technology for military purposes and to provide guarantees for applying nuclear energy solely for peaceful purposes actually began at the time of the discovery and the use of the atomic bomb in 1945. Already at that time states and international organisations were making efforts to solve the dilemma posed by nuclear energy and its potentials.

The first attempt to control the development and dissemination of nuclear technology as a peaceful source of energy, while at the same time preventing the proliferation of nuclear weapons, was based on an American report, known as the Acheson−Lilienthal Report (1945). The Report emphasised the positive aspects of control and insisted on the need to reserve certain 'dangerous' activities in nuclear energy development as matters for international ownership and control. It called also for the creation of an international atomic energy authority which would own and operate all nuclear facilities ranging from uranium mines to research and production plants throughout the world.

Although the Charter of the United Nations, which was signed prior to the use of the atomic bomb, does not contain provisions relating either to the bomb or to the use of nuclear energy, the first resolution of the General Assembly of the United Nations, adopted unanimously on 24 January 1946, dealt with control and use of nuclear energy. By this resolution the UN General Assembly established the Atomic Energy Commission and asked the Commission to make specific proposals: for an exchange of basic scientific information in the interests of using nuclear energy for peaceful purposes; for control of atomic energy in order to ensure its use only for peaceful purposes; for elimination from national armaments of atomic weapons; and for effective safeguards, through inspection and other means, in order to exercise the necessary control.[2] These principles continue to serve as the basis for all future efforts exerted in the area of nuclear energy and its peaceful uses. As will be demonstrated later in this chapter, problems which the United Nations already faced in 1946 have still not been solved.

The United States presented to the UN Atomic Energy Commission a control plan (known as the Baruch plan) based on proposals already made in the Acheson–Lilienthal Report. The plan failed to gain acceptance by the Soviet Union which feared an American monopoly in this new technology. In the following years the negotiations conducted between the great powers and within the UN to reach an agreement on the international control of the use of nuclear energy and to prohibit nuclear weapons did not result in the conclusion of international treaties. This was a result of the gradual deterioration of relations between the United States and the Soviet Union. The nuclear monopoly of the United States soon came to an end with the explosion of a nuclear device by the Soviets in 1949. At the time of the Baruch plan, the United States was the only known possessor of the technology for fabrication of nuclear explosive weapons. It had already refused to share the A-bomb secrets with its wartime allies, Great Britain and Canada. By its Atomic Energy Act of 1946, it even cut off the flow of information on civil nuclear power development anticipated under options on technical co-operation provided for in wartime agreements.

This action only increased the determination of these countries to go alone. As a result Great Britain launched its own military and civil programmes and succeeded in exploding its first nuclear device in 1952, while Canada confined its efforts to civil programmes. France demonstrated an ability to develop and explode a nuclear device in 1960. Thus Great Britain and France separately and independently joined the so-called 'nuclear club'.

The Soviet Union for its part initiated close co-operation with China in the nuclear field by supplying a research reactor and helping to develop China's uranium resources. Considerable know-how was transferred and thousands of Chinese scientists received training in the Soviet Union. Although this co-operation was ended in 1959, China carried out a nuclear weapon test in 1964. According to one opinion, 'the limitation and counter-productive effects of the principle of denial of technology as a main element of policy has thus been established and "horizontal" proliferation was already a reality' at that time.[3]

Following the Americans' failure to gain international acceptance of their proposals for international ownership and control of nuclear energy and facilities, they initiated in 1953 the 'Atoms for Peace' programme to share the benefits of peaceful application of nuclear energy with other countries. Although several reasons could be advanced to explain this far-reaching decision, it suffices to point to the fact that, after the American monopoly in nuclear weapons had been broken by the Soviet Union, it was no use denying peaceful nuclear technology to friendly countries in Western Europe and elsewhere. The result of the Atoms for Peace programme was a large-scale and world-wide transfer of peaceful nuclear technology. This programme also led to the creation of the IAEA in 1957.

The IAEA was created 'to encourage and assist research on, and development and practical application of, atomic energy for peaceful uses throughout the world' and to provide for 'development of and practical application of nuclear energy for peaceful purposes, including the production of electric power, with due consideration for the needs of the under-developed areas of the world', as well as 'to establish and administer safeguards designed to ensure that special fissionable and other materials are not used in such a way as to further any military purpose' (Article III, A, 1, 2 and 5).

Although the number of nuclear weapon states has not increased further, it soon became clear that the increased application of nuclear technology for peaceful purposes could lead to proliferation because of the possibility of using nuclear energy for military purposes unless adequate measures were adopted. The earliest efforts in the United Nations to draft a treaty which would insure that atomic energy would be used exclusively for peaceful purposes had as one of its aims the prevention of the spread of nuclear weapons. The first proposals dealing directly with the spread of nuclear weapons were advanced by the Soviet Union and the United States in the Sub-Committee of the Disarmament Commission in 1956–57. During these discussions two different approaches to the problem of preventing the spread of nuclear weapons were developed, namely, the creation of NWFZs from which all nuclear weapons would be prohibited, and secondly, agreement on a treaty which would specifically ban the dissemination of nuclear weapons by the nuclear powers and the acquisition of nuclear weapons by states not possessing them.

The question of conclusion of a treaty on non-proliferation of nuclear weapons was raised for the first time in the General Assembly in 1958, by Ireland, and at the following session the General Assembly adopted, on 20 November 1959, resolution 1380 (XIV). This resolution pointed to the danger of an increase in the number of states possessing nuclear weapons, and it was suggested, *inter alia*, that the Ten Nation Disarmament Committee should explore possibilities for preventing such a danger, 'including the feasibility of an international agreement, subject to inspection and control, whereby the powers producing nuclear weapons would refrain from handing over the control of such weapons to any nation not possessing them and whereby the powers not possessing such weapons would refrain from manufacturing them'.[4]

Along with the efforts to halt the wider dissemination of nuclear weapons, suggestions were made that an agreement to ban the testing of nuclear weapons could be considered as a separate measure pending progress towards an agreement on more comprehensive forms of disaramament. The numerous proposals and discussions in the United Nations, and especially the trilateral negotiations between the Soviet Union, Great Britain and the United States, led finally to the Treaty Banning Nuclear Weapons Tests in the Atmosphere, in Outer Space and Under Water, signed in Moscow on 5 August 1963. Later that year and during the following years the General Assembly called upon all states to become parties to the Treaty and up to 31 December 1979 111 states had become signatories.[5] It must, however, be stressed that, according to some writers, a concern about the public health hazards of radioactive materials being deposited in the atmosphere, rather than a direct campaign in non-proliferation terms, was the genesis of the pressure for a ban on nuclear weapons tests.[6]

Parallel with the efforts to halt proliferation of nuclear weapons, two other kinds of measures deserve mention: the prevention of the militarisation, or military nuclearisation, of areas or environments; and the creation of NWFZs. The first kind of measures led to the conclusion of several agreements. These include: the Antarctic Treaty of 1959, which declares the Antarctic an area to be used exclusively for peaceful purposes by prohibiting any measures of a military nature, such as the establishment of military bases and fortifications, and carrying out of military manoeuvres or testing of any type of weapon, as well as the disposal of radioactive material waste in Antarctica; the Treaty on Principles governing the Activities of States in the Exploration and Use of Outer Space, including the Moon and other Celestial Bodies (1967), which prohibits the placing in orbit around the Earth of any objects carrying nuclear weapons or any other kind of weapons of mass destruction, the installation of such weapons on celestial bodies, or the stationing of them in outer space in any other manner; and the Treaty on the Prohibition of the Emplacement of Nuclear Weapons and other Weapons of Mass Destruction on the Sea-Bed and the Ocean Floor and in the Subsoil thereof (1971). Although there have been many proposals for creation of nuclear-weapons-free zones, the only treaty signed up to now is the Treaty for the Prohibition of Nuclear Weapons in Latin America (1967) which prohibits the testing, use, manufacture, production or acquisition by any means, as well as the receipt, storage, installation, deployment and any other form of possession of any nuclear weapons by Latin American countries. The parties to the Treaty are to conclude agreements with the IAEA for application of safeguards to their nuclear activities. The proposals for creation of NWFZs with respect to different geographical areas including the Balkans, the Mediterranean, the Middle East, Africa, South-East Asia and the Indian Ocean have not so far led, in spite of numerous resolutions of the UN General Assembly, to the signing of agreements.

It should be also mentioned that the United States and the

Soviet Union have signed several arms control agreements, among the most important of which are the Treaty on the Limitation of Anti-Ballistic Missile Systems (1972), the Interim Agreement on Certain Measures with Respect to the Elimination of Strategic Offensive Arms (SALT I, 1972), the Agreement on the Prevention of Nuclear War (1973), the Protocol to the Treaty on the Limitation of Anti-Ballistic Missile Systems (1974), the Treaty on Limitation of Underground Nuclear Weapons Tests (1974), the Joint US–Soviet Statement on the Question of Further Limitation of Strategic Offensive Arms (1974), the Treaty on Underground Nuclear Explosions for Peaceful Purposes (1976) and several documents signed in Vienna in 1979 of which the most important are the Treaty on the Limitation of Strategic Offensive Arms (SALT II) and the Protocol to the Treaty on the Limitation of Strategic Offensive Arms.[7] (Not all of these measures are yet operational at the time of writing.)

Although one cannot ignore the importance of these agreements, particularly for US–Soviet overall relations, it should be stressed that they are of marginal importance from the point of view of halting so-called vertical proliferation and even more from the point of view of general and complete disarmament.

The Non-Proliferation Regime under the NPT

Fears of so-called horizontal proliferation to Nth countries led in 1968 to signing of the NPT. The NPT is considered to be one of the major arms control agreements thus far concluded. It has set up a regime of non-proliferation which has been effective during the last 10 years in spite of the fact that many state parties have serious objections as to its discriminatory character while many other countries refused to accept it mainly for the same reasons. But in spite of shortcomings of the NPT, the main aim should be to strengthen the regime thus created, while at the same time efforts should be made to find more equitable and more efficient means to halt further proliferation.

From the text of the NPT one may deduce that the term 'nuclear weapon proliferation' implies the acquisition, by manufacture or transfer, of nuclear weapons or devices, by any state which had not manufactured or exploded a nuclear weapon or other nuclear explosive device prior to 1 January 1967 (Articles II and IX.3).

Also, it is clear from the Preamble of the Treaty that the proliferation of nuclear weapons is undesirable because it is believed
that 'the proliferation of nuclear weapons would seriously enhance
the danger of nuclear war'. This belief, coupled with some recent
developments in peaceful uses of nuclear energy, which will be discussed later in this chapter, has created serious problems and has
even at some junctures brought into question the very existence of
the regime created by the NPT.

Before dealing with problems which have emerged during the
last few years in the field of nuclear energy and the interrelation-
ship between the military and peaceful uses of nuclear energy, it
will be useful to point out the main features of the regime created
on the basis of the NPT. The core of the non-proliferation regime
is the obligations undertaken in Articles I and II of the NPT.
Under Article I NWSs have undertaken an obligation 'not to
transfer to any recipient whatsoever nuclear weapons or other
nuclear explosive devices or control of such weapons or devices' as
well as not to 'assist, encourage or induce any non-nuclear-weapon
state to manufacture or otherwise acquire' such weapons or
devices. As a counter-obligation, NNWSs have undertaken 'not to
receive . . . nuclear weapons or other nuclear explosive devices' or
'control over such weapons or explosive devices' either through
transfer, manufacture or any other manner from other states.
Although there is no explicit prohibition in the Treaty, it should
be interpreted in such a way as prohibiting NWS parties to the
Treaty from extending such assistance to or encouraging NNWSs
non-parties to the NPT from manufacturing such weapons. NWSs
retained their right – in addition to retaining their nuclear
arsenal – to assist one another in the development of nuclear warheads and in further testing of the same. They also retained the
right to receive from any state material and equipment needed for
the implementation of their nuclear programmes as well as the
right to station nuclear weapons on the territories of other states.

Article III of the NPT relates to control and inspection. This
Article actually reflects the discriminatory status to which NNWSs
are subjected. Safeguards were only accepted by the NNWSs,
while there are no provisions on the verification of the obligations
assumed by NWSs with respect to nuclear weapons or nuclear
explosive devices used for peaceful purposes. In other words, only
nuclear activities of NNWSs intended for peaceful purposes are
subject to control. The purpose of the control, in effect, is to

prevent nuclear energy for peaceful purposes being used for military development. The same article specifies an obligation of signatory states not to supply fissionable materials and equipment to NNWSs whether or not signatory of the NPT, the only exception being material subject to control under the NPT. This is to say that even those states that have not signed the NPT must accept the IAEA safeguards over the sources of special fissionable materials used for peaceful purposes. Also, at the request of developed NWSs, a provision was incorporated whereby the control exercised in pursuance of the NPT would not in any way retard or prevent the development of nuclear energy and its application for peaceful purposes. There are two problems arising from this article. First, not all parties to the NPT have concluded agreements with IAEA. By December 1979 only 66 out of 108 NNWSs had fulfilled this obligation. Many of the states which have not signed such agreements are states which as yet have no significant nuclear activities, although this does not absolve them from observing the Treaty provisions.[8] The most serious problem, however, is the discriminatory application of Article IV regarding NWSs and nuclear supplies from parties to non-parties of the Treaty. Although NWSs are not obliged to apply IAEA safeguards to their peaceful nuclear activities, this question has been raised both by other industrial countries and by developing countries. After the First Review Conference, Great Britain has voluntarily submitted its non-military nuclear installations to safeguards under IAEA supervision, while negotiations to the same end between the United States and IAEA are under way. France, which is not party to the NPT, signed an agreement under which part of its nuclear facilities will be placed under IAEA safeguards. However, the right of these states to withdraw nuclear material from civilian activities and to use it for military purposes has remained unaffected. This kind of verification has more psychological effect because safeguarded peaceful activities in countries with unrestricted military nuclear programmes seem meaningless.

Article IV of the NPT was introduced at the insistence of NNWSs as a counterbalance to their obligation not to produce nuclear weapons or nuclear explosive devices. It recognises an inalienable right of all contracting parties to develop, produce and use nuclear energy for peaceful purposes without discrimination, in conformity with Articles I and II of the NPT. Moreover, NWSs assume an obligation to facilitate the exchange of equipment, materials and scientific and technological information for the use of nuclear energy in peaceful programmes, bearing in mind the special needs of the developing areas of the world. They also acknowledge the obligation to provide services, at low prices, in order to promote peaceful applications of nuclear explosions (Article V of the NPT). There is to be no discrimination in this area and these states are to exercise this right through appropriate international bodies.

Provisions of Article VI of the NPT relate to disarmament measures. It was the NNWSs that insisted upon this provision in order to establish a balance between 'horizontal' and 'vertical' proliferation. Since NWSs refused to introduce into the NPT a commitment regarding specific disarmament measures or time limits, the notion was promoted that the NPT should serve as a transitory phase in the process of nuclear disarmament. However, the obligation assumed by the NWSs was not to disarm, but to negotiate 'in good faith' to end the nuclear arms race as soon as possible and eventually to proceed towards nuclear disarmament by signing an agreement on general and complete disarmament. Even though the two superpowers have been conducting negotiations for an extended period of time, the results are very modest and relate only to some partial measures in the field of arms control, while genuine disarmament measures are absent.

It is obvious from this brief description of the NPT provisions that it is primarily concerned with the interests of the leading nuclear powers. They achieved what they had hoped to achieve from the very outset: the conclusion of an agreement which would only serve to prevent the further horizontal proliferation of nuclear weapons. Because of the specific nature of the NPT, the nuclear weapons of these powers have remained outside the scope of legal regulation, and consequently they are free to act as they consider in their best interests, avoiding precision about their rôle in the solution of some other questions directly associated with the non-proliferation.

The NPT has been signed and ratified by 114 countries. All NNWSs which are parties to the Treaty are obliged to open their nuclear facilities to IAEA safeguards. Only three of five NWSs, that is states which prior to 1 January 1967 had manufactured and exploded a nuclear weapon or other nuclear explosive device, are parties to the Treaty. France has stated that, while it would not sign the NPT, it would behave in future in that field exactly as the states adhering to the Treaty.[9] China has stated that it is firmly against using the NPT to deprive NNWSs or countries with few nuclear weapons of their sovereignty. In practice it has not, however, acted contrary to the non-proliferation objectives.[10] Also, a considerable group of so-called 'near-nuclear' countries are not parties to the NPT. India, Pakistan, Israel and South Africa all refused to sign the Treaty. In Latin America certain states with major nuclear programmes (Argentina and Brazil) are not parties to the NPT.

The efforts of the non-aligned and developing countries to remedy the shortcomings of the NPT were aimed first at improving the Treaty as such at the First Review Conference held in Geneva in 1975. The Conference took place in an atmosphere which reflected the dissatisfaction of many of the NNWS parties to the Treaty with the way in which it had been implemented by the NWSs. From the outset, divergent views were expressed with regard to the objectives of the Conference, the implementation of the provisions of the Treaty and the measures that should be taken to strengthen it. The NWSs and some of the NNWSs stressed that the principal purpose of the Conference was to strengthen the Treaty by encouraging a wider adherence to it and by taking measures towards a more effective safeguards system designed to prevent the diversion of nuclear material and technology to military purposes. Those states felt, on the whole, that the Treaty had its primary purposes both as an instrument to prevent the spread of nuclear weapons and as the most appropriate framework for international co-operation in the peaceful uses of nuclear energy. On the other hand, many NNWSs, including a number of developing countries, held that the Conference's main objective was to make a thorough, critical examination of the Treaty's operation in order to determine whether all its provisions were being implemented and to adopt the measures required to fill in gaps and remedy any inadequacies that might emerge from such an examination. Most of these countries believed that, while it was vital that the Treaty should be strengthened and that all states should accede to it, the goal could be best accomplished on the basis of an acceptable balance of mutual responsibilities and obligations of the nuclear and non-nuclear parties to the Treaty.

In the discussion of the provisions of the Treaty relating to the non-proliferation of nuclear weapons all participants agreed that Articles I and II had been fully observed by the parties to the

Treaty. In the debate on the provisions of the Treaty relating to the peaceful application of nuclear energy, virtually all speakers commended the IAEA for the manner in which it had thus far carried out its safeguards activities pursuant to Article III of the Treaty. Many participants stressed the need to improve and strengthen the IAEA safeguards further; some countries specifically advocated the standardisation and universal application of these safeguards. Several non-nuclear countries contended that Article III placed the NNWS parties to the Treaty at a disadvantage in comparison with states who were not parties to the Treaty, in that the latter countries could import nuclear materials and equipment without having to submit all their peaceful nuclear activities to IAEA safeguards.

A number of non-nuclear weapon developing countries expressed dissatisfaction with the implementation of Article IV, in particular with what they regarded as the inadequacy of technical assistance in the field of nuclear energy given to developing countries party to the Treaty. They pointed out that non-parties to the Treaty, including some relatively advanced countries, had benefited considerably more from the transfer of nuclear technology and equipment than countries parties to the Treaty, and stated that developing countries should be given preferential treatment and increased technical assistance through IAEA.

It was further pointed out at the Conference that nuclear assistance had been extended more readily to non-parties of the Treaty than to parties. If non-nuclear parties were not receiving the benefits provided by Aricle IV, it was because nuclear assistance was being sold for commercial profits or awarded as a political prize to prospective friendly states not necessarily NPT parties. Thus the Declaration noted that state parties to the NPT should 'give due weight' to NPT adherence in reaching decisions regarding the provision of nuclear material or technology for peaceful uses.

The most controversial views were expressed in regard to Article VI of the Treaty. The majority of the NNWSs, in particular developing countries, held that the NWSs had not adequately fulfilled their obligations to negotiate effective measures to halt the nuclear arms race and achieve nuclear disarmament. Many states, developed and developing, pointed out that over the preceding 5 years the pace of the nuclear arms race, far from slackening as envisaged in Article VI, had actually accelerated. A large number of NNWSs, including some of the developed countries, expressed the view that, while the immediate objective of the Treaty was to prevent 'horizontal' proliferation of nuclear weapons, the Treaty would lose its credibility unless efforts were also made to prevent 'vertical' proliferation; the two were regarded as interrelated processes which, in order to redress the original inbalance of the NPT, should be achieved simultaneously. Some asserted that the failure of the Treaty depended primarily on the implementation of Article VI by the nuclear powers.

In reply to this view, both the United States and the Soviet Union maintained that the arms control agreements concluded since the Treaty had gone into effect, including three major agreements to limit offensive and defensive strategic weapons reached in the SALT negotiations and at Vladivostok in 1974, represented considerable progress towards the implementation of Article VI.[11]

Another major issue at the Conference was the question of security assurances and guarantees to NNWSs. A number of states held that the security assurances provided in Security Council Resolution 255 (1968) and the declarations made by the three nuclear powers in that connection were inadequate and should be replaced by more comprehensive and effective guarantees. In the view of many of these countries, the NWSs should undertake legally binding commitments not to use or threaten to use nuclear weapons against NNWS parties to the Treaty — the so-called 'negative assurances'. The nuclear powers opposed these proposals.

The Review Conference concluded its work with the adoption, by consensus, of a Final Declaration. However, the Declaration adopted can in no way be considered a satisfactory document from the standpoint of the verification of measures undertaken towards arresting vertical proliferation of nuclear weapons as well as towards more equitable participation of all states parties in the peaceful uses of nuclear energy. The Declaration, for the most part, reflects the interests of NWSs and does not reflect in a true light the positions and conclusions of a large number of participating states in the Conference, especially developing and non-aligned countries. It does not contain a critical analysis of the 5-year period of the implementation of the NPT, nor of the behaviour of member states of the NPT towards their commitments, nor conversely of adequate measures to improve the existing situation which remains unchanged. Although the Final

Declaration was adopted by consensus, as has already been mentioned, a number of delegations expressed dissatisfaction about the outcome of the Conference, made interpretive statements contradicting the consensus or objected outright to various formulations.

Non-Proliferation and Developing Countries

During the last few years there has been a heated debate among states and scientists on the meaning of some of the provisions of the NPT. Although during this debate many different views have been expressed, it seems that the question of the relationship between the provisions on prohibition of transfer and acquisition of nuclear weapons and those concerning the peaceful uses of nuclear energy have been central. These differences exist not only among NWSs and NNWSs, but more and more they are becoming a stumbling block between developed and developing countries. Within this spectrum of opinions two extremes stand out: first, the opinion of those who consider that the NPT is primarily an arms control agreement and that as a result provisions of Articles I and II should prevail over other provisions of the Treaty and, secondly, the opinion of those who consider that priority should be given to Article IV which deals with the right of parties to develop the peaceful uses of nuclear energy and to receive assistance for this purpose from other states.

No-one can deny the fact that the primary objective of the NPT is non-proliferation of nuclear weapons. But at the same time one should not discard the fact that Article IV was originally included as a compensation for countries forgoing their rights to acquire nuclear weapons. The NPT, at the time of negotiation, not only recognised the urgency and importance of preventing the spread of nuclear weapons as a measure in reducing the danger of nuclear war, but it also accepted the importance of intensifying international co-operation in the development of the peaceful application of nuclear energy. In return for co-operation in facilitating the application of IAEA safeguards, it was accepted that all signatory states had an 'inalienable' right to engage in research, production and use of nuclear energy for peaceful purposes, and would be able to acquire sources and special fissionable materials, as well as equipment for the reprocessing, use and production of nuclear material for peaceful purposes. As a result during the late 1960s and early 1970s several important transactions took place between supplier states and developing countries concerning power reactors, heavy water and fuel fabrication plants and other facilities. At that time it seemed that IAEA safeguards constituted an adequate guarantee for the prevention of nuclear proliferation. In 1975 France concluded agreements with the Republic of Korea and with Pakistan. Agreements for safeguards in respect of both plants were concluded between the states concerned and the IAEA. Apparently under pressure from the United States, South Korea, however, seems to have decided not to go in for reprocessing and the agreements with France have consequently lapsed. With regard to Pakistan it was reported that France decided to withdraw its sale of reprocessing equipment to Pakistan and offered some substitute but Pakistan did not accept. Similarly, West Germany concluded in 1975 an agreement with Brazil for the export of all elements in the nuclear fuel cycle, including reprocessing and enrichment facilities. At the same time the Agency concluded safeguards agreements with some non-signatories such as Argentina, India and Pakistan with regard to their respective power reactors supplied to them by West Germany and Canada. This was also the era of considerable optimism about the future of nuclear power and a number of advanced countries were interested in marketing power reactors in developing countries.

Taken together the NPT and IAEA safeguards worked satisfactorily for a period of time but in the mid-1970s the prospect of an increased spread of nuclear power, the separation of plutonium from spent nuclear fuel, more economic methods of enriching uranium, projected acquisition of so-called sensitive facilities by several countries with limited nuclear power programmes, and the prospect of introducing fast breeder reactors, all led to a growing concern about the adequacy of the current NPT/IAEA safeguards regime. Moreover, parties whose non-nuclear intentions were already enshrined in their ratification of the NPT appeared to be incurring disadvantages as compared with non-parties of the Treaty.

Since the mid-1970s, and particularly since the Indian nuclear explosion of 1974, there has been a marked tendency to regard all activity in the field of nuclear energy as contributing to proliferation. This fact, coupled with increased efforts by several countries to acquire so-called sensitive nuclear technology, triggered a process of major reappraisal throughout the world concerning general proliferation risks and the adequacy of existing non-proliferation measures.

Before dealing with the latest development in the proliferation/non-proliferation dilemma, it is appropriate to point out some of the views expressed regarding nuclear proliferation. According to one view, the resistance of the NWSs to meaningful strategic arms reductions is the principal obstacle to curbing proliferation. Years of negotiations over the levels and testing of strategic arms have failed to produce reductions or a comprehensive test ban. Those who advocate this view believe that until the NWSs stop accentuating the importance of nuclear weapons and themselves begin a process of denuclearisation, there will be an inexorable ground-swell of interest among other states in developing weapons of their own.

According to another opinion, nuclear proliferation is so severe a problem that those with power to impede it should do so whatever the cost. Hence there have been such dramatic proposals as those favouring a general moratorium on nuclear power, joint Soviet–American or unilateral nuclear guarantees to states with valid nuclear security concerns, and severe economic and diplomatic sanctions against states that acquire nuclear weapons.

A third view centres on the belief that proliferation is neither generally nor, in most cases, specifically undesirable. The diffusion of nuclear capabilities, like the diffusion of power more generally, will, in the judgement of many observers, erode the hierarchical features of the international system and help right the imbalance by which the powerful remain rich and the weak impoverished. To them proliferation is an element in a general pattern of challenge to an unjust *status quo*.

Finally, some would maintain that a world of 10 or 20 nuclear powers could be as stable as today's world provided there was enough time and enough wisdom to adopt security relationships to the shifting configuration of power.

To forestall an uncontrolled spread of nuclear technology and to eliminate commercial competition as a factor in negotiating safeguards, the major nuclear countries, led by the United States, established a Nuclear Supplier Group which came to be known as the London Suppliers Club (1975). The initial membership of seven nations later increased to fifteen including some states from Eastern Europe. According to its members, the main motivation behind the establishment of this group was to strengthen the non-proliferation regime by controlling the supply of nuclear-related equipment, materials, technology and services. It should be noted, however, not only that the membership of this group is heterogeneous, but also that their interests differ a great deal. Only three members are self-sufficient in nuclear technology and materials, while others are suppliers and recipients of material and/or technology. Their interests are, therefore, not entirely identical.

The guidelines were first conceived in 1975 and published in 1978.[12] The suppliers' policies are based on a common 'trigger list' of nuclear and other materials, equipment and facilities that are to be exported on certain conditions. The conditions include the following: formal assurance from the recipient government explicitly excluding uses that would result in any nuclear explosive device; effective physical protection by the importing countries to prevent any unauthorised use and handling of the materials and facilities; and application of IAEA safeguards with duration and coverage provisions conforming to the guidelines established by the IAEA Board of Governors in 1974. The guidelines call for restraint in the transfer of sensitive facilities and technology − meaning those involved in reprocessing, enrichment and heavy water production − and weapons-grade materials. IAEA safeguards would apply to all sensitive facilities. In addition, the transfer of sensitive facilities would trigger the application of IAEA safeguards to any facility of the same type constructed during an agreed period in the recipient country. In addition, the safeguards envisaged in the guidelines include, *inter alia*, restrictions on re-export from the importing country and on uranium enrichment and plutonium reprocessing. Several individual suppliers have indicated that they would impose additional requirements with regard to their nuclear exports and they have done so. These include West Germany, France, Canada, Australia and Sweden.[13]

Although it has been said that the signatories of the NPT will not be affected by these guidelines because their programmes are fully safeguarded, most of the developing countries view them with scepticism and concern. They view this step as yet another example of an organised and deliberate effort on the part of the advanced countries to deny technology to the developing countries and impose onerous restrictions on its transfer, which is tantamount to constricting the growth of their civil nuclear programmes.[14]

Some developing countries have spoken of the Club as a 'cartel' that, for political and commercial purposes, has been given a moral façade of non-proliferation. Obviously this is strongly disputed by the suppliers. Others claim that the guidelines are directed primarily against non-signatories of the NPT and are designed to convince them that any development of independent nuclear programmes without joining the fold of the NPT would be both difficult and expensive to pursue. However, in practice these guidelines adversely affect signatories of the NPT. Many of the developing countries that have signed the NPT resent them and consider them to be contrary to the spirit of Article IV of the NPT wherein they are promised unrestricted access to and sharing of nuclear technology for their safeguarded nuclear programmes. As the nuclear technology is not confined to one specific narrow discipline, applying the guidelines means that in order really to block the transfer of technology for potential military nuclear applications, one would have to restrict the flow of basic knowledge in numerous technological areas not necessarily confined to the nuclear field. It has been also pointed out that for the members of the London Club it will become increasingly difficult to draw the line between what is exclusively related to nuclear technology and what is not.

The guidelines apply not only to supplied facilities, equipment and physical processes but to new 'sensitive' facilities utilising technology derived directly from transferred 'sensitive' facilities and know-how. They also impose safeguards for a period of 20 years or more on certain basic physical processes which are not entirely nuclear. In connection with this restriction it is stressed that essential information on these processes has been already published and it seems illogical to impose restrictions on its use. However, it is considered that unless governments of supplier states impose severe restrictions on the exchange and release of basic scientific information and data both internally and externally, the spread of new technologies which could contribute indirectly towards the advancement of nuclear technology cannot be contained.

The understanding reached among the supplier states to strengthen IAEA safeguards by giving them necessary technical and political support is considered by some states as contrary to IAEA statutes and as a discrimination in favour of signatories of the NPT *vis-à-vis* non-signatories in matters of technical assistance. Furthermore, the IAEA has been asked by certain supplier states to accept the concept of sensitive technologies and not to grant technical assistance related to them without asking for safe-guards.[15]

The most far-reaching restrictions on nuclear facilities which could spread nuclear-weapons-usable material are embodied in American policy on nuclear energy. It is considered that at least two events of global significance have influenced American non-proliferation policy during the second half of the 1970s. First, the increase in crude oil prices made nuclear power economic; simul-taneously, export of nuclear power plants and nuclear technology became commercially attractive. The dispersal of nuclear power plants is perceived by the United States as creating the tech-nological infrastructure for the weapons option. Secondly, the Indian nuclear test of May 1974 heightened American anxieties that a proliferation chain-reaction would follow.[16]

Although the changes in American policy were discernible earlier, it should be noted that Carter assumed office with a strong personal commitment to non-proliferation. This is evident from his nuclear-power policy statement of 7 April 1977, in which he perceived 'the risk that components of the nuclear power process will be turned to providing atomic weapons'. The elements of the new American non-proliferation strategy are embodied in the United States Nuclear Non-Proliferation Act (NNPA) of 10 March 1978.

The NNPA outlines a number of initiatives to be taken by the United States to provide adequate nuclear fuel cycles, combining action at the national and international levels. For instance, the United States is to take action to ensure its capacity to provide a reliable supply of nuclear fuel and to initiate international discus-sion to develop international approaches for meeting future world-wide nuclear fuel needs. In particular, negotiations are to be undertaken with a view to the establishment of an international fuel authority to provide nuclear fuel services; and repositories for the storage of spent fuel under effective international auspices and inspection, including arrangements under which nations placing spent fuel in such repositories would receive compensations for the energy content of the spent fuel. Pursuant to the NNPA, the benefits of such international undertaking should be available to NNWSs only if such states accept IAEA safeguards on all their peaceful nuclear activities, do not manufacture or otherwise acquire any nuclear explosive device, do not establish any new enrichment or reprocessing facilities and place any such existing facilities under effective international auspices and inspection. In line with American interests in the strengthening of IAEA safeguards, the NNPA sets forth actions to be taken together with other nations to improve the IAEA safeguards system and to assist IAEA in its effective implementation.

The NNPA defines the criteria governing the issue of export licences for individual items and stipulates a set of nearly identical requirements for newly-negotiated agreements for co-operation in the peaceful uses of nuclear energy. In addition, existing agreements are to be renegotiated to conform to the same requirements as new ones. The export criteria applicable to export licences and agreements for co-operation are the following: application of safeguards to exported items; prohibition of use for explosive devices; provision of adequate physical security; application of all statutory requirements to any material or facility derived from exported sensitive technology; prohibition of reprocessing or alteration of material exported by the United States or material produced through the use of such exported material without American approval; and prohibition of retransfer to a third party without American approval. As an additional export criterion, the NNPA requires that IAEA safeguards be maintained with respect to all peaceful activities of the recipient NNWSs at the time of the export. That requirement, which is to be included in new agreements for co-operation with NNWSs and renegotiated agreements, will apply to export licences covering shipment taking place 2 years after the date of the enactment of the law and to any export licence application filed 18 months after that date.

The President is required to take 'immediate and vigorous steps' to obtain the adherence of other nations to export criteria similar to those adopted by the United States as well as their agreements to certain conditions regarding their peaceful nuclear programmes, including commitment to refrain from enrichment or reprocessing and to limit the fabrication or stockpiling of plutonium, uranium-233 or highly enriched uranium to facilities under effective international auspices and inspection. Such facilities should be few in number, carefully sited and managed so as to minimise proliferation and environmental risks, and conditions should be established to limit the access of NNWSs to sensitive technology.[17]

It is said that American policy was primarily motivated by the conviction that the plutonium-producing technology could not be properly safeguarded. US Government spokesmen explained that the restrictions on technology were intended as temporary measures to be applied until such time as these sensitive parts of the fuel cycle could be made technically or institutionally safe. They denied that these steps in any way weakened American commitments under Article IV of the NPT. Rather, they were undertaken to strengthen the commitments in Article I not to assist NNWSs in developing nuclear weapons. The NNPA included the Carter initiative for a 2-year INFCE which was to seek alternatives to a plutonium-producing fuel cycle. The hope was that INFCE would result in some technical or institutional innovation to produce nuclear energy for generating power without making weapons material. But NNWSs and especially developing countries did not interpret these measures in the same light.

Many developing countries resent any restriction on the export of nuclear technology. They consider that such measures drastically weaken the commitments accepted by the industrialised states, in particular the NWSs, under article IV of the NPT. This sentiment was already expressed clearly during London Club meetings. The NNPA caused even greater dissatisfaction. It was regarded as a way of perpetuating the supremacy of the industrialised countries over the developing ones. Moreover, confidence in the United States as a dependable supplier has been shaken by unilateral, unexpected cut-offs of American-supplied fuel. However, one should have in mind the fact that the attitudes of developing countries are also not homogeneous and are influenced by their political situation, their state of nuclear development and their security perspectives.

But on the whole, preventing the transfer of nuclear technology and techniques is tending to further widen the gap between the developed and developing countries. It hampers the normal development of productive forces and of science on terms of equality for all countries. It violates the right to full development of natural resources. Dissatisfied with the results of the First Review Conference on the NPT and with the more and more restrictive policy of supplier states, the non-aligned and developing countries have shifted their activities in the direction of securing a more equitable position in respect to the use of nuclear energy within the framework of the IAEA and the UN, as well as relying more and more on the co-operation between themselves.

As a result and in accordance with the action programme for

co-operation of non-aligned and developing countries in the field of nuclear energy, Yugoslavia initiated, at the 20th General Conference of IAEA in 1976, a move for the establishing of an international pool for the nuclear fuel cycle. The idea of organising this pool is based on the association of states for the purpose of ensuring financial, material and technological conditions for securing all the phases of the nuclear fuel cycle. Similar proposals were made during INFCE discussions.[18]

At its 32nd Session, the UN General Assembly adopted, on the initiative of non-aligned countries, a resolution on the peaceful uses of nuclear energy. The General Assembly invited all states to consider convening an international conference or conferences aimed at promoting international co-operation in the peaceful uses of nuclear energy and required states to strengthen their existing programmes for the development of the peaceful use of nuclear energy in the developing countries. The principles set forth in this resolution are the following: the use of nuclear energy for peaceful purposes is of great importance for the economic and social development of many countries; all states have the right, in accordance with the principle of sovereign equality, to develop their programmes for the peaceful uses of nuclear technology, for economic and social development, in conformity with their priorities, interests and needs; all states, without discrimination, should have access to and should be free to acquire technology, equipment and materials for the peaceful uses of nuclear energy; and international co-operation in the field covered by the said resolution should be under agreed and appropriate international safeguards applied through the IAEA on a non-discriminatory basis in order to prevent effectively the proliferation of nuclear weapons.

The dissatisfaction of developing and non-aligned countries and their opposition to the restriction of export of nuclear technology influenced to a great extent the Final Document at the UN General Assembly Special Session on Disarmament. While the Document contains relatively little about the question of proliferation of nuclear weapons due to the insurmountable differences between NWSs and NNWSs, it reflects in some degree the approach of developing countries towards peaceful uses of nuclear energy. It stressed:

Non-proliferation measures should not jeopardize the full exercise of the inalienable rights of all states to apply and develop their programmes for the peaceful uses of nuclear energy for economic and social development in conformity with their priorities, interests and needs. All states should also have access to and be free to acquire technology, equipment and materials for peaceful uses of nuclear energy, taking into account the particular needs of the developing countries. International co-operation in this field should be under agreed and appropriate international safeguards applied through the IAEA on a non-discriminatory basis in order to prevent effectively the proliferation of nuclear weapons.[19]

It should be also mentioned that on the initiative of non-aligned and developing countries the UN General Assembly decided at its 34th Session to convene an international conference on the peaceful uses of nuclear energy to be provisionally held in 1983.

Parallel with these actions within the UN and IAEA, the non-aligned and developing countries have realised that they have to organise themselves and that the co-operation among them in peaceful uses of nuclear energy should be intensified so that these countries become less dependent on the developed countries and especially in the field in which they could achieve a higher level of self-sufficiency. In this light one should look upon the meetings of the Group of Non-Aligned Coordinating Countries on Peaceful Uses of Nuclear Energy held in Belgrade in 1978 and in Buenos Aires in 1980.[20]

Although not much could be achieved at the Second Review Conference on the NPT in 1980 given the differences between NWSs and NNWSs, there were some developments which indicate that supplier states have realised that unless they seek common solutions with recipient states, there will be no progress towards halting further proliferation of nuclear weapons. One such development was the recently completed INFCE study in which 66 countries (39 developing countries) and five international organisations participated. At this point it is appropriate to mention only two aspects of the INFCE study. One was the distinct appreciation on the part of the participants of the need for international action to tackle the nuclear energy proliferation dilemma. This means that the time is ripe for concerted steps towards co-operation between suppliers and recipients leading to internationalisation of the sensitive parts of the nuclear fuel cycle. In this way the technologies could be operated in the interests of the world community both in avoiding the spread of nuclear weapons and assuring the necessary supplies and services for peaceful nuclear programmes. Secondly, it was recognised that it was impossible to find a technical solution to the proliferation-prone nature of the sensitive technology, especially reprocessing, and consequently it was concluded that the proliferation of nuclear weapons is primarily a political problem for which political solutions should be sought. These findings of INFCE have also strengthened the hand of those who hold that nuclear energy is expected to increase its rôle in meeting the world's energy needs and can and should be widely available to that end; that effective measures can and should be taken to meet the specific needs of developing countries in the peaceful uses of nuclear energy; and that effective measures can and should be taken to minimise the danger of the proliferation of nuclear weapons without jeopardising energy supplies or the development of nuclear energy for peaceful purposes.[21]

Conclusions

On the basis of foregoing discussion several conclusions could be deduced:

1. The efforts of the international community to end the arms race, and especially the nuclear arms race, have not resulted in such measures as would constitute genuine disarmament.
2. Instead of reducing the stockpiles of nuclear weapons, the world is witnessing an ever-growing arms race and particularly a nuclear arms race between two superpowers.
3. From the point of view of further nuclear proliferation, vertical proliferation is considered by most NNWSs as a principal incentive for horizontal proliferation.
4. From the point of view of horizontal proliferation, the non-proliferation regime under the NPT has been, at least for the time being, functioning satisfactorily and that in spite of its deficiencies it should be strengthened by encouraging universal adherence.
5. To make the non-proliferation regime more reliable and more effective, all parties to the NPT − NWSs and NNWSs − should fulfil their obligations in good faith.
6. The main task in strengthening the existing non-proliferation

regime should be more elaborated and effective IAEA safe-guards.

7. As nuclear power is the only practical and viable alternative available at the present time for meeting a great part of the energy needs of many countries, it should be expected that an increased number of countries, especially developing, will be interested in obtaining their own nuclear power, if other energy-related technology does not become available in the near future.

8. The NWSs should accept the fact, known since the beginning of the atomic age, that the peaceful and military aspects of the use of nuclear energy could not be separated.

9. The spread of nuclear energy for peaceful uses does not neces-sarily mean the proliferation of nuclear weapons, although such a possibility cannot be excluded.

10. The question whether a country becomes a nuclear weapon country or not is a primarily political question for which a political decision is necessary, and hence should be solved by political means.

11. It should be accepted that there are no technical means by which any one fuel cycle can be made proof against abuse.

12. The nuclear states should accept that all states have an inalienable right to apply and develop their programmes for the peaceful uses of nuclear energy for economic and social development in conformity with their priorities, interests and needs.

13. Nuclear supplier states and recipient states should seek to establish agreed and mutually acceptable principles on the basis of which co-operation between the two groups of states should be carried out in future.

14. That effective measures should be taken to meet the specific needs of developing countries in the peaceful uses of nuclear energy.

15. Last, but not least, necessary arrangements should be under-taken to solve global and regional security problems, as a pre-condition for all other measures in the field of nuclear energy.

Notes

1. SIPRI, *World Armaments and Disarmament: SIPRI Yearbook, 1980* (London, 1980) pp. xlii–xliii.

2. Resolution of the UN General Assembly, I (1).
3. R. Imai and R. Press, *Nuclear Non-Proliferation: Failures and Prospects* (International Consultative Group on Nuclear Energy, New York and London, 1980) p. 3.
4. UN, *The United Nations and Disarmament, 1945–1970* (New York, 1970) pp. 258–62.
5. SIPRI, *Yearbook, 1980*, p. 447.
6. Imai and Press, op. cit., p. 3.
7. US Arms Control and Disarmament Agency, *Arms Control and Disarmament Agreements: Texts and History of Negotiations* (Washington, DC, 1977); and US Department of State, *SALT II Agreement* (Washington, DC, 1979).
8. SIPRI, *The NPT: The Main Political Barrier to Nuclear Weapon Proliferation* (London, 1980) pp. 17–18.
9. UN General Assembly, Twenty-Second Session, Plenary Meetings, 1672nd Meeting.
10. ibid., Twenty-Eighth Session, First Committee, 1969th Meeting.
11. UN, *The United Nations Disarmament Yearbook*: Vol. I: *1976* (New York, 1977) pp. 102–8.
12. See IAEA Document, INFCIRC/254.
13. B. Sanders, 'Nuclear Exporting Policies' in SIPRI, *Nuclear Energy and Nuclear Weapons Proliferation* (London, 1979) pp. 241–50.
14. For more details on the views of developing countries see M. A. Khan, *Nuclear Energy and International Co-operation: A Third World Perception of the Erosion of Confidence* (International Consultative Group on Nuclear Energy, New York and London, 1979) esp. pp. 13–18.
15. ibid.
16. P. R. Chari, 'An Indian Reaction to U.S. Non-Proliferation Policy', *International Security*, fall 1978, p. 57.
17. UN, *The United Nations Disarmament Yearbook*: Vol. II: *1978* (New York, 1979), pp. 251–3.
18. M. Osredkar, 'A Nuclear Fuel Cycle Pool or Bank?' in SIPRI, *Internationalization to Prevent the Spread of Nuclear Weapons* (London, 1980), pp. 129–34.
19. UN, Tenth Special Session, S-10/2, Final Document of the Tenth Special Session of the General Assembly, para. 68.
20. E. Kljun, 'The Non-Aligned Countries and Peaceful Uses of Nuclear Power', *Review of International Affairs*, xxviii (1978) 10–12.
21. IAEA, *INFCE, Summary Volume*: Vol. IX (Vienna, 1980) pp. 1–53, 276.

PART III
REGIONAL STUDIES

15 The Dilemma of European Theatre Nuclear Arms Control

Lawrence Freedman

Introduction

'It is said the appetite develops with eating.' This comment is reported to have been made by President Brezhnev at the Moscow Summit with Chancellor Schmidt in July 1980. Taken as a statement on Soviet foreign policy, Brezhnev's comment might appear quite sinister, but put in context as an observation on arms control it is quite profound. Arms control has represented an attempt to codify 'balances', and because these balances never seem complete, the inclination has been to include more and more weapon types in the accounting system – medium-range aircraft in the case which prompted Brezhnev's remark. The initiative taken at the Moscow Summit in July 1980 led to a new set of negotiations which began in preliminary form on 16 October 1980. These negotiations extend further the boundaries of arms control and exemplify all the attendant problems.

They have been stimulated by politics rather than strategy, so that they are already overloaded with expectations and responsibilities, including sustaining what remains of detente in Europe. They have been entered into, at least on the Western side, without a clear view of their likely outcome. A principle of equality is believed to be at stake, but it is hard to see how realistically this can be turned into a credible agreement. The two sides start with completely different notions of the scope of the talks: the United States wishes to restrict matters to medium-range missiles that can hit European targets; the Soviet Union has a much broader concept encompassing all systems capable of reaching her soil.

The unpromising nature of the whole enterprise is illustrated by the difficulties found in describing the preliminary talks. To the Soviet Union discussions are 'Related to Nuclear Arms in Europe', which to the West begs the question of Soviet weapons that can attack Europe from bases in Asia. The American alternative 'Discussions of Questions related to the Limitation of Certain US and Soviet Forces' does not even convey a vague sense of an agenda.

Arms control has been set a critical test which it is ill-equipped to meet. There is a real danger that, whatever the motives in reassuring domestic opinion or preserving a modicum of detente, the result will be more prolonged and acrimonious negotiations followed by disappointment and recriminations. This, in turn, could lead to the discrediting of even limited forms of East–West discussions on military issues.[1]

One objective of this chapter is to describe the background to these talks and the practical impediments to their successful conclusion. Another objective is to suggest one possible way out of the difficulties, which is to fully integrate the talks on theatre systems with those on central systems, presuming SALT can be put on course once again. This analysis warns of the pitfalls of proceeding with theatre negotiations in the absence of SALT.

NATO's Position

During the 1970s the position adopted by the Alliance on the advisability of negotiating on European-based systems has been reversed. At the start of SALT the threat to Europe posed by Soviet medium- and intermediate-range ballistic missiles (MR/IRBMs) was recognised but there was reluctance to raise this because it would involve conceding the Soviet point on including the forward-based systems (FBS) – the American medium-range aircraft based in and around Europe. The fear in Western Europe was that this issue would allow the Soviet Union a means of breaking the links between the US nuclear arsenal and the defence of Europe.[2]

There were a number of reasons for moving away from this approach, six of which are:

1. The desire for arms control to provide complete, comprehensive coverage of all weapons pointed to theatre systems as a key lacuna, a 'grey area' somewhere between SALT and MBFR.

2. The acknowledged strategic parity focused attention onto disparities elsewhere. The first signs of modernisation of the Soviet theatre systems in the mid-1970s (Backfire/SS-20) emphasised this particular disparity.

3. Once the Soviet Union managed to entangle cruise missiles in SALT II the fate of this option for countering the Soviet theatre advantage was bound up with the future of the negotiations. The mention of ground-launched cruise missiles (GLCMs) in the Protocol to SALT II, and the promise in the Declaration of Principles for SALT III to resolve the protocol issues confirmed the entanglement.

4. In justifying the NATO programme to modernise its long-range theatre nuclear forces (LRTNF), based on the Tomahawk GLCM and the Pershing ballistic missile, great play was made with the Soviet SS-20 IRBM so that the futures of the two programmes were inevitably seen to be linked.

5. It was necessary to be sensitive to dissenting opinion in Europe, which had emerged during the neutron bomb episode of 1977−78 opposed to the introduction of any new nuclear weapons.

6. Arms control has been seen as a medicament for detente. This came to be stressed in 1980 as the health of detente was seen to wane.

During 1979 it became accepted wisdom in NATO that the LRTNF programme could not go ahead without some 'parallel' arms control offer. On 6 October 1979 Brezhnev hinted at substantial concessions if the NATO programme was abandoned, but unpleasant consequences if it went ahead. This led to a debate on whether arms control negotiations should precede deployment, if not development and production, of the Pershings and Tomahawks in order to allow the Soviet Union to demonstrate its good faith.[3] Although this particular approach was rejected, both Belgium and the Netherlands have made it clear that their participation in the programme, as hosts to cruise missiles, is conditional on progress in arms control.[4]

Those drawing up the actual force plans in 1979 were working within a range of 200–600 missiles. The final figure of 572 missiles (108 Pershing and 464 Tomahawk) tended on the high side which can, in part, be seen as anticipating some future cuts in deference to arms control. As an additional sweetener it was agreed to withdraw 1000 nuclear warheads from Europe 'as soon as feasible'. The actual arms-control proposal involved the following principles:[5]

1. Any future limitations on US systems principally designed for theatre missions should be accompanied by appropriate limitations on Soviet theatre systems.
2. Limitations on US and Soviet long-range theatre nuclear systems should be negotiated bilaterally in the SALT III framework in a step-by-step approach.
3. The immediate objective of these negotiations should be the establishment of agreed limitations on US and Soviet land-based long-range theatre nuclear missile systems.
4. Any agreed limitations on these systems must be consistent with the principle of equality between the sides. Therefore, the limitations should take the form of *de jure* equality both in ceilings and in rights.
5. Any agreed limitations must be adequately verifiable.[6]

Adopting SALT as the most appropriate forum recognised that cruise missiles were already bound up with SALT, the 'decoupling' implications of having completely separate talks, and the advisability of keeping the negotiations bilateral. Confusion was likely to result from attempting to involve all interested parties, and then in talking seriously within such a body. The unwillingness of the British and French to expose their small nuclear forces confirmed the bilateralism. Only American missiles from the NATO side were to be discussed. Restricting future negotiations to 'land-based missiles', reflected the popular perception of the issue at hand. Excluding aircraft would also keep matters simple.

The American concept has been essentially to see SALT III as a central negotiation mainly concerned with reducing the SALT II ceilings with a series of distinct, peripheral negotiations on discrete issues, such as anti-satellite weapons and depressed-trajectory missiles as well as LRTNF.[7] There is much to be said for this concept, but there are now two obvious problems. First, notwithstanding President Reagan's expressed determination to negotiate a better SALT II, neither side seems prepared for serious negotiations on 'deep cuts' for some time. This seems an unlikely sun around which all else must revolve, especially when one of the satellite negotiations is close to being joined. Secondly, as will be discussed later, LRTNF cannot easily be contained.

The Soviet Position

One reason for doubting whether a theatre negotiation can be kept short and simple is the Soviet attitude. The Soviet Union has consistently demanded that American FBS be included in SALT because they threaten the Soviet homeland. On similar grounds she has argued for the inclusion of British and French nuclear forces.

In SALT I the Soviet Union received no formal credit for either FBS or the British and French forces.[8] These same issues were raised in the early stages of SALT II. However, in the Vladivostok Agreement of November 1974 no mention was made of FBS. Henry Kissinger observed that agreement had been possible partly because the USSR had dropped her insistence on including FBS in the totals.[9] However, the Vladivostok *aide memoire* did include 'air-launched missiles', which provided the Soviet Union with an opportunity to get a handle on cruise missiles.

After signing SALT II in June 1979, she quickly placed European-based systems on the agenda for SALT III. Meeting with the press on 25 June, Soviet Foreign Minister Andrei Gromyko proposed drawing other countries and their weapons into SALT and covering the FBS issue.

A willingness to negotiate on missiles based in Europe had been indicated by Brezhnev as early as March 1979,[10] but the most direct appeal was the one made on 6 October 1979. Then he spoke of a readiness 'to reduce, compared with the present level, the quantity of medium-range nuclear missiles deployed in the western parts of the Soviet Union: but, of course, only in the event that there is no additional deployment of medium-range missiles in Western Europe'. In the period leading up to 12 December this offer was stressed, although its ambiguities were never clarified, particularly as to whether the SS-20 was to be included.[11]

After the NATO decision the main question was whether the Soviet Union would agree to talk at all. The initial reaction was

that the 'basis' for talks had been destroyed, but by July, and
Schmidt's visit to Moscow, a new basis had been found. The new
Soviet position was agreed by the Politburo on 4 July 1980:

> Without withdrawing the proposals put forward earlier, [the
> Soviet Union] could also agree to a discussion of issues relating to
> medium-range weapons even before ratification of SALT II. At
> the same time, the discussions must involve not only medium-
> range missiles, but also US forward-based nuclear weapons.
> Both these problems must be discussed simultaneously and in
> organic connection. . . . Possible accords could be imple-
> mented only after the SALT II Treaty comes into force.[12]

In terms of the subject matter of the negotiations, therefore, the
key difference between the two sides is the FBS question. The other
long-standing Soviet objective, the inclusion of British and French
forces, appears to have been postponed for the moment as something more relevant to SALT III proper.

The Forces

The two sides possess systems with such variations in numbers,
types and quality, and held for such disparate purposes as to
render a proper comparison extremely difficult. There is a
boundary problem as LRTNFs blend into battlefield nuclear
forces, and as wholly nuclear systems make way for dual capable
tactical air or anti-ship systems. At the other end there are the 400
Poseidon warheads that have officially been assigned to SACEUR
and the Soviet SS-11 ICBMs in IR/MRBM fields, which are
already SALT accountable. Any drawing of boundary lines must
be quite arbitrary.

Missiles
NATO has not had any land-based missiles in Europe since the
Thor and Jupiter, both of which were moved by the mid-1960s,
apart from 18 French IRBMs and 180 short-range Pershing I
missiles (72 of which are operated by West Germany under a dual-
key system).[13] The two new systems − Pershing II and the Tomahawk GLCM − will not become operational until December 1983
at the earliest.[14] By mid-1986 the 108 Pershing IIs should all be

deployed, but only 160 of the Tomahawks will be deployed. It will take until 1989 for the full force of 464 to be ready.[15]

The Soviet missile force reached a peak in 1964 with 733 SS-4s and SS-5s (598 in soft launchers and 135 in hardened launchers). By the late 1960s a few had been withdrawn, but the major move came in 1968 when about a quarter were removed to positions in the Far East facing China. At the time the Soviet Union was attempting to develop a solid-fuelled (for quicker reaction) follow-on system. A missile, designated the SS-14 by NATO, was tested using the last two stages of the SS-13 ICBM.[16] The SS-13 did not turn out to be a very popular ICBM and its low rating appears to have reflected on the SS-14, which was never deployed.[17]

From 1969 to 1971, perhaps as a result of this failure, 120 SS-11 ICBMs were deployed as an expedient in MR/IRBM fields. These SS-11s were unambiguously linked to the theatre tasks, though they were counted in the SALT totals.[18] They are still deployed in this mode.[19]

The SS-20 IRBM first became operational in 1976. It is of 4400 km in range and is derived from the first two stages of the SS-16, the latest, and unsuccessful, attempt to develop an efficient, solid-fuelled ICBM. The most recent estimate is that 160 SS-20s are now in place. They are found in 23 sites in the broad areas in the Soviet Union, in the Western Military Districts facing NATO, in the Far East facing China, and in the centre of the country in swing sites, capable of being directed against Europe or China. This latter location is significant for any attempt to design a nuclear free zone for Europe or in assessing proposals to cut back on missiles located in the 'Western parts of the Soviet Union'. Estimates suggest that two-thirds of the SS-20s will be capable of attacking Europe. It is commonly assumed that the planned force level will be 250 SS-20s but that is only an assumption.[20]

There are 440 of the older missiles still deployed (380 SS-4 and 60 SS-5). It would appear that these are now wholly concentrated on Europe and the installations in the Far Eastern Districts are no longer operational.[21]

No SS-4s (but some SS-5s) have been dismantled since autumn 1979. This may reflect a desire to maintain a bargaining card for negotiations. At the June 1980 meeting of NATO's Nuclear Planning Group, Ministers 'noted with concern the continued retention of Soviet SS-4 and SS-5 missile launchers. This, coupled with the continuing deployment of SS-20 missiles could lead to an even larger superiority in LRTNF in the mid-1980s than previously anticipated.'[22] The previous estimate had been 50 SS-4s by the mid-1980s.[23]

Aircraft

Many aircraft that the Soviet Union appears to include under the FBS heading, the carrier-based A-6s and A-7s, and the F-4s, are dual-capable and generally unsuitable for strikes into Soviet territory. Technically, it would be very difficult to include them in an agreement. For example, if the carrier-based aircraft were included there would have to be some rules as to the patrols and composition of the US 6th Fleet in the Mediterranean.

Moreover, if these systems were included then the United States would probably demand the inclusion of comparable Soviet systems and this in turn would lead to great confusion. Although one can vary the picture according to the range/combat radius level chosen, the Soviet position at every point looks the strongest. Furthermore, as shorter-range aircraft are held in much larger numbers, they soon come to dwarf the longer-range,and more unambiguously strategic TNFs. The position can at least be simplified by identifying the key long-range systems. It is best not to attempt to do this solely by range, because this is by no means a fixed measure.

On the American side it is very difficult to exclude the 170 F-111s based in Great Britain, which are included in official descriptions of NATO long-range TNFs.

On the Soviet side the most obvious systems would be the medium-range bombers under the control of the Soviet Long-Range Aviation Force. This would involve the Tu-16 Badger, the Tu-22 Blinder and the Tu-22M Backfire. At the moment the Soviet inventory includes 288 Badgers, 125 Blinders and 75 Backfires.[24] The Backfires are expected to increase at the rate of 30 per year, the maximum permitted following Brezhnev's June 1979 undertaking to Carter. The Badgers, which are now well over 20 years old, will be gradually phased out, though the Blinders, which were first deployed in 1962, will probably linger on for some time. As with the missiles, about a third of these aircraft are based close to China.[25]

When it comes to negotiating, a further problem could be those Soviet systems assigned to the Naval Air Force — in mid-1980, 280 Tu-16, 40 Tu-22 and 70 Tu-22M. At the moment on the NATO side, American systems are supported by 57 British Vulcans and 33 French Mirage IVs. However, these will all be phased out by 1985.

Prospects for Agreement

From all this, what are the prospects for an agreement? On the basis of past experience with SALT it must be considered unlikely that the condition of parity, required as one of NATO's five principles, can be created through arms control unless it virtually exists already. To construct equality out of inequality requires the stronger to make extra concessions. This has not been the habit in the past.

There are four possible points of parity. First, by about 1985 there may be an equality in land-based missiles, at a level of some 250 missiles, halfway through the NATO programme and at the probable conclusion of the SS-20 programme. Codifying parity at this point might well appeal to the Soviet Union, even without FBS, but for the United States it would mean cancelling half her planned force without any compensating concessions on the Soviet side. It would also mean disregarding any older SS-4s and 5s that had not been retired. Providing an incentive to the Soviet Union to double her planned SS-20 production by fixing a ceiling to accommodate most, if not all, of the TNF programme is equally unappealing. From the NATO point of view another key objection is that no allowance is made for the three warheads on each SS-20 as against the single warhead Tomahawks and Pershings.

There are ways of addressing this last point. The first is through counting launchers rather than missiles, which has been normal in SALT. Strictly speaking the Tomahawks are carried and launched in batches of four on a GLCM Transporter−Erector−Launcher (TEL). The problem with trying to create a parity on this measure is that the programmes of each side hardly begin to meet at the end of the decade. To achieve a ceiling at say 160 launchers, the NATO programme would be cut by 64 launchers, half of which might well be Pershings. The Soviet Union would have to hold her SS-20 force at about the current level, and dismantle all her SS-4s and SS-5s.

Current NATO studies prefer to count warheads rather than launchers, which would be more innovatory in SALT terms.[26] However, the required adjustments to existing programmes are similar to those of a launcher ceiling. If, as expected, the Soviet Union continues to build up her SS-20s for the duration of the talks, then adoption of either of these ceilings will require her to accept dismantling her own modern systems while American forces are continuing to grow.

A final approach to parity recognises Soviet concern over FBS by including the F-111 but in return draws in larger numbers in the Soviet Long Range Aviation Force. If both programmes are allowed to run their course (and the Soviet Union does not drastically increase SS-20 production or hold on to obsolescent systems) then a form of parity might arrive naturally by 1989. An arms-control agreement which merely acknowledged this fact would hardly be taken seriously. A ceiling of 450 for delivery vehicles might prove attractive to the USSR only in her older systems. For the same reason it would not appeal to NATO.

There is another obvious difficulty. About one-third of all Soviet medium-range forces are facing China. To bring them into an agreement would seriously upset the calculations. From the Soviet perspective these systems have nothing to do with the European theatre: from the NATO perspective they could be turned against it, either as a result of a Sino–Soviet *rapprochement* or just through reinforcement measures in an emergency. It has been suggested that SS-20s could be transported to new sites by air. Whether or not NATO would feel able to exclude them might depend on how well such a movement could be observed. Certainly the movement of aircraft from one theatre to another would present no problems. The movement of aircraft based in the United States which could be sent to Europe in a crisis, might be relevant to a compromise here.[27]

It is possible that an unequal deal would be accepted, despite offending the principle of parity, by which the Soviet Union would accept a firm limit on her force at, say, 200 SS-20s with a rapid run-down of SS-4s and SS-5s in return for a significant cut by NATO, for example the 108 Pershing II missiles which apparently alarm the Soviet Union more than cruise missiles. Their combination of accuracy and speed reduces warning time. Such a deal would have a number of problems: Pershing is generally considered a better missile than Tomahawk within NATO;[28] a deal of this sort would not seem very radical in Europe, merely confirming that arms control legitimises military programmes rather than restrains them; and it would not address the generalised hostility to cruise missiles in Europe. Another possibility might be to include the US F-111s but no Soviet aircraft. The Soviet Union may have something like this in mind but given the fuss about Backfire in SALT II it would seem a non-starter.

With all the options discussed thus far it is difficult to identify the mixture of incentives that might bring the negotiations to a successful conclusion. The Soviet objectives of severe limitation and cancellation of NATO's LRTNF programme and acceptance of the principles that account should be taken of American FBS, are not compatible with the NATO position of only considering missiles and tolerating restraints in its own programme only to the extent that these are fully reciprocated by the Soviets. Furthermore, the Soviet Union is in a strong bargaining position, with her modernisation programme well advanced (and her final goal uncertain), while NATO's programme remains politically controversial.

This all suggests that without a substantial concession by one side or the other, there can be no agreement based on the principle of parity at the theatre nuclear level and it is even difficult to find one that accepts some permanent disparity. Politically this creates the prospect of East–West acrimony rather than comity, with both sides using the occasion for publicly shifting the blame to the other for a new arms race, adding to arms control's bad name and disappointing those in Europe anxious to see both the SS-20 and TNF programmes either abandoned or substantially reduced through mutual agreement.

The Integrative Approach

There is an alternative possibility: to merge discussions on theatre systems with those on central systems. This approach has some appeal in Europe but has found little favour in Washington where it has been felt that the main business of SALT III will be to achieve 'deep cuts' in the ceilings agreed in SALT II, and that the inclusion of peripheral matters, such as LRTNF, will only complicate and delay. However, as this now provides the sole motor for SALT, the hierarchy of concerns no longer seems appropriate. Moreover, as we have seen, the prospects for a contained negotiation on theatre systems are not encouraging.

For NATO there are good arguments for a merger. It is profoundly 'coupling' in recognising the strategic unity of the alliance and emphasising that American nuclear weapons provide a continuum of deterrence. A deal achieved solely within a European framework would inevitably encourage notions of a separate theatre balance, even if reached and enforced within some specially broadened SALT context.

One objection is that it will force difficult choices on Washington between the two types of systems and the competing demands of domestic and alliance constituencies. However, the existence of separate negotiations will not prevent links developing between the two, with concessions in the different negotiations being traded. Suspicions will inevitably grow within NATO that the United States is assigning top priority to central systems and will not squander precious negotiating capital on the secondary matter of theatre systems. If an all-inclusive ceiling can be achieved within SALT III with a freedom-to-mix arrangement, then the allies can sort out the proper balance between central and theatre systems among themselves, without the Soviet Union sitting in, acting almost as an arbiter. Lastly, at least for Washington, all these systems can reach the Soviet Union, while Moscow would have to make far more serious choices among its different adversaries.

Nevertheless, the Soviet Union ought not to have fundamental objections. It fits in with previous demands for FBS to be brought into SALT. It need not offend the principle of no amendment to SALT II until the Treaty is ratified.

The proposal is to add 400, either to the eventual ceiling for central systems under SALT II, 2250, or to a lower figure if further cuts in central system levels are agreed. Into this raised ceiling can be included theatre missiles and aircraft as already specified, but to levels either less or more than 400 depending on the priorities of each side.

The United States, for example, might still be interested in going beyond 400 in theatre systems to take up some of the gap between the SALT II ceiling and the currently planned force levels.[29]

Because this proposal is based on launchers rather than warheads it does not take account of the SS-20's three warheads.[30] This could be remedied by including the SS-20 under one of the existing sub-ceilings for MIRVed missiles, the most likely would be the 1320 ceiling which currently gives the United States a 120 credit for bombers carrying air-launched cruise missiles (ALCMs). An equivalent 120 credit for MIRVed medium-range missiles could well seem appropriate.[31]

Within these sort of totals the 66 US FB-111s could not be excluded. The more politically awkward problems of the Soviet forces facing China and the British and French forces will remain. They may become linked, so that they are either brought in together or kept out together.[32]

It has not been possible to suggest anything more than expedients to many of the obvious difficulties over what to exclude and include, to be faced whatever the conceptual framework. The problems already identified will not evaporate by placing the negotiations in a different setting, and some new ones will emerge. There is a major mitigating factor: what appears as 20 per cent of some theatre balance will only represent a couple of per cent of the overall balance.

Arms control always involves a compromise between strategic logic and political convenience, and this case is no exception. The proposals outlined above are designed more to respond to a developing political situation and make no pretence to manufacture some new strategic stability – an elusive concept in these circumstances. The only real strategic benefit would be to couple theatre with central systems in an overall SALT ceiling, serving to reinforce an important piece of NATO symbolism. Nor is it claimed that major political benefits can be gained. The current requirement is to avert a political crisis.

This analysis warns of some pitfalls in the coming talks, and, in suggesting integration with the main body of SALT, also cautions against attempting to rescue SALT by persevering with European negotiations in isolation. It illustrates the general difficulties inherent in this sort of arms control, guided by the dubious precept of parity and dominated by the imperfect science of weapon counting. In offering any directions in this area the old *Punch* cartoon comes to mind – 'to get there, I wouldn't be starting from here'.

Notes

1. The present writer's scepticism as to the approach to arms control informing these talks is expressed in Lawrence Freedman, 'Time for a Reappraisal', *Survival*, xxi (1979) 198.
2. Uwe Nerlich observed: 'To some West Europeans, FBS had taken on

symbolic functions, and American handling of the FBS issue was seen as the one indicator of future accountability to European interests of American strategic power in Europe.' *The Alliance and Europe*: Part V, *Nuclear Weapons and East–West Negotiations* (Adelphi Papers no. 120, London, 1976) p. 4.

3. See, for example, Klass de Vries, 'Responding to the SS-20: An Alternative Approach', *Survival*, xxi (1979) 251–5. A key objection to this conciliatory approach was that it was unlikely that the US Congress would authorise funds to be spent on systems when there was a chance that they would never be deployed.

4. The Netherlands' position is that she will only consider opting into the programme in mid-1981 depending on the state of arms-control negotiations. Belgium apparently took a firmer stand in December 1979, implying that she would confirm participation after 6 months. However, the continuing political crisis in Belgium meant that a decision was postponed. In September 1980 the Belgium Cabinet announced that it would review the position every 6 months, monitoring the negotiations, but could on balance be expected to accept the cruise missiles: 'In the event of negotiations between the United States and the Soviet Union not reaching a conclusion, Belgium, in solidarity with its allies, will take all the measures agreed between the NATO partners.' *International Herald Tribune*, 20–21 September 1980.

5. The preparation of the NATO arms-control position was the responsibility of the Special Group, up to December 1979. They operated from April 1979 in parallel to the High Level Group which was responsible for the actual force plans. In 1980 the Special Group was reconstituted as the Special Consultative Group. It has met a number of times to refine the NATO proposal. Now that talks are to begin it will act as the main consultative mechanism to enable the American negotiators to be aware of the interests of all NATO members.

6. NATO Communiqué, *Special Meeting of Foreign and Defence Ministers* (Brussels, 12 December 1979).

7. This desire to push TNF to one side is reflected in one of the few published detailed studies on US strategies for SALT III, William E. Hoehn Jr, *Outlasting SALT II and Preparing for SALT III* (Santa Monica, California, 1979): '. . . SALT III negotiations must emphasize strategic ceilings and missile verification measures. Other important issues – the resolution of many protocol items, "grey area" and theater systems, etc., – must be the core issues for "SALT IV" conducted in parallel but separately' (p. x).

8. In a unilateral statement after the signing of the Interim Agreement on Offensive Arms in May 1972, the Soviet Union argued that she was entitled to increase the number of her nuclear ballistic missile-firing submarines (SSBNs) in line with any increases in those of American allies, implying that the extra numbers she was allowed under the submarine-launched ballistic missile (SLBM) ceilings took account of British and French forces. The United States refused to accept this argument and it has not been raised again since, even when France actually brought an extra submarine into operation.

9. 'The progress that has been made in recent months is that the Soviet Union

gradually gave up asking for compensations for the forward-based systems party because most of the forward-based systems, or I would say all of them, are not suitable for a significant attack on the Soviet Union.' Press Conference of Secretary of State Henry Kissinger, Vladivostok, 24 November 1974. To be found, with a rich collection of source material, in Roger P. Labrie (ed.), *SALT Handbook: Key Documents and Issues*, 1972–1979 (Washington, DC, 1979) p. 285.

10. Leonid Brezhnev, speech to a meeting of the Baumansky constituency in Moscow, 2 March 1979; '[The USSR] has already repeatedly said that it stands not for the accumulation but the restriction of nuclear-missile and other weapons by agreements based on full reciprocity. The same applies to medium-range weapons in Europe, taking into account the presence of American military bases there, of course.'

11. There were only hints from Eastern European sources that SS-20 production might cease if the NATO programme was abandoned. See Milton Leitenberg, 'NATO and WTO Long-range Theatre Nuclear Forces' in Karl E. Birnbaum (ed.), *Arms Control in Europe: Problems and Prospects* (Laxenburg, Austria, 1980) p. 34.

12. *Pravda*, 7 July 1980. The Soviet Union has argued that this was an alternative to previous proposals for the reduction of her medium-range weapons if no additional US weapons were deployed in Western Europe, or else a discussion in the framework of SALT III after the SALT II Treaty enters force. See *Pravda*, 15 July 1980.

13. Sea-based missiles include 64 British and 80 French SLBMs and the 400 *Poseidon* warheads (essentially the contents of two SSBNs) assigned to SACEUR by the United States.

14. It was reported in October 1980 that delays in the GLCM development programme, particularly with regard to the software and hardware for the control systems, have used up all the spare time built into the programme, so that 'if further delays occur they would affect the operational commitment to NATO'. *Aviation Week and Space Technology*, 20 October 1980.

15. The current intention is for the 108 Pershing II to be based in West Germany, with her, Great Britain, Italy, Belgium and Holland respectively taking 96, 160, 112, 48 and 48 cruise missiles each.

16. There was also some work on a version using the first and third SS-13 stages to produce a longer-range missile – 3000 as against 1100 nautical miles.

17. There may have been a sighting in the Far Eastern region close to the Mongolian border. If true, this confirms the importance of the 'China threat' in stimulating Soviet MR/IRBM development.

18. In the now declassified presentations of the US Secretary of Defense to Congress (from which much of the above information is taken), these SS-11s were first discussed separately from the rest of the SS-11s and other ICBMs. However, in public presentations of the 'threat' they were brought together. See Lawrence Freedman, *US Intelligence and the Soviet Strategic Threat* (London 1977) pp. 158–9.

19. The relevant SS-11s, at the Derazhnya and Pervomaysk sites, are deployed in their silos at such an angle that they are clearly aimed at European targets and could not be retargeted against the United States. They have now been supplemented by 60 SS-19s at these sites and might eventually be replaced by

more of this particular missile. There are reports of training exercises with
the SS-19 that show it being prepared for theatre use (*Armed Forces
Journal International*, December 1979). The point is that the SS-19s are in
vertical silos and can therefore be targeted against the United States or
Europe.

20. The 23 bases already operational or under construction are capable of
supporting over 200 SS-20s.

21. See Harold Brown, *Department of Defense Annual Report, Fiscal Year 1981*
(Washington, DC, 1980) p. 93.

22. NATO Nuclear Planning Group, *Final Communiqué*, M-N PG-1(80)13
(Bodö, 4 June 1980). As the SS-4s and SS-5s are in different sites there is no
necessity for a one-to-one replacement. The most relevant considerations are
manpower and maintenance requirements.

23. See Harold Brown, op. cit. in note 21. He notes that this decline 'is based
upon current trends. It is possible, however, that the Soviet Union may wish
to retain a larger proportion of the current force, perhaps for use as a
bargaining chip in future arms control negotiations' (p. 93).

24. IISS, *The Military Balance 1980–81* (London, 1980). This excludes 280
Badgers, 40 Blinders and 70 Backfires attached to the Naval Air Forces.

25. If the F-111 is included then there is a case for including the 370 Su-19
Fencers. This is the closest Soviet aircraft to the F-111. Furthermore, there
has been a suggestion that it might be a medium bomber rather than a close
support aircraft. However, while its combat radius is not dissimilar from the
F-111, its weapons load at 8000 lb compares unfavourably with the F-111 at
28,000 lb and certainly does not warrant medium-bomber status (*The
Military Balance 1980–81*, pp. 90–91). Furthermore, once one starts
including aircraft such as the Su-19 then it becomes difficult to exclude
others essentially designed for combat support.

26. However, the fractionation limit in SALT involves a move in this direction.
Counting the GLCM-TEL as a single launcher might well seem contrived.
The normal inclination would be to count launch tubes (as in a submarine).

27. Potentially available in the United States are 44 F-111 E/F and 237 of the
much older and less capable F-111 A/D. In addition there are 66 long-range
FB-111s which are part of Strategic Air Command.

28. Furthermore, if the problem it creates for the Soviet Union is reduced
warning time then the only significance this might have would be in confus-
ing any plans for launch on warning. Persuading her of the impracticality of
such a dangerous plan would seem a wholly desirable objective – stabilising
in the traditional arms control sense.

29. One American problem is that all new missiles are likely to be MIRVed so
that as old systems are phased out they will be unable to be replaced with new
missiles because they will come up against the sub-ceilings for MIRVed
missiles and there are no new bombers coming into production. There are
plans to 'stretch' 66 FB-111s and 89 F-111Ds between 1983 and 1986 and to
turn them into 'Ersatz' long-range bombers. (*Aviation Week and Space
Technology*, 16 June 1980).

30. It is assumed here that GLCMs will be counted in individual tubes rather
than in batches of four on TELs.

31. It would obviously be very attractive for the United States if the SS-20 could

be used to cut into the Soviet MIRVed ICBM (820) or even MIRVed ICBM and SLBM (1200) sub-ceilings.

32. Differentiating between Soviet bombers and missiles, as discussed earlier, might be matched by differentiating between French (which are not assigned to NATO) and British (which are) forces, particularly as it is now known that Great Britain will now have no more than five SSBNs until well into the next century. Neither Great Britain nor France could prevent the United States allowing the Soviet Union a credit for their systems.

16 Nuclear-weapon-free Zones: the Latin American Experiment

Félix Calderón

Introduction

Prima facie, the idea of establishing nuclear-weapon-free zones (NWFZs) is very interesting inasmuch as it implies the regional proscription of nuclear weapons through renunciation by the regional states and the inhibition of the external nuclear powers. Nevertheless, a more thorough study of its theoretical implications and practical usefulness shows us that it is not an easy undertaking and that its effectiveness has not been totally proved.

The establishment of a NWFZ has, *stricto sensu*, two aspects. One relates to its adoption *de jure*, and the other relates to its validity *de facto*. The first implies the solution of a series of problems of a theoretical nature and the fulfilment of a series of requirements, whereas the second involves a process which can be prolonged *sine die*, if new or different factors appear. Every one is aware that the Treaty for the Prohibition of Nuclear Weapons in Latin America was at the moment of its adoption a great achievement, given the many existing theoretical difficulties. But the creation *de jure* of a NWFZ is one thing and its *de facto* application is another.

This chapter is intended to make evident those difficulties related to the establishment of a NWFZ. To that end, it is necessary first to explain some elements that make up the theoretical framework. Next, an assessment of all the initiatives so far formulated will be given. And, finally, the Tlatelolco Treaty will be examined in order to set forth the real possibilities of creating more NWFZs. (It is worth noting that the analysis will focus on the establishment of NWFZs in inhabited areas, even though the military non-nuclearisation of empty spaces is not entirely disregarded.)

Theoretical Aspects

As has been pointed out, the difficulties in establishing the NWFZs are first of all of a theoretical nature because of the lack of consensus among experts regarding the meaning and scope of the NWFZ concept. A typical example of this was the condensed study carried out in 1975 by the *ad hoc* group of qualified governmental experts. This did not include a definition of the NWFZ. Nor did it resolve other crucial questions (linked to the same concept) such as transit, the zone of application and nuclear explosions for peaceful purposes.[1]

This misunderstanding at the theoretical level, which could not but affect the interest in NWFZs, could be explained basically by the different approaches made by the experts in the study on the NWFZs. As a logical consequence, neither the ideas on the usefulness of the concept nor those on its viability and scope are the same.

At present, it seems that the main tendency associates the concept of the NWFZ with the regime of horizontal non-proliferation of nuclear weapons. This is mainly due to the adoption of the Treaty for the Prohibition of Nuclear Weapons in Latin America (better known as the Treaty of Tlatelolco); to the Indian nuclear explosion of 18 May 1974; and to intense debate in the UN which followed that event.

DEFINITION OF NWFZs

Definitions of NWFZs are numerous. Some have only been confined to the simple use of synonyms; others have put emphasis on legal formalities; and yet others have tried to combine both with the political dimension of the concept. With reference particularly to the latter, there exists only one definition which has received international acceptance. This is the one adopted by the

UN General Assembly in its Resolution 3472B of 11 December 1975. This can be broken down into two different elements: the legal formalities necessary for the creation of a NWFZ; and the intrinsic nature of the NWFZ. It reads:

> A nuclear-weapon-free zone shall, as a general rule, be deemed to be any zone recognized as such by the General Assembly of the United Nations, which any group of States, in free exercise of their sovereignty, has established by virtue of a treaty or convention whereby: (a) The statute of total absence of nuclear weapons to which the zone shall be subject, including the procedure for the delimitation of the zone, is defined; (b) An international system of verification and control is established to guarantee compliance with obligations deriving from that statute.

A careful analysis of this definition, from the point of view of the aforementioned elements, leads to the identification of at least two inescapable problems: first, the reference to recognition of the NWFZ by the UN General Assembly, and secondly, its asymmetry or imbalance because of its exclusive reference to the statute of total absence of nuclear weapons. In relation to the first point, the problem not only arises because of the legal and political superiority of a treaty over a UN resolution, but also because of the absence of any practical effects of such recognition when it is given after the adoption *de jure* of the NWFZ, but before its application *de facto* (the real and effective application in the whole area). With respect to the second point, the problem is obviously of greatest magnitude inasmuch as it has to do with the rationality itself of the concept of NWFZ. In effect, the issue at stake is not that of banning nuclear weapons for the sake of banning them (as those who accept this definition appear to believe), but to create a situation of privilege which is only achieved when the zone in question is excluded from an eventual nuclear war as a sort of compensation for the prohibition of the military atom. Hence, even though this definition, accepted by the General Assembly (in reality, the General Assembly did no more than endorse the proposal presented by Mexico), has been politically endorsed by a large number of states, it suffers from major difficulties that obstruct its use in operation as much because of an excess of legal formalities, as because of its lack of weight *vis-à-vis* the political atmosphere necessary for the creation of a NWFZ.

So, how should we define a NWFZ? A study of the only regional project for the banning of nuclear weapons in an inhabited region of the planet, the Treaty of Tlatelolco, leads to the identification of two fundamental aspects common to all the NWFZs: aims and essential characteristics. With regard to aims, there are two. First is the immediate one of the strengthening of the security of all the states involved, which is attained with the adoption *de jure* of the NWFZ and its application *de facto*. Second is the long-range aim, which concerns the promotion of nuclear disarmament. With respect to the essential characteristics, there are also two. On the one hand, there is the statute of total absence of nuclear weapons within a determined geographical area, and, on the other hand, the guarantees that that geographical area will remain free from any nuclear confrontation (the so-called 'negative security assurances').

In other words, the concept of NWFZ implies a perfectly balanced mechanism which responds to certain aims and which by no means could be considered as an isolated measure implying only obligations of a negative nature for the regional states. From this point of view, the NWFZ can very well be interpreted as a measure of regional nuclear non-armament (to prevent the horizontal proliferation or the 'dissemination' — in the sense of scattered abroad — of nuclear weapons); or as a measure of regional nuclear disarmament. In any case, it should imply the creation of a sanctuary in a particular geographical area as well as the promotion of an auspicious climate towards making total nuclear disarmament possible.

It is worth noting that whatever form a NWFZ takes its establishment is, *per se*, a process which starts with its adoption *de jure* and continues until it is put into effect *de facto*. For even though the constituent treaty may be negotiated by the states of the region if it is to be put into effect it also needs the agreement of the nuclear powers. It is this fact which raises the question of whether or not it would be convenient to include the nuclear powers in the NWFZ negotiations from the beginning.

GUIDELINES AND REQUIREMENTS

One of the questions on which the *ad hoc* group of qualified governmental experts reached a consensus concerned the singularity of each region, which imposes a 'pragmatic and flexible approach'. This certainly does not mean that each NWFZ has to be a *sui generis* model, but that it is necessary to adapt the same model to the peculiarities of each geographical area. This unique model which defines legally the NWFZ is considered by some experts as a series of principles. However, in practice it is no more than a group of guidelines which are fulfilled according to the specific procedures adopted to put into effect the different projects on NWFZs. In general terms, the establishment of a NWFZ in a region where there has never been nuclear weapons is not the same as its creation where it is necessary to eliminate those existing. These guidelines include:

(a) the statute of total absence of nuclear weapons which involves the renunciation of nuclear weapons as well as the acceptance of the complementary system of verification and control;
(b) the so-called 'negative security assurances';
(c) the conditions for the entry into force of the treaty establishing the NWFZ; and
(d) the duration of that treaty as well as the right to withdraw from it.

Apart from the degree of emphasis which may be placed on any of these guidelines, they contain certain basic concepts which cannot be rejected without placing in jeopardy the NWFZ as a whole. On the other hand, these guidelines are only adopted once some political requirements have been satisfied. In other words, the adoption of a treaty related to the establishment of a NWFZ implies the previous fulfilment of certain conditions so as to create the appropriate climate for it. There is no sense in trying to work out those guidelines in a region where the highest priority for establishing a NWFZ does not reside in the legal field but in the political one. These requirements include:

(a) free initiative of the interested states and their voluntary adhesion to the resulting treaty;
(b) participation in the project of all the states of military importance in the region;
(c) absence of serious tension or fundamental difference between the states involved;
(d) the existence in the region of a certain homogeneity and of a high degree of understanding;

(e) preservation of the regional *status quo*;
(f) consensus with respect to the regime which governs the NWFZ; and
(g) the nuclear powers' agreement to the 'mise en oeuvre' of the NWFZ. (In the light of the experience of Tlatelolco it is not in fact necessary for this condition to be met *a priori*.)

It is quite clear that if any one of these requirements is not fulfilled, it would be difficult for a projected NWFZ to materialise. This conclusion is underlined by the record of the failure of numerous initiatives, as will be seen in the following section.

NWFZ's Initiatives

The first initiative to establish a NWFZ came from the Soviet Union and was concerned with regional nuclear disarmament. On 27 March 1956 Andrei Gromyko put before the Sub-Committee on Disarmament in London a new plan for the reduction of armed forces and conventional weapons. The third section of this dealt with the creation within Europe of an area, consisting of both parts of Germany and their neighbouring countries, for the limitation and inspection of weapons where the installations of nuclear weapons, amongst other things, would be prohibited.[2] Of course, this gesture by the Soviets was certainly not motivated by altruism. However, it did have the merit of placing on the table of multilateral discussions a relatively new idea which would be returned to many times, although not always with the original aim of regional nuclear disarmament in mind.

From 27 March 1956 to date, 17 initiatives have been presented, all of which come under the regional context. Of these only six have had the same objective as the Soviet proposal (military denuclearisation). The remaining eleven have instead been concerned with the prohibition of nuclear weapons (non-dissemination and non-horizontal nuclear proliferation). Obviously this categorisation does not take subtle distinctions into account but, in general terms, it provides a good illustration of the trends which have been observed since 1956.

With reference to those initiatives concerned with nuclear disarmment, four have developed beyond the initial stages (the Rapacki Plan and the projects for the Indian Ocean, the South

Pacific and Africa). The other two never crossed the threshold of the initial declaration (the Unden Plan and the East Asia proposal). But they all have in common the fact that none of them resulted in a treaty being signed, either because it would have threatened the military equilibrium of the region established by the superpowers or because the proposals were simply a response to particular circumstances.

The Rapacki Plan (an improved version of the 1956 Soviet proposal), the Unden Plan (which focused on Central and Northern Europe) and the proposals to create a 'zone of peace' in the Indian Ocean and to denuclearise the South Pacific (1975), could be considered as a threat to the *status quo*. The two proposals which were the result of special circumstances were the one for East Asia (made in November 1971 when the Vietnam War was in progress) and the one related to Africa which was originally put forward in December 1960 following the French explosions in the Sahara (today the African situation is ambigious because of the suspicions that South Africa possesses nuclear bombs).

With reference to the initiatives concerned with the prohibition of nuclear weapons, because of the superpowers' wish to exclude the areas involved from all open military confrontation, four have actually resulted in treaties (the Antarctic Treaty, the Outer Space Treaty, The Tlatelolco Treaty and the Sea-Bed Treaty). The remaining seven have not progressed beyond the initial declaration stage, with the sole exception of the projects for the Middle East and Southern Africa. They are either attempts to maintain the *status quo* of the region unaltered when confronted with its imminent change or in attempts to change it in view of the supposed existence of the bomb. They are, in chronological order: the Romanian proposal to establish a 'zone of peace' in the Balkans (1957), to which 2 years later the Russians added the Adriatic Sea; the Soviet proposal to create a 'zone of peace' in the Baltic Sea (1959); the initiative of the People's Republic of China to create a NWFZ in Asia and the Pacific (1960); the Soviet project to establish a NWFZ in the Mediterranean (1963); the Kekkonen Plan to prohibit nuclear weapons in the Scandinavian countries (1963); the Iranian proposal to establish a NWFZ in the Middle East (1968); and the project which related to Southern Asia (1974).

To summarise, from 1956 to date the concept of NWFZ has been used in an indeterminate way to promote nuclear disarmament, non-dissemination or, simply, horizontal non-proliferation (the last two imply non-nuclear armament), although with most emphasis on the first two. Nevertheless the only proposal which has successfully resulted in a treaty, with the exception of those which relate to the uninhabited areas, has been the one which was in fact linked to horizontal non-proliferation. This was the Brazilian initiative of 7 November 1962 which resulted in the signing of the Treaty of Tlatelolco on 14 February 1967. This outcome raises a series of questions as to what scope and viability NWFZs really have.

It is now appropriate to consider how the Latin American undertaking of non-military nuclearisation has been put into effect and up to what point it can be taken as a model for other regions.

The Treaty of Tlatelolco

The initiative to establish a NWFZ in Latin America was a result of the missiles crisis of 1962, when the Cold War moved to the Caribbean. Although a variety of proposals for NWFZs had been put forward at several different forums, it was the danger of the actual presence of missiles in Cuba in the future which aroused the interest of the Latin American states in the prohibition of nuclear weapons.

The first proposal was made by Brazil in 1962, and in 1963 it was taken up by Mexico. From that date this country, through its representative Alfonso García Robles, played such a leading rôle in bringing the project into existence that the success of that negotiation is often attributed to Mexico, and to Ambassador García Robles in particular.

The President of Mexico, A. López Mateos, formally proposed the non-nuclearisation of Latin America in a letter dated 21 March 1963 addressed to four Heads of State (Bolivia, Brazil, Chile and Ecuador). This proposal was taken up a few weeks later in a joint declaration signed by these five leaders (29 April). Furthermore, this declaration formed the basis for the Resolution 1911 (XVII) which was adopted by the General Assembly of the UN on 27 November of the same year. Afterwards, it was also Mexico's decisive participation which set in motion the Preparatory Commission for the Denuclearisation [sic] of Latin America (COPREDAL) and finally made possible the adoption of the treaty.

What is now known as the Treaty of Tlatelolco (the title of Tlatelolco comes from the name of the district in which COPREDAL met four times) consists of the Treaty itself plus two complementary protocols. In fact these three legal instruments form a unique juridical complex which cannot be split up. It is based on the nature of the NWFZ.

On 31 March 1980 the main Treaty was in force in 22 Latin American states (signature, ratification and dispensation stipulated in Article 28, paragraph 2): The following states were not participants for a variety of reasons. Argentina, Brazil, Cuba, Chile and Guyana. The Additional Protocol I had not yet been ratified by the United States and France. The Additional Protocol II had already been accepted by the five nuclear powers, although with some observations.

As has earlier been seen, the establishment of a NWFZ depends not only on the states of the region renouncing nuclear weapons, but also on a corresponding undertaking from states outside the region (this applies to the nuclear powers in particular) not to introduce in any form weapons of mass destruction. This being the case, the most appropriate methodology to use is to examine the Treaty of Tlatelolco as a whole, taking as a starting point its two essential characteristics, which are also very closely linked. These are the statute of total absence on nuclear weapons and the so-called 'negative security assurances'.

THE STATUTE OF TOTAL ABSENCE OF NUCLEAR WEAPONS

The term 'total absence' of nuclear weapons should be understood to mean the general rather than absolute absence of these weapons of mass destruction, because the latter would be an abstraction.

The statute of total absence of nuclear weapons has two fundamental aspects: the undertaking by the states both within and outside the region to prohibit nuclear weapons in the area; and the complementary system of verification and control to ensure that this undertaking is respected. The Tlatelolco Treaty as a whole deals with both these aspects in great detail (the main Treaty, Additional Protocol I and Articles 1 and 2 of Additional Protocol II). Nevertheless, as will be seen below, there are some omissions and ambiguities which leave the door open for the dissembled presence of nuclear devices in the area.

The Prohibition of Nuclear Weapons. Nuclear weapons are totally prohibited in Latin America in Article 1 of the Main Treaty, in the Additional Protocol I and in Articles 1 and 2 in the Additional Protocol II. Although the obligations of the states within the region (the so-called involved states) are more explicit than those of other states (states which have dependent territories in the area in addition to the nuclear powers), they are fundamentally similar. In any event, they both have the same objective: to ensure the total absence of nuclear weapons. These obligations read:

Main Treaty, Article 1:
1. The Contracting Parties hereby undertake to use exclusively for peaceful purposes the nuclear material and facilities which are under their jurisdiction, and to prohibit and prevent in their respective territories: (a) The testing, use, manufacture production or acquisition by any means whatsoever of any nuclear weapons, by the Parties themselves, directly or indirectly, on behalf of anyone else or in any other way, and (b) The receipt, storage, installation, deployment and any form of possession of any nuclear weapons, directly or indirectly, by the Parties themselves, by anyone on their behalf or in any other way.
2. The Contracting Parties also undertake to refrain from engaging in, encouraging or authorizing, directly or indirectly, or in any way participating in the testing, use, manufacture, production, possession or control of any nuclear weapon.

Additional Protocol I, Article 1:

To undertake to apply the statute of denuclearization [*sic*] in respect of warlike purposes as defined in Articles 1, 3, 5 and 13 of the [Main Treaty] in territories for which, *de jure* or *de facto*, they are internationally responsible and which lie within the limits of the geographical zone established in that Treaty.

Additional Protocol II, Article 1:

The statute of denuclearization [*sic*] of Latin America in respect of warlike purposes as defined, delimited, and set forth in the

[Main Treaty] of which this instrument is annex, shall be fully respected by the Parties to this Protocol in all its express aims and provisions.

Additional Protocol II, Article 2:

The Governments represented by the undersigned Plenipotentiaries undertake, therefore, not to contribute in any way to the performance of acts involving a violation of the obligations of Article 1 of [the Main Treaty] in the territories to which the Treaty applies in accordance with Article 4 thereof.

According to Article 5 of the Main Treaty, 'a nuclear weapon is any device which is capable of releasing nuclear energy in an uncontrolled manner and which has a group of characteristics that are appropriate for use for warlike purposes', the term 'nuclear weapons' involves fission and fusion arms regardless of whether they are offensive or defensive. It also involves both strategic and theatre nuclear weapons.

In comparison to what is stipulated in Articles I and II of the NPT, the obligations contained in the Treaty of Tlatelolco are more far-reaching. Consequently, the supply or installation of any nuclear weapons in the region is completely prohibited. Similarly, so is any assistance which an involved state may give to a nuclear or non-nuclear power in the manufacture of any of these nuclear devices.

Nonetheless, these far-reaching obligations are affected by the gaps and ambiguities to be found in the Tlatelolco Treaty. These include the problem of transport (which is simply ignored), the delimitation of the zone of application and peaceful nuclear explosions. These gaps and ambiguities, one way or another, conspire against the statute of total absence of nuclear weapons and, in the end, against the whole concept of NWFZ.

The Transit Problem.   Specialists differentiate between what is strictly speaking transport and transit. The former refers to the movement of nuclear weapons on ships and airplanes which belong to those states which are members of the area concerned. The latter refers only to the movement through the zone of nuclear weapons on ships and aeroplanes belonging to other states. In the case of transit, entry to ports and airports is also covered.

Those who drafted the Treaty omitted any specific reference to either, in any of its three legal instruments. This omission is not in fact due to negligence on the part of the negotiators but rather to the problems which the *sui generis* legal status of the Panama Canal presented at the time. (The United States had always maintained that the inclusion of the Panama Canal in the NWFZ should not affect its right to free transit which is established by contract. This right to free transit has also been recognised by the new Panama Canal Treaty.)

The COPREDAL, well aware of the implications of this omission, decided before completing their work to issue a declaration giving some interpretation of the subject. This made clear that transport remained subject to the conditions contained in Article 1 of the Main Treaty whilst decisions about transit were to be left to the individual states, always assuming that no agreement had been reached between involved states and nuclear powers.

In fact, with the exception of Mexico and Panama, which have both expressly forbidden the transit of nuclear weapons through their territory, none of the Latin American countries has unilaterally implemented similar decisions nor has any reached a multilateral agreement. Furthermore, some of them, such as Brazil, have legalised the transit of nuclear-powered ships through their territorial waters.

The nuclear powers hold two official positions on the subject. First there is that held by the United States, France and Great Britain who reject any total prohibition of the transit of nuclear weapons through the zone which is affected. Secondly, there is the position held by the Soviet Union and China which is that transit, in whatever form, is incompatible with the principles of the NWFZ.

If it is accepted that the total prohibition of nuclear weapons in a NWFZ is not absolute, then the main problem is arguably not the transit of ships and aeroplanes, but rather how this is to be monitored. In any event, so long as some nuclear powers do not share the Soviet position this, in realistic terms, will remain the main point in question. This being the case, it is therefore imperative that regulations to control the transit of nuclear weapons within the NWFZ be drawn up. If this is not done there will be nothing to prevent the false or hidden presence of these destructive weapons. This is a risk which exists today in Latin America.

The Delimitation of the Zone of Application.   One problem which is closely linked to the above relates to the spatial delimitation of the NWFZ. In theory the zone of application referred to in a treaty which creates a NWFZ should be an internationally recognised geographical area. Otherwise, which comes to the same thing, the zone should consist solely of those territories belonging to the member states and not of any areas which do not come under their sovereignty. Any other solution which has not been negotiated would be open to debate. Which formula was adopted in the Treaty of Tlatelolco? As far as can be deduced from reading Article 4 of the Main Treaty two zones of application have in fact been adopted. The first zone, which may be called the one of provisional delimitation, consists solely of the territories belonging to the states which are full participants in the Treaty of Tlatelolco (paragraph 1). The second zone, which may be called the one of definitive delimitation, consists of the whole of Latin America plus certain parts of the high seas to the East and West of the continental and insular mass (paragraph 2). Apart from the objections which this Article in itself gives rise to (the Treaty of Tlatelolco in reality creates two NWFZs: one provisional and one definitive), both zones of application are also open to different interpretations, which works against their being internationally recognised.

With reference to the provisional zone of application, the definition of the term 'territory' in Article 3 of the Main Treaty raises the question of how extensive the zone is. Should it include the 200 mile maritime zone over which some Latin American States claim sovereignty and jurisdiction? In accordance with Article 3 the term 'territory' shall include the territorial sea, air space and 'any other space over which the state exercises sovereignty in accordance with its own legislation'. So, it would appear that the 'exclusive economic zone' is excluded from this term because it allows the coastal state sovereignty over the resources but not over the zone itself, which is why free navigation is permitted. The United States, France, Great Britain and the Soviet Union have emphasised that the reference to 'own legislation' to be found in that Article should be taken within the context of its compatibility with the norms of the international law. However, this interpretation is not necessarily shared by all the Latin American countries. This has resulted in a controversy as to what the real limits of the provisional zone are. In any case, the provisional NWFZ does not cover so far half of the continental and insular surface of Latin America because of the absence of, among others, Argentina and Brazil, both of which have a large territorial surface.

With reference to the definitive zone of application, in addition to the controversy relating its extensiveness, there are three other points about which there are discrepancies. First, it is not known how the principle of free navigation stands in relation to the enforcement of individual national laws. If the idea is to preserve the integrity of this principle then there would appear to be little sense in including vast portions of the high seas in the NWFZ. (At least, all the nuclear powers have declared themselves in favour of freedom of navigation on the high seas being applied to the zone of definitive delimitation.) On the other hand, if the idea is to regulate this principle only where the transit of nuclear weapons is concerned, then a decision as to who should have responsibility for this would have to be made. It would evidently not be realistic to exclude the nuclear powers from the drawing-up of these regulations. Lastly, there is also some doubt as to the practical validity of a zone of application where there are conflicting laws. In effect both the Tlatelolco Treaty and the Interamerican Treaty of Mutual Assistance share the same stage, with the difference that the former prohibits the use of nuclear weapons on that stage whereas the latter, by implication, does not exclude them. A conflict provoked by Cuba or the Soviet Union within the zone in which both treaties are superimposed could well '*vider de sa substance*' the Treaty of Tlatelolco.

In conclusion, in the case of the Tlatelolco Treaty a clearly defined zone of application which enjoys international recognition does not exist. Further, the differences of opinion which are generated by the different interpretations of Article 4 itself make it difficult to predict, for the present, that any agreement will be reached between the involved states and the states outside the zone (particularly the nuclear powers) which will resolve this impasse. As a logical consequence it is quite possible to imagine situations in which nuclear powers could ignore Article 4 without legally violating the undertaking in Article 1 and 2 of the Additional Protocol II. One possible example of this would be the presence of a ship or submarine carrying nuclear warheads in the 'exclusive economic zone' of any of the coastal Latin American States.

Peaceful Nuclear Explosions.   The negotiations for the Treaty of

Tlatelolco took place in the midst of an upsurge of expectations as to the possible peaceful use of nuclear explosive devices. (Speculation as to the possible civilian use of nuclear explosions began in 1958. Today the outlook is rather sombre.) This explains why the right to conduct nuclear explosions was included among its dispositions, as also was the mechanism to control these nuclear explosions. Even though it was already possible to predict the potential military use of these nuclear explosive devices, it seems that reaching an agreement on the subject was more important to the negotiators than the implications of what effect such a disposition might have on the status of the NWFZ.

Up to what point can peaceful nuclear explosions be compatible with the statute of total absence of nuclear weapons? In general terms, so long as non-military nuclear explosive devices have any military significance there is no doubt that any legitimisation of their use within a NWFZ remains a flagrant contradiction of that statute. If the intention is to ensure that the involved states have access to the benefits to be derived from their non-military application, it would be sufficient simply to adopt an improved version of the contents of Article V of the NPT rather than turn to the recognition of a right which may well open a Pandora's Box.

Within this context the formula contained in Article 18 of the Main Treaty is an error and is dangerous. Not only has the right to conduct nuclear explosions been recognised but also, which is equally questionable, an ambiguous formula has been used which opens the door to that right being utilised in an arbitrary fashion according to individual interpretations. Paragraph 1 of this Article reads:

> The Contracting Parties may carry out explosions of nuclear devices for peaceful purposes − including explosions which involve devices similar to those used in nuclear weapons − or collaborate with third parties for the same purpose, provided that they do so in accordance with the provisions of this Article and the other Articles of the Treaty, particularly Articles 1 and 5.

Prima facie, to be able to conduct civil nuclear explosions using devices which are similar to nuclear weapons without violating Articles 1 and 5 of the Main Treaty would appear to be a contradiction. Nevertheless, from the legal point of view this ambiguity makes possible more than one interpretation. The

United States, Great Britain, the Soviet Union and some of the involved States such as Mexico have made the point that Article 1 and 5 exclude, for the present, the implementation of Article 18 given that today's technology does not differentiate, *de facto*, between nuclear devices for military or civilian purposes. (There is one fundamental characteristic which both have in common: the releasing of large quantities of energy from a relatively small, light device in a space of time measured in millionths of a second.) Nevertheless, Argentina and Brazil, amongst others, hold a different opinion. They consider that Article 18 does not ignore that similarity but rather underlines it.

The basic question to be determined is how far Article 18 is subordinated to Articles 1 and 5. In principle, when Article 18 establishes the right to carry out civil nuclear explosions 'including explosions which involve devices similar to those used in nuclear weapons', it recognises by tacit inference two basic premises. First, it is perfectly possible to conceive a nuclear explosive device different from nuclear weapons. Secondly, a nuclear explosion with peaceful aims, even in the case of using similar devices to a nuclear bomb, does not necessarily involve a violation of Articles 1 and 5. In other words, it is feasible to carry out peaceful nuclear explosions without contravening these articles.

If conducting a peaceful nuclear explosion must always imply as a condition *sine qua non* the previous manufacturing of a nuclear explosive device different to the nuclear weapon, then the word 'similar' (from the Latin *similis* which means alike, of the same nature or quality) would not make any sense. So, although Article 18 does not exclude the eventual use of a nuclear device different from a nuclear weapon, neither does it forbid the use of a device, technically speaking, equivalent to such a weapon of mass destruction.

Therefore, the distinction between Article 18 and Articles 1 and 5 is dependent upon the author's intention (the state which conducts the nuclear explosion) rather than in the technicalities, leaving in this way important channels for ambiguities and a game of chances. Thus including the right to conduct nuclear explosions in the Treaty of Tlatelolco and, in addition, making it ambiguous, was a mistake. Even though carte blanche has not actually been offered to the involved states given the parallel existence of safeguards (Article 18, paragraphs 2 and 3), there is no guarantee at present that nuclear explosions with potential military use will never happen in Latin America. At least for those Latin American countries which remain out of NPT (Argentina, Brazil, Colombia, Cuba and Chile), the option to conduct peaceful nuclear explosions is still open.

The System of Verification and Control.   The undertaking by the states both within and outside the region to prohibit nuclear weapons in it, does not have, in theory, any sense if it is not accompanied by a system of verification and control to ensure its fulfilment. Normally, the system of verification and control must have two kinds of safeguards in every NWFZ: first, one applicable to all the installations and nuclear materials of the regional states, in order to assure the absence of illicit use of nuclear energy for peaceful purposes; and secondly, one designed to make evident any secret introduction of nuclear weapons into the area, thereby involving the states outside the region, in particular the nuclear powers.

Naturally, the Tlatelolco Treaty includes references to both types of safeguards, as well as special safeguards to prevent the misuse of the peaceful nuclear explosions (Article 12 of the Main Treaty). Nevertheless, those safeguards only refer to the regional states, and there is no single disposition covering the commitments of the states outside the zone. Thus the safeguards are in some respect questionable. The IAEA is in charge of enforcing the first kind of safeguards (Article 13 of the Main Treaty), and shares with the Agency for the Prohibition of Nuclear Weapons in Latin America (OPANAL) the verification and control of the peaceful nuclear explosions (Article 18, paragraphs 2 and 3). The second kind of safeguards have been assigned, mainly, to OPANAL (Article 16, paragraph 1, sub-paragraph (b), and from 2 to 8).

The first kind of safeguards, which comprises full-scope safeguards over all nuclear activities of the contracting parties of the Main Treaty and of the non-independent territories covered by the Additional Protocol I, is based on the comparison of information submitted by the inspected state with the verification and observations carried out independently by the IAEA. Thus its efficiency greatly depends on the goodwill of the recipient state. In order to have an idea of its level of credibility, it could be pointed out that it is impossible, technically speaking, to watch nuclear materials when they are only some days or weeks away from being used in a bomb.

Besides, safeguards have been designed to guard what is already declared, not to disclose illicit activities.

Regarding the second kind of safeguards, the problem remains that it only refers to the contracting parties of the Main Treaty and neglects control of any military activity of a nuclear power in the disputed areas of the zone of application. So a legal imbalance regarding control exists. In addition, the illicit or dissembled presence of nuclear weapons in the region is encouraged.

Finally, the international control that the Tlatelolco Treaty establishes on a peaceful nuclear explosion carried out by an involved state does not forbid in any way the state (always providing that it stays outside the NPT) using in the future the information for military purposes. Nor is it forbidden to assist a similar effort that could be made by another state which is not bound by the treaty of regional non-nuclearisation.

Moreover, Article 30 of the Main Treaty provides a clause of denunciation that gives the contracting parties more freedom of action than the pertinent clause of the NPT (Article X) if it wishes to get rid of the commitments acquired under Article 1 of that legal instrument. This greater freedom of action appears through the fact that the denunciation could take place if there 'may arise circumstances . . . which affect [the] supreme interest [of the contracting parties], or the peace and security of one or more contracting parties'. Therefore, not only is there no control over the activities of the nuclear powers, but also a contracting party with an advanced technology could, theoretically, escape from the treaty through the unexpected use of its right to denounce it.

THE 'NEGATIVE SECURITY ASSURANCES'

The term 'negative security assurances', as this guarantee is also known, certainly is not the most appropriate one. Nonetheless, it is used here as it is well understood in the diplomatic world.

The statute of total absence of nuclear weapons does not constitute the only basis for the rationality of NWFZ. Logic also demands a guarantee by the nuclear powers to exclude the whole zone from any nuclear confrontation. Such a guarantee would mean the interdiction of use, or threat of use of weapons of mass destruction against the involved states. It is in fact nothing more than a commitment of a negative nature, designed to counterbalance the importance of the renunciation by the regional states of nuclear weapons. The qualification of negative guarantee is made contrary to the one named positive guarantee, which means to support the immediate assistance of a non-nuclear state, victim of an act or subject to a threat of aggression, which implies the use of nuclear weapons. An example of the latter is given in the Resolution 255 (1968) of the UN Security Council, adopted so as to satisfy the security requirements of the non-nuclear states within the context of the NPT.

The Tlatelolco Treaty contains this guarantee in Article 3 of the Additional Protocol II. Reservations have been forbidden (Article 4), and its complete enforcement is subject to, in principle, the adherence of all nuclear powers to that legal instrument. In theory, this negative guarantee, as contained in the Additional Protocol II, does not give rise to further objections. Nevertheless, controversies arise when one analyses the way it operates within the context of the Tlatelolco Treaty. First, there is the problem of its application in terms of time. According to the interpretations given by the United States, Great Britain and the Soviet Union, this guarantee would be frankly unnecessary if it was being enforced only during peacetime. And that is so, because they have reserved their right of suspending the fulfilment of their commitments in the eventuality of an attack carried out by a regional State with the support of a nuclear power. (The Soviet position is more ambigious, as it refers to an aggression only and it is sufficient that a regional state becomes a participant in aggression.)

Secondly, there is also the problem of its application in terms of space, due to the existing legal superposition regarding zones of application between the Tlatelolco Treaty and the Interamerican Treaty of Mutual Assistance. A possible scenario, according to Article 3 of the Interamerican Treaty, is that a Soviet nuclear attack against the United States would oblige the Latin American States to give assistance to the latter. But if these countries give priority to the regional non-nuclearisation treaty, then the Interamerican Alliance would lose its *raison d'être*.

Finally, it is arguable that this guarantee, as well as the whole Tlatelolco structure, would be placed at risk as a consequence of the rise of a new power possessing nuclear weapons (Article 28, paragraph 4 of the Main Treaty). The problem itself might not be so much to get the adherence of a new nuclear-weapon state to the

Additional Protocol II, but to determine what is understood by a new nuclear-weapon state.

Along with the chronological criteria followed by the NPT ('For the purpose of this Treaty, a nuclear-weapon state is one which has manufactured and exploded a nuclear weapon or other nuclear explosive device prior to 1 January 1967'), there are arguably up to three ways of defining a nuclear-weapon state: one that manufactures and tests nuclear weapons; one that manufactures and tests a peaceful nuclear explosive device; and one that is assumed to have a bomb-making capacity.

What was the criterion adopted by the Tlatelolco Treaty? Nothing on this subject has been foreseen in the Treaty itself or the two Additional Protocols. However, according to the interpretation given by the General Secretary of OPANAL, Gros Espiell, the determining criteria would be the second of these, which means that not only India, but every state that carries out peaceful nuclear explosions, would be obliged to sign the guarantee. Even states belonging to the zone, such as Brazil or Argentina, would be so obliged.[3]

Conclusion

The establishment of a NWFZ is a measure of a political nature which has as its primary aim the strengthening of the security of a group of states and subsequently of making a contribution to the total banning of nuclear weapons from the earth. In spite of the theoretical difficulties involved, the NWFZ could be a concrete measure of regional nuclear disarmament, of non-dissemination of nuclear weapons, or simply of horizontal non-proliferation. In any case, in practice, it is a specific measure of limited scope and of questionable efficacy.

As the NWFZ does not go further than a determined geographical area, it does not imply the absolute proscription of nuclear weapons. Its scope is thus limited. And its efficacy is subject to controversy, as far as its creation implies for the involved states a 'marchandage' which does not necessarily respond to the immediate aim of the NWFZ.

The process of non-nuclearisation in Latin America certainly is not excepted from these limitations of a practical kind. On the contrary, these limitations have been amply confirmed even though at its birth this Treaty was a great achievement, as it involved, for the first time, an inhabited zone. Thus the Tlatelolco Treaty is far from providing a permanent solution to the problem of proscribing nuclear weapons in Latin America. Furthermore, technological progress has increased its gaps and ambiguities. The necessity for its renegotiation is accordingly bound to be increasingly recognised.

At present the Latin American stage is quite different from that existing at the time of adoption of the Tlatelolco Treaty. At that time the use of nuclear weapons for peaceful purposes was, for most of the countries of the region, a long-term possibility. Now we see the civil atom becoming commonplace. In some cases this has been accompanied by an increase in the possibilities of potential military use, with all the consequences that that implies. In these circumstances the Tlatelolco Treaty, as well as all the other agreements relating to disarmament and arms control, must not be regarded as of a static character. It must be adapted to changes of circumstances so that it does not become obsolete. Hence the case for its renegotiation.

No spread of NWFZs can at present be foreseen, not even in the long term, unless a firm and irrevocable process of nuclear disarmament is set in motion. The application of the Tlatelolco Treaty has shown that the definitive establishment of a NWFZ is not easy. And sometimes one has the impression that the concept of NWFZ is not the most appropriate means to strengthen the security of a group of countries. At least, that is the result, for the time being, of the Latin American experiment. Hence while, in general terms, the NWFZ is an attractive idea, it has uncertain support. For the fate of a NWFZ does not only depend on the political will of the involved states; it also relies on the political will of the nuclear powers.

Notes

1. United Nations Conference of the Committee on Disarmament (CCD), *Comprehensive Study of the Question of NWFZs in all its Aspects* (New York, 1975).
2. United Nations Disarmament Sub-Committee Records, 1/41, 27 Mar. 1956.
3. See OPANAL, *Informes y Declaraciones de los Secretarios Generales* (Mexico City, 1975) p. 71.

17 International Security Regimes: the Case of a Balkan Nuclear-free Zone

Athanassios G. Platias and R. J. Rydell

Introduction

That the study of international regimes is undergoing a renaissance should come as no surprise to the informed observer of contemporary world affairs. The irony lies in its timing. The superpowers appear to be arming for yet another phase of the Cold War; the developing world is increasingly challenging the political and economic terms that have governed postwar North–South relations, and prolonged domestic economic hardships are threatening a resurgence of protectionism within the industrialised world. Yet despite this apparent throwback of world politics to its older semi-gladiatorial mode, students of international relations are giving renewed emphasis to the study of international co-operation as manifested in the creation and growth of regimes.

An everyday definition of a regime is 'a mode or system of rule or government'.[1] In contemporary theory of international relations, however, regimes consist of procedural and normative guides to state behaviour. These include rules, procedures, norms, principles and institutions – all artifacts of co-operative actions of nation states – which constrain the inherent tendency of countries to act exclusively in the light of short-term perceived self-interests.

Although *Realpolitik* may often lead a state to join a regime or regulate its behaviour after becoming a member, it is the Grotian rather than the Machiavellian tradition of international relations that accounts for the growth of regimes in the modern era.

International regimes have grown most recently in the areas of outer space, the oceans, telecommunications, weather modification, trade in commodities, and the protection of natural wildlife. Various types of international regimes have existed for centuries in such areas as the law of the sea, monetary affairs, trade and communications. But the technological, political and economic forces which have brought nations into these more recent 'webs of interdependence'[2] have extended deeper than ever before into provinces that had once been within the exclusive jurisdiction of national governments: arms control, domestic economic policy, export controls, collective security arrangements, foreign economic assistance and energy policy are all issue areas that are increasingly becoming co-ordinated by international regimes. It is not the existence of regimes *per se* but their incredible geographical and functional diversity that are hallmarks of world politics in this century.

According to the logic of international functionalism pioneered by David Mitrany the root causes of war and disharmony could be extricated if neglected welfare tasks could be managed on an international basis. Hence international co-operation in the relatively 'non-political' areas of health, education, environment and natural resources would develop national habits of acting with others to solve common problems; once the beneficial results emerged for all to see, 'spill-over' would occur as national political and security interests would progressively be incorporated into this liberal vision of a global 'harmony of interests'.[3] In fact, however, functionalists observed that few areas are truly non-political: national rivalries continued, albeit in different forums.

The failure of the functionalist 'spill-over' hypothesis has spawned other approaches to international regimes, including one which turns functionalism on its head and suggests the incremental development of regimes in areas that bear directly upon core security interests of states. Alliance systems, one variant of such a regime, are as old as the city-state. Other 'adversary regimes'[4] are represented in such arrangements as regional defence pacts, the SALT process, non-proliferation agreements and measures taken to restrict national development of chemical and biological weapons. Like all regimes, security regimes serve the interests of their parties by reducing uncertainty, stabilising expectations, and encouraging the 'routinisation' of conflict. Moreover, both types of regimes are shaped both by structural characteristics of international society and by the emergence of shared beliefs about the ends and means of participation in the regime.[5] Regimes will differ, however, in the extent to which these various features are balanced.

This chapter represents an effort to analyse the notion of a nuclear-weapon-free zone (NWFZ) as an adversary security regime. By selecting a regime dealing intimately with sensitive national and international security interests and by assessing the applicability of this regime to the Balkans (included in this region are Bulgaria, Romania, Yugoslavia, Albania, Greece and Turkey), a politically volatile area once known as the 'powderkeg of Europe', the authors seek to shed some light on the wider problems of forming and maintaining security regimes. The Balkans represent an excellent area for research on regime-building because of the extent to which the region mirrors conditions existing in international society. The globalist ideologies of Maoism, Titoism, Marxism–Leninism, Stalinism, capitalism, democratic socialism and Islamic revivalism are all prominent in the Balkans. The heterogeneity of the region also extends to the governmental structures, including past or present parliamentary democracies (Greece and Turkey), socialist governments (Yugoslavia and Romania) a centralist pro-Soviet communist state (Bulgaria), and a hybrid (Stalinist–Maoist) socialist people's republic (Albania). To the extent that the region in many ways represents a microcosm of international society, we believe that it represents a classic case for research on security regimes.

The chapter thus represents an attempt to create the conditions for what Harry Eckstein has called a 'critical case study'[6] – that is a case selected specifically for the purpose of building generalisations or testing hypotheses about some wider universe of activity. In sum, the chapter sheds some light on questions concerning the creation of new international regimes where great 'complexity' prevails, namely conditions of cultural and ideological diversity, interstate rivalries, mutual distrust, the existence of non-state actors, heightened perceptions of security interests at stake, and great political uncertainty and risk.

Security Regimes for Nuclear Arms Control in the 1980s

International efforts focused on controlling the use or effects of nuclear weapons in the 1980s will be concentrated in three diplomatic areas. The regulation of competition in strategic weaponry will continue to be a relatively high priority of the United States and Soviet Union. In the European context, the modernisation of theatre nuclear weapons by both East and West will provide opportunities for talks on the disposition and possible reduction of such weapons. Lastly, further international proliferation of nuclear weapons poses dangers that will continue to attract a great deal of attention by countries which supply and consume nuclear power technology.

Yet there are some enormous difficulties ahead. The future of the SALT process is clouded by the erosion of detente following the Soviet invasion of Afghanistan and the pending collapse of the SALT II Treaty during the Reagan Administration. If the prospects for immediate reductions of strategic arsenals appear dim, so are the chances for reductions in European-based nuclear and conventional forces, given the current international climate of East–West mistrust and suspicion. Moreover, efforts to arrest the spread of nuclear weapons are likely to encounter difficult problems as many non-nuclear-weapons states develop technical capabilities and political motivations for manufacturing nuclear explosive devices. Analysts of non-proliferation are thus increasingly shifting their attention away from stopping proliferation to a greater concern for slowing its rate or scope, or as one analyst put it, 'managing nuclear multipolarity'.[7]

Parties to the NPT, assembling in August 1980 in Geneva for the NPT's quinquennial Review Conference, failed to reach a consensus on the foundations of the international regime for nuclear power. Unlike the 1975 conference, participants at the 1980 Review Conference could not even agree on a joint final communiqué. Both conferences reveal the outlines of what is becoming a schismatic international dialogue about the non-proliferation regime, where non-nuclear-weapons states (NNWSs) attempt to link non-proliferation to wider themes relating to the structure of international society such as the New International Economic Order while the nuclear weapons states (NWSs) and their allies try to decouple non-proliferation from these themes by narrowing the discussion to technical issues associated with the nuclear fuel cycle. In this and in virtually all other fora on arms control and non-proliferation, the notion of a NWFZ has been obscured by this diplomatic *pas de deux* between advocates of technical fixes and proponents of a restructured nuclear world order.

The 1980 Review Conference gave very little attention to NWFZs, focusing instead upon the Treaty's provisions on disarmament and its promise of open access to peaceful nuclear technology. Among the non-governmental organisations (NGOs) attending the Review Conference, both Pugwash and the World Without War Council submitted memoranda that included NWFZs among other proposals for strengthening the regime.[8] The Secretariat of the agency monitoring the Tlatelolco Treaty (the Latin American NWFZ) also advocated continued extension of the NWFZ concept.[9] All of these memoranda stress the importance of both positive and negative security assurances (discussed below), the continuing utility of safeguards, and support of the Great Powers as conditions encouraging the formation of NWFZs. The Netherlands and Bulgaria submitted working papers that stressed security assurances and NWFZs as 'effective means of curbing the spread of nuclear weapons . . . [which] contribute significantly to the security of those states [which participate in them]'.[10]

In terms recently developed by Ernest Haas, the recent NPT Review Conference is rich with examples of 'fragmented issue linkage',[11] especially in the efforts of OECD nations to maintain an international consensus on the discriminatory premises of the non-proliferation regime articulated in the NPT and the attempts by less-developed nations to harmonise their positions on nuclear disarmament and access to peaceful technology. Thus, despite little agreement about the causes and effects of proliferation, each bloc conceptualised issue-linkages in accordance with perceived security and economic interests. Little 'substantive issue linkage' occurred: the level of intellectual coherence evident in the debates was very low.

Nuclear-Weapon-Free Zones: Concept and History

In brief, a NWFZ is a spatial area (land, sea, air, extraterrestrial) defined by international treaty wherein nuclear weapons may be neither developed nor stored. Implicit in this brief definition are

T ABLE 5   *NWFZ dates*

2 October 1957	Rapacki proposal in UN General Assembly for NWFZ covering both Germanies, Poland and (later) Czechoslovakia
8 January 1958	Soviet Premier Bulganin proposes Nordic NWFZ to Norwegian Premier Gerhardsen
25 June 1959	Soviet Union proposes Balkan NWFZ
1 December 1959	Antarctic Treaty
28 March 1962	Second Rapacki Plan
20 May 1963	Soviet Union proposes Mediterranean NWFZ
28 May 1963	Finnish President Kekkonen proposes Nordic NWFZ
5 August 1963	Partial test ban treaty in air, space, sea
21 July 1964	African NWFZ proposed in declaration by Heads of African Governments
30 November 1965	Soviet Union proposal for African NWFZ
14 February 1967	Tlatelolco Treaty creates Latin American NWFZ
10 October 1967	Outer Space Treaty
11 February 1971	Seabed Treaty
16 February 1971	UN General Assembly resolution for Indian Ocean as 'Zone of Peace'
15 October 1974	Soviet President Podgorny promises Soviet Union will guarantee non-nuclear status of Nordic NWFZ if established
9 December 1974 and 11 December 1975	UN General Assembly resolutions on NWFZs for South Asia, Africa, Middle East, South Pacific and Definition of NWFZ
30 May 1975	NPT Review Conference approves NWFZ concept
13 November 1980	Israel proposal in UN for Middle East NWFZ

four essential concepts: initiative from the parties themselves; means of verification; international recognition; and consonance with the regional and strategic military balance and security perceptions. From a legal point of view, the notion of a NWFZ is thus entirely consistent with UN Charter provisions dealing with sovereign equality, the proscription of the threat or use of force, the right to collective self-defence, the peaceful settlement of disputes and co-operation among states.[12] The significance of the concept as a security regime comes from its close association with vital interests of the parties to the agreement. In essence, the NWFZ can serve the interests of the NNWSs by reducing regional suspicions and risks of attack while also promoting the collective interest in halting the spread of nuclear weapons.

As indicated in Table 5, NWFZs have been proposed repeatedly in the postwar period. When a comparison is made between the claims and results of other proposals of arms control and disarmament in this period, it is clear that NWFZs are one of the few concrete achievements to which reference can be made. First, geographical denuclearisation has been accomplished in the following uninhabited areas: Antarctica (1959), outer space including the moon and other celestial bodies (1967), and the seabed (1971).[13] Secondly, the Treaty of Tlatelolco established in 1967 a NWFZ covering most of South America; although Argentina, Brazil, Chile and Cuba are not yet full parties, the Tlatelolco Convention has established the largest NWFZ yet attempted in an inhabited area.[14] Other regions where NWFZs have been proposed include: the South Pacific, Africa, the Middle East, South Asia, the Indian Ocean, Central Europe, Scandinavia, the Balkans, and a 'worldwide NWFZ'.[15]

Despite this long-standing international interest in NWFZs as instruments of arms control, the last major effort at analysing the concept and its implementations was completed in 1975.[16] Since then, arms control literature and policies have dealt with nonproliferation by examining the civilian nuclear fuel cycle, tightening up safeguards, imposing strict conditions on nuclear exports and emphasising conventional arms transfers and security guarantees as 'incentives' not to proliferate. Thus despite a growing consensus that proliferation is a political not a technical problem there is an evident tendency for public policies and arms control literature, especially in advanced countries, to concentrate on narrow technical and economic issues, such as 'proliferation-resistant' fuel cycles, criteria for nuclear exports and economic disincentives against early decisions to reprocess. This is fragmented issue linkage, *par excellence*.

One of the foremost reasons why NWFZs are greeted with scepticism is that they have often been used as instruments of policies that have little to do with arms control or non-proliferation. As seen in Table 6, for example, many NWFZs have been proposed as political responses to a particular disturbing event rather than as a studied, analytical move aimed at the narrow objective of controlling proliferation. Warsaw Pact countries have in particular shown a predilection for calling for the establishment of a NWFZ

TABLE 6   *NWFZs as Responses to Events*

Date	NWFZ region	Precipitating event
1957	Central Europe	US missiles into West Germany
1959	Adriatic and Balkans	Jupiter IRBMs proposed for Italy, Greece, Turkey
1961	Africa	French Algerian nuclear tests
1963	Mediterranean	MLF Proposal: NATO Polaris submarines in Mediterranean
1963	Nordic Area	Multilateral force
1967	Latin America	Cuban missile crisis
1974	South Asia/Indian Ocean	Indian nuclear test
1974	Middle East	1973 Yom Kippur War and evidence of Israeli bomb
1974	Africa	Nigerian proposal, upon reports of South African bomb
1980	Middle East	Israeli proposal upon reports of Iraqi and Pakistani efforts to acquire the bomb

when perceived security interests were jeopardised. In the ter-
minology developed by Haas, this corresponds to 'tactical issue
linkage', where policies are pursued with the aim of securing *ad
hoc* advantages rather than the reconstruction of regimes along
the lines of substantive rationality.[17]

Thus in 1957, Poland proposed a NWFZ for Central Europe
after a NATO decision to instal American IRBMs in West Germany; the Soviets favoured an Adriatic and Balkan NWFZ in 1959
after the installation of Jupiter IRBMs in Italy and Turkey; and
the Soviet Union also favoured a denuclearised Mediterranean in
1965 when NATO was considering a nuclear multilateral force
(MLF) in the region. Similarly, Iran proposed a Middle East
NWFZ shortly after the 1973 Yom Kippur War when it was
evident that Israel had the bomb; and Pakistan proposed a South
Asian NWFZ after the May 1974 Indian nuclear explosion. In
each of these cases, a NWFZ was used as an instrument for attaining tactical policy goals which often had little to do with the wider
objectives of non-proliferation, world peace and national
economic development.

Although both NWFZs and the NPT share a common objective
of curtailing the geographic (or horizontal) spread of nuclear

weapons, both also serve other national security interests of member states. By reinforcing a diplomatic commitment of the peaceful uses of nuclear energy, both of these instruments enable a state to shape an environment more conducive to international trade in nuclear power technology. Many NNWSs also like the idea of their neighbours relinquishing the option of developing nuclear weapons which could be used in local conflicts. Whereas the 'NPT bargain' consists of NNWSs giving up their weapons option in exchange for peaceful nuclear technology transfers and reductions of strategic arsenals, NWFZs extend this deal to include a ban on the possession of foreign-controlled nuclear weapons on NNWSs' soil. By agreeing to this arrangement, NNWSs stand to gain security benefits in the form of reduced risks of direct involvement in nuclear war and Great Power security assurances. Opportunities thus abound in NWFZs for fragmented and tactical issue linkages; the deeper problem of the relationship between NWFZs and world peace (the problem of substantive issue linkage) remains non-consensual.

The NWFZ concept also relates to some additional themes in the theory and practice of international relations and regime-building. The intellectual heritage of the NWFZ includes past experience with demilitarised zones (DMZs).[18] For example, the need for verification, international recognition, consent of local parties, Great Power acquiescence, and legal codification are shared by all such zones. The possible breakdown of NWFZs will therefore be likely to occur for reasons similar to those which account for the end of other DMZs: termination through negotiation, unilateral abrogation, incomplete verification, covert action, or military responses to changes in regional power balances.

The NWFZ concept is also related to a wider debate over the question 'whether arms cause conflicts, or vice versa?' Those who, like Norman Angell, Philip Noel-Baker, and Prince Kropotkin[19] feel that arms *per se* are causes of war would have great sympathy for NWFZs since the absence of nuclear arms logically prevents their use by local countries. Those who place conflict before arms, however, are likely to remain sceptical about the ability of NWFZs to remain non-nuclear in all conflicts. With respect to nuclear war, proponents of this view posit that it is the nature of the local conflict that will determine whether nuclear weapons are used. They can point to the ill-fated interwar disarmament conferences organised by the League of Nations as illustrations of the fatuity of seeking peace through simple quantitative restraints on arms. The longevity of security regimes thus depends critically upon some measure of substantive issue linkage; the long-term effects of clashing interests and cognitive disunity increase the likelihood that the regime will be, as Thomas Hobbes might have put it, 'nasty, cruel, mean, brutish and short'.

A Prototypical NWFZ

With this background, we can outline the features of a composite of the various NWFZ regimes surveyed above. Although variations will clearly occur in different regional contexts due to different political military and social conditions, a prototype NWFZ can be sketched to serve as a benchmark for analytical reference.

With respect to the *timing* of NWFZ proposals (in populated areas), the following conditions contribute to fruitful international negotiations: prior existence of a disturbing (or potentially disruptive) international event of political–military significance; local perceptions of security advantages from a NWFZ; forceful and persistent advocacy in international arenas; and Great Power acquiescence.

With respect to the *substantive content* of this prototypical NWFZ, the following characteristics are suggested from past experience:

1. Legal status: international recognition; treaty of unlimited duration; voluntary and initiative consent of local parties; verification by *ad hoc* regional organizations.
2. Membership: geographically contiguous but without any requirement for all-inclusive membership; include all major regional powers and other states within regional perimeter of zone.
3. Political–military: NWFZ must not destabilise existing military security managements including alliances; support by superpowers and other nuclear states (nations developing nuclear technology and weapons); selective conventional arms assistance sufficient to lessen incentives in selected nations to develop nuclear options; regime should not discourage peaceful uses of atomic energy.

4. Obligations: no development, deployment, or storage of nuclear weapons of any sort; NWS security guarantees against threats of using nuclear weapons against any NWFZ member; agreement with UN Charter and other international obligations.

Lastly, the establishment of a NWFZ requires the resolution of a number of collateral issues. They include the problems of transit rights, 'peaceful nuclear explosions', effects on alliance commitments, and the colonial territories of NWSs.

A Balkan NWFZ: Geopolitical Considerations

The Balkan region has historically been characterised by chronic strife at both intra- and inter-state levels, often involving conflicting Great Power interests. As one historian once put it, the Balkans were where 'the politics of British Empire, Russia, France and Germany were practiced before their extension to the Afro-Asian continents'.[20] In the nineteenth century and the first half of the twentieth century the Balkans were one of the most explosive areas of the world. From the outbreak of the First World War at Sarajevo (1914) to the continuing disputes between Greece and Turkey, the area has been characterised by great political, social and military instability.

In many respects, the collapse of the Ottoman Empire produced historical consequences resembling those following the collapse of the British and French colonial empires at the end of the Second World War. National boundaries were carved before and after the First World War that often ignored the ethnic identities of the Balkan peoples and conformed primarily to the administrative and political convenience of the Great Powers.[21] The Balkan map was consolidated in its present form at the Paris Peace Conference of 1919. Consequently not a single Balkan country emerged as monoethnic, and practically all Balkan states have entertained irredentist notions against one another.[22]

Much is now being written about the instability of NATO's southern flank. In the aftermath of the 1974 Turkish invasion in Cyprus, Greece withdrew from the military structure of the Atlantic Alliance and ended home-porting rights to the US Sixth Fleet. Turkey responded to an American arms embargo of 1975 by closing 25 American bases. Thus, despite recent events, including Greek reintegration into the military sector of NATO, and the re-opening of US bases in Turkey, regional politics have reached the point where, in Stephen Larrabee's words, 'Greece and Turkey have better relations with most countries in the Warsaw Pact than they do with each other or with some members of the Atlantic Alliance'.[23]

With the recent demise of Josip Tito, the disputes within the southern flank of NATO and the continuing suspicions and mis-trust in the area, the whole situation increases the long-term risk that nuclear weapons might some day be developed or used either as nationally controlled devices or via introduction by outside powers. The capability of Balkan countries to do the former is a function of the nuclear technology in the region, both current and planned. One index of this capability is the number of power and research reactors in the region (see Table 7) which could conceivably be geared to the production of bomb-grade fissile material.

TABLE 7   *Nuclear reactors in the Balkans (in megawatts)*

	Current and past	*Planned*
Romania	1 research reactor (3 MW)	9 (at 600 MW)
Bulgaria	2 power reactors (at 408 MW) 1 research reactor (1 MW)	2 (at 408 MW)
Yugoslavia	3 research reactors (all <7 MW)	3 (at 1000 MW), 2 (at 1200 MW), 1 (at 632 MW)
Greece	1 research reactor (5 MW)	1 (at 600 MW) 2 (at 900 MW)
Turkey	3 research reactors (<6 MW)	2 (at 1000 MW), 1 (at 600 MW)
Albania	—	—

SOURCES: 1. Nuclear Assurance Corporation, 'Nuclear Megawatt Status Report', October 1981 (Atlanta: NAC, 1981). 2. IAEA, *Research Reactors in Member States*, 1980 edn (Vienna: IAEA, 1980). 3. US Congress, Senate Committee on Governmental Affairs, *Nuclear Proliferation Factbook* (Washington, DC: GPO, September 1980).

The data suggest rather ambitious nuclear development plans, especially in the region's Warsaw Pact countries. Romania, for example, has recently contracted for four 600 MW CANDU reac-tors worth over $3 billion, making it Canada's 'best power reactor export market to date'.[24] According to *Nuclear News*, the Canadians have authorised licensing agreements for an eventual 16 units.[25] By 1990 Romania plans to rely on nuclear power for 18 per cent of its energy capacity, while progressively assuming more of the manufacturing work from Canada. The CANDU, moreover, produces about twice the amount of plutonium per year as conventional light water reactors.[26] Similarly, Turkey, a country now under martial law, announced in June 1979 that it was purchasing its first nuclear power plant as part of an industrial deal with the Soviet Union valued at $8 billion; in addition, the Swedish firm ASEA-ATOM is now negotiating with the Turkish Electricity Authority for the building of another 600 MW nuclear plant. Although Sweden, Canada and the Soviet Union all require strict safeguards on their exports, it is clear that by the end of the century several Balkan nations will have the skills, equipment and materials to manufacture a nuclear explosive and/or to export sensitive components, if such a decision is made.

The mere stockpiling of an ally's nuclear weapons also poses some risks that through theft, sabotage, accident, military capture, or a variety of additional means (such as terrorism and host-country capture) nuclear weapons might be deployed or used in the area. Moreover, given some local fears that external nuclear weapons could be targeted for the Balkans (such as pre-emptive attack or retaliation), there might well be some 'substantive' grounds for all local parties to reach some basic agreement on the need to exclude such weapons from the region. Yet such an agreement would be vacuous unless external NWSs agreed to respect the integrity of the regime through positive and negative security assurances.

Continuing instability in the region also produces some perceived incentives to permit and even encourage the presence of nuclear weapons in the area, or at least the perpetuation of the option of their introduction if strategic circumstances require them. In particular, it seems highly unlikely that NATO will discard its nuclear options given the superiority generally conceded to conventional Warsaw Pact forces in the area. As one State Department Desk Officer for Turkish politics once commented when asked about a possible Balkan NWFZ, 'such a proposal would knock a hole in the southern flank of NATO'.[27]

There are a variety of specific bilateral conflicts that continue to work against regional co-operative efforts for a NWFZ. The two areas of major conflict (actual or potential) remain the ongoing disputes between Greece and Turkey over Cyprus,[28] the Aegean Sea, and over national minorities. Another possible area of serious military conflict is between Yugoslavia and Bulgaria over the status of Macedonia (boundaries and minorities).

TABLE 8   *Local conflicts*

	Countries	Subject
Main conflicts	Greece and Turkey	Cyprus* Aegean Sea† Continental Shelf Military and civilian air traffic control Territorial Waters Militarisation of the Greek Islands National Minorities
	Yugoslavia and Bulgaria	Status of Macedonia‡ Territorial disputes Minorities
Underlying or potential conflicts	Albania and Yugoslavia	Albanian minority (in Kossovo)
	Greece and Yugoslavia	Minorities (Macedonia)
Less important conflicts that might escalate under the right conditions	Bulgaria and Romania	Territorial disputes (Dobrudja)
	Greece and Albania	Greek minority (in Northern Epirus)
	Hungary and Romania	Hungarian minority (in Transylvania)
	Hungary and Yugoslavia	Hungarian minority (in Voyvodina)

* The issue is the Turkish invasion and continued occupation of approximately 38 per cent of Cyprus.
† The main dispute is over the Aegean Sea Continental Shelf and territorial waters. With regard to the Continental Shelf, the issue is whether the Greek Islands possess their own Continental Shelf (Greek position) or are merely extensions of the Turkish Continental Shelf and have no rights in the seabed of the Aegean Sea (Turkish position). The dispute on the territorial waters arises from the possibility that Greece might extend her 6-mile territorial waters to 12, an extension that Turkey considers *casus belli*.
‡ The origins of the Macedonian dispute lies in the nineteenth century. Currently it constitutes a most divisive issue between Yugoslavia and Bulgaria (and to a lesser extent between Greece and Yugoslavia). Yugoslavia recognises a *unique* Macedonian nationality (and encourages the use of the Macedonian language). This is against Bulgarian policies which claim that Macedo-Bulgarians are indistinguishable by historical or cultural tradition from the Bulgarians. This makes Yugoslavs suspicious of Bulgarian ambitions to annex part of the Macedonia and/or to use the Macedonia quarrel as an instrument for the advancement of the Soviet aims in the region.

In addition to the many disputes cited in Table 8, a number of uncertainties continues to affect regional security, including: the future of post-Tito Yugoslavia; the resolution of the Cyprus problem; the direction of policy in Albania after Enver Hoxha; and the long-term effects of continued deterioration of the Turkish economy. All of these instabilities must be seen in the context of the numerous crises currently under way in the Middle East region, whose escalation would directly or indirectly affect the area. The close proximity of Greece and Turkey to Middle East oil accounts for a considerable degree of NATO's interest in restraining these disputes.

Uncertainties extend also to the future of the NPT regime for countries in the region. At the 1975 NPT Review Conference, for example, Romania and Yugoslavia[29] expressed strong reservations about the discriminatory nature of the NPT bargain, with Belgrade threatening to reconsider its continued adherence to the treaty. Although Turkey has recently ratified the NPT (leaving only Albania outside the NPT regime), several leaders in both Greece and Turkey have spoken of the possibility of indigenous development of nuclear weapons.[30]

A Balkan NWFZ and the European Theatre Nuclear Balance

As Table 9 shows, there has been a variety of proposals for a Balkan NWFZ. All of these proposals have originated in Warsaw Pact countries, all have been unilateral initiatives from the statesmen who advocated them, all have been proposed at a high level of generality and all were announced without prior consensus between the superpowers. A brief look at the history of those proposals illustrates the relationship between calls for a Balkan NWFZ and local concerns about the stability of the wider balance of power in Europe.

The Romanians, at the level of Prime Minister, proposed in September 1957 that a 'peace zone' be established in the area; in June 1959, they made explicit reference to denuclearisation, a position supported diplomatically by the Soviet Union.[31] In 1959, 1963 and on numerous occasions in the UN the Soviet Union has reiterated its call for a Balkan NWFZ; in each case, however, the proposal has been preceded by some action by NATO that stimulated

TABLE 9 *Proposals for a Balkan NWFZ*

Date	Country	Proposal	Forum	Result
10 September 1957	Romania	NWFZ: Balkans as an area of peace with no foreign military bases	Official	Reiterated
May 1959	Soviet Union	Balkans as region of peace	*Isvestia* 29 May 1959	Romania supported and urged treaty on NWFZ with Great Power guarantees
25 June 1959	Soviet Union	Notes to Balkan states, United States, and Great Britain regarding Balkan and Adriatic	Diplomatic Notes	Yugoslavia, Romania, Bulgaria, Albania supported. United States rejected
17 May 1963	Soviet Union	NWFZ of all Mediterranean	Diplomatic note to the 18-nation Committee on Disarmament	United States rejected
1968	Bulgaria Yugoslavia	Balkans and Mediterranean NWFZ	1968 Conference of NNWSs	NATO rejected
1972	Romania	Proposal for conference of Balkan states to deal with Balkan NWFZ	Conference of the Committee on Disarmament	NATO rejected

some diplomatic response by the Warsaw Pact. These actions have included new missile deployments, the MLF proposal, and force modernisation efforts. American responses to these proposals for a Balkan NWFZ have come in the form of summary dismissals. In particular, NATO countries have stressed the necessity of a nuclear means of countervailing Soviet conventional forces, the threats posed by long-range tactical nuclear weapons deep in the Soviet Union, and the alleged propagandistic and hypocritical nature of these proposals.

There are three basic reasons why tactical nuclear weapons have been justified as being in the interest of NATO. The first reason is political: these weapons help reinforce the American commitment to defend Europe in the event of a massive military attack from the Warsaw Pact. Secondly, they allegedly help reduce the economic burden of mobilising a European conventional force sufficient to deter a Warsaw Pact ground offensive. Thirdly, according to the military doctrine of 'flexible response', NATO must retain the capability to escalate to the nuclear level if necessary to counter-balance alleged Soviet advantages in conventional forces.

The United States has been estimated to possess roughly 31,000 nuclear weapons of all types; roughly 9000 of these are strategic and 22,000 are tactical.[32] About 7000 of these tactical weapons are based on European territory, while another 1000 are deployed in the Atlantic fleet. NATO theatre weapons in Europe are stored in over 100 Special Ammunition Storage Sites (SAS) that consist of igloos and protective facilities; the location of these sites is presumed to be known by the Soviet Union.

The authors were unable to obtain data on the number of SAS in Greece and Turkey, the proportion of the 7000 European tactical nuclear weapons that are based in the Balkan area (if any) and future modernisation plans. Although the exact number and location of nuclear weapons based in the area remains classified, it can be surmised from available data that these weapons are small in number, antiquated and incapable of striking targets deep in the Soviet Union. One index of the actual number of warheads is provided by existing information on the types of equipment that could be used to deliver a nuclear explosive. Table 10 summarises the current deployment of nuclear-capable delivery vehicles in the area. When these modest capabilities are compared to the 7000 aggregate total of European theatre nuclear weapons it is apparent that the Greek and Turkish nuclear contribution to NATO is minimal. Furthermore, the modest Soviet deployment of short-range Scud and Frog missiles in Romania and Bulgaria could probably be removed without seriously jeopardising the required balance. No regular Soviet troops are currently stationed in Balkan member states of the Warsaw Pact.

TABLE 10   *Nuclear-capable delivery systems in the Balkan region*

Country	Weapon system	Number	Range (miles)	Yield (KT)	Year of initial development
Greece	F-4 fighter–bomber	56 (est. 1985)	1400(+)	—	1960
	F-104G fighter–bomber	31	1450(+)	—	1968
	155 mm howitzer	240	$4-30 \times 10^3$ metres	2	1942
	8 in. howitzer	n.a.	$14-16 \times 10^3$ metres	1	Early 1950s
	Honest John (surface-to-surface)	8	5–22	20	1951
	Nike-Hercules (surface-to-air)	n.a.	84	1	1958
Turkey	F-4	49 (1978)	As above		
	F-104S	30 (1978)	As above		
	155 mm howitzer	190	As above		
	8 in howitzer	n.a.	As above		
	Honest John	18	As above		
	Nike-Hercules	170	As above		
Romania	Frog SSM	30	10–45	1	Early 1960s
	Scud SSM	20	50	1	1965
Bulgaria	Frog	36	As above		
	Scud	20	As above		
Yugoslavia	155 mm howitzer	n.a.	As above		
	Frog-7	n.a.	As above		

SOURCES: IISS, *The Military Balance, 1979–1980; Jane's Weapons Systems, 1979–1980; Defense and Foreign Affairs Handbook, 1980.*
n.a. = not available.

Even without serving as depots for nuclear weapons, both Greece and Turkey would still contribute invaluable benefits to NATO in the form of overflight and base rights, intelligence and communications facilities, command and control systems, radar installations, ammunition and supply storage, and manpower. Moreover, ever since the Truman Doctrine was announced in 1947 the United States has given a commitment to the security of both countries concerning Soviet bloc aggression. These security assurances were reaffirmed after the Cuban missile crisis and the subsequent withdrawal of Jupiter IRBMs from Turkey. It is thus by no means clear that a treaty establishing a NWFZ would *ipso facto* constitute a security threat to Greece, Turkey or NATO. Indeed, a report from the US Congressional Budget Office has argued that the retirement of outdated theatre nuclear force (TNF) systems could yield some added security to both countries and Europe as a whole. According to that study, 'it may be desirable to increase US and NATO efforts to . . . reduce or eliminate marginally or highly vulnerable and destabilising theater nuclear systems such as Honest John, ADM (atomic demolition munitions), nuclear Nike Hercules and QRA (Quick Reaction Alert) forces'.[33] These are precisely the systems which now remain in Greece and Turkey.

The Rôle of Security Assurances

Countries will join together to create NWFZs when it is in their apparent interests to do so. Countries will not join when great uncertainty exists with respect to internal compliance or recognition of the zone by nuclear-armed states. Certification of compliance can be arranged through a variety of means, ranging from inspections by the IAEA or some regional organisation (such as OPANAL, the Agency for the Prohibition of Nuclear Weapons in Latin America), to national means of verification including bilateral agreements and pooling of intelligence data. The Tlatelolco Treaty states have approached the problem of recognition by seeking assurances by all NWSs (in Protocols I and II) that the zone and all colonial territories therein will remain free of nuclear weapons. Hence, although a group of countries could declare a *de jure* NWFZ, such a declaration would in itself amount to little unless the NWS agreed to respect the zone. Countries are reluctant to relinquish the same instruments with which they may be attacked.

Considerable attention has recently been given in such fora as the UN Special Session on Disarmament, the 1975 and 1980 NPT Review Conferences and in Conferences of Non-Aligned Nations, to superseding the relatively legalistic approaches offered above with more concrete policy statements by the NWSs regarding the non-use of nuclear weapons. In particular, UN Security Council Resolution 255 (19 June 1968) has called for 'immediate' international assistance for any NNWS that is the victim of a nuclear attack by a NWS; such assistance − known as 'positive security assurances' − is currently supported in principle by all the NWSs.[34] Pledges of no first-use of nuclear weapons under any circumstances against a NNWS, or 'negative security assurances', have so far only been issued by the Chinese.[35] Conditional assurances of this variety have been issued by the following countries:[36]

Soviet Union:	non-use against any country which neither possesses nuclear weapons nor seeks to acquire them;
United States and Great Britain:	non-use against any NNWS party to the NPT, or any other binding agreement not to acquire nuclear weapons, *except* in the event of an attack on the United States/Great Britain or its allies by NNWSs 'allied to' or 'associated with' a NWS;
France:	non-use pledge offered only for members of NWFZs.

The inability of the NWSs to agree on a common position on negative security assurances reveals the prevalence of tactical and fragmented issue linkages and the absence of major substantive international agreement on the rules of the game of weapons development and use. Thus the Soviet position would permit an atomic attack on Europe, the American and British positions would allow first-use in South Korea and the Middle East, and the French position would permit nuclear strikes against all countries except the 22 full parties to the Tlatelolco Treaty (an area not posing any security threats to France). Moreover, since the Chinese are undoubtedly aware that any Chinese nuclear attack upon a NNWS would probably draw in other NWSs to the detriment of China, they lose little in security terms by proffering non-use pledges to NNWSs.

Merits and Demerits of a Balkan NWFZ

The critical variables behind the implementation of a Balkan NWFZ thus appear to be political and military. The military acceptability of such an arrangement to NATO will depend upon the concessions that can be extracted from the Soviet Union on such issues as the exclusion of the eastern Mediterranean from the zone, a reduction in the numbers and readiness of Soviet conventional forces near the Balkan region inside the Soviet Union, restrictions on Soviet deployments of MRBMs and the Backfire bomber, and superpower security assurances and verification procedures. Because the Soviets have been proposing a Balkan NWFZ for over 20 years, it is perhaps time for NATO to test the seriousness of these proposals by preparing a list of demands that could provide a basis for negotiation.

Political opposition to the NWFZ would be more likely to come from non-Balkan members of NATO rather than from the regional parties themselves, many of whom have supported a Balkan NWFZ in principle for decades. Parliamentary and Congressional opposition could be expected from political circles which would associate the establishment of a Balkan NWFZ with appeasement of Soviet interests in the area. Some European allies might oppose any such scheme on the grounds that it might symbolise a political 'decoupling' of American security policy from the defence of Europe.

While not minimising the substantial political obstacles associated with negotiating and implementing a Balkan NWFZ, the authors believe that the concept merits further analysis aimed at establishing a NATO position on the matter. If established, such a zone would break a long-standing pattern of limiting NWFZs to unpopulated areas and regions at the periphery of the international system. Summary dismissals, such as the American statement in 1959 that 'this proposal is similar to other Soviet proposals to accomplish piecemeal the design of rendering the Western nations incapable of deterring aggression',[37] serve no purpose other than the prolongation of a shaky *status quo*. And in the light of the rapid diffusion of nuclear technology and the numerous political crises brewing in the area, the *status quo* might ultimately prove to be more disruptive to regional security than alternative defence arrangements which are supplementary to NATO, including a NWFZ.

The major demerits of a Balkan NWFZ include the following: political obstacles from European countries fearful of any American decoupling from European security; difficulties in defining a range of collateral issues such as transit rights, nuclear-related installations, peaceful nuclear explosions, and sanctions for apparent violations; the likely difficulty in obtaining major concessions from the Soviet Union with regard to force deployments and capabilities within the Soviet borders; the lack of any consensus on security guarantees; and political problems associated with attempting to negotiate new nuclear arms control agreements in a climate of renewed superpower antipathy.

Conclusion

In its 1976 evaluation of NWFZs, the *SIPRI Yearbook* contained the following pessimistic assessment:

> Further fruitless consideration of the subject may even detract attention from the need to ensure the universality of the NPT and provide an excuse for certain countries to postpone indefinitely a decision on the renunciation of a nuclear-weapon option, as well as an alibi for the nuclear-weapon powers to eschew, also indefinitely, an undertaking not to use nuclear weapons against non-nuclear-weapon states.

At the other extreme, William Epstein has characterised the NWFZ as a potentially more effective means of controlling proliferation than the NTP.[38] This chapter does not advocate the immediate establishment of a Balkan NWFZ; its major goal has been neither to praise nor bury the notion of an NWFZ, but to analyse it.

As surveyed above, the politics of NWFZs have been most notably characterised by fragmented and tactical issue linkages. Most countries have shown considerable resistance to the idea of voluntarily relinquishing their sovereign right to acquire a national capability to make nuclear weapons. In the absence of a solid international consensus on the substantive linkages between NWFZs and world order and economic development, it seems likely that approaches to nuclear proliferation will continue to proceed on a piecemeal basis; yet another example of disjointed incrementalism. Grandiose schemes, like the international ownership of the entire nuclear fuel cycle, carry little weight in countries which already have more than their share of uncertainties and risks with which to cope.

A growing number of analyses of international regimes are

turning from globalist or holist approaches to intractable regulative and distributive problems of international society to more modest undertakings, especially those grounded on the basis of substantive issue linkage. As Robert Rothstein has argued:

> In an environment of conflict and uncertainty, separate systems with different but interlocking sets of rules may be more realistic than the quest for global rules . . . [this] should increase the possibility that problem solving and negotiation can be moved somewhat closer to the individuals, the sectors, or the countries most significantly affected by a decision.[39]

Further progress in the establishment of NWFZs is now stalemated by forces which are inherent in the nation-state system. Nationalism, simplistic cognitive images of national threats, an international preoccupation with state sovereignty, complex linkages to superpower politics and continuing strategic instability − all of these frustrate the establishment of NWFZs.

In sum, the future of NWFZs as a means of nuclear arms control rests upon two pillars. First, NWFZs will not be favoured in time of great strategic uncertainty. This is not to suggest a structuralist explanation for the creation of NWFZs. Indeed, the Tlatelolco, Outer Space and Seabed Treaties were all signed during a period of great strain between the superpowers. However, looking beyond the political problems associated with Czechoslovakia, Vietnam, and Cambodia, one must recall that this period was characterised by greater strategic stability than had previously existed between the superpowers. The Soviets had announced 'peaceful co-existence', a nuclear 'essential equivalence' had been reached, and the SALT process was ultimately under way. The Cuban missile crisis helped to forge Soviet−American support for a Latin American NWFZ and the NPT. Strategic stability would thus appear to be a necessary but not sufficient condition for the establishment of NWFZs. The second pillar consists of the emergence of a cognitive consensus on the definition of the central problems concerning the proliferation of nuclear weapons. There is little doubt, given the number that have already been established, that the *notion* of a NWFZ has widespread international support as a complementary means of pursuing nuclear arms control. Other areas of general agreement are: the acceptability of international safeguards, the undesirability of uncontrolled national stockpiles

of plutonium, the need for an international repository of spent
fuel, the desirability of multinationally controlled reprocessing
centres (if large-scale reprocessing takes place), and the need for
further controls and reductions of strategic arms. Furthermore,
the superpowers now are in agreement about the undesirability of
further proliferation and the importance of strict controls over
nuclear technology. Since the larger problems of world order and
justice will likely remain intractable, and since the diffusion of
nuclear technology will continue apace, it is desirable from the
standpoint of the current non-proliferation regime to pursue all
alternatives for collaboration where substantive issue linkage is
possible. The authors believe NWFZs are one such area.

In the past NWFZs have been subjects of incrementalist
bargaining associated with tactical and fragmented issue linkage.
At present substantive issue linkage is increasingly evident in international fora where the prospects of further nuclear proliferation
are deliberated. The future of NWFZs will ultimately rest on the
extent to which they are believed by local parties and the NWSs to
be in the interest of international security.[40]

Notes

1. *Random House Dictionary of the English Language* (New York, 1970).
2. Ernest Haas, *Tangle of Hopes*, (Englewood Cliffs, New Jersey, 1969).
3. David Mitrany, *A Working Peace System* (Chicago, 1966).
4. Paul R. Viotti and Douglas J. Murray, 'International Security Regimes: On
   the Applicability of a Concept', paper presented at American Political
   Science Association Convention, Washington, DC, August 1980.
5. Ernest Haas, 'Why Collaborate? Issue-Linkage and International Regimes',
   World Politics, xxxii (1979–80); and idem, 'Is There a Hole in the Whole?'
   International Organization, xxix (1975).
6. Harry Eckstein, 'Case Study and Theory in Political Science', in Fred I.
   Greenstein and Nelson W. Polsby, *Handbook of Political Science*, vol. 7,
   (Reading, Massachussets, 1975).
7. John J. Weltman, 'Managing Nuclear Multipolarity', paper presented at a
   conference on 'The Future of Arms Control', Harvard University, Center for
   Science and International Affairs, 15–16 May 1980.
8. See Yolanda White, 'Working Paper for the Second Review Conference of
   the State Parties to the Nonproliferation Treaty', (New York, 1980); and
   Pugwash Council, 'Statement from the Pugwash Council on the Second NPT
   Review Conference', *Pugwash Newsletter*, Jan. 1980.
9. *Second Review Conference of the Nonproliferation Treaty*, NPT/
   CONF.II/9, 14 May 1980, Geneva (Latin American memorandum).

10. ibid., NPT/CONF. II/C. 1/9, 27 Aug. 1980 (Netherlands paper).
11. Haas, 'Why Collaborate?', loc. cit., p. 372.
12. See, *inter alia*, Articles 1 and 52 of the UN Charter. According to the provisions of Article 1, states undertake '. . . to take effective collective measures for the prevention and removal of the threats to the peace . . . to develop friendly relations among nations . . . and to take other appropriate measures to strengthen universal peace'. Also, the concept of the NWFZs is consistent with the provisions of Article 52 which envisages the existence of regional arrangements or agencies for dealing with matters relating to the maintenance of international peace and security as are appropriate for regional action.
13. UN, *Treaty Series* (New York, 1962), vol. 422, no. 5778, pp. 71–107; ibid., vol. 610, no. 8843.
14. US Arms Control and Disarmament Agency, *Documents on Disarmament, 1967*, (Washington, DC, 1968) pp. 69–83.
15. See Roderick Alley, *Nuclear-Weapon Free Zones: The South Pacific Proposal*, (Stanley Foundation Occasional Paper no. 14), 1977, pp. 40–3; William Epstein, 'A Nuclear-Weapon Free Zone in Africa?', in ibid., pp. 23–4; Kathleen Teltsch, 'Iran Asks UN Action to Keep Region Free of Nuclear Arms', *New York Times*, 13 June 1974; Bernard Nossiter, 'Israel in Policy shift to see Mideast Ban on Nuclear Weapons', *New York Times*, 8 November 1980; UN General Assembly Resolution 3265B (xxix) on a 'Nuclear Weapon-Free Zone in South Asia', 9 Dec. 1974; Devendra Karshik, *The Indian Ocean: Toward a Zone of Peace* (Delhi 1972); Betty Goetz Lall, 'On Disarmament Issues: The Polish Plan', *Bulletin of the Atomic Scientists*, June 1964; Jay C. Mumford, 'Problems of Nuclear-Free Zones: The Nordic Example', *Military Review*, March 1976; Statement by Soviet Government on Baltic Nuclear-Free Zone, 25 June 1959, US Department of State, *Documents on Disarmament 1945–1959* (2 vols, Washington, DC, 1960) ii, 1423–6; and Bernard Feld, 'A New Look at Nuclear Weapon-Free Zones', *Pugwash Newsletter*, May 1977.
16. UN, *Special Report on the Conference of the Committee on Disarmament: Comprehensive Study of the Question of Nuclear-Weapon Free Zones in All its Aspects* (New York, 1976).
17. Haas, 'Why Collaborate?', loc. cit., p. 372.
18. NWFZs, in fact, can be thought of as selective demilitarisation. Here, the emphasis has been placed upon the absence of nuclear weapons instead of the absence of fortifications and troops. The underlying rationality, however, is almost the same as the following definition indicates: 'Demilitarization . . . denotes the agreement of two or more States by treaty not to fortify or station troops upon, a particular zone of territory; the purpose usually being to prevent war by removing the opportunity of conflict as the result of frontier incident or to gain security by prohibiting the concentration of troops on the frontier.' See L. F. L. Oppenheim, *International Law* (London, 2 vols, 1965 ed.) ii, 24 n. 1.
19. Norman Angell, *The Great Illusion* (New York, 1910); Philip Noel-Baker, *The Arms Race* (London, 1960); and Prince Kropotkin, *Memoirs of a Revolutionist* (Boston, 1899).
20. Nikolaos Stavrou, 'Greek–American Relations and their Impact on Balkan

Cooperation', in Theodore Couloumbis and John Iatridis (eds), *Greek–American Relations* (New York, 1980) p. 150.

21. ibid., p. 151.
22. ibid., p. 151.
23. Stephen Larrabee, unpublished paper, Harvard University, Center for Science and International Affairs, 1979. Also see idem, *Balkan Security* (Adelphi Paper no. 135, London, 1977).
24. *Nuclear News*, Feb. 1979.
25. ibid.
26. *Nuclear Proliferation Factbook* (1980 edn) p. 220.
27. Interview, April 1980.
28. The official Greek position on the Cyprus question is that this problem is essentially a matter for the two communities on the island and cannot be considered within the context of bilateral Greek–Turkish relations.
29. About Yugoslavia and nuclear weapons, see *Survival* XVIII (1976), 116–17; and XIX (1977), 127–9.
30. See, Andrew Wilson, *The Aegean Dispute* (Adelphi Paper no. 156, London, 1980) p. 41 n.60; and SIPRI, *World Armaments and Disarmament: SIPRI Yearbook, 1976* (Cambridge, Massachussets, 1976), p. 389.
31. See UN, *Study of Nuclear-Weapon Free Zones*, p. 22.
32. See, '30,000 U.S. Nuclear Weapons', *Defense Monitor*, Feb. 1975; *Monitor*, Center for Defense Information, Mar. 1980, p. 6; and US Congress, Congressional Budget Office, 'Planning U.S. General Purpose Forces: The Theater Nuclear Forces', Jan. 1977.
33. US Congressional Budget Office, 'Planning U.S. General Purpose Forces: The Theater Nuclear Forces', Budget Issue Paper (Washington, DC, 1977).
34. Further details on the distinction between positive and negative security assurances can be found in Jozef Goldblat and Sverre Lodgaard, 'Non-Use of Nuclear Weapons', *Bulletin of Peace Studies* (1980).
35. See Cyrus Vance, 'Chinese Positions on Negative Security Assurances', in US Congress, House Committee on Foreign Affairs, Subcommittee on International Security and Scientific Affairs, Hearing on 'The Second Nuclear Nonproliferation Treaty Review Conference', 96th Congress, 1st Session, 16 July 1979, pp. 24–6.
36. Goldblat and Lodgaard, loc. cit.
37. Statement by the Department of State Regarding the Soviet Proposal for an Atom-Free Zone in the Baltic-Adriatic Region, 11 July 1959, US Department of State, *Documents on Disarmament 1945–1959*, II, 1435.
38. William Epstein, 'Nuclear-Free Zones', *Scientific American*, Nov. 1975.
39. Robert L. Rothstein, *Global Bargaining: UNCTAD and the Quest for a New International Order* (Princeton, New Jersey, 1979), p. 272.
40. The authors wish to thank A. Carnesale, L. Eriksson, P. Katzenstein, J. Murphy, B. Posen, G. Poukamisas, R. Rainer, J. Sharp, D. Siotis and S. Van Evera for their helpful comments on an earlier draft of this chapter. All errors and opinions are of course the responsibility of the authors. The Ford Foundation and Cornell University Peace Studies Program have provided financial support during the preparation of this chapter.

18 Greece and Nuclear Weapons

Kosta Tsipis

Introduction

Recently there has been considerable debate in Greece regarding
the advisability of equipping the Greek defence forces with nuclear
weapons. There has been much debate but little technical analysis
of the costs, benefits and the scale of magnitude of the resources −
natural, human, and manufacturing − required for such an
effort.

This chapter will not address the advisability or not of nuclear
weapons acquisition by Greece. It will only identify and discuss six
technical and military issues involved in the process of accumulat-
ing a nuclear arsenal. First, the study will examine the circumstances under which Greece would want to acquire nuclear
weapons. Secondly, it will deal with the methods of acquisition
and their relative practicality. Thirdly, the study will identify the
requirements in terms of manpower, facilities and materials
implicit in some of the more realistic methods. Fourthly, the
technical details of fabrication of nuclear warheads from uranium
and plutonium will be examined. Fifthly, the costs, both direct
and indirect, of such an effort will be estimated. Finally, the
possible utility of nuclear warheads for Greece under several
conditions will be examined.

Putative Circumstances Favouring Acquisition

There are several possible reasons, some logically founded, some

299

not, for which Greece may want to accumulate a nuclear arsenal. These include:

1. deter a nuclear rival or neighbour from attacking Greece with conventional weapons;
2. deter an opponent from attacking Greece with nuclear weapons;
3. deter attempts of nuclear blackmail of Greece by an opponent that demands political, geographic or other concessions under the threat of nuclear attack;
4. use nuclear weapons to intimidate a non-nuclear rival or strengthen one's bargaining position in war or peace;
5. attempt to gain enhanced international status by exhibiting possession of nuclear weapons;
6. initiate a military—scientific technological base occasioned by the decision to acquire a nuclear arsenal;
7. follow the example of other nations of similar size and level of development;
8. create a nuclear deterrent following withdrawal from or collapse of existing military-alliance structures.

Although some of the circumstances listed here are dependent on external factors beyond the control of the Greek Government, and others are implicitly matters of internal political decision, this chapter does not seek to evaluate them or rank them in any order either of importance or of probability of occurrence. The occasion for such a decision may be triggered by a number of events including:

1. nuclearisation of neighbours or potential adversaries;
2. breakdown of international constraints of nuclear proliferation;
3. diminution or elimination of the technological and feasibility gap that separates use of nuclear energy for production of electric power from use in the manufacture of weapons;
4. reduction in perceived protection afforded by an alliance;
5. rise of hostile or imperialistic tendencies in neighbouring countries.

The rise of unforeseen circumstances that may add weight in domestic arguments in favour of the acquisition of nuclear weapons is an ever-present possibility that should not be neglected or overlooked.

Methods of Acquisition of Nuclear Weapons

There are, of course, a number of methods by which Greece could in principle at least acquire one or more nuclear weapons. They can be broadly divided into three classes:

1. illegal acquisition, either overt or covert;
2. purchase of weapons or of essential components requiring only final assembly;
3. manufacture them from their constituent raw materials.

Clearly, illegal acquisition (for example, overtly to capture weapons based on Greek soil, or covertly to become the recipient of weapons that somehow have been stolen from existing arsenals) is a conceivable but not a probable mode of acquisition. This is in part because of the enormous security, diplomatic and political costs, and in part because most probably only a token number of weapons could be acquired in this fashion. Consequently, this method of acquisition will not be considered acceptable in the context of this chapter and will not be pursued further.

Under the present international circumstances purchase of nuclear warheads or of essential components of warheads is impossible. It is, of course, conceivable that a complete breakdown of the NPT some time in the future will result in an international market in nuclear weapons. However, the trend is certainly moving in the opposite direction: the United States, certainly until the defeat of Carter, has vigorously pursued efforts to restrain as much as possible the opportunities for additional countries to acquire nuclear weapons or the capacity to manufacture them. The French and West German Governments tacitly agreed with American proposals and future diplomatic activity among the supplier countries will tend to strengthen the NPT and minimise or postpone for considerable periods of time the probability of emergence of additional nuclear-armed countries. In conclusion, then, it can be asserted that purchase of nuclear weapons will remain impossible until at least the end of this century.

The only method for acquisition remaining is to manufacture nuclear warheads, either from uranium or from plutonium. Throughout this chapter it will be assumed that as a matter of fact the fabrication of fusion weapons (colloquially but inaccurately known as the 'hydrogen bomb') both requires the possession of, and is one technological level more sophisicated than the fabrication of, fission weapons. Therefore this chapter will not address at all the question of fusion weapons, and will concentrate only on analysing the requirements for the assembly of fission weapons based on uranium or plutonium. This basic assertion is supported by historical fact, since all countries in possession of fusion weapons (the United States, the Soviet Union, Great Britain, China and France) first mastered the technology of fabrication of the simpler fission weapons that subsequently can be used either as the trigger device of a fusion explosive or as part of a fission-fusion fission device based on the 'booster principle'.

Fabrication of Warheads from Uranium or Plutonium: Fissile Material Requirements

There are only three materials suitable for the production of nuclear fission weapons. Uranium-235 (U_{235}), Uranium-233 (U_{233}) and plutonium-239 (Pu_{239}). The first two are found in nature as isotopes of the much more abundant, but not fissionable U_{238}. Plutonium is a man-made element generated in nuclear reactors by the absorption of one neutron by U_{238} that becomes U_{239}. This isotope decays immediately to Neptunium 239 which after a few days is spontaneously transformed to Pu_{239}, a relatively stable element. U_{233} has never been used in nuclear weapons because its presence in uranium ore is negligible. It can be produced in reactors containing thorium 232 by a neutron capture and the subsequent rapid decay of the formed Protactinium into U_{233}. The fission properties of U_{233} vary little from those of U_{235}. Therefore in all subsequent discussion only U_{235} and Pu_{239} will be considered. These two elements possess three properties that make them suitable materials for a nuclear explosive device:

1. They can be fissioned by a neutron, releasing in addition to energy several neutrons capable of splitting other nuclei. Therefore they can sustain a chain reaction.
2. The neutron generation time (the average time between the creation of a neutron by fission and the time this neutron produces another fission) is small compared to the time it takes for a pressure wave to travel through the core of fissile material inside a warhead.

3. The critical mass (the minimum amount of material needed to maintain a chain reaction and therefore produce an explosion) is small, about 50 kg for U_{235} and 8 kg for pure δ-phase metallic Pu_{239}. Since these materials are on the average 18–20 times more dense than water, a critical mass of uranium occupies the volume of an ordinary orange while that of plutonium is about the size of a table-tennis ball.

In assembling a nuclear weapon it is useful to surround the uranium or plutonium with a material that reflects neutrons back into the core of the weapon, thereby reducing the necessary amount that constitutes a critical mass: if U_{235} is surrounded by a lining of several centimetres of U_{238}, a good neutron reflector, the critical mass is reduced to about 12 kg. The corresponding critical mass of plutonium surrounded by 10 or more centimetres of beryllium is 4 kg. Consequently it is here assumed that 12 kg of U_{235} or 4 kg of Pu_{239} are enough for criticality. It must be noted that the advanced nuclear technology of the United States has reduced these values considerably. Thus a modern American weapon with an explosive yield of 20,000 tons of TNT has a nuclear core that weighs about 10 kg. It will be assumed, however, that any country such as Greece will be obliged at least *ab initio* to use nuclear explosives technology that will require considerably larger amounts of Pu_{239} or U_{235} for a 20 kiloton weapon. Thus it is here assumed that a weapon of this explosive yield will require at a minimum 20 kg of plutonium or *50–60 kg* of 93 per cent pure U_{235} with a 7 per cent U_{238} admixture. These figures will form the base of all subsequent calculations concerning methods of production of U_{235} and then of Pu_{239}.

1. U_{235}
Natural metallic uranium contains 0.7 per cent of U_{235} and 99.3 per cent of U_{238}. Since each ton of average uranium ore as extracted from the ground contains about 1.5 kg of metallic uranium, one requires roughly 6000 tons of metallic uranium which contains 50 kg of 93 per cent U_{235} needed for one weapon. Each kg of uranium metal costs \$20–40 to extract from the ore. It is expected that the 40\$/kg (1976 dollar) price must be taken as the lowest limit of the cost of uranium metal extraction for the case of Greece, if the country were in possession of uranium deposits. Probably the actual cost will be considerably higher because of

royalties and licensing costs of imported technology and know-how. Thus the price of uranium metal per weapon will be at least

$$(0.93 \times 50/0.7 \times 10^{-2}) \times 40 = 2.7.10^5\$.$$

Since, however, metallic uranium contains only 0.7 per cent U_{235} it is necessary to subject the natural uranium to a process that would enrich it to the necessary 93 per cent U_{235} concentration suitable for weapons fabrication. It takes about 300 separation work units per kg of 0.7 per cent U_{238} natural uranium to be enriched to the necessary 93 per cent U_{235} suitable for weapons fabrication. The current cost of a separation work unit is \$100. Therefore the separation cost per weapon is $50 \times 300 \times 100 = 1.5 \times 10^6\$$. There are four known methods for the enrichment of natural uranium: gaseous diffusion, gas centrifuge, the Beckler nozzle and laser separation. The gaseous diffusion enrichment method is the only proven working method for producing weapons-grade material. It requires extensive facilities with capital cost exceeding US \$1 billion (1965) for a plant that processes about 10,000 tons of natural uranium per year. A smaller plant would cost less, but the capital investment does *not* scale with the size of throughput; therefore even a small gaseous diffusion plant with a capacity of a few hundred tons per year would cost several hundred million dollars. In addition, gaseous diffusion consumes large amounts of power. For 10,000 tons throughput the annual power consumption is 6 million kW, and the annual operating cost about \$1 billion (1976). Thus even if the complex technology of gas diffusion enrichment were completely at hand such a facility would be prohibitively expensive for Greece. The gas centrifuge method is more suitable for production of smaller quantities of enriched weapons-grade uranium. However, the process is still in the stage of early development and no firm costs can be quoted. The Unrenco/Centec group has a pilot plant in operation that can produce enough U_{235} for ten weapons per year. The estimated capital cost is about $200 \times 10^6\$$ and the operating expense of the order of $15-20 \times 10^6\$$ per year. At this cost, and without investment amortisation, the cost of U_{235} per weapon will be between \$1.5 and 2.0 million (1976). Gas centrifuge technology is also highly classified and requires the ability to produce light but very strong cylinders and very low friction bearings. Neither of these two metallurgical technologies is developed in Greece. Their development will require additional investment and a considerable period of time. On the other hand, it may be possible at some future date to purchase key centrifuge components from France, the Netherlands, Great Britain, the United States or Japan. The Beckler nozzle isotope separation method is still in its preliminary stage of development and it is unlikely that any significant quantities of uranium will be separated by that method for a number of years. The costs of this method are expected to be roughly the same as the gas centrifuge method.

Laser isotope separation is in principle possible but not a single atom of uranium has been separated by this method as yet. It is expected that the method will not be in practical application (if it ever succeeds) for at least another 10 years. Several serious technical difficulties remain to be practically resolved and as a result it is impossible at this time to predict the capital investment and operating costs of a uranium enrichment facility using laser separation.

To summarise: the total cost of 50 kg of 93 per cent enriched U_{235} enough for one 20 kiloton weapon is $\$2.7 \times 10^5$ for natural uranium $+ 1.5 \times 10^6\$$ for enrichment $\simeq 2$ million dollars (1976). The cheaper of the two enrichment facilities that would produce enough U_{235} for a few weapons per year is expected to cost $\$200$ million (1976) to construct and between $\$15$ and $\$20$ million to operate. (The latter number divided by the number of weapons produced per year is the per weapon enrichment cost listed above as $1.5 \times 10^6\$$ per weapon assuming a production of enough U_{235} for ten weapons per year.) This figure is in complete agreement with the cost estimate derived independently on the basis of the necessary separation work units. Both methods of enrichment involve highly secret advanced technologies unavailable to Greece at this time. Therefore to the above costs one must add an indeterminate amount for technology acquisition.

2. Pu_{239}

Pu_{239} is produced in reactors when U_{238}, the abundant isotope of uranium, is irradiated by neutrons. This process can take place in any type of reactor, power, research, or the pool type available at Democritos Research Center. The annual Pu_{239} production (in kgs per MW electric energy per year) for various types of reactors is given below:

Boiling water	0.23 kg/MWe/yr
Pressurised water	0.23 kg/MWe/yr
Pressurised heavy water	0.29 kg/MWe/yr
Gas-cooled	0.25 kg/MWe/yr

A 1000 MW power reactor then would produce of the order of 250 kg of plutonium per year at 75 per cent load factor. Under these circumstances the plutonium produced will be a mixture of Pu_{239} and Pu_{240}. The latter isotope does not fission, is more likely to capture a neutron and become Pu_{241} and therefore both increases the neutron generation time and raises the critical mass value necessary for an explosive device. In addition, Pu_{240} fissions spontaneously with the emission of several neutrons, one of which may start the chain reaction before the plutonium core has reached its supercritical state and therefore may cause the untimely predetonation of the nuclear charge. This, aside from the obvious risks of an accident, has two undesirable effects: first, it makes the explosive yield of the weapon unpredictable and second it may reduce it by a factor of 10 or more, that is instead of the expected 20 kT yield the device may 'fizzle' and yield 1 or 2 kT TNT equivalent. In order to keep the proportion of Pu_{240} small in the fuel rods of a power nuclear reactor these rods must be burnt only to 10 per cent of their useful uranium content. This, however, is extremely uneconomical. Accumulation of Pu_{239} from the operation of power reactors entails a very large economic penalty.

Instead of a power reactor one could install a dedicated plutonium production reactor similar to the Dimona facility in Israel or the proposed Osiris metallurgical research reactor of Iraq. Such a reactor, if it would be possible to acquire it from one of the supplier countries, would cost approximately 50×10^6\$ (1976) and would have an annual operating cost of \$4 million. This figure does *not* include the cost of fuel or amortisation of capital investment. For a reactor that could produce about 100 kg or plutonium a year, this cost would be about \$340,000 per kg. For a reactor that would produce 40 kg of Pu_{239} a year the cost per kg would be about \$650,000. A heavy water moderated reactor of 20 MWe power rating would produce about 10 kg of plutonium per year. This reactor would have to be imported from Canada but Ottawa does not license the export of such reactors as part of the NPT efforts.

Finally, it is worth considering the capabilities of the small experimental reactor at Democritos. The time needed to produce 10 kg of plutonium with this reactor under several operating conditions varies between 5 and 35 years. The 5-year time span requires 90 per cent enriched uranium fuel that the US government exports with great difficulty and the proviso of on-site inspection of its use. Needed alterations of the core of the reactor will require 1–2 additional years and about $1.5–2.0 million. The times listed imply continuous irradiation of the rods excluding any other use of the reactor at Democritos.

A complete plutonium production facility with an output of 40 kg plutonium per year will require, in addition to the reactor, a uranium ore-processing and refining plant, a fuel element fabrication facility, a plutonium separation plant (reprocessing) in which the plutonium produced by irradiation in the fuel rods will be separated from the uranium by chemical means, and a plutonium metal reduction plant. The total complex is estimated to cost about $50 million and requires about 5 years to install *given the technological know-how*. The annual cost will be about $25 million.

Plutonium is a highly toxic and radioactive substance and its handling and processing requires special remote-handling and sealed facilities. The cost estimate for a complete plutonium-handling complex assumes less than completely safe installations in the plutonium (fuel element) reprocessing plant. It is therefore to be expected that accidents or fatalities of workers by radioactive or toxic exposure may occur. A completely safe facility may cost an additional $5–10 million. The overall costs of a plutonium production reactor cum the complete plutonium-handling facility result in a price per kg of plutonium roughly the same as would result from using a power reactor somewhat inefficiently to produce Pu_{239} in its fuel rods, if the annual plutonium production is about 40 kg. For smaller quantities a power reactor appears more economical while for larger quantities a dedicated plutonium production reactor results in lower costs per kg of plutonium. Assuming that 20 kg of 90 per cent or better Pu_{239} metallic plutonium is necessary for a 20 kT weapon, one arrives at a price per plutonium weapon of about $10–20 million. This is sharply higher than the cost of a similar warhead in the United States. The difference is due both to the economies of size and the advanced nuclear warhead technology of the United States.

Weapon-fabrication Manpower and Facilities Requirements

The fabrication of a weapon, given adequate supplies of suitable fissile material, requires a number of activities such as design and fabrication of the explosive core itself, design and fabrication of the arming and fusing mechanisms, measurement of the properties of the fissile material at hand, some testing of this material, design and fabrication of fail-safe mechanisms to protect the device from unauthorised or premature use, and design and installation of protective measures that will protect the device from catastrophic events such as accidental release from an aircraft in flight, fire, earthquake or other extreme environments. The explosive core will usually consist, in an implosion-type weapon, of the fissile material, the surrounding neutron reflector (tamper) and the necessary explosive shaped charges and associated electronic and fusing components necessary to render the mass of the fissile material supercritical. Considerable expertise is needed for the design and manufacture of this assembly. Once the assembly is ready it has to be integrated into the weapon which will presumably be an air-droppable bomb that must weigh no more than 1000 kg and preferably half of that if it is to be carried by an F-4 fighter—bomber or other aircraft of that type. The entire weapon must then be tested in underground facilities and careful and extensive instrumentation is necessary in order to evaluate its performance. Considerable know-how in diagnostic physics will be necessary for that task. Finally, storage facilities for the weapons must be designed and constructed. These facilities must be both readily available to suitable aircraft, and safe from unauthorised entry, surprise attack, and accidents.

The fabrication of a nuclear weapon using plutonium is additionally complicated by the complex metallurgical processes involved, the toxicity, chemical reactivity and radioactivity of the material. The capital investment in a facility that could assemble ten warheads a year would be about $15 million, and the annual operating costs about $2 million. Three to five years at the very minimum will be required for the design and initial assembly of a device *once the necessary personnel is assembled*. Longer periods of time must be contemplated if anything less than a massive effort is made to acquire nuclear-weapons capability. The number of scientists and engineers required for a total programme for the production of fissile material, and the design, initial assembly and testing of a fission weapon, is estimated by several independent analysts to be about 500 scientists, of which 50 at least must be at the doctoral level, that includes physicists, chemists, metallurgists, electronics, computer and explosives experts. In addition, the effort will require 1500 engineers, mainly nuclear, chemical and electronic. If Greece will have to train twenty to thirty Ph.D. scientists (4–8 years needed) and 300 other scientists (4–5 years needed) the total cost for *training* alone is $30 million over a period of 4–8 years. In addition, assuming that 1000 engineers are to be trained, the cost will be approximately $90 million over a period of 4–8 years. Most of this money will have to be in foreign currency since the majority of the training will have to take place abroad. In addition, a fraction of the scientists and engineers currently gainfully employed in the Greek industrial sector will have to be siphoned off into the nuclear-weapon effort, drastically reducing both the productivity and the rate of growth of Greek industry. This will represent an unknown cost in lost opportunities and retardation of the further industrialisation of Greece.

The task of designing a weapon will require extensive computational capability for calculations and simulation studies. This computational capability does not exist today in Greece and will have to be imported. Several million dollars will be required for that.

The testing of the device will cost between $11 and 20 million, depending upon the availability or not of a suitable mine for the test. This figure includes the cost of instrumentation but not of the device tested.

Direct and Opportunity Costs of the Programme

In addition to the direct costs of the programme outlined in the last two sections that amount, for a plutonium device, to a capital outlay of nearly $250 million, there are several other types of costs that can only be briefly outlined.

One, namely the loss of the services of a sizeable portion of the Greek scientific and engineering potential to the nuclear-weapons programme for periods up to 10 years, has already been hinted at. While Greece is in the process of becoming increasingly industrialised in order to better fit in the European Economic Community (EEC), such a diversion of scientific and technical manpower will have serious economic and perhaps political side-effects. Additionally, any overt attempt by Greece to acquire a nuclear arsenal will result in immediate retaliatory measures from the supplier countries such as the United States, France, West Germany, and

Great Britain. These measures will no doubt involve embargoes of essential technological imports to Greece, economic penalties such as loss of most-favoured trade status in the United States, and loss of privileges in the EEC. But, most importantly, such an attempt at nuclearisation will deny Greece access to nuclear technology and nuclear fuel essential for its nuclear power reactor programme. A nuclear reactor is such a vastly complex and massive engineering system that Greece simply cannot construct it. Fuel elements for this reactor could be in principle fabricated in Greece *if* the country had enough uranium ore to support it for the 30-year normal lifetime of the installation. But Greece does not, and even if such ore were available it would cost much more to fabricate the fuel elements locally rather than to purchase them from a supplier country. Thus the per kilowatt cost of power from the reactor would become prohibitively high. It is a fact that further industrialisation of Greece to the end of the century will require the installation of a nuclear power reactor, and therefore the reactor cannot be abandoned in favour of acquiring a nuclear arsenal. Once the reactor is in operation, it would in principle be possible to divert a number of 10 per cent burnt fuel elements and extract the plutonium from them. That, however, would jeopardise further supplies of fuel for the reactor and therefore it would be equivalent to shutting down the reactor permanently for the sake of diverting plutonium for weapons fabrication.

Diplomatic and security costs must also be considered. Abrogation of the NPT, of which Greece is a signatory, is bound to evoke the most profoundly negative response both from supplier countries and from the community of nations such as Sweden that have been championing the NPT. Diplomatic isolation may in the end erode the position and security of the country more drastically than the acquisition of nuclear weapons could restore (to say nothing of the 5–10-year hiatus during which Greece will not have nuclear weapons, but will be known to be developing them).

By far the most serious indirect cost of the initiation of development of nuclear weapons in Greece will be the actual diminution of its security that will result. Such development will undoubtedly force neighbouring countries to initiate a counter-development aimed at eventually providing them also with a nuclear arsenal. Greece then will become involved in a regional nuclear arms race that will end with the country having one or more opponents possessing nuclear weapons, a threat that it does not face now.

Thus the long-term security of the country will be diminished drastically. On the other hand, the situation is symmetrical: if a putative adversary of Greece launches a nuclear weapons development programme, Greece would have to re-examine the entire issue in a new light.

Finally, expenditure of sums, mainly in foreign currency, for a nuclear weapons development programme is bound to affect the economic ability of the country to support and improve the conventional armed forces. Thus it may well be that the several hundred million dollars necessary for the development of a nuclear arsenal could buy more security for the country if spent procuring high-technology conventional weapons or strengthening the industrial and technological base of the economy, than buying nuclear weapons that, as the experience of all the existing nuclear countries has shown, cannot be used for political or military ends other than deterrence. Thus possession of nuclear weapons did not prevent the defeat of American forces in Vietnam or improve the political or military ability of the British to impose their will in Rhodesia, Ireland and elsewhere. Neither has any of the nuclear powers parleyed the possession of nuclear weapons into successful coercion or military advantage.

Utilities of a Nuclear Arsenal

A nuclear arsenal consisting of a modest number of tested, air-deliverable weapons could prove quite useful under certain circumstances. These cirumstances, however, have at this time and in the foreseeable future very small probability of occurrence, and therefore the overall utility of nuclear weapons should be viewed in that frame of reference. For example, possession of nuclear weapons could prove an effective deterrent against a nuclear adversary bent at blackmailing or coercing Greece. They would in all probability dissuade him from attacking Greece, although it is not certain that, if in possession of superior conventional forces, such an adversary could not attack and occupy a portion of Greek territory. In the last analysis, then, a nuclear arsenal can only deter nuclear attack or nuclear blackmail from another nuclear power. It will also most probably, but not certainly, discourage a non-nuclear adversary from attacking Greece. It must be borne in mind that to date nuclear weapons have not proved helpful in resolving favourably conventional conflicts.

A useful by-product of a programme to develop a nuclear arsenal in Greece will be the establishment of a strong nuclear-technology base and the rapid improvement and expansion of the scientific and technological potential of the country. The decision to build nuclear weapons in France resulted in a rapid development of nuclear and electronics technology in that country. On the other hand, it must not be forgotten that France already possessed an advanced technological base at the time the nuclear weapons programme was initiated. Finally, if the Greek Government decided to improve the scientific and technological potential of the country, it can certainly do so without the initiation of a nuclear-weapons project.

Air-deliverable nuclear weapons may find in some cases battle-field applications such as against concentrations of hostile forces. They could be used with impunity, however, only if the adversary did not possess nuclear weapons. In addition, it must be remembered that use of nuclear weapons on the battlefield requires dedicated units for delivery, and extensive training of all forces that would be involved in such use. These conditions tend to abbreviate the conventional capabilities of the armed forces, and as NATO has already experienced, this proves to be a costly effort both financially and in terms of combat units and equipment available for conventional operations. At any rate, before one can decide on the cost-effectiveness of nuclear weapons for battlefield use, one must carefully examine all alternative munitions and systems that could perform the same mission with similar, or better, results.

Conclusion

This brief analysis tends to confirm that, if for any reason Greece decided to develop a nuclear weapons arsenal, it would be possible to do so. The fabrication of deliverable, tested nuclear weapons does not present in principle any insurmountable technical obstacles. If Greece were ready to pay the costs, both in finance and in political, diplomatic, and security disadvantages, she could eventually acquire a nuclear arsenal. This study has pointed out that if Greece is in possession of useful uranium ore deposits, that is of deposits that yield above 1.0 kg of uranium metal for every ton of ore, in enough quantity to provide not only the necessary fissionable material for weapons, but all the necessary fuel for the nuclear power reactor needed for energy production, then Greece could contemplate abrogating the NPT and charting a course of nuclear technology development independently of the supplier countries. Such action could postpone acquisition of a power reactor until the beginning of the next century, and fabrication of nuclear weapons until the mid-1990s. If Greece wants to avail herself of technology and fuel necessary for the projected power reactor, she has *no alternative* in the foreseeable future but to remain a signatory of the NPT. Diversion of fissionable material from an operational power reactor is both a dangerous violation of treaty obligations that Greece has signed and does not in itself make nuclear weapons available. The processing and fabrication of this purloined material into weapons *cannot be performed secretly*. At any rate, any credible nuclear weapon requires testing which will obviate all previous secrecy.

The development of the facilities for the production of weapons-grade fissile material, of the weapons' assembly plant, of the design, testing and fabrication of the weapon and of assorted subsidiary activities will require 10,000–15,000 man-years and the expenditure of more than $250 million over a period extending between 5 and 8 years. Subsequent to this initial investment, it is expected that the established facility will be able to produce two 20 kT nuclear weapons a year at a cost of roughly $10 million each (1976). A higher rate of production will require more fissile material but will affect the overall cost in manpower and funds only marginally. Finally, while there are serious costs of opportunity in excess of the direct manpower and monetary costs that may in effect amount to a sum larger than the direct costs mentioned above, the utility of a nuclear arsenal for Greece appears for the foreseeable future confined to marginal circumstances that have small probability of occurrence. The disutilities, on the other hand, that stem mainly from the connection between nuclear weapons and nuclear power, and the explicit desire of the supplier nations to discourage and penalise proliferation of nuclear weapons, are immediate, certain, and enormously threatening to the economic and industrial development of Greece.

19 Nigeria's Nuclear Potential

Robert D'A. Henderson

Introduction

In his 1979 Reith Lectures on BBC Radio, Professor Ali Mazrui suggested that 'those African countries which signed the non-proliferation treaty (NPT) should review their positions, and consider setting up a continental nuclear consortium allied to a strategy of developing a small military nuclear capability, first in Nigeria and later on in Zaire and black-ruled South Africa' as a means of enhancing their national identities and their international status.[1] At present only six countries on the African continent have had, have, or are actively seeking a nuclear energy capability.

Among the North African states, Egypt has trained nuclear scientists and a modest research facility with a 2 MW Soviet-built reactor which has been operating since 1961. Egypt has only recently ratified the NPT, in February 1981, with an IAEA safeguards agreement coming into force in August 1982. In 1974, the Richard Nixon Administration offered to sell two 60 MW power reactors to Egypt as part of a linked arrangement to sell the same type of reactor to Israel. A purchase agreement with Egypt was signed in August 1976, but by 1978 the agreement had not been submitted for US Congressional approval.[2] The other potential nuclear state in North Africa is Muammar Qaddafi's Libya, constructing a 2-MW research reactor supplied by the Soviet Union. Libya, which ratified the NPT in May 1975 and has since entered into an IAEA safeguards agreement, currently lacks trained personnel though its oil revenue would enable it to purchase the necessary facilities and perhaps foreign expertise.

In Subsaharan Africa, Zaire (formerly the Belgian Congo) has had a small nuclear reactor installed by the Belgian Government a year prior to its 1960 independence. In fact, the uranium for the Allied Powers' Manhattan Project during the Second World War came from the Katanga mines in Zaire.[3] In February 1961 Kwame Nkrumah's Ghana signed an agreement with the Soviet Union for a research reactor, fuel rods, construction of a research facility at Kwabenya (near Accra) and the training of Ghanaian personnel.[4] The facility began operating in 1964, although the reactor itself was still under construction. After the 1966 ouster of Nkrumah, however, the new military leaders closed down the entire research facility, and the Soviet technicians were sent home. Recently a government committee was formed to investigate the possibility of re-starting the nuclear research programme utilising the trained personnel from the original programme who are still available from their posts in the national universities and technical institutes. Both Zaire and Ghana are signatories to the NPT and have concluded IAEA safeguards agreements. But by far the most controversial nuclear state in Africa is in the southern part of the continent.

While engaged in a very substantial nuclear programme, South Africa has consistently refused to sign the NPT. Beginning in 1953, South Africa became a major supplier of uranium to the United States and Britain. As a result of the American 'Atoms for Peace' programme of peaceful nuclear co-operation in 1955, the United States–South African Agreement for Co-operation Concerning Civil Uses of Atomic Energy was signed in July 1957.[5] This Agreement was amended and extended in 1962, 1967, and 1974. According to the President of the South African Atomic Energy Board in 1974, in view of its uranium resources and uranium enrichment expertise and technology, South Africa could develop in the direction of marketing part of its uranium in the form of enriched uranium and eventually in the form of fuel elements for power reactors in the future. But such a development 'can be carried out meaningfully only if our engineers and scientists can gain experience with the behaviour of nuclear fuel in power reactors under operating conditions, and are given the opportunity to test their own nuclear fuel under practical conditions in power reactors'.[6] In addition to its own internally developed uranium enrichment technology, South Africa purchased its Safari I 20 MW thermal research reactor, located at Pelindaba, from the United States in 1961 (Safari I was operational in 1965 and Safari II in 1968), established its own pilot enrichment plant at Valindaba in 1971 (a commercial enrichment plant is expected to be operational by 1984), and awarded a French consortium the contract to build its first nuclear power reactor Koeberg A for start-up in November 1982 (Koeberg B is expected to start up in 1983).

Much of South Africa's nuclear programme is not under any IAEA safeguards. And in August 1977 both the Soviet Union and the United States accused South Africa of planning to detonate a nuclear device in its Kalahari desert area; in any event, no nuclear explosion took place.[7] But recently there has been some evidence of a nuclear explosion in the southern Indian Ocean below South Africa, and though the South African Government has denied all knowledge of or involvement in the event, a South African naval task force was reported to be conducting a secret exercise at sea at the time, according to an American Central Intelligence Agency (CIA) report.[8]

The sixth African country is Nigeria, which ratified the NPT on 27 September 1968 but has no IAEA nuclear safeguards agreement in force. Nigeria at present utilises no nuclear reactors or fissionable materials. It has publicly committed itself to the peaceful uses of nuclear energy and has supported calls for a nuclear-weapon-free zone (NWFZ) for Africa (including South Africa). After the French nuclear test in the Algerian portion of the Sahara Desert in February 1960, Nigeria joined other independent African states in protesting against nuclear testing on the African continent and supported a move for a continental NWFZ. Then, in 1974, Nigeria proposed such a continental zone before the United Nations, partly in response to widespread press reports that South Africa's intensive nuclear programme was intended to establish a weapons production capability.

In a well-argued article, Ashok Kapur recently claimed.

The new Third World orientation is to create third party interference in superpower planning and to create the intellectual and resource foundation to strengthen the capacity to interfere. Resource diplomacy, conventional arms proliferation and use, and nuclear option-building are different instruments but they are products of this new orientation in regional life.[9]

In relation to Nigeria, research has already been conducted into its resource diplomacy and conventional arms proliferation and use.[10]

This chapter seeks to investigate Nigeria's nuclear option-building in terms of its technical expertise, mineral resources, nuclear energy facilities, the transfer of nuclear technology, and the bureaucratic/intellectual constituencies of that nuclear technology. By analysing these various components, it is hoped that it will be possible to discern the Nigerian outlook for nuclear policy decision-making for the 1980s and 1990s.

Technical Expertise

On 24 August 1976 the Nigerian Federal Military Government (FMG) established by decree an atomic energy commission with responsibility for 'the promotion and development of atomic energy and for all matters relating to the peaceful uses of atomic energy'.[11] Under the then military government, nuclear research programmes were to be situated at 'centres of excellence' at the University of Ife (in the southern part of the country) and Ahmadu Bello University (in the north). The University of Ife alone sent twenty graduate students abroad for postgraduate training in nuclear technology; many of these students went under an exchange agreement with McMaster University in Canada. Even so, for the near future, Nigeria will lack enough highly trained nuclear scientists, engineers, and technicians to support a modest nuclear research programme. But there have been calls for a major Federal Government investment for the development of indigenous nuclear expertise. The Vice-Chancellor of the University of Nigeria (Nsukka), Professor F. N. Ndili, recently called for the establishment of a national institute for nuclear studies in the country; he went on to urge the Federal Government to embark on a programme to train more physicists and mathematicians.[12] Similar calls were made at the National Energy Policy Conference in Jos in August 1978.

A second option would be to recruit foreign nuclear expertise from either industrialised or Third World (semi-industrialised) nuclear states for this nationally sensitive industry. Among possible Third World countries with nuclear expertise (though at various levels) are India, Pakistan, Brazil, and Egypt. To pursue this option, if only for the short term, India is a particularly likely candidate in view of its own domestic nuclear industry. Besides exploding a nuclear device in 1974, India currently operates two nuclear power stations for electricity production, two more are nearing completion, and a fifth one is to begin construction. Further, India now has extensive experience using natural uranium fuel and heavy water as moderator, and is beginning to gain more advanced nuclear technology with its fast breeder test reactor at Kalpakkam.[13] Regardless of which option will be pursued (possibly both complementary), the present Nigerian civilian government has continued Federal financial support for nuclear technology training in line with the objectives of the previous FMG.

Mineral Resources

During 1976–77, the Nigerian FMG and the parastatal Nigerian Mining Corporation carried out a feasibility survey of uranium ore deposits in the Gombe area of Bauchi State. As a result of this survey, the FMG in partnership with the French Minatome Company in the following year formed the Nigerian Uranium Mining Company (NUMCO) for the purposes of uranium exploration, exploitation, processing and marketing. The Nigerian Mining Corporation, which represented the Federal Government, held 60 per cent of the NUMCO shares and the Minatome Company, which provided the technical expertise for the project, had 40 per cent. By early 1980 NUMCO had established its headquarters in Gombe, though it has had its activities restricted to that area as 'other suitable and interested organisations are allowed to explore in defined areas without detriment to national interest'. In March 1980 the Nigerian Minister for Mines and Power, Alhaji Mohammed Ibrahim Hassan, announced that 'priority attention' would be given to the development of uranium ore deposits in Benue, Niger, Sokoto, Cross River, and Bauchi states.[14]

Another possible source of uranium ore is the huge deposits being mined in the French-speaking northern neighbour Niger. These deposits are currently estimated to comprise approximately 10 per cent of the world's known commercially exploitable uranium deposits (at the present world market price of $80 per kg). Of course, if the world price rises, other known uranium deposits could become commercially viable in several countries around the world. These deposits are presently being mined and processed into yellow cake, and then milled and refined, under the technical expertise of foreign companies, including the French Commissariat for Atomic Energy. Nigeria has a 16 per cent participation share in the exploration of uranium in Niger, while Niger itself retained a 45 per cent share.[15] Other possible sources of uranium from among Nigeria's African neighbours are the Central African Republic and Gabon, whose deposits are being developed by French concerns. But it is not known at this time if Nigeria has any plans to establish a mill and refinery to process uranium ore.

Nuclear Energy Facilities

At present Nigeria has no operational nuclear energy facilities. It has been planned that a van de Graaf accelerator be established as part of the nuclear research programme at the University of Ife, though neither the research centre nor the accelerator facility has begun to be constructed. An estimated 2-year construction period would be necessary before the research facilities would be operational, after which a research reactor is to be installed and commissioned at a later date. At the time that Nigeria established its atomic energy commission, it was reported that talks with West Germany had begun on the purchase of a nuclear power station. During his 1976 visit to Bonn the Nigerian Chief of Staff, Brigadier Shehu Yar'Adua (acting in the capacity of FMG Prime Minister), discussed the proposed scheme with West German Chancellor Helmut Schmidt. As Nigeria was a signatory to the NPT, talks were started between the West German Kraft Werke-Union AG, which constructs nuclear power-generating stations, and representatives of the Nigerian government for the purchase of a 450 MW medium-sized reactor. The scheme was then valued[16] at about DM 1,000 million. Though discussions were also reported to have been held with the Canadian Government over the possible purchase of a 600 MW CANDU reactor, no agreement was reached in either case.

If Nigeria does decide in the future to purchase a nuclear power reactor, it will, in theory, have three options. First, it could buy a natural uranium/heavy water type, such as the Canadian CANDU. In that case, at least initially, it would need to depend on foreign assistance not only to mill and refine local uranium and convert it into fabricated fuel elements but also to supply heavy water or the technology required to produce it. Second, it could purchase an enriched uranium/light water reactor of the pressurized water reactor (PWR) or boiling water reactor (BWR) types favoured in the United States, France or West Germany. In that case, foreign assistance would be essential not only to process and fabricate local uranium but also to have the uranium enriched in one of the three or four plants operated by major industrial countries. Third, it could eventually hope to buy one of the fast breeder reactor types still under development, which need uranium but which, more significantly, both consume and produce plutonium in their fuel cycles. Apart from the fact that this last option is more speculative and could not be taken up until a clearly commercial fast breeder reactor design was internationally available − well into the 1990s − it would, however, represent a leap into a new generation of nuclear technology, for exploiting or operating which Nigeria could hardly hope to have the qualified personnel. In practice, therefore, the choice is almost certain to lie between the first and second options.

Two things stand out clearly. One is that Nigeria, whichever reactor option it decides to pursue, would be heavily dependent, especially in the earlier stages of a programme, not only on foreign nuclear experts but also on foreign nuclear suppliers. Even if it made economic sense to build up a complete nuclear infra- structure locally, involving uranium processing, fuel fabrication and plants for producing heavy water, enriching uranium and/or reprocessing spent fuel, in order to support only one or two power reactors − which is most implausible − Nigeria would be unlikely to shift from current priorities the huge share of government resources needed to purchase the relevant technology and equip- ment 'off the shelf'. More probably, therefore, it would have to rely on foreign suppliers to provide heavy water or enrichment services, and even to fabricate fuel elements.

The other thing which stands out is that Nigeria, as a party to the NPT, is already under an obligation to conclude a 'full-scope' safeguards agreement with the IAEA, involving regular inspection of all its current and future nuclear activities, and would clearly have to make such an agreement before it began to operate a power reactor or even a small research reactor. In addition, any foreign supplier of reactors, fuel elements, heavy water or enrich- ment services would almost certainly insist not only on the applica- tion of IAEA safeguards but also on its own right to ensure the peaceful use of the materials or equipment concerned, possibly including its right to take back spent fuel elements containing plutonium and probably including a right of 'prior consent' by the supplier to the disposition of such spent fuel.

Nigeria is unlikely to purchase a nuclear power reactor in the foreseeable future. In any case, given the lead-time for building and commissioning such a plant, it could not have a power reactor in operation before the 1990s.[17] It might well, of course, prefer to begin by importing and installing a research reactor, to gain experience and to train technicians. What is evident, however, is that by committing itself firmly to any part of this process, Nigeria, despite its access to local uranium reserves, would in effect commit itself also to international safeguards and inspection and to a considerable measure and period of technical and commercial dependence on foreign suppliers.

Transfer of Nuclear Technology: the Politico-strategic Context

Nigeria has repeatedly denounced South Africa's intensive nuclear research and development programmes, based on Western nuclear co-operation and sales with South Africa and on South Africa's own indigenous nuclear technology (i.e. its enrichment process). Under the 'Atoms for Peace' programme and then through the sale of research reactors and new nuclear power reactors, South Africa has received extensive nuclear technology and facilities from Western countries, including the United States, Britain, West Germany and France. It has been reported that South Africa now has a nuclear exchange agreement with Israel, and it is generally accepted that South Africa has the capacity (in expertise, facilities, and nuclear materials) to produce nuclear explosive devices. Whether it also has the capability to produce a nuclear weapon of a size which could be delivered onto a distant target is still questionable. But South Africa does possess jet bombers (Canberras, Buccaneers, and Mirage) which could carry a conventional-size bomb to a target within the southern African subregion.[18] It has also developed the technology to assemble and operate surface-to-air guided missiles (the Cactus system), but it is unlikely that it currently has the capability to produce an intermediate-range missile to carry a nuclear warhead or to produce a smaller tactical nuclear weapon, despite suggestions that Israel could provide this expertise. Thus for the foreseeable future, South Africa is unable to threaten Nigeria territorially with 'nuclear blackmail'.

But South Africa's nuclear capability is seen as a physical threat to its neighbouring Black-ruled states in Southern Africa and as a 'psychological' threat to the African continent in that it is a further support for the maintenance of its *apartheid* system. Nigeria's Ambassador to the United Nations, Leslie O. Harriman, as Chairman of the February 1979 UN Seminar on Nuclear Collaboration with South Africa, pointed out in his concluding statement that South Africa had not acceded to the NPT, so that it could continue with its nuclear programme and threaten African states, and that it had challenged the Organization of African Unity's commitment to the denuclearisation of Africa.[19] President Alhaji Shagari in his recent address to the Foreign Policy Association in New York continued to support the position that Nigeria 'will not allow Africa to be subjected to nuclear blackmail' by South Africa and the need to keep Africa as a nuclear-free zone. He went on to point out that 'resources wasted on the stockpiling of weapons of mass destruction can be better utilised in solving the problems of want and in improving the material conditions of human existence'.[20] Yet only days before, at a press conference on the 20th Anniversary of Nigeria's Independence, he stated that although Nigeria did not consider a nuclear capability as one of her priorities, it 'reserved the right to do whatever she could to protect herself if racist South Africa persisted in acquiring nuclear weapons to threaten the continent'. But he agreed that Nigeria had not reached the stage for such acquisition though 'everything depended upon developments in the international community' in relation to self-determination and the abolition of *apartheid* in Southern Africa.[21]

Nigeria has consistently pursued its anti-*apartheid* policy in a number of international forums where the issues of nuclear energy and nuclear disarmament are discussed. When the Ten-Power Committee was expanded into an Eighteen-Nation Disarmament Committee in 1960, Nigeria was one of the eight non-aligned countries invited to join. Though renamed the Conference of the Committee on Disarmament (CCD) in 1969, Nigeria continues to play an active rôle in this body. As a member of the Board of Governors of the IAEA, Nigeria was one of the main instigators for the expulsion of South Africa from the Board in June 1977 and for its replacement by Egypt, though South Africa still remained a full member of the IAEA.[22] In 1978 Nigeria was elected to the 'African' seat on the UN Security Council. Among Nigeria's proposed objectives, Ambassador Harriman listed such 'activist' Council steps as an oil and arms embargo and a foreign investment ban against South Africa's *apartheid* regime and action to denuclearise the African continent.[23] From its chairmanship of the UN Special Committee against *apartheid*, Nigeria initiated the afore-mentioned 1979 seminar on nuclear collaboration with South Africa. During the September 1979 Conference of the Non-Aligned Movement, Nigeria was one of the main supporters for the inclusion in the Conference's Declaration of a call for convening another international conference on the peaceful uses of nuclear energy, tentatively scheduled for 1983 by the UN General Assembly.[24]

Partly as a result of its active participation in these international fora and partly in recognition of its emerging economic and military rôle in Africa, Nigeria's views on African affairs are increasingly being sought. In 1976 during the US Senate hearings on the proposed sale of light-water reactors to South Africa, the State Department spokesman on African Affairs stated that consultations with the Nigerian Foreign Minister had been held in New York. When asked if the Foreign Minister expressed his opposition to the sale, the spokesman confirmed that 'he expressed his deep concern regarding it'.[25] In addition to Nigeria's diplomatic opposition to South Africa's *apartheid* policy and its nuclear programme, it was reported that Nigeria was threatening to use its enlarged naval force to seize any sea-borne uranium shipments from the Rossing mine in Namibia and that the decision to set up a uranium air shuttle might have been as a result of this perceived threat.[26] Nigeria has recognised that South Africa's nuclear weapon capability or potential capability gives it 'a diplomatic resource in a non-crisis situation and a potential military resource if the state is forced into a "back to the wall" crisis', in the words of Kapur.[27] This factor, plus Nigeria's anti-*apartheid* policy, could lead to greater government investment in a nuclear energy programme, though even with greater political will it is unlikely that Nigeria could develop its nuclear technology and facilities to the level of weapons production by the turn of the century.

But such a national nuclear development programme could

further enhance Nigeria's regional power status in West Africa. At present, in addition to its large population (estimated at between 80 and 100 million) and its huge oil deposits, Nigeria has established a large and increasingly effective military capability along with an emerging industrial production infrastructure. These factors have ensured it of a major voice in the Economic Community of West African States (ECOWAS). If Nigeria did pursue a nuclear programme it could provide the basis for nuclear energy production for the ECOWAS member-states. At the July 1980 Conference of the West African Science Association, the Nigerian Federal Minister for Science and Technology, Sylvester U. Ugoh, stated that the nations of the sub-region should pool their resources so as to achieve solutions within the shortest time and at minimal cost, and called for greater co-operation in the area of energy production, including nuclear and solar energy. Notwithstanding the mutual economic advantage of a joint regional approach to future energy production it must be borne in mind that, should some West African countries choose the nuclear energy option, they could seek French (or other nuclear states') nuclear expertise and technology as opposed to any nuclear assistance which Nigeria might be able to offer in the future. Indeed, the then French Industry Minister, André Giraud, in a recent interview, urged the expansion of civilian nuclear power as a means of preventing war over conventional energy sources. He went on to say: 'We must be more liberal in our approach to peaceful nuclear power and avoid creating a mood of discrimination against non-nuclear countries. Otherwise, you push some countries into starting their own programmes, and then there are no sanctions left if they add a military programme, too.'[28]

Transfer of Nuclear Technology: the Socioeconomic Context

Although Nigeria is a member of the Organisation of Petroleum Exporting Countries (OPEC) and a net exporter of oil, current estimates of its oil reserves suggest that they could be exhausted by the year 2000 at present rates of production. The country's energy requirements are supplied from either hydroelectric power resources or thermal power stations utilising non-renewable reserves of oil, natural gas or coal. The major electricity generating plants are the Kainji Dam (installed capacity of 760 MW) and the more recently commissioned gas-fired steam turbine power station at Sapele (720 MW). Two additional hydroelectric stations are under construction at Jebba (540 MW) and Shiroro (600 MW), and feasibility studies are under way for similar schemes at Lokoja, Ikom and Makurdi. In addition to the gas-fired Sapele station, smaller gas turbine power stations at Afam (256 MW) and Delta (312 MW) have been using natural gas as fuel for some time; all three of these stations are located near the oil fields. But the biggest potential consumer for natural gas is the planned Lagos 750 MW thermal plant which is unlikely to start up until after 1985. Even so, the gas being flared off at the oil fields (amounting to 95 per cent of the gas associated with the oil deposits) is to be halted by the end of 1983. There are also isolated oil-fired steam turbine stations in such towns as Katsina, Minna, Yola and Makurdi, as well as a few remaining coal-fired plants in the East such as the one at Oji.

In 1977 the maximum power demand on the national grid was 753 MW (up from 256 MW in 1970), with a projected growth to 2189 MW by 1982. The 1972—77 period showed an average 20 per cent annual growth rate in the demand for power. The prediction for the 1977—82 period is an average of 25 per cent each year.[29] Part of this increased demand will be met by the additional hydro-electric stations on the Niger—Benue rivers, while in the south greater use can be made of the gas reserves (especially those not associated with the oil deposits) or to a lesser extent the coal deposits in the eastern section of the country. According to the Guidelines for the Fourth National Development Plan 1981—85[30], the Government is to encourage a greater use of coal and gas for power generation to reduce the country's dependence on hydro-electricity, and to pursue developments in solar energy. This is partly due to the effects that further damming of the tributaries of the Niger—Benue rivers will have on water and storage levels of the existing and proposed dams. This environmental factor was high-lighted during the 1977—78 drought when low water levels at the Kainji Dam resulted in a drop of electricity output, leading to nationwide power cuts.

In the north, with its increasing industrialisation, there is a constantly growing demand for electric power. At present, most of the northern areas are connected by transmission and distribution networks to the Kainji Dam, with additional networks being added. With the October 1980 commission of Nigeria's third oil refinery at Kaduna with a 740 km oil pipeline connection to the coast, some of the fuel problems in the north will be eliminated; also recently a contract was given for the construction of an electricity generating plant to be linked to the refinery. And to improve the distribution of the finished petroleum products, pipelines have been built from the refinery to Kano (via Zaria) and Maiduguri (via Jos). But what other energy sources are available? There appear to be good prospects (and costs) for exploiting wind and solar energy renewable sources by those African countries bordering on the Sahara or which have a coastline. Due to variations in wind speeds, and the need to compensate for them, wind-generated electricity could prove more expensive than other energy sources. In the case of solar energy, both the technology and the equipment are available for small-scale uses, such as water heating, water pumping, and household power generating. While relatively inexpensive, this energy source is currently more relevant to rural energy requirements (i.e. households) than to towns and cities.

In Nigeria's case, though perhaps more so in the northern part of the country, the cost of transporting fuel (for example, by a gas or oil pipeline network) to regional thermal power stations plus the stations themselves could prove to be just as expensive as nuclear plants. And natural uranium/heavy water reactors have a record of commercial operation in such countries as Canada and India; while the expected life of a power reactor is comparable to that of a large thermal generating plant. Also, nuclear power stations hold out the prospect that, even if it involved continuing dependence on the outside world, they would at least provide an alternative to relying exclusively on the few remaining foreign suppliers of fossil fuels as when Nigeria's own petroleum and gas resources run out. It needs to be noted that these resources will still be steadily consumed by the country's expanding petrochemical industries even if they are no longer utilised as an energy source. With its growing population and industrial sector, it is reasonable to expect that Nigeria will be able to use all its energy production (from whatever source) for the foreseeable future. It is very likely that nuclear power stations could become a viable and necessary policy option by the year 2000. But it is unlikely that any single power station would be constructed which could contribute more than 15 per cent of the total electricity generation in the national power grid. This is because if the station failed or had to be shut down the whole grid could suffer power cuts similar to the 1977–78 cuts. It is significant that the Guidelines for the Fourth National Development Plan make no mention of nuclear energy as a possible power source, though the actual Plan is yet to be released.

Bureaucratic/Intellectual Constitutencies

Kapur has pointed out that new bureaucratic and intellectual constituencies have emerged in favour of a stronger emphasis on the nuclear factor in Third World decision-making.[31] In addition to those Third World countries which already have national nuclear energy programmes, Nigeria fits into the category of those which have nominal programmes but with the future potential to expand them; this is as opposed to Third World countries which know that they are unlikely to have the financial and technical resources to pursue such programmes even in the future. Who constitutes these interest groupings and what rôle do they play in Nigerian decision-making? Basically, they include political and military leaders, the diplomatic service, and university lecturers and research scientists.

Focusing on the national domestic audience, political leaders can point to a nuclear programme as a further symbol of national power and national identity,[32] that such a programme places the country within that 'upper class' minority in world affairs with the technological capability. It enhances their claims to having their country's views taken into consideration and for their inclusion at the 'High Table' of international discussions. Further, it reinforces their claims to regional power status as well as to speak for the independent states of Black Africa. Such a programme can be seen as a further method of consolidating the national identity internally, and promoting the nation's status externally. On the other hand, there appears to be little support among the military leadership towards diverting national resources towards such a programme. In terms of national security priorities, there would seem to be several reasons for such disinterest. First, Nigeria has no regional neighbour armed with nuclear weapons. While South Africa is believed to possess such a capacity, its delivery systems only have a targeting range within the southern African region. Next, the financial and technological resources to pursue such a programme would almost certainly reduce such resources available for developing the country's conventional military power as well as its domestic security-related industries. And finally the military leadership has placed major emphasis upon improving the armed forces' efficiency, modernising its conventional fire-power and creating a regional mobility for its forces.

The pursuit of a national nuclear programme would strengthen Nigeria's claim for diplomatic participation in numerous, special-ised international forums. Its diplomats and their views would be accorded heightened status in those forums where they already participate, such as the IAEA Governing Board, the Committee on Disarmament (CD), the UN Security Council and Special Committee against *apartheid*, and the Non-Aligned Movement. Lobbying of their views and votes would provide additional bargaining chips both within such forums themselves and in other parallel international discussions, which might be unconnected to nuclear energy issues (i.e. the North–South dialogue). As a 'membership card' into higher diplomatic discussions and as a way to give greater weight to the views expressed by its diplomats abroad, the Foreign Ministry could find that it was in its own interest to support a highly visible though perhaps modest nuclear programme.

Finally there are the university lecturers and research scientists, who view a national programme as a further claim upon scarce government resources. Such a programme could guarantee funds for research projects and technical equipment, where such require financial support in millions of Naira rather than in thousands; it could lead to the creation of additional university posts or whole new departments, and even to the establishment of specialised research centres. It would require increased national representa-tion at international conferences on the uses of nuclear energy and on sponsored inspection tours of operational nuclear facilities. Further their scientific expertise would necessitate their involve-ment in national policy-making, if only in the rôle of scientific advisors and consultants.

Outlook for Policy Decision-making

For both politico-strategic and socioeconomic reasons, Nigeria will pursue a nuclear energy strategy, if only at the level of establishing a pool of trained scientists and technicians for a small-scale nuclear research centre. Its bureaucratic/intellectual constituencies would support a policy which gave a 'high profile' to the decision-making on the nuclear option (in the form of a national nuclear energy policy) while still accepting a 'low priority' and proportional funding for nuclear research and development. This would be a lower level adaptation of Kapur's 'dual nuclear decisions' in the Third World (namely, no nuclear weapons at present and intensified research and development to build the nuclear option).[33] But Nigeria's ratification of the NPT has not resulted in the level of assistance and transfer of nuclear technology expected. At the 1979 Havana Non-aligned Conference, Nigeria was a key promoter of the view that Third World countries have an inalienable right to develop nuclear power programmes in relation to their own priorities, interests and needs. While Third World countries may have been overly optimistic in their understanding of the level of nuclear technology transfer as a result of the NPT (Article 4 of which stated that nuclear states party to the NPT would assist non-nuclear signatories to develop their nuclear capacity for peaceful purposes), their complaints are not unlike similar complaints on the low level of industrial technology transfer as seen in the North–South dialogue.

Nigeria is not at this time prepared to have its right of decision-making on a nuclear option for peaceful purposes restricted. Rather for the present, it will follow the 'high–low' policy outlined above as this approach would be consistent with both its current level of technical expertise and industrial development and its present need to finance declared national priorities, such as industrial production, transport infrastructure, universal education and health services. Shagari's comments on nuclear policy at the 20th Anniversary press conference support this order of priorities.

If Nigeria should decide to pursue a major national nuclear development programme in the future, and it is unable to achieve a transfer of nuclear technology from one of the industrialised nuclear powers, it will have two possible paths. First, it can pursue a difficult and very expensive 'go-it-alone' development programme, not unlike that followed by France and China. Pakistan at present appears to have adopted this approach in its own nuclear programme, albeit outside the NPT. Or it can pursue a 'shop-around' approach for nuclear assistance from one of the developing countries which already has a major nuclear programme but which may not be party to the NPT. Precedents for this approach include the 1961 Indian–Egyptian nuclear co-operation agreement, the reported nuclear collaboration between South Africa and Israel, and the recent nuclear co-operation accord between Brazil and Iraq; of these states only Iraq, and recently Egypt, has ratified the NPT.

Looking into the future, both these paths would appear to be possible though expensive options. Yet what Nigeria is seeking is more of an 'open door and helping hand' international transfer policy for peaceful nuclear technology and *not* a 'closed door and secret password' one within which it can make its decision on a national nuclear option in the coming decades.

Notes

1. Ali A. Mazrui, 'Africa's Nuclear Future', *Survival*, XXII (1980) 79.
2. See Ernest W. Lefever, *Nuclear Arms in the Third World: U.S. Policy Dilemma* (Washington, DC, 1979) pp. 71–4.
3. The present writer is grateful to Ian Smart for bringing this point to his attention, as also for several others, particularly on nuclear energy facilities.
4. Robert Legvold, *Soviet Policy in West Africa* (Cambridge, Massachussets, 1970) p. 134.
5. Testimony of Myron B. Kratzer, Department of State, in 'US Policy toward Africa', Hearings before the Committee on Foreign Relations, the Senate, 94th Congress, 2nd Session, 26 May 1976 (Washington, DC, 1976) p. 277.
6. A. J. A. Roux, 'South Africa in a Nuclear World', *South Africa International* (Johannesburg) Jan. 1974.
7. For two differing viewpoints of this event see Carel Birkby, 'New Storm over Nuclear Weapons', *To the Point* (Johannesburg) 2 Sept. 1977 and 'Does South Africa have the Bomb?', *New African* (London) Oct. 1977.
8. See Thomas O'Toole, 'New Zealand "Confirms" Mystery Atom Test', *The Guardian Weekly*, 25 Nov. 1979 and O'Toole, 'SA Ships "in zone of suspected N-Blast"', *The Guardian*, 31 Jan. 1980.
9. Ashok Kapur, 'The Nuclear Spread: A Third World View', *Third World Quarterly*, Jan. 1980.
10. See James Mayall, 'Oil and Nigerian Foreign Policy', *African Affairs* (London) July 1976; and Robert D'A. Henderson, 'Choices and Changes in Nigeria's Defence Policy in the 1970s', a paper presented at the 8th Annual Conference of the Nigerian Society of International Studies, Lagos, Feb. 1980.
11. *The New York Times*, 5 Sept. 1976.
12. 'V-C wants institute for nuclear studies', *New Nigerian* (Kaduna) 4 Mar. 1980.
13. *International Herald Tribune*, Dec. 1979, Special Report on India.
14. *New Nigerian*, 28 Nov. 1979, 7 Feb. 1980, and 31 Mar. 1980; and *Daily Times* (Lagos), 29 Mar. 1980.

15. 'What Uranium does for Niger', *West Africa* (London), 21 Jan. 1980; and *New Nigerian*, 24 Mar. 1980.
16. *Daily Times* (Lagos), 1 Sept. 1976.
17. According to the IAEA, an overall time schedule for a first nuclear plant to become operational is 11 years (including 6 years for construction); see IAEA, *Steps to Nuclear Power* (Vienna, 1974).
18. See Zdenek Cervenka and Barbara Rogers, *The Nuclear Axis* (London, 1978) ch. 7.
19. United Nations Special Committee against Apartheid, *Report of the United Nations Seminar on Nuclear Collaboration with South Africa* (New York, 1979) p. 44.
20. *Daily Times* (Lagos) 6 Oct. 1980.
21. *Daily Sketch* (Ibadan) 30 Sept. 1980; *Daily Times* (Lagos) 30 Sept 1980; and *National Concorde* (Lagos) 30 Sept. 1980.
22. Roger Murray, 'Why the Atom Authority kicked South Africa out', *New African*, Oct. 1977, pp. 970–1.
23. Jane Rosen, 'Nigeria in the UN driving seat', *Guardian Weekly*, 23 Jan. 1978.
24. Stockholm International Peace Research Institute, *The NPT: The Main Political Barrier to Nuclear Weapons Proliferation* (London, 1980) p. 28.
25. Testimony of James Blake, Deputy Assistant Secretary for African Affairs, Department of State in 'US Policy toward Africa', loc. cit., p. 306.
26. *Sunday Times* (London) 9 Dec. 1979.
27. Kupur, loc. cit., p. 60.
28. *International Herald Tribune*, 30 Jan, 1980.
29. Federal Republic of Nigeria, *Guidelines for the Fourth National Development Plan, 1981–85* (Lagos, 1980) p. 53.
30. ibid., p. 55.
31. Kapur, loc. cit., p. 61.
32. By way of comparison see B. W. Augenstein, 'The Chinese and French Program of the Development of National Nuclear Forces', *Orbis*, XI (1967) 846–63.
33. Kapur, loc. cit., p. 73.

Index

A-6 aircraft, 242
A-7 aircraft, 242
Academy of Science (USSR), 96
Acheson—Lilienthal Report, 207, 208
Adriatic, 258, 280, 288
Aegean, 286
Afghanistan, 18, 23, 118, 120, 175,
  176, 177, 189, 201, 202
Africa, 1, 2, 19, 145, 211, 158, 278,
  279, 280, 314, 315
Afro—Asian Solidarity Committee
  (USSR), 108
Ahmudu Bello University, 317
Albania, 275, 284, 286, 287, 288
Allison, Graham, 85
Almelo, 183
American Legion, 114
Amin, Idi, 1, 24
Angell, Norman, 281
Angola, 23, 118
Antarctic Treaty, 211, 258, 278, 279
Anti-Ballistic Missile systems, 114,
  115, 120
Argentina, 7, 38, 151, 172, 187, 189,
  190, 191, 201, 216, 220, 260, 265,
  267, 268, 279
Arms Control and Disarmament
  Agency (US), 68, 70, 86, 88, 89,
  90, 93, 94, 95, 96
Arms Control and Disarmament
  Research Unit (UK), 90, 95, 96
Asia, 145, 236
Atlantic, 72
Atomic Energy Act (US), 169, 178, 208

Atomic Energy Commission, 208
Atomic Energy of Canada Ltd, 190
Atoms for Peace, 184, 209, 315, 321
Australia, 222
Austria, 92

B-52 bomber, 51
Backfire bomber, 14, 71, 237, 242,
  245, 250, 293
Badger bomber, 242, 250
Balkans, 211, 258, 275, 278, 280,
  283, 284, 285, 286, 287, 288, 289,
  290, 291, 292, 293, 294
Baltic, 258
Bari, 70
Baruch, Plan, 208
Bastian, G., 70
Belgium, 92, 97, 146, 151, 154, 194,
  237, 248, 249, 315
Belgrade, 228
Berger, Markus, 71
Berlin, 109
Berlin Wall, 56
Bertram, Christoph, 53, 83
Bhutto, Z. A., 188
Biological Warfare Convention, 19,
  49
Blinder bomber, 242, 250
Bolivia, 259
Brazil, 7, 38, 151, 183, 187, 195, 216,
  259, 260, 265, 267, 268, 279, 317,
  330
Brezhnev, L. I., 107, 108, 109, 110,
  111, 115, 235, 237, 239, 242

332

Britain, *see* Great Britain

British Broadcasting Corporation, 314

Brookings, 66, 73

Brown, Harold, 34, 38, 65, 69, 73, 250

Brown, Neville, 45

Brzezinski, Zbigniew, 55

Buccaneer, 321

Bulganin, Nikolai, 278

Bulgaria, 275, 277, 279, 284, 286, 288, 289, 290

Bundy, McGeorge, 58

Burhop, Eric, 172, 173

Cairo, 170

Cambodia, 295

Campaign for European Nuclear Disarmament, 29

Campaign for Nuclear Disarmament (UK), 29

Canada, 91, 92, 93, 94, 96, 178, 183, 208, 209, 220, 222, 284, 285, 306, 317, 319, 326

Canberra bomber, 321

CANDU, 284, 285, 319

Caribbean, 259

Carter, Jimmy, 56, 65, 67, 68, 73, 114, 117, 118, 119, 122, 125, 175, 177, 180, 184, 186, 187, 188, 191, 192, 193, 194, 196, 197, 198, 202, 224, 242, 301

Central African Republic, 319

Central Intelligence Agency, 316

Chalfont, Lord, 90

Chile, 259, 260, 268, 279

China, 38, 40, 41, 44, 118, 169, 170, 172, 203, 209, 216, 241, 242, 244, 246, 249, 258, 263, 292, 302, 329

Churchill, Winston, 117, 168

Clarke, Robin, 106

Cogena, 194

Colombia, 268

Commager, Henry Steele, 37

Commissariat Énergie Atomique, 189, 203, 319

Committee for European Security and Cooperation (USSR), 108

Committee on Disarmament, 328

Comprehensive Test Ban, 8, 49

Conference of the Committee on Disarmament, 288, 322

Conference on Security and Cooperation in Europe, 11, 15, 28, 53, 55, 60, 61, 77, 92, 94, 98, 101

Congress of Vienna, 114

Conseil de Politique Nucléaire Extérieure, 186

Convention on Prevention of Nuclear War, 67

COPREDAL, 259, 260, 263

Costa Rica, 26

Cox, Arthur M., 66

Cruise missile, 10, 24, 28, 40, 66, 68, 70, 71, 72, 85, 237, 238, 239, 240, 241, 243, 244, 246, 248, 249, 250

Cuba, 117, 260, 265, 268, 279

Cuban Missile Crisis, 115, 259, 280, 290, 295

Cyprus, 283, 286, 287, 298

Czechoslovakia, 56, 116, 117, 190, 278, 295

Daedalus, 82, 85

de Gaulle, Charles, 181

Democratic Party (US), 119

Democritas, 305, 306, 307

Denmark, 91, 92, 93, 94, 95, 97, 148

Deutsch, K. W., 55

Dimona, 202, 306

Dobrudja, 286

Dulles, John Foster, 55, 89, 169

East Germany, *see* German Democratic Republic

Ebenhausen, 90

Eckstein, Harry, 275

Economic Community of West African States, 324

Ecuador, 259

Egypt, 9, 172, 314, 317, 330

Eighteen-Nation Disarmament Committee, 43, 171, 288, 322

Eisenhower, Dwight D., 24, 88

Electricité de France, 188

Epirus, 286

Epstein, William, 294

Erhard, Ludwig, 90

Erler, Fritz, 90
Espiell, Gros, 271
Euratom, 153, 160, 178, 194, 196, 202, 316
Eurochemic, 154
Eurodif, 154, 155, 157, 161, 179
European Court of Justice, 195
European Economic Community, 309, 310
European Nuclear Energy Agency, 154
Evron, Yair, 52

F-4 aircraft, 242, 290
F-104 aircraft, 290
F-111 aircraft, 242, 245, 250
Feld, Bernard T., 33, 83
Finland, 91, 92, 93, 95, 96, 97, 148, 190; see also Kekkonen Plan
Ford, Gerald, 48, 180, 184, 185, 187, 191, 192
Ford Foundation, 96
Foreign Policy, 36
Fortune, 122
Forward-based systems, 236, 239, 241, 244, 245, 246, 247, 248
Framatome, 188, 190, 203
France, 5, 7, 19, 38, 40, 41, 45, 55, 64, 72, 91, 92, 93, 94, 97, 151, 154, 157, 169, 172, 176, 177, 178, 179, 181, 182, 183, 184, 185, 186, 188, 189, 190, 192, 193, 194, 195, 196, 197, 198, 202, 203, 209, 214, 215, 220, 222, 238, 239, 240, 243, 246, 248, 249, 251, 258, 260, 263, 264, 280, 283, 292, 301, 302, 305, 309, 312, 316, 318, 319, 320, 321, 324, 329

Gabon, 319
Gambia, 26
Gandhi, Mahatma, 42
Gateshead, 25
Gelb, Leslie, 82
George, Alexander, 101
Germany (Imperial), 283
Ghana, 315
Giraud, André, 203, 324

Giscard d'Estaing, Valery, 185, 186, 195
Gnat aircraft, 44
Gorleben, 199
Great Britain, 27, 29, 40, 41, 44, 45, 49, 50, 51, 55, 72, 78, 90, 91, 92, 93, 94, 95, 151, 154, 169, 172, 173, 178, 190, 195, 206, 208, 209, 214, 238, 239, 242, 243, 246, 248, 249, 251, 263, 264, 267, 270, 283, 288, 292, 302, 305, 311, 315, 320
Gray, Colin, 36
Greece, 275, 280, 283, 284, 286, 289, 290, 291, 298, 299, 300, 301, 302, 303, 304, 305, 306, 307, 308, 309, 310, 311, 312, 313
Gromyko, Andrei, 239, 257
Group of Non-Aligned Coordinating Countries on Peaceful Uses of Nuclear Energy, 228
Guyana, 260

Haas, Ernest, 277, 280
Hague, The, 73
Haig, Alexander, 65, 80
Harriman, Leslie, 322, 323
Hassan, A. M. I., 318
Havana, 329
Helsinki Final Act, 28, 76
Hiroshima, 32, 105
Hobbes, Thomas, 282
Honest John, 290, 291
Hoxha, Enver, 287
Hudson Institute, 36, 86
Hungary, 56, 286

Ifé, University of, 317, 319
Ikle, F. C., 58
India, 5, 42, 44, 141, 151, 169, 176, 183, 201, 202, 216, 220, 253, 271, 278, 280, 317, 318, 326, 330
Indian Ocean, 211, 257, 258, 279, 280, 316
Institute for the United States and Canada (USSR), 96
Institute for World Economy and International Relations (USSR), 96
Interamerican Treaty of Mutual Assistance, 270

International Atomic Energy Agency, 7, 18, 149, 153, 160, 162, 178, 182, 184, 188, 200, 203, 209, 211, 214, 215, 217, 219, 220, 222, 223, 224, 225, 226, 227, 228, 230, 268, 291, 314, 315, 316, 320, 322, 323, 328

International Herald Tribune, 37

International Institute for Strategic Studies, 72

International Nuclear Fuel Cycle Evaluation, 176, 177, 188, 194, 195, 196, 197, 198, 199, 200, 204, 226, 227, 228, 229

Iran, 175, 177, 183, 189, 203, 280, 306, 330

Iraq, 5, 175, 188, 189, 191, 201, 203, 280, 306, 330

Ireland, 170, 210

Israel, 5, 169, 172, 173, 202, 216, 278, 280, 306, 321, 322, 330

Isvestia, 288

Italy, 5, 92, 97, 151, 188, 190, 194, 203, 249, 280

Japan, 126, 138, 151, 183, 190, 196, 197, 198, 305; *see also* Hiroshima, Nagasaki

Jordan, 25

Jos, 317

Jupiter missile, 280, 291

Kahler, Miles, 69

Kainji Dam, 324, 325

Kalahari, 316

Kalpakkam, 318

Kapur, Ashok, 316, 323, 329

Katanga, 315

Kekkonen Plan, 258, 278

Kennan, George, 62, 116

Kennedy, John F., 169, 170, 171

Kennedy, Robert, 169, 170

Kennedy, Robert (US Army College), 66

Kissinger, Henry, 65, 239, 249

Kistiakowsky, G. B., 79

Kossovo, 286

Kraft Werke-Union, 189, 190, 319

Kropotkin, Prince, 281

Kwabenya, 315

La Hague, 189, 194, 195, 196

Larrabee, Stephen, 284

Laser weapons, 12, 13, 139

Latin America, 19, 145, 176, 216, 280, 295; *see also* Tlatelolco Treaty

Law of the Sea Conference, 7

League of Nations, 282

Libya, 190, 201, 314

London, 172, 193, 257

London Suppliers Group, *see* Nuclear Suppliers Group

Ludz, Dieter, S., 71

Macedonia, 286

McMahon Act, *see* Atomic Energy Act (US)

McMaster University, 317

McNamara, Robert, 35, 114

Madrid, 11, 15, 28

Manhattan Project, 178, 315

Martinique, 185

Mateos, A. López, 259

Mazrui, Ali, 314

Mediterranean, 72, 211, 242, 258, 278, 280, 293

Mexico, 148, 254, 259, 263, 267

Middle East, 52, 56, 116, 177, 211, 258, 278, 279, 287

Minatome Co., 318

Minuteman, 34, 68

Mirage bomber, 243, 321

Mitrany, David, 274

Mol, 154

Morris, Frederic, 85

Moscow, 110, 172, 210, 235, 240

Mosely, Philip, 118

Mountbatten, Lord, 28, 29

Multilateral Force, 178, 280, 288

Murphy Commission, 87, 89

Mutual Balanced Force Reduction Talks, 25, 41, 49, 55, 94, 121

Mutual Force Reduction Talks, *see* Mutual Balanced Force Reduction Talks

MX missile, 32, 34, 66, 119, 120

Myrdal, Alva, 90, 93

Nagasaki, 105

Namibia, 323

National Security Council (US), 8, 90, 93
Ndili, F. N., 317
Nehru, Jawaharlal, 42, 43, 46, 47
Nerlich, Uwe, 247
Netherlands, the, 73, 91, 92, 93, 94, 95, 96, 97, 151, 154, 183, 194, 237, 248, 249, 277, 305
Neutron bombs, 140, 177
Newhouse, John, 114
New Society, 27
New York Times, 67
Niger, 19, 318, 319
Nigeria, 19, 201, 315
Nike-Hercules, 290, 315
Nixon, Richard, 48, 89, 116, 314
Nkrumah, Kwame, 47, 315
Noel-Baker, Philip, 281
Non-Governmental Organisations, 277
Non-Proliferation Treaty, 4, 5, 8, 18, 38, 45, 48, 59, 121, 149, 151, 155, 171, 176, 178, 181, 182, 183, 184, 207, 212, 213, 214, 215, 216, 217, 218, 219, 220, 222, 223, 226, 228, 229, 262, 266, 268, 269, 270, 271, 276, 277, 281, 291, 292, 294, 295, 301, 306, 310, 312, 314, 315, 319, 320, 322, 329, 330
NORAD, 125
North Atlantic Treaty Organisation, 10, 31, 32, 37, 38, 39, 40, 48, 52, 62, 64, 65, 69, 70, 71, 72, 73, 75, 76, 77, 78, 91, 94, 110, 111, 168, 169, 171, 172, 173, 177, 178, 236, 237, 238, 239, 240, 241, 242, 243, 244, 245, 246, 247, 248, 249, 251, 280, 283, 284, 285, 287, 288, 289, 290, 291, 292, 312
North Sea, 203
North Vietnam, 118
Norway, 91, 92, 93, 94, 95, 96, 97, 278
Nuclear News, 285
Nuclear Non-Proliferation Act (US), 177, 187, 188, 194, 196, 198, 199, 202, 224, 225, 226
Nuclear Regulatory Commission (US), 202

Nuclear Suppliers Group, 9, 149, 177, 185, 186, 187, 190, 221, 222, 223, 226
Nye, Joseph, 204
Nyerere, Julius, 26

OPANAL, 268, 271, 291
Organisation for Economic Cooperation and Development, 145, 146, 147
Organisation of African Unity, 322
Organisation of Petroleum Exporting Countries, 324
Osirak, 189, 203
Ottoman Empire, 283
Outer Space Treaty, 211, 258, 278, 279, 295

Pacific, 258, 265
Pakistan, 5, 172, 176, 183, 186, 195, 201, 202, 203, 216, 220, 280, 317, 329
Panama, 263
Panama Canal, 263
Paris, 169, 181
Paris Peace Conference (1919), 283
Partial Test Ban Treaty, 115, 210
Pawelczyk, Alfons, 78
Peace Committee (USSR), 108
Peace Fund (USSR), 108
Pelindaba, 315
Pentagon, 28, 65
Pershing I, 240
Pershing II, 10, 28, 68, 70, 72, 85, 237, 238, 240, 243, 244, 249
Persian Gulf, 23, 37
Phantom aircraft, 78
Poland, 28, 92, 97, 175, 278, 280; *see also* Rapacki Plan
Polaris, 280
Poseidon, 72
Pravda, 110
Princeton University, 69
Progressive, 138, 139
Pugwash, 33, 101, 277
Punch, 247

Qaddafi, Muammar, 314
Quebec Agreement, 178

Quester, George, 52

Rand Corporation, 86, 119
Rapacki Plan, 257, 258, 278
Reagan, Ronald, 25, 80, 199, 204,
    238, 276
Republican Party (US), 57, 119
Rhodesia, 311
Ridgway, R. L., 61
Robles, García, 259
Rogers, B. W., 60
Rölling, B. V. A., 84
Romania, 92, 97, 258, 275, 284, 286,
    287, 288, 289, 290
Rothstein, Robert, 295
Ruehl, Lothar, 71
Russia (Tsarist), 283

SACEUR, 249
Sahara, 169, 258
Sarajevo, 283
Saudi Arabia, 203
Scandinavia, 258
Sea-Bed Treaty, 211, 258, 278, 279,
    295
Schlesinger, James, 67, 69
Schmidt, Helmut, 78, 235, 240, 319
Serena, 194
Shagari, Alhaji, 322, 329
Simes, Dmitri, 119
Snow, C. P., 30
South Africa, 1, 5, 38, 151, 172, 173,
    203, 216, 315, 316, 321, 322, 323,
    327, 330
South Korea, 183, 188, 201, 203, 220,
    292
Spain, 151, 202
Soviet Union, 2, 8, 9, 10, 11, 12, 16,
    24, 27, 28, 29, 30, 31, 32, 33, 34,
    35, 36, 37, 38, 41, 48, 49, 50, 52,
    53, 54, 55, 56, 57, 58, 59, 64, 66,
    67, 68, 69, 71, 72, 73, 75, 77, 78,
    79, 80, 82, 85, 92, 94, 95, 96, 107,
    108, 109, 114, 115, 116, 117, 118,
    119, 120, 121, 122, 139, 151, 168,
    169, 170, 171, 172, 175, 177, 190,
    201, 205, 208, 209, 210, 212, 218,
    235, 236, 237, 238, 239, 240, 241,
    244, 245, 246, 247, 248, 249, 250,

251, 257, 258, 263, 264, 265, 267,
    270, 276, 278, 280, 285, 286, 287,
    288, 289, 290, 292, 293, 294, 295,
    302, 314, 315, 316
SS-4, 53, 72, 241, 242, 243, 244, 250
SS-5, 53, 72, 241, 244, 250
SS-11, 240, 241, 249
SS-13, 241, 249
SS-14, 241
SS-19, 249
SS-20, 11, 12, 28, 53, 71, 72, 85, 237,
    239, 241, 243, 244, 245, 246, 249
Stalin, Joseph, 27
Stanford Arms Control Group, 56
Stanford University, 101
Stassen, Harold, 89
Stockholm International Peace
    Research Institute, 72, 205, 294
Strategic Arms Limitation Talks, 14,
    15, 16, 17, 25, 41, 48, 49, 50, 55,
    62, 63, 67, 77, 78, 79, 93, 94, 96,
    114, 115, 116, 117, 118, 119, 120,
    121, 122, 123, 177, 206, 212, 218,
    236, 237, 238, 239, 240, 241, 242,
    243, 245, 246, 247, 248, 249, 258,
    274, 276
SU-19, 249
Sverdlovsk, 120
Sweden, 3, 45, 90, 93, 95, 96, 146,
    190, 198, 222, 285
Switzerland, 92, 146, 187, 190
Symington Amendment, 202

Taiwan, 201
Tanzania, 1, 26
Tarapur, 202
Teller-Ulam principle, 139
Ten-Nation Disarmament
    Commission, 42, 210, 322
Thor missile, 240
Three Mile Island, 145
Tito, Josip, 284
Tlatelolco, Treaty of, 19, 211, 252,
    253, 255, 259, 260, 261, 262, 263,
    264, 265, 266, 267, 269, 270, 271,
    272, 277, 278, 279, 291, 292, 295
Tomahawk, see Cruise missile
Transylvania, 286
Treverton, Gregory, 72

Tricastin, 154, 179, 189
Trident, 24, 25, 34, 40, 66, 68
Truman Doctrine, 290
Turkey, 275, 280, 283, 284, 285, 286, 287, 289, 290, 291, 298

Uganda, 1, 26
Ugoh, Sylvester U., 324
Unden Plan, 258
Union of Soviet Socialist Republics, see Soviet Union
United Kingdom, see Great Britain
United Nations, 3, 26, 45, 46, 64, 91, 92, 93, 94, 105, 110, 121, 170, 171, 172, 210, 211, 218, 226, 227, 228, 253, 254, 257, 259, 270, 278, 280, 283, 287, 291, 297, 316, 322, 323, 328
United Nations Educational, Scientific and Cultural Organisation, 113
United Reprocessors, 154
United States, 2, 5, 7, 10, 11, 12, 14, 16, 23, 24, 31, 32, 33, 34, 35, 36, 37, 38, 39, 41, 44, 48, 49, 51, 52, 53, 55, 56, 57, 59, 62, 64, 66, 67, 68, 69, 70, 71, 72, 73, 75, 76, 78, 79, 80, 82, 83, 85, 91, 92, 93, 94, 95, 96, 97, 98, 99, 108, 114, 115, 116, 117, 120, 121, 122, 125, 139, 145, 151, 168, 169, 170, 171, 172, 173, 175, 176, 177, 178, 179, 180, 181, 182, 183, 184, 185, 186, 187, 188, 189, 191, 192, 193, 194, 195, 196, 197, 198, 199, 200, 201, 202, 203, 204, 205, 206, 207, 208, 209, 210, 211, 212, 214, 218, 220, 224, 225, 235, 236, 238, 239, 242, 243, 244, 245, 246, 247, 248, 249, 250, 251, 260, 263, 264, 267, 270, 276, 283, 284, 285, 288, 289, 290, 291, 292, 293, 295, 301, 302, 303, 305, 306, 307, 309, 310, 311, 314, 316, 320, 321, 323
Uranium Institute, 204

Urenco, 154, 155, 157, 161, 183, 304
Uruguay, 91

Valindaba, 316
Vienna, 25, 41, 64, 114
Vietnam, 23, 39, 85, 115, 258, 295, 311; see also North Vietnam
Vladivostok, see Strategic Arms Limitation Talks
Voyvodina, 286
von Schubert, Klaus, 74
Vulcan bomber, 51, 243

Walker, Paul, 89
Warnke, Paul, 79, 93
Warsaw Pact, 10, 41, 48, 54, 63, 64, 65, 68, 69, 71, 72, 73, 75, 76, 109, 110, 111, 112, 279, 284, 285
Warsaw Treaty, see Warsaw Pact
Washington, 172
West African Science Association, 324
West Germany, 5, 52, 56, 64, 71, 78, 90, 92, 93, 94, 95, 96, 97, 98, 151, 154, 169, 173, 176, 177, 179, 181, 182, 183, 184, 185, 186, 187, 188, 189, 190, 191, 193, 195, 196, 197, 199, 202, 220, 222, 240, 249, 257, 278, 280, 288, 289, 301, 309, 319, 320, 321
Wilson, Harold, 90
Wilson, Woodrow, 117
World Federation of Scientific Workers, 172
World Without War Council, 277
Würzbach, Peter Kurt, 71

Yar'Adua, Shehu, 319
Yom Kippur War, 280
Yugoslavia, 227, 275, 284, 286, 287, 288, 290

Zaire, 314, 315
Zangger Committee, 182, 185
Zia, Mohammed, 188

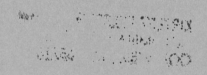